The Gilbert Collection

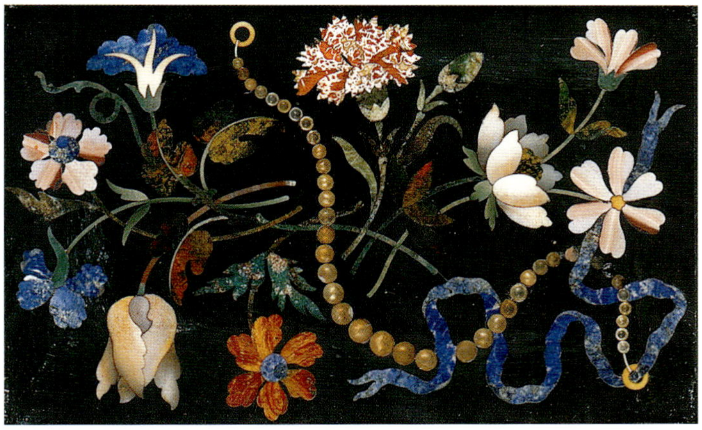

Hardstones

ANNA MARIA MASSINELLI

with contributions by JEANETTE HANISEE GABRIEL

PHILIP WILSON PUBLISHERS

IN ASSOCIATION WITH THE GILBERT COLLECTION

First published in 2000 by
Philip Wilson Publishers Limited
143–149 Great Portland Street
London W1N 5FB

Distributed in the USA and Canada by
Antique Collectors' Club Limited
Market Street Industrial Park
Wappingers' Falls
NY 12590

ISBN 0 85667 510 5

This publication has been made possible by a
grant from the Heritage Lottery Fund.

Heritage
Lottery Fund

Designed by Peter Campbell
Copy-edited by Melissa Larner

Printed and bound in Italy
Società Editoriale Lloyd, Srl, Trieste

Contents

were much more costly than the thread-like opaque glass rods used for micromosaics. The medium was also arguably a more potent vehicle for artistic expression.

During the seventeenth century the technique was used in the production of some of the most magnificent luxury objects in Italy, made for the great private and ecclesiastical patrons of the day. The repertoire of these great commissions, as well as the craft's gradual path in the nineteenth century towards a wider and more commercial market is fully charted in this remarkable collection.

We are grateful to the authors of these two catalogues, Anna Maria Massinelli and Jeanette Gabriel, Sir Arthur Gilbert's private curator, for their commitment to the publication, carried out at a difficult time during the transport of the collection from Los Angeles to London and the installation of the new museum for the Gilbert Collection at Somerset House. I would also like to add my own thanks to Rachel Layton, Assistant Curator, for her tireless liaison between authors, publisher, photographers and editor, without which it would have been impossible to complete this project.

Timothy Schroder
Keeper of the Gilbert Collection

Contents

Acknowledgements

GRATITUDE MUST BE EXPRESSED first to Sir Arthur Gilbert for giving me the opportunity to work on his unique collection of Hardstones, and to Lady Gilbert for her kindness and generous hospitality. Special recognition should go to the staff of the Gilbert Collection Trust, particularly Jacqueline Strologo, Timothy Schroder and Rachel Layton. Lastly, thanks to the following indivduals who helped make the author's task less arduous:

Andrea Baldinotti
Rodolfo Bargelli
John Barone
Leslie Bowman
Marco Cassi
Martin Chapman
Curzio Cipriani
Simonella Condemi
Greg Dobie
Peter Fusco
Cristina Giorgetti
Roger Jones
Mary Levkoff
Patrice Marandel
Mario Massinelli
Piera Bocci Pacini
Luisa Poggi
Robert Seawer
Ditta Ugolini

The other contributor to this volume, Jeanette Hanisee Gabriel, Arthur Gilbert's private curator, wishes to extend her profound thanks to the following scholars and associates who contributed to her research on this catalogue:

Arte dell' Mosaico
Brian Consadine
Katharina Bott
Robbie Diamond
Rudolph Distelberger
Ronald Freyberger
Karyn Frykholm
Angelo Gabriel
Christopher Gilbert
Anna Maria Guisti
Alvar González-Palacios
Archduke Geza von Habsburg
Anne Jackson
Dr J. H. Leopold
Stephen Markel
Dr Karl Schlossmacher
Kenneth Snowman
Charles Truman
Caroline Venables
Sebastian Whitestone
John Winter
Lucy Wood

Foreword

The Gilbert Collection of Italian mosaics has been formed over a thirty-five-year period by Sir Arthur Gilbert, who was born in London but made his home in California in 1949. The gift of his collection to the British nation brings to this country something that is unique not only among British collections, but also among the museums of the world. The collection comprises works in two different media, Roman micromosaics and Florentine *pietre dure*, and this catalogue has been conceived as two independent volumes, each providing a thorough overview of the development of the craft and the social and political circumstances in which it flourished.

Arthur Gilbert was first drawn to Roman micromosaics when he was briefly deceived by the painterly qualities of a pair of mosaic pictures he happened to notice in an auction house in Los Angeles. His purchase of these curiosities proved to be the starting point of a collecting odyssey, resulting in the formation of a collection whose comprehensiveness bears comparison only with those of the Vatican Museum in Rome and the State Hermitage in St. Petersburg.

The art of mosaics is of ancient origin and enjoyed its first great period during the Roman Empire when it was used for the creation of geometric patterns and pictorial decoration in floors. During the early Christian period it was elevated to the walls and domes of churches in the creation of some of the most intensely spiritual images in Christian art. Over the ensuing centuries, however, it became almost exclusively associated with Byzantium and eastern-looking Venice, until its revival in sixteenth-century Italy.

Eighteenth- and nineteenth-century Rome saw a resurgence of the craft, fuelled by affluent tourists with money to spend. Souvenirs of the Grand Tour were provided in the form of views of Rome and images from ancient history exquisitely worked in a technique reminiscent of the civilisation they sought to evoke. But these mosaics differed from their ancient prototypes in being painstakingly worked with infinitely smaller tesserae in a technique now known as 'micromosaic'. This technique became an end in itself as the best workshops competed to produce ever more finely executed images composed of ever smaller tesserae. The range of material to which the technique was applied was enormous, from jewellery and snuffboxes to large pictures and tabletops. All of these forms and subjects are comprehensively represented in the Gilbert Collection.

At the same time as he was starting to collect micromosaics, Gilbert was also attracted by Florentine hardstones, or *pietre dure*. These brilliantly virtuoso works were made from cut and polished stones, carefully selected for colour and texture and assembled into sophisticated pictures or geometric designs. The materials for the finest work in this technique were much more costly than the thread-like opaque glass rods used for micromosaics. The medium was also arguably a more potent vehicle for artistic expression.

During the seventeenth century the technique was used in the production of some of the most magnificent luxury objects in Italy, made for the great private and ecclesiastical patrons of the day. The repertoire of these great commissions, as well as the craft's gradual path in the nineteenth century towards a wider and more commercial market is fully charted in this remarkable collection.

We are grateful to the authors of these two catalogues, Anna Maria Massinelli and Jeanette Gabriel, Sir Arthur Gilbert's private curator, for their commitment to the publication, carried out at a difficult time during the transport of the collection from Los Angeles to London and the installation of the new museum for the Gilbert Collection at Somerset House. I would also like to add my own thanks to Rachel Layton, Assistant Curator, for her tireless liaison between authors, publisher, photographers and editor, without which it would have been impossible to complete this project.

Timothy Schroder
Keeper of the Gilbert Collection

The Origins and Development of Mosaics in Semiprecious Stone

The Italian word *commesso*, deriving from the Latin *committere* (to join together), is used to describe a type of mosaic executed in coloured marble, *pietre dure* (hardstones), and *pietre tenere* (softstones). The sophisticated artistic taste of late Mannerist Florence and the richness and splendour of the Grand Ducal Medici court created the ideal conditions for the development of elaborate *commesso* works composed of semiprecious stone pieces fitting perfectly together like wood marquetry, but not fixed to a ground or base. The origin of Florentine mosaics is to be found in two different technical predecessors: *pietre tenere* mosaics made in Rome, and Milanese hardstone sculpture.

The earliest references to the revival of stone-mosaic work date from the mid-sixteenth century and relate to the creations of craftsmen in Rome, where antique-marble mosaics survived or were unearthed during archaeological excavations, thus keeping alive the Roman taste for opulent mosaics in polychrome marble. The development of modern mosaic techniques in the sixteenth century was one of the outcomes of a widespread interest in Roman antiquities among the educated classes, an interest that helped make the city a focal point for artists, intellectuals and antiquarians from all over Europe. In a guidebook compiled by Lucio Mauro in 1550, published by Ulisse Aldrovandi (1522–1605) in 1562, which was written to sing the praises of the classical antiquities conserved in the palaces of Rome, the only furnishings referred to are contemporary items in stone mosaic. Mauro noticed in one of the rooms overlooking the Belvedere Courtyard in the Vatican an 'octagonal table, intricately and beautifully inlaid, and opposite it a small study decorated with the same inlay, an exquisite sight'. In the house of the Most Reverend Gaddi (Niccolo Gaddi, a Florentine collector) could be seen a 'most beautiful table made of mottled green, 5 spans long and 3 ½ wide, edged in gilded copper with a decorative ebony border half a span wide'.[1]

From the 1550s on, Milan was the most important centre in Europe for the production of carved vessels and engraved rock-crystal panels. The material was available locally, near Saint Gotthard in the Alps. Whole families of stone carvers were involved; their patrons were the most prestigious courts of Europe.

Craftsmen such as these concentrated on making engraved crystal panels bearing sacred or mythological scenes, plant designs, or portraits, which were used to decorate furniture, particularly cabinets and caskets. Vases and drinking vessels, carved from rock crystal as well as from other kinds of semiprecious stone, were also popular items. They would often be carved in curious shapes, inspired by the natural form of the block of crystal or stone. The shapes that recurred most frequently were fantastic animals, birds, fish, and ships. Ewers and vessels would have elaborate handles with decorated ends shaped like monsters, or covers topped with a bird or a lion. The carved stone would be set in an elaborate mount of engraved and enamelled gold.

Paolo Morigia (1525–1604), who provides information on the activity of the Milanese stonecutters, also records the execution of *pietre dure* ornamentation for furniture, such as an ebony table for the Emperor Rudolf II (r. 1576–1612) made in the workshop of Gasparo Miseroni (1518–73). The design, by Giuseppe Arcimboldo (c. 1530–93), was made in jasper, lapis lazuli and rock crystal by Giuseppe Guzzi (Morigia 1595, p. 375). In Florence, the first phase of hectic activity in the field of hardstone mosaics, encouraged by the Grand Dukes Cosimo I de' Medici (r. 1569–74) and his son Francesco de' Medici (r. 1574–87), is documented as early as 1568 in the celebrated pages of Giorgio Vasari's (1511–74) *Lives of the Artists*. It was Ferdinand I de' Medici (r. 1587–1609), however, brother of Francesco and his successor to the title, who gave official status to the manufacture of mosaics, granting a 'letter patent' on 3 September 1588, in which the Roman aristocrat Emilio de' Cavalieri (c. 1550–1602) is named as the superintendent of all the craftsmen (except for Giambologna, Jacques Bylivelt, and Anton Maria Archibusiere).[3]

The combined experience of the Roman mosaicists and the Milanese stone carvers was exploited in Florence during the reigns of Cosimo and Francesco, when artists like Bernardino di Porfirio, from Leccio (who made mosaic tables in Rome), and the Milanese craftsmen Ambrogio and Stefano Caroni (documented 1572–1606 and 1572–99 respectively) and Giorgio Gafurri arrived at court, bringing their skills with them.[4] During his years as a cardinal, living in the Villa Medici on the Pincio in Rome (1575–87), Ferdinand de' Medici witnessed the establishment of the production of stone mosaics there before overseeing the hardstone work promoted by his brother in Florence. He steered the stoneworkers towards the improvement of their mosaic skills, employing painters such as Jacopo Ligozzi (1547–1626), Lodovico Cigoli (1559–1613), and Cigoli's pupil Jacques Bylivelt (1576–1644) to provide cartoons for them.

The objective of producing a perfect 'stone painting', now pursued with the assistance of painters as well as skilled stone carvers, helped guide Florentine mosaic work away from the conventional geometric models produced by Roman craftsmen. Because such a picture was dependent on the variety of colours at the artist's disposal, the search for hardstones during Ferdinand's reign became feverish, involving enormous expense.

The activity of the many artists, architects, painters, stone carvers, and metalsmiths working in the court workshops, located first in the Casino di San Marco and then, after 1586, in the Uffizi, was directed towards the manufacture of luxurious furnishings for the residences of the Grand Dukes, for foreign royalty, and for the creation of a magnificent mausoleum for the Medici family in the church of San Lorenzo.[5]

The intentions of the first three Medici Grand Dukes were furthered by their successors, Cosimo II (r. 1609–21), Ferdinand II (r. 1621–70), Cosimo III (r. 1670–1723), and Gian Gastone (r. 1723–37). During the seventeenth century, the artists who came for short periods to the court workshops diversified the scope of *pietre dure* craftsmanship.

In the 1600s, while the pictorial and figurative scope of flat mosaic work was being developed, a kind of relief sculpture in mosaic was also being tried out. In 1605, for example, four small statues of the Evangelists were carved to designs by Orazio Mochi (1625–c. 1670) for the ciborium of the Cappella dei Principi in San Lorenzo (now in the Museo degli Argenti, Florence). The various parts of the saints' bodies, their clothes, and their attributes were all carved in different coloured stone.[6] One of the most elaborate and unusual works of this type – a bust of the Grand Duchess Vittoria della Rovere portrayed in the habit of the oblates of Montalve[7] – was made by Giuseppe Antonio Torricelli (1662–1719) in 1697.[8]

From 1694 to 1725, activity in the court workshops depended on the sculptor and architect Giovanni Battista Foggini (1652–1725), who brought a delicate baroque feel to the subject matter of Florentine mosaic work. He endorsed the prevalent taste for plant designs and amalgamated flat mosaics with reliefs in his garlands of fruit worked in different stones (see cat. no. 10).

After the death in 1737 of Gian Gastone, the last Medici Grand Duke, the court went through a period of stagnation, but the workshops continued to function. Furnishings and valuable *objets d'art* continued to be made after the tradition of the latter days of the Medici, using the typical compositions of birds and flowers on a black marble ground. Under the new Grand Duke, Francis I of Lorraine (r. 1737–65), and his son, Pierre Léopold (1747–92), resident in Florence between 1765 and 1790, a complete renewal of the decorative language took place. This was due to the activity of Louis Siries, who was artistic director of the workshops from 1748 until he was replaced by his son Luigi (1743–1811) in 1789. The traditional tangle of plants on a black ground was abandoned once and for all, and the colour schemes were changed. Florentine mosaics now began to be characterised by well-lit landscapes and charming figurative scenes.

Giuseppe Zocchi (1711–67), active in the manufacture of mosaics between 1750 and 1767, and Antonio Cioci (d. 1792), who succeeded him between 1771 and 1782, were leading exponents of the mosaic style current in the Grand Ducal workshops during the regime of the dukes of Lorraine.[9] In 1798, the court workshop was moved from the Uffizi to a new location, at the Opificio delle Pietre Dure.

When Napoleon's troops arrived in Florence in 1799, the court workshops were closed down. A few years later, however, when the kingdom of Etruria was established, work started again. With the return to Florence in 1814 of Duke Ferdinand III of Lorraine (r. 1790–1801, 1814–24), a period of decline set in, which, during the second half of the century, became irreversible.

Until 1854, the factory had been directed by Carlo Siries (d. 1854), who succeeded his father, Luigi, in 1811. During the nineteenth century, exceptionally skilled stoneworkers such as Giovan Battista Giorgi (1815–51), Niccolò Betti (1806–82), Edoardo Marchionni (1873–1923) and Paolo Ricci (active 1855–92) interpreted the eclectic taste of the period in a series of sophisticated pieces in which the floral element is dominant.

The output of the mosaic workshops was exhibited at international exhibitions in the nineteenth century, frequently winning awards, including the gold medal in Paris in 1855.[10] At the Esposizione Nazionale Italiana, held in Florence in 1861, the products of the Opificio swept the board.

The pieces were displayed in a suitable setting – the so-called Hall of Jewels (a reference to the *sala delle gemme* in the Uffizi, where the *pietre dure* vases, gems, cameos, and jewellery of the Grand Ducal collection had been exhibited since the reign of Pierre Léopold). Here, among other items, were Betti's table (Museo dell'Opificio, Florence) decorated with fruit, flowers, and birds,[11] a cabinet in ebony and *pietre dure*, and a walnut wardrobe with two seventeenth-century mosaic panels on the doors.[12] In the section devoted to 'deluxe objects and furnishings, and decoration' there were items from the many private workshops that proliferated in Florence in the second half of the century, such as those of Gaetano Bianchini, Enrico Bosi, Cesare Piazzini, Santi Ciotti, and Giocondo Torrini.[13] Demerio Carlo Finocchietti wrote warmly about certain aspects of the exhibition but lamented the general decline in originality.

Participation in the International Exhibition in London in 1862 brought forth less positive comments. Finocchietti was present as a member of the jury and complained of the difficulty craftsmen faced in preparing new work at such short notice. A replica of the *Tomb of Cecilia Metella* (cat. no. 70) was not finished in time, so a tabletop realised in Egyptian nephrite and a 'jewel casket' were sent instead. Unfortunately, these failed to impress the jury, which was 'grieved not to see anything as conspicuously meritorious as in former years'. Finocchietti seems to have tried to negotiate the first prize for the state workshop in Florence, whose supremacy was gravely threatened by the comparison of its products with those of the imperial Peterhof factory in Russia

> which were a most magnificent sight and caused me great anxiety, even though I was convinced that the Russian entry was in some respects inferior to the entry from Florence. The novelty and elegance of the Russian designs, and the perfection of the display, in particular a small lapis lazuli table, made me afraid that the Florentine entry might be at risk in the face of such well-aimed and rigorous competition.
>
> Competition with the imperial factory of Russia, because of the novelty of their designs and the high quality of stones they used, threatened Florence's claim to the first prize, but in the end both were judged worthy of a medal.By giving such a reward to the Tuscan *pietre dure* workshop, the jury made it clear that they hoped in any subsequent exhibition to see objects of a significance to convince them that the Italians have not lost their creative genius nor their appreciation of beauty.

The largest of the private Florentine workshops were represented alongside the Opificio. Finocchietti also provides some insight into their activities:

> Once the *pietre dure* items had been judged, we examined Florentine mosaics made in various private workshops, most of which have been in existence producing so-called Florentine mosaics for at least fifty years. Their products are not always made with silicate stone, being most frequently mixed with calcareous stone, shells, and other softer materials that the craftsmen think more suitable and

more likely to enhance the intricate designs employed in these workshops. This different attitude towards design is motivated by the private workshops' eagerness to offer for sale objects which, for this reason and because their price is somewhat lower, will be more likely to tempt the public to buy them.

Florentine mosaic work, which has made remarkable progress over the previous half century, is better known abroad than any other. For this we should be grateful to the mosaicists of Florence, and in particular to the distinguished Gaetano Bianchini, who has given time and resources to the furtherance of this noble industry, one of the ornaments not only of Florence, but of Italy.

In all the great exhibitions the Florentine mosaic has always given a good account of itself and has won approval and honour.

In the Italian exhibition of 1861 the Florentine craftsmen vied with one another to display the most splendid products; not all of those, however, who exhibited in Florence deemed it convenient to take part in the International Exhibition in London.

Those sending work included only: Giocondo Torrini and Carlo Vichi, the Montelatici brothers, Francesco Betti, Giovanni Binazzi, and Gelasio Barbensi.

Gaetano Bianchini, who had promised to send a selection of tables, sent only two that had already been exhibited elsewhere and that are the property of an English gentleman.

The large workshop of Enrico Bosi was unable to send its mosaics in time to be considered by the judges, who had already completed their deliberations. Although they arrived last, however, Bosi's products were popular with the public and sold more readily than other objects. His workshop was able on this solemn occasion to sell objects to the value of twenty thousand *lire*.

The council of the jury did not limit their inspection of these valuable entries to a single visit, but examined them carefully several times before deciding on a reward; in this way they were able to establish a carefully considered and fair comparison between the Russian, English, and Maltese mosaics that we saw in competition with the Italians.

The result of their thoughtful deliberation was a medal for the workshops of Giocondo Torrini and Carlo Vichi, and an honourable mention for Francesco Betti and Giovanni Binazzi.

Although an honourable mention in an exhibition like the one in London corresponds to a medal in a provincial exhibition, in my opinion the judges of the second section were a bit too hard on the work of Betti and Binazzi; I had tried hard to ensure that they were awarded the medal, as I had also tried to ensure that Montelatici and Barbensi should be awarded the honourable mention. [14]

The Opificio was represented again at exhibitions in Padua in 1869 and Vienna in 1874 with a table decorated with musical emblems executed by Niccolò Betti in 1868.[15] The fortunes of the factory were going into irreversible decline, however, whereas the private workshops, with techniques and designs borrowed from the Opificio, were finding their niche commercially with work that, as Finocchietti had noted, combined *pietre dure* with less costly materials like calcareous stone and shells.

In addition to the workshops that exhibited in Florence and London, there was also a workshop set up by Giovanni Ugolini in 1868 in Via dei Fossi; it moved in 1900 to the Lungarno Acciaiuoli, where it can still be found. Ugolini's products won great acclaim abroad and were awarded prizes at exhibitions in Brussels in 1897 and Paris in 1900 (fig. 1). The alabaster workshops of Volterra too began to flourish, producing furniture with carved

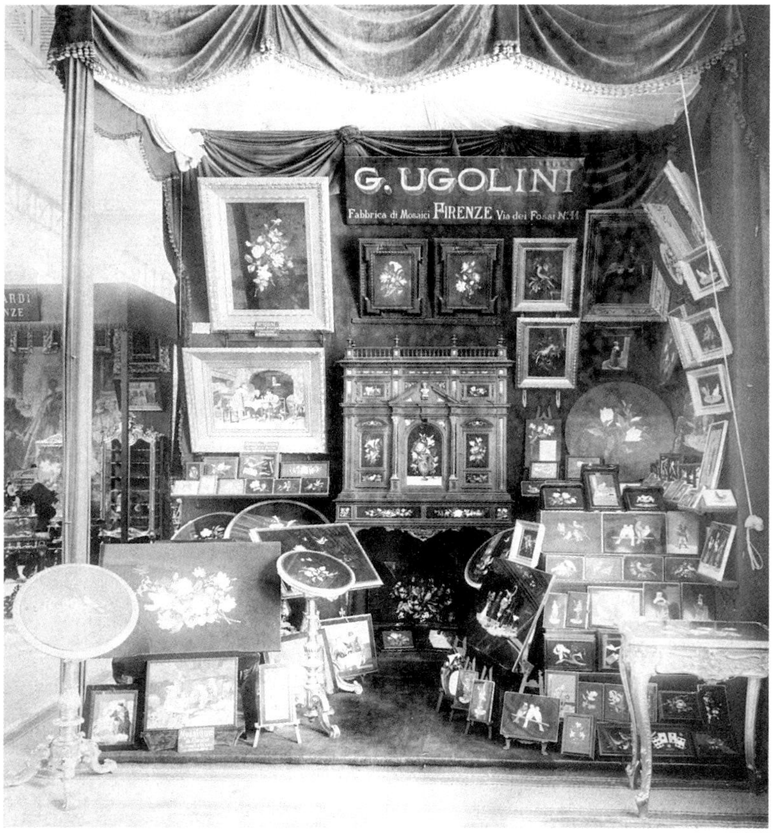

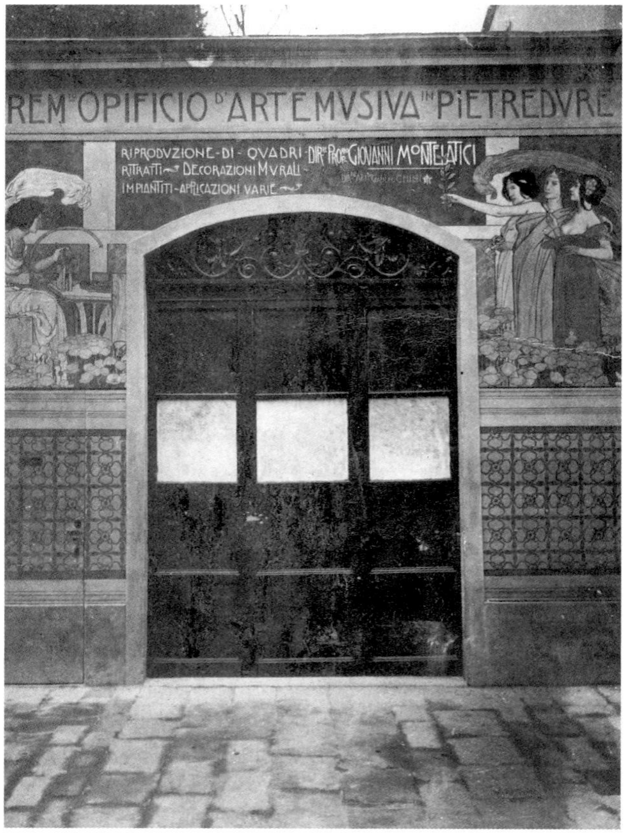

FIG. 1 The Ugolini stand at the Paris Exposition Universelle, 1900.

FIG. 2 The façade of the Montelatici workshop in Via Arnolfo.

pillars and floral motifs inspired by Florentine mosaic work.[16]

Finocchietti, however, noticed a change in the quality of mosaic work being produced. While exhibiting virtuoso skill in craftsmanship, it was lacking imagination in design:

> In the general artistic decadence that ensued, design was neglected or corrupted by forms and taste that were far from the true spirit of the Italian school; the objects produced by the workshop in question were not worthy of public esteem. Something is lacking in a perfectly executed mosaic if excellent workmanship is not combined with imaginative and beautiful design and harmonious colours; arranging pieces of different stone with greater or lesser exactitude requires the diligence of a craftsman, whereas combining and matching the colours and the composition of a painting in stone mosaic requires the intelligence and good taste of an artist.[17]

Giovanni Montelatici (1864–1930), presumably the son of the Montelatici who, according to Finocchietti, went unrewarded at the International Exhibition in London in 1862, reiterated Finocchietti's views on the decline of Florentine mosaics. Giovanni made an attempt to restore artistic dignity to this type of work by setting up a joint venture in 1898 with Galileo Chini (1873–1957), an artist from Mugello (near Florence). Chini, who was in touch with artistic trends in Europe, was made artistic director of Montelatici's workshop in Via Arnolfo (fig. 2).[18] The collaboration brought the partners a gold medal at the Paris Exhibition in 1900, where they displayed a large table bearing an inlaid picture of the Annunciation. (For more information on Montelatici and Chini, see the Hardstone Pictures section.)

STONE MOSAICS ELSEWHERE IN ITALY

The impetus given to *pietre dure* mosaic work by the Grand Ducal workshops in Florence encouraged the training of a large number of craftsmen, who then spread their skills all over Italy, setting up studios from the first half of the seventeenth century onward.

Pietro Paolo Corbarelli (1589–1649), recorded as being in Padua from 1639, created the polychrome marble and *pietre dure* decorations on the high altar in the church of Santa Giustina between 1637 and 1643 and the mosaics for the altar of the Santissimo Sacramento in 1648. The tabernacle on the altar in Santissimo Sacramento was made by his sons Simone (documented 1656), Antonio (documented until 1682), and Francesco (documented until 1683). Another son, Benedetto, worked mainly in Vicenza, moving there in 1671. He was responsible, along with Antonio and other members of the family, for decorating the altar in Santa Corona. In 1676 Antonio, in collaboration with Francesco, decorated the altar in the Capella della Croce in the Basilica del Santo in Padua. Francesco and his sons ran a flourishing workshop in Brescia after 1683; the activity of the sons is documented right through the first half of the eighteenth century.

The design repertory used by the Corbarelli craftsmen in their mosaic panels – floral motifs, birds, insects, arabesques, figurative scenes from the Bible, townscapes, and still lives with musical instruments – is reminiscent of the work produced by the Grand Ducal workshops in Florence.[19] Benedetto Corbarelli also set up his own workshop in Modena from 1680 to 1689; this was established for the working of *pietre dure* 'in the Florentine manner'.

In his memoirs, made known by Campori [20] we learn of Benedetto's trips to Tuscany in search of hardstones, and of the execution of a 'large cabinet' and table, completed in 1683. He ran a workshop located near the church of the Corbarelli relying on the ducal stores for items such as diamonds and stonecutting tools. Cavalier Donzi was the manager of the stonecutters; the painter Francesco Stringa looked after the creative side of the business.

In Naples, records in the archives reveal that artisans from Florence and Carrara specialising in polychrome marble and *pietre dure* were active in the city from the end of the sixteenth century and throughout the following one. Here, too, their work was connected with certain types of ecclesiastical commissions, particularly altar frontals and decorated altars. These usually contained many polychrome marbles and softstones combined with lapis lazuli and reverse-painted rock crystal.

The mosaic decorations in the church of Santa Maria Nova (1605–7), by Mario and Constantino Mariasi of Carrara, contain ornamental elements, such as candlesticks and plant motifs. Other Tuscan craftsmen working in Naples in the second and third decades of the seventeenth century included Francesco Balsimelli and Jacopo Lazzari.[21] Plant designs still predominate in their work, betraying their allegiance to the ornate Florentine taste of the Mannerist period. Their use of these motifs, however, lacks the naturalistic, three-dimensional effect of the Florentine work, showing increasing signs of abstraction.

Cosimo Fanzago (1591–1678), the leading exponent of Neapolitan baroque mosaic work, developed an ornamental language that was completely liberated from any Tuscan model. His decorative themes are characterised by an over-abundance of plant ornamentation with designs sometimes based on embroidered altar frontals.

On the initiative of the Bourbon King Charles III (r. 1759–88), a *pietre dure* workshop modelled on those of Florence was established in Naples at San Carlo alle Mortelle. It was organised by Francesco Ghinghi (1689–1762), a craftsman from the Grand Ducal workshops in Florence and a pupil of Giovanni Battista Foggini. It survived until 1861, when it was closed by royal decree. The products of the Neapolitan court workshop were of a similar type to their Florentine counterparts. They consisted mainly of tabletops and inlaid panels, with a prevalence of ornamental (usually plant) motifs on a black marble background, but also included cameos, snuffboxes, and jewellery (like the parure in the Gilbert Collection, cat. no. 109).

Carlo Celano (1617–93) supplies information about the workshop:

> It was set up first and foremost to make pieces for the Royal House: the altar in the chapel in the Palace in Caserta and other particular items in oriental granite were our first attempts. The Tabernacle on the aforementioned altar is perhaps the noblest and richest in existence, being made of amethyst, lapis lazuli, petrified wood, granite, carnelian, agate, and jasper of amazing beauty; equally beautiful are two carved topazes which serve as doors to two ciboria. The bas-reliefs on the carved topazes bear the effigy of the Redeemer.
>
> These two topazes were originally one piece weighing eleven and a half pounds, and are now reduced to three quarters of a span each.[23] As time went by, the early masters disappeared; for political reasons the necessity for maintaining the arts diminished, even if it did not disappear completely, and with it the need to conserve this glorious training ground. But then King Francesco I had the idea of returning the Neapolitan workshop to its former glory. In 1829 Signor Orazio Angelini was sent to Florence to learn the techniques and to learn other ways of achieving success in such work. He was ready to cut and polish stones and employ further artists.
>
> Thanks to his admirable determination and to further provision of funds, the workshop has been able to produce a number of beautiful objects. The cupboards are well stocked with tools and stones, neatly arranged. One of the stones may be the only example of its kind in the world: a mass of petrified wood from the orient, almost circular in shape and 8.75 spans in diameter, composed of sardonyx, chalcedony, and agate; the minerals resemble the concentric circles of a cross-section of a tree trunk.
>
> People remember that this rock lay for a long time unnoticed on the pier in this city and no one knew how it had been transported or by whom, nor whence it came. A large part has now been used to make different objects.[24]

Celano's information about the great lump of petrified wood is endorsed by the large amount of such stone used in the Neapolitan workshop. One of the objects made from the block may be an oval table in the Museo Nazionale di Capodimonte, Naples.[25]

The taste for lapidary mosaic later spread rapidly through the world of baroque decoration in Sicily. The island was rich in coloured marbles: *cot ognino* (quince marble) was mined at Monte Pellegrino, grey marble at Bellolampo and Cefalù, *rosso di libici* (red) at Trapani, and yellow at Castronovo. *Pietre dure* was also to be found in abundance, with agates at Giuliana and jasper at Collesano and Taormina.[26]

Mosaic decorations in mixed marbles (so-called *mischi e tramischi)* existed in Messina as early as the first half of the seventeenth century. Initially, the coloured marble was used as a smooth finish for sarcophagi and memorial plaques but, as the century advanced, the taste for intarsia with plant motifs grew; opulent spirals and tendrils and vases of flowers were depicted in patches of dense colour. These schemes diverged from the controlled, naturalistic Florentine models in the direction of more abstract, stylised patterns that seem to be based on textile designs for damasks and brocades. This is exemplified by the mosaics from the church of San Gregorio, now in the Museo Nazionale di Messina.[27]

Vincenzo Tedeschi (d. 1643), who worked in the Duomo in Messina, is thought to have been the intermediary through whom the techniques of stone intarsia, and the taste for such work, travelled from Tuscany to Sicily. Although technically less assured than their Neapolitan counterparts, the Sicilian mixed-marble mosaics, with their riotously decorated surfaces are closer in style to Neapolitan mosaics than to Florentine ones. This link was demonstrated in the late seventeenth century when two master craftsmen from Fanzago's workshop in Naples, Andrea Gallo and Innocenzo Mangani, were summoned to Messina to enrich the already opulent stone mosaics in the churches of the city with plaster putti and garlands.

During the last twenty years of the seventeenth century, flat mosaics alternated with relief mosaics. Besides plaster reliefs, white marble decorations, including female heads, festoons, putti, and scrolls, began to appear on top of the mosaic grounds. Ornamental cycles of this type occur frequently in the churches of Palermo. In San Francesco d' Assisi the interior decoration dates from 1690; in the Chapel of the Crucifix in the Duomo in Monreale, the decorations were added between 1687 and 1690.

This kind of ornamentation, based on the prevalent colours of Sicilian marble – black, red, and white – with relief carvings standing out from the tangled web of the background inlay, persisted for the following century, becoming one of the most typical features of Sicilian craftsmanship.[28]

STONE MOSAICS ELSEWHERE IN EUROPE

By the second half of the sixteenth century, the taste for highly coloured and costly mosaic decorations had taken hold all over Europe. There are examples of the use of *pietre dure* in furniture-making in the second half of the sixteenth century in Dresden. A sculptor from Lugano, Giovanni Maria Nosseni (1544–1620), was summoned there in 1575 to oversee the search for, and extraction of, semiprecious stones. At Schloss Pillnitz, Dresden, of the suite made by him comprising a table, stools, and a bed, some ebony stools remain, in which jasper panels are mounted.[29]

The success of *pietre dure* decoration in Bohemia can be attributed to the patronage of Emperor Rudolf II, who established a specialised workshop in Prague. Glyptic work was supervised by Ottavio Miseroni (1567–1624) of Milan; *pietre dure* mosaic work, by the Castrucci family of Florence.[30]

In the early part of the seventeenth century, the city of Augsburg in Bavaria was becoming known in the rest of Europe for producing cabinets, some of them decorated with *pietre dure* designs.[31] Landgrave Karl of Kassel (1654–1730) was also associated with Florentine mosaics and established a specialised workshop at court, summoning the craftsman Francesco Mugnai (d. 1710) from Florence at the end of the seventeenth century. Mugnai worked in Kassel until his death and was responsible for making several large cameos and an unfinished tabletop depicting the goddess Minerva in relief on a landscape background of *pietre dure* mosaic (Landesmuseum, Kassel). His work was carried on in Kassel by German artists, including Johann Albrecht Lavillette (1663–1743), born in Dresden, who specialised in small mosaic reliefs.

In the eighteenth century, stone carving and engraving in Dresden achieved international renown with Johann Cristoph Neuber (documented to 1733), who specialised in cameos, Johann Melchior Dinglinger (1664–1731) and Johann Christian Neuber (1736–1808). The latter furnished an enormous international clientele with his small, exquisite items in carved stone, some of the most successful of which were his snuffboxes inlaid with *pietre dure* from Saxony and decorated for the most part with delicate geometric patterns.[32]

Frederick II of Prussia (r. 1740–86), known as Frederick the Great, was also interested in precious stones and used them abundantly in the interior decoration and furnishings of his palace at Potsdam. The King ordered inlaid-stone tabletops from Florence; his fabulous 'Grottensaal' in the Neuen Palais, encrusted with blocks of precious minerals, demonstrates a characteristically German taste. He was a great collector of hardstone boxes, as the examples in the Gilbert Collection demonstrate (see cat. nos. 53–59).

A further example of the popularity of Florentine mosaic work in eighteenth-century Germany is the Florentiner Zimmer (1711–29) in the castle of La Favorita in Rastatt, designed for the Margravine Sibilla Augusta (1673–1733). The ceiling and walls are inlaid with panels of Florentine mosaics bearing designs from nature and landscapes; these are repeated on the tabletop in the centre of the room.[33]

An interesting insight into the popularity of *pietre dure* work at the French court is provided by the presence of glyptic items in the collection of Louis XIV (r. 1643–1715). At the centre of the collection are several vases in sardonyx, lapis lazuli, and agate, mounted in enamelled gold. The colours of the enamel are particularly brilliant against a white background; the delicate designs are characterised by a dragon motif (other decorative motifs include putti, masks, and harpies). These vases were the work of a Parisian goldsmith, Pierre Delabarre, who was active during the first half of the seventeenth century; the *pietre dure* elements of his works were sometimes drawn from other sources.[34]

It was Cardinal Mazarin (1602–61) who disseminated the taste for *pietre dure* mosaics in France. He had in his possession valuable cabinets in ebony with inlaid panels, similar to the type produced in the Grand Ducal workshops in Florence. The cardinal's vast correspondence with the Florentine abbot, Luigi Strozzi, testifies to his constant interest in the *pietre dure* items to be acquired in Tuscany.[35]

There were too few craftsmen capable of producing artefacts in *pietre dure* of Florentine quality to satisfy demand at the French court. In 1668, seven years after the death of Mazarin, records show that there were three Florentine stone carvers in Paris – Ferdinando and Orazio Migliorini and Filippo Branchi – all working in the Gobelins factory. Gian Ambrogio Giachetti joined them in 1670. Two exquisite cabinets, built by the Italian cabinetmaker Domenico Cucci (1635–1704) and decorated with fourteen *pietre dure* panels, both in relief and flat mosaic, were executed by these craftsmen at the Gobelins in 1683; these cabinets are now at Alnwick Castle, Northumberland.

During the last twenty years of the seventeenth century, records show that two tabletops inlaid with animal and plant motifs were produced, as were mosaic panels for the decoration of furniture. There are noticeable stylistic affinities between the Gobelins products and Florentine work, both in their technique and ornamentation. Differences of taste can be seen in the division of space, choice and combination of plant motifs, reiteration of animal themes, and a marked preference for pieces of stone with larger striations.

At the beginning of the eighteenth century, interest in this kind of work began to decline, even though Jean La Tellier, one of the Parisian craftsmen working alongside the Tuscan masters, continued to make mosaic work until 1727, with his son Louis as apprentice. In the mid-eighteenth century, *pietre dure* techniques were used primarily for making *objets de vertu*, and the art of stone engraving saw a considerable revival. Jacques de Gault, Adrien-Jean Maximilian Vachette (1753–1839), and Louis Siries (who moved to Florence in 1746) were specialists in this type of work.

During the neoclassical period, hardstone decoration returned to fashion; vases in carved jasper, amethyst, or polychrome marble, with elaborate gilt-bronze mounts, were popular. Pierre Gouthière (1732–1813) created the mounts for a perfume burner in jasper (Wallace Collection) and vases in serpentine (Louvre), both of which belonged to the Duc d'Aumont, a keen enthusiast for semiprecious stones and furniture with panels inlaid with hardstones.

After the departure from Naples of Charles III in 1759, the new King of Spain started a mosaic factory at the court in Madrid, at the Buen Retiro. Again, craftsmen from Florence were asked to assist, and in 1761 Domenico Stecchi and Francesco Poggetti left for Spain. A few months later, Alonso Cruzado (d. 1791) reached Madrid from Paris. Between 1763 and 1764 five craftsmen are recorded as having been instructed by the Florentine stoneworkers; Poggetti's son, Luigi, was active there until the destruction of the workshop during the Napoleonic wars, in 1808.[36] One of their most celebrated products was a series of eight *tondi* (Museo del Prado, Madrid) with pictorial panels similar in style to Giuseppe Zocchi's Florentine work, bearing garlands of fruit, flowers, and birds, reworking motifs from late seventeenth-century Florence.[37]

NOTES

1 Aldrovandi 1562, pp. 137, 189.
2 Tuena 1990; Massinelli 1990, pp. 54–57.
3 Various aspects of the Grand Ducal workshops in Florence are examined in later chapters. A bibliography of the subject includes Zobi 1853, written by the first historian of the mosaic factory. For more recent contributions see Rossi 1967; Giusti, Mazzoni, and Pampaloni Martelli 1978; and Baldini, Giusti, and Pampaloni Martelli 1979. Indispensable essays by Alvar González-Palacios are gathered together in González-Palacios 1986. See also *Splendori di pietre dure* 1988; Giusti 1992; and González-Palacios 1993.
4 On the activity of the court stonecutters and goldsmiths, see Fock 1972; 1974.
5 Baldini, Giusti, and Pampaloni Martelli 1979; *Splendori di pietre dure* 1988, pp. 67–73.
6 *Splendori di pietre dure* 1988, pp. 134–37
7 Formerly in the Conservatorio 'La Quiete' Florence, now in the Museo degli Argenti.
8 *Splendori di pietre dure* 1988, p. 174.
9 González-Palacios 1986, vol. 1, pp. 84–85, 87–99.
10 Giusti, Mazzoni, and Pampaloni Martelli 1978, p. 315, fig. 371.
11 Giusti, Mazzoni, and Pampaloni Martelli 1978, p. 227.
12 Coccoluto 1861, p. 14; Massinelli 1993, p. 116.
13 Coccoluto 1861, pp. 276–77.
14 Finocchietti 1863, pp. 8–11.
15 Giusti, Mazzoni, and Pampaloni Martelli 1978, p. 278, no. 20.
16 Cozzi 1986.
17 Finocchietti 1863, p. 8.
18 Cefariello Grosso 1993, p. 11.
19 Massa 1983, p. 712.
20 Campori 1879, pp. 1–10.
21 Ruotolo 1974.
22 The history of the workshop and its products has been carefully reconstructed in González-Palacios 1977c, which includes Ghinghi's autobiography. See also *Civiltà del '700 a Napoli* 1979, pp. 71–151; González-Palacios 1982b, pp. 51–75; *Splendori di pietre dure* 1988, pp. 250–59.
23 One of the two topazes with Christ giving the blessing is now in the Museo Nazionale di S. Martino, Naples.
24 Quoted in Rossi 1967, p. 142.
25 *Splendori di pietre dure* 1988, p. 256, no. 76.
26 Piazza 1992, p. 18.
27 Accascina 1963.
28 Piazza 1992.
29 Mackowsky 1904, pp. 27–29; Quellmalz 1990, pp. 28–30, pl. 29.
30 See cat. no. 1; Neumann 1959; Prague 1988.
31 Alfter 1986.
32 See cat. nos. 78–79; Quellmalz 1990.
33 Rossi 1967, pp. 154–60.
34 Alcouffe 1988a.
35 González-Palacios 1982b; González-Palacios 1988c.
36 The production of the Buen Retiro workshop has been carefully catalogued in González-Palacios 1982b, pp. 66–77, and González-Palacios 1988b.
37 *Splendori di pietre dure* 1988, p. 264; Giusti 1992, pp. 223–53.

NOTE TO THE READER

This catalogue groups objects into the following categories:
1) cabinets, caskets, and clocks; 2) tables; 3) ecclesiastical objects; 4) snuffboxes; 5) hardstone pictures; 6) miscellaneous objects. Works are generally listed in chronological order within these categories.

Dimensions are usually provided as height by width by depth; height by diameter (round tables); length by width (tabletops); or height by width (hardstone pictures). Dimensions do not include frames (hardstone pictures); for other objects, measurements include the entire surface area.

Inventory numbers are provided for each catalogue entry, and comprise the Museum's accession number followed in brackets by Sir Arthur Gilbert's personal inventory number.

Short citations for sources are provided in the text; a complete listing of references can be found in the Bibliography. Similarly, a short form for exhibitions has been provided, where applicable, in the entries; a complete exhibition history follows the Bibliography.

When known, life dates are provided.

Abbreviations for some of the documentary sources referred to in the text are as follows:

A. A. G.	Archivio dell'Accademia dei Georgofili, Florence
A. S. F.	Archivio di Stato di Firenze
A. S. N.	Archivio di Stato di Napoli
B. N. F.	Bibliotheque Nationale Centrale, Florence
B. U. F.	Biblioteca della Galleria degli Uffizi, Florence
G. D. S. U.	Gabinetto Disegni e Stampe degli Uffizi, Florence
G. M.	Guardaroba Medicea
G. N. S	Gabinetto Nazionale delle Stampe, Rome
Y. I. R. C.	Imperiale e Real Corte Lorenese
M. M.	Miscellanea Medicea

Cabinets, Caskets and Clocks

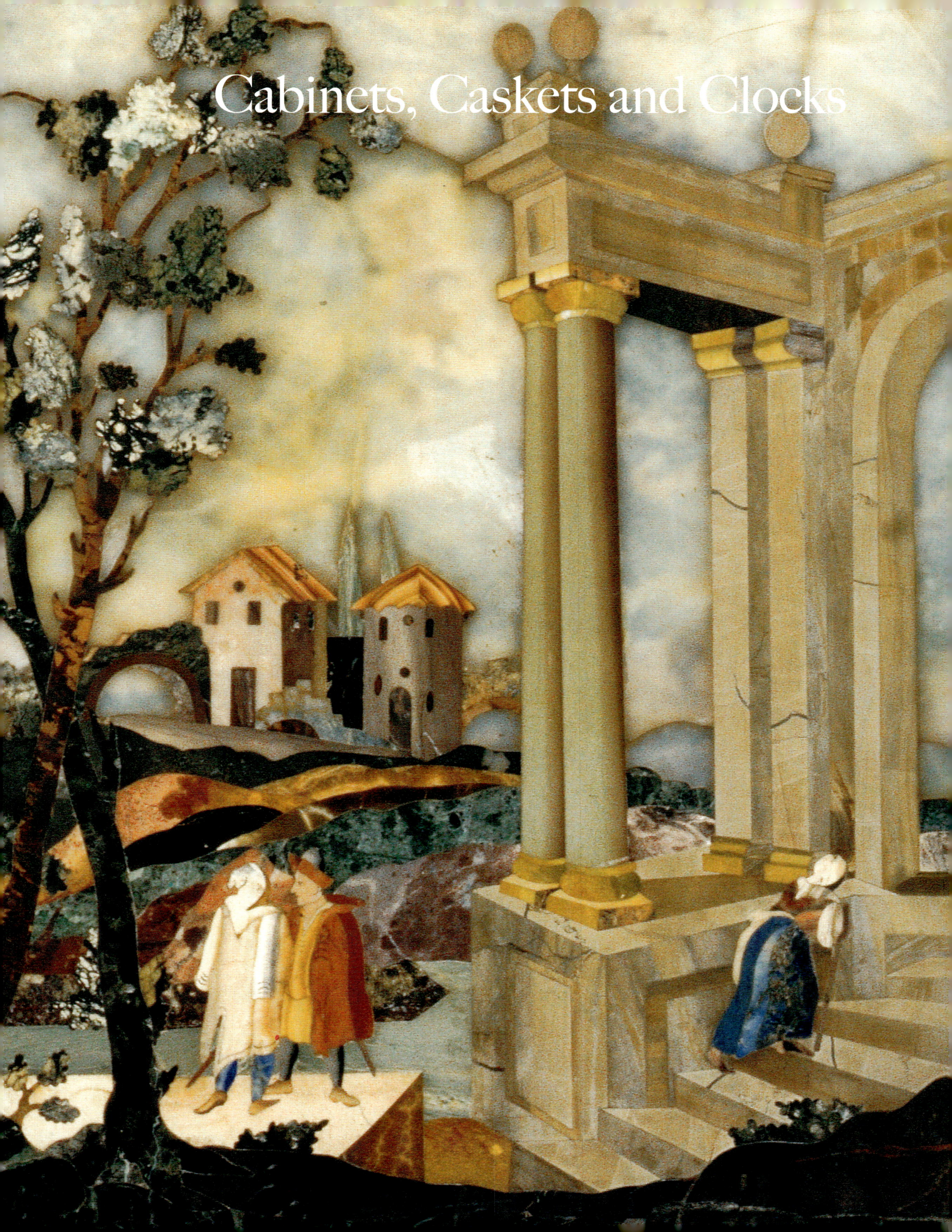

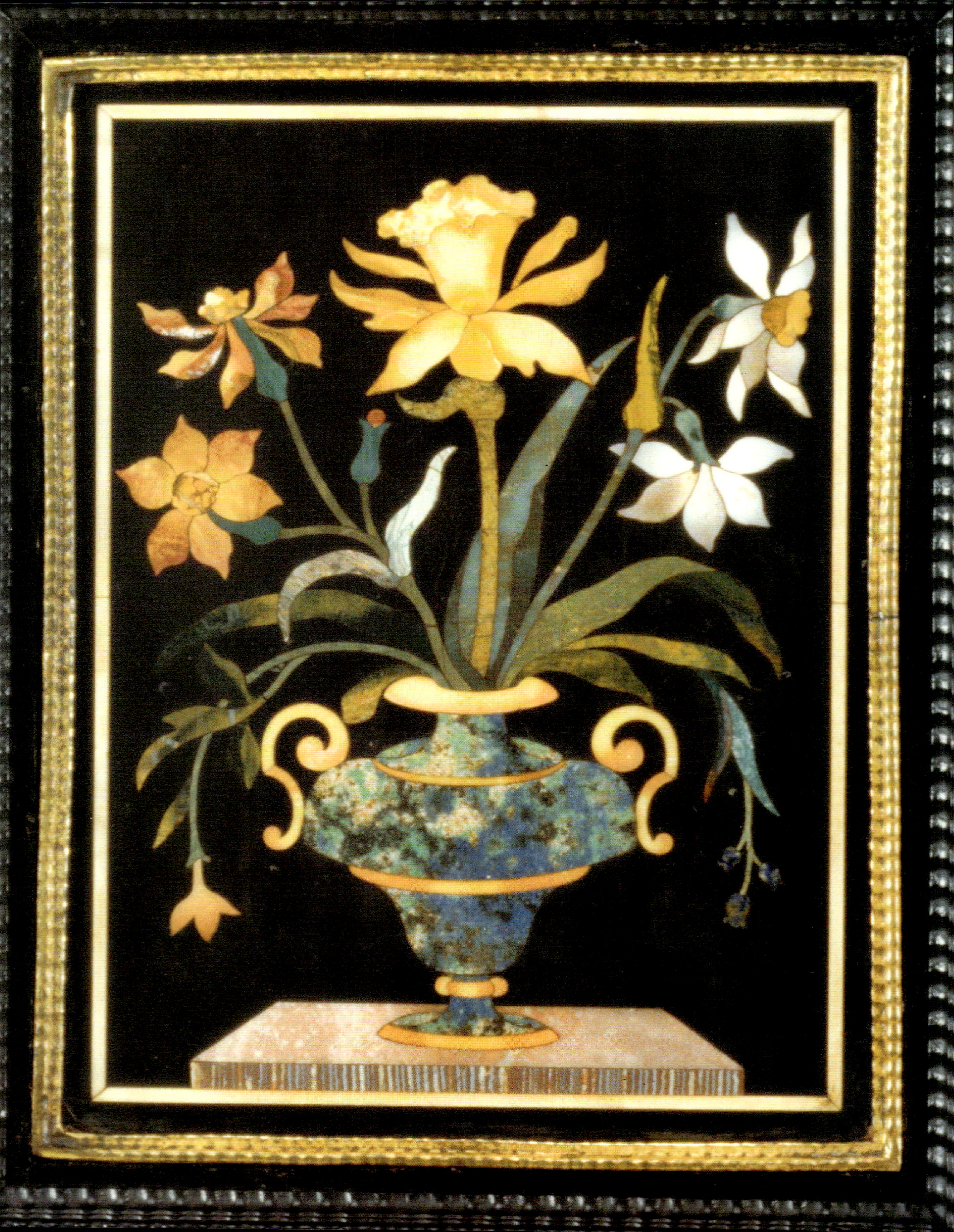

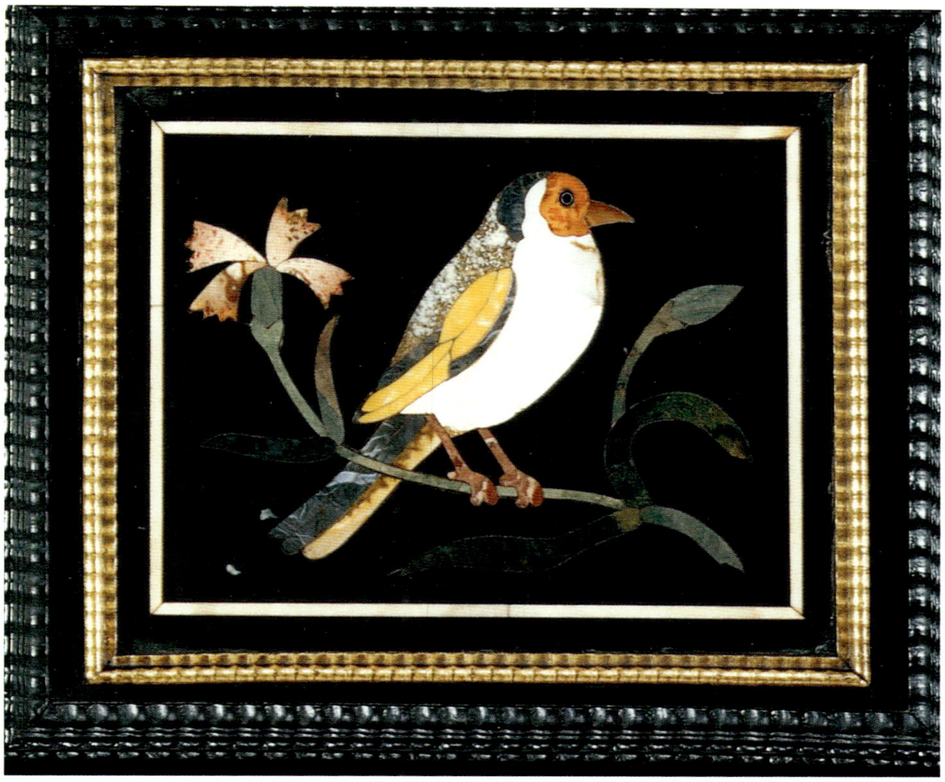

FLORENTINE CABINETS decorated with semiprecious stones became popular in Italy in the second half of the sixteenth century with the production of *studioli* – writing cabinets of architectural form. Most of these are now lost, but they are well known through contemporary inventories and illustrations.

The distinctive feature of these elaborate pieces of furniture was their structure. They displayed all the characteristic elements of Mannerist architecture – a pediment, corbels, pilasters, columns, and terminals – on a façade hiding a whole warren of small compartments: the *segreti* (secret drawers). The design of Renaissance cabinets was closely connected with the sixteenth-century passion for collecting; often the original function of a cabinet was to hold a collection of jewels, antique medals, or cameos. The appearance of these cabinets was strongly influenced by the archaeological interests of the collectors who commissioned them, as is evidenced by decorative details such as a series of small bronzes – either classical or derived from famous sculptures of antiquity – distributed in niches, on the pediment, or on the upper part of the façade.

In the documents that have survived to the present day, the names of all the major architects of the latter half of the sixteenth century are mentioned in relation to the design of cabinets. In Florence, Bernardo Buontalenti (1536?–1608), the court architect, designed three ebony cabinets inlaid with semiprecious stones (now lost) for Francesco and Ferdinand de' Medici. The first is mentioned in a famous passage by Raffaello Borghini (1541–c. 1588):

Previous page
Detail of cat. no. 6

Opposite
Detail of cat. no. 4

Above
Detail of cat. no. 4

> The Grand Duke has had made to [Buontalenti's] design an ebony writing cabinet constructed from all the orders of architecture, with columns of lapis lazuli, bloodstone, agate, and other gems, and the facade bears a number of gold terminals made with the collaboration of Benvenuto Cellini, Bartolomeo Ainmannati, Giambologna, Vincenzo Danti, Lorenzo della Nera, and Vincentio de' Rossi. In this marvellous work of art there are many stones, precious ones, inlaid with beautiful symmetry; on the stones, Bernardo, with diligent hand, has painted some miniatures depicting stories of Pallas Athene and portraits of some of the most beautiful women in Florence, and truly it is a lovely thing to see. But whoever wants all these adornments, the friezes, the borders, and all the details that contribute to making this a thing of consummate beauty, plus the ingenious locks, the little secret drawers, and the marble table inlaid all over with gemstones that stands in front of it – if you should want to possess all this, then I must tell you that it is a lengthy and difficult undertaking and cannot be achieved in a short time.[1]

In Prague, Emperor Rudolf II – who maintained very close relations with the Grand Dukes of Florence and the Milanese *pietre dure* ateliers, set up a workshop with aims very similar to those of Florence. Ottavio Miseroni arrived in Prague in 1588; Cosimo Castrucci is documented there from 1596. The two craftsmen were required to make lapidary mosaics, and from the outset they managed to give their work an individual pictorial quality and identifiably northern flavour. The colour of the local stones they used (the range of tones was fairly restricted) was ideally suited to the depiction of picturesque Germanic landscapes. The output of the Castrucci family (Cosimo's son Giovanni arrived in Prague in 1608) is known through a number of cabinets and caskets, including a casket in the Gilbert Collection (cat. no. 1).

In the furniture made in the Prague workshop, architecture was only of secondary importance; the structure of the caskets was mainly designed to hold and display the hardstone panels. The cabinets that can be reliably attributed to the Castrucci workshop cannot be identified as such on architectural grounds; some of them were constructed at a later date using *pietre dure* panels constructed in the workshop for different pieces of furniture. The number of pieces recovered today suggests that the workshop was highly productive.

During the second decade of the seventeenth century, activity in the imperial workshops in Prague slowed down, and mosaic decoration passed into the design repertory of the cabinetmakers of Augsburg. The city had been celebrated since the second half of the sixteenth century for its cabinet-makers; highly elaborate cupboards and writing desks were made there and exported all over Europe. There is evidence of the use of stone mosaic decoration in Augsburg from the end of the sixteenth century.[2]

The Mannerist cabinets that have survived are virtuoso works. Opulent, and refined in their architecture, they were made to order for clients and collectors whose tastes they reflect. Throughout the seventeenth century, the Florentine workshops continued to produce examples that were unique in the complexity of their design and ornamentation. Once the jewel-work style (see Tables section) had been put to one side in the early seventeenth century, stoneworkers began producing cycles of mosaic panels bearing landscape and floral designs in both hardstone and softstone.

From the mid-seventeenth century and throughout the following century, Florentine mosaics became associated throughout Europe with expensive and ostentatious furniture. Whether decorated with flowering branches, birds, fruit, vases of flowers, landscapes, views of Florence, or mythological motifs, Florentine cabinets remained popular throughout the Continent.

From the early years of the seventeenth century, the production of cabinets was augmented by the manufacture of caskets. By the end of the century, these, along with clocks, would become some of the items most frequently made in the court workshops.

When Giovanni Battista Foggini was named architect-in-chief and manager of the court workshops in 1694–95, production of caskets was stepped up and began to assume a more ceremonial character, thanks to their opulent decoration with panels of *pietre dure* and bronze statuettes to Foggini's designs. Alvar González-Palacios, who has collated all the archival material relating to these objects with various of Foggini's drawings and certain caskets traced to a number of different collections, has been able to expose the salient features of this stream of objects.[3] There are different styles and qualities of caskets in Foggini's output. Generally, they are made of ebony with mosaic panels, usually in relief, inlaid in the lid and sides. The mosaics bear the usual naturalistic motifs: flowers, fruit, and birds. He was also responsible for an elegant clock, now in the Gilbert Collection (cat. no. 10). This clock sums up, with the caskets of ebony and *pietre dure*, the main field of activity of the Grand Ducal workshops in the final ten years of the reign of Cosimo III.

At the Exhibition of the Products of French Industry in Paris in 1844, there could be seen – among the various styles of reproduction furniture – cabinets of wood veneered in ebony and embellished with *pietre dure* panels. It was the Esposizione Universale Fiorentina in 1855, however, that conferred status on revivals of the styles of the Renaissance, Louis XIV, Louis XV and Louis XVI. The adulation of Queen Marie-Antoinette (1755–93) by the Empress Eugénie (1826–1920) encouraged the fashion during the Second Empire for Louis XVI furniture.

The eclectic tastes of the late nineteenth century stimulated a return to the production of cabinets decorated with lapidary mosaics in Florence. Older mosaic panels were frequently used on newer pieces of furniture. According to Paolo Ferroni, antique furniture 'could be used without too great an outlay by making it into the artistic furniture that today is in such great demand; if left in oblivion these pieces will perish'.[4]

In the mid-nineteenth century, the Opificio and some of the independent workshops also produced cabinets and caskets in the seventeenth- and eighteenth-century styles, with a preference for floral decoration on a ground of black marble. The construction was generally quite simple, the mosaic decorations being mounted on a frame of wood or metal.

A large cabinet, exhibited by the Ugolini workshop at the Exposition Universelle in Paris in 1900, is evidence of the persistence of the fashion for furniture in the Medici style. The presence of works from the past, and their continuing prestige, forged strong links with previous styles among local craftsmen. The furniture remaining in the Palazzo Vecchio and the Palazzo Pitti and that which had been cropping up regularly in the salesrooms since the end of the eighteenth century stimulated the curiosity of modern craftsmen and made them wish to emulate it. They were often witnesses to acts of terrible destruction. It was a cabinetmaker at the beginning of the nineteenth century (and his remark would have been just as pertinent at the end of the century) who observed bitterly: 'Such beautiful cabinets were kept in the Guardaroba, but now very few are left. There were equally beautiful ones in private houses, but the number is ever decreasing and now, when such a cabinet comes up for sale, modern artists rush to see it and profess themselves overwhelmed'.[5]

NOTES

1 Borghini 1584, p. 610; Heikamp 1963; Massinelli 1990.
2 See Alfter 1986.
3 González-Palacios 1986, vol. 1, pp. 42–47.
4 (B. U. F. 1862, c. 16; Giusti, Mazzoni, and Pampaloni Martelli 1978, p. 287).
5 A. A. G., Carte Bartolozzi, Busta 179, ins. 56, c. 264r.

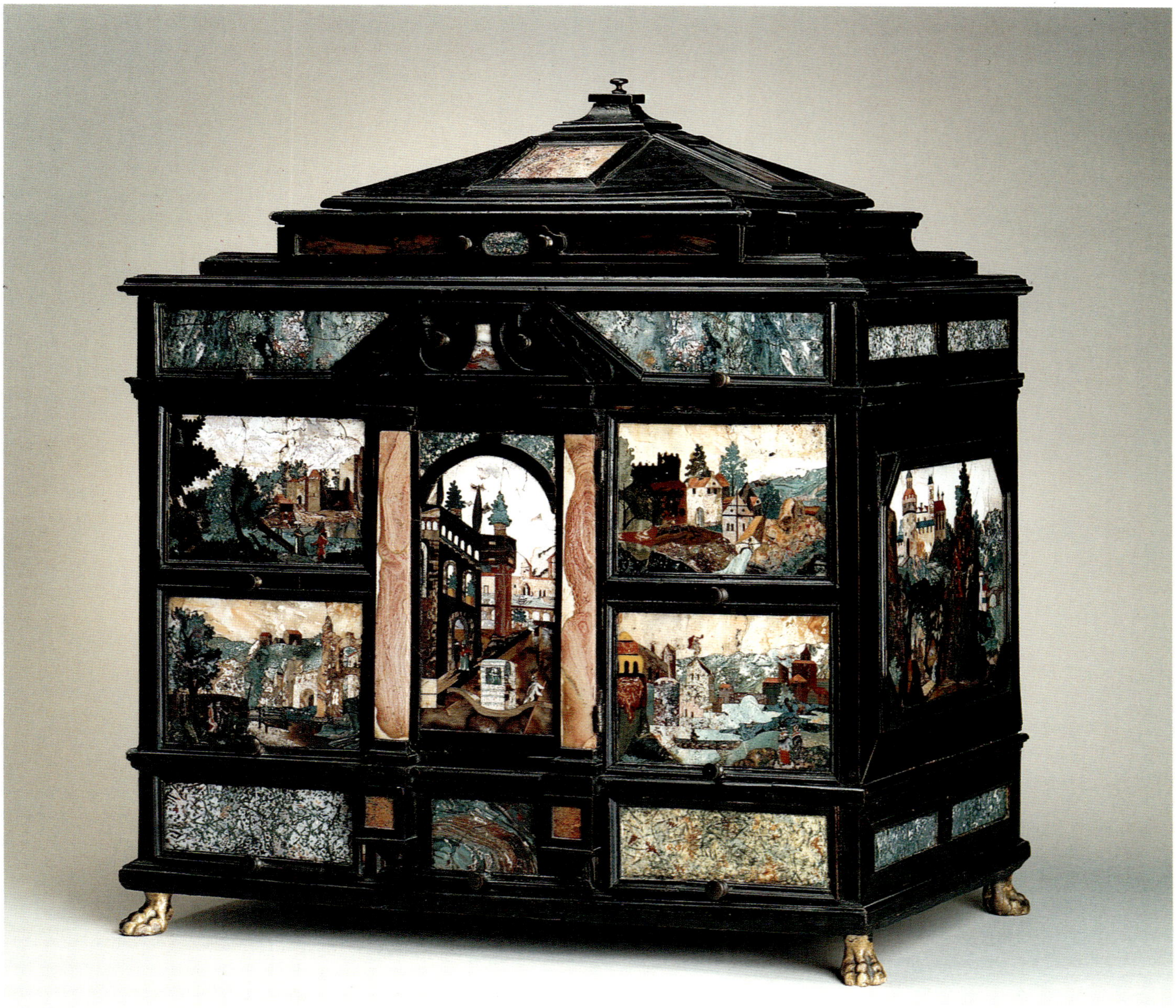

1. COLLECTOR'S CABINET

Castrucci workshop, probably Cosimo the elder, Prague, c. 1610
Pietre dure, ebonised and gilded wood, 48.6 × 46.7 × 25.4 cm (19⅛ × 18⅜ × 10 in)
1996.210 (MM39)

PROVENANCE: Hradchin Palace, Prague; Le Beau, New York 1966; Los Angeles County Museum of Art.

LITERATURE: Sherman 1971; Avery and Emperatori 1975, no. 47; González-Palacios 1977a, no. 1; Johnson 1977, p. 40; Distelberger 1980, p. 62; González-Palacios and Röttgen 1982, no. 1; Liechtenstein 1985, p. 45; Giusti 1992, p. 164.

EXHIBITIONS: Los Angeles, 1975; London, 1975; Los Angeles / Atlanta / San Antonio / Richmond / Seattle, 1977–79.

DESCRIPTION: A collector's cabinet of ebonised wood set with seven pictorial *pietre dure* panels and several more of hardstone. The door in the centre of the façade is faced with a panel of stone mosaic depicting a Venetian *capriccio*. This panel is flanked by two smooth, jasper pilasters with simple capitals and bases of ebonised wood.

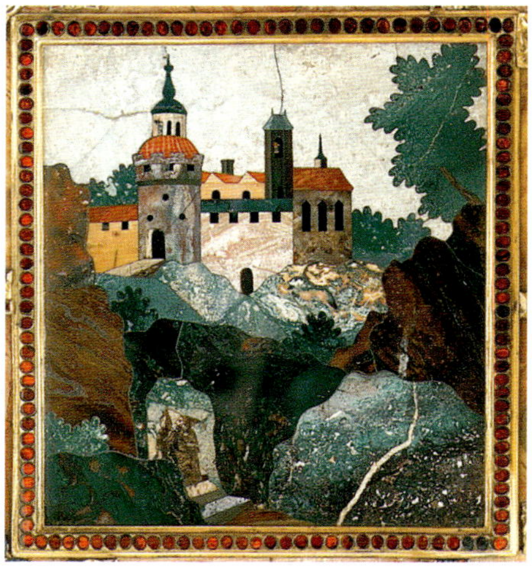

FIG. 3 Detail of casket, Castrucci workshop. Liechtenstein Collection

On either side of these are two pairs of panels, one above the other, with narrow moulded frames. The central door is attached to the right-hand panel by two hinges. When the door is opened, the side panels can be slid in the grooves toward the centre to reveal six inner drawers, three on each side. The upper part of the front of the cabinet is occupied by a long drawer faced with jasper; in the centre, above the central door, there is a wooden triangular shape forming a broken pediment. The lower band has three drawers, the central and left-hand ones being faced with jasper; the right-hand one, with imitation jasper. On top of the cabinet, a pyramidal roof bears four square panels of stone framed on each of its four sides. The base of this pyramid contains a very narrow drawer with bands of jasper on the front. All the drawers have small brass handles in the shape of flattened spheres. On the sides of the cabinet, rectangular mosaic panels with canted corners are framed in wood. The upper and lower sides have two rectangular bands of jasper. The chest stands on four lion's feet in gilded wood.

COMMENTARY: According to Rudolph Distelberger, the hardstone plaques on this casket were made in the Castrucci workshop in Prague around 1610 by the elder Castrucci.[1] The wooden construction is of the period. The Castrucci workshop exploited natural variations of colour and pattern in each mineral to create the mountainous landscapes with castles, towns, and people depicted on the panels. While hardstone work is generally associated with Italy, this variant style unquestionably evolved in Prague.

Artists in every medium made extensive use of print sources. Engravings made around 1600–18 by the Flemish painter and engraver, Aegidius Sadeler (1570–1629) after designs by Pieter Stevens (c. 1567 –after 1624) seem likely to have been the inspiration for scenes on this and other Castrucci plaques. Sadeler came to work at the royal Prague workshops in 1598, as did Pieter Stevens, another Flemish artist whose work influenced Saedler. The hardstone panels on the Gilbert Collection cabinet can be compared with other works made in the Prague workshops. A *pietre dure* scene of the same design is on the front of a casket made for Prince Karl von Liechtenstein (1569–1627), now in the royal collection in Liechtenstein (inv. no. 599).

On the left front of the Gilbert Collection cabinet is a view of Krumay Palace, Bohemia, with two hooded monks under a stone arch. This view is also on the lid of the Liechtenstein casket fig. 3, on a seventeenth-century Dresden cabinet using Prague *pietre dure* panels (Dresden, Grünes Gewölbe), and on an individual panel in the Umeleckopromyslové Muzeum (Museum of Decorative Arts) in Prague.[2] Another framed plaque depicting a boatman is at the Museo Civico in Turin.[3] The panel with cut corners on the left side of the Gilbert Collection cabinet is the same as the middle panel on the right side of the Liechtenstein casket (fig. 4).[4]

NOTES

1 Thanks to Rudolph Disteberger of the Kunsthistorisches Museum, who examined this object at Los Angeles in 1988.
2 Bukovinska 1972, p. 365, fig. 3.
3 *Splendori di Pietre Dure* 1988, no. 414.
4 Liechtenstein 1985, no. 25.

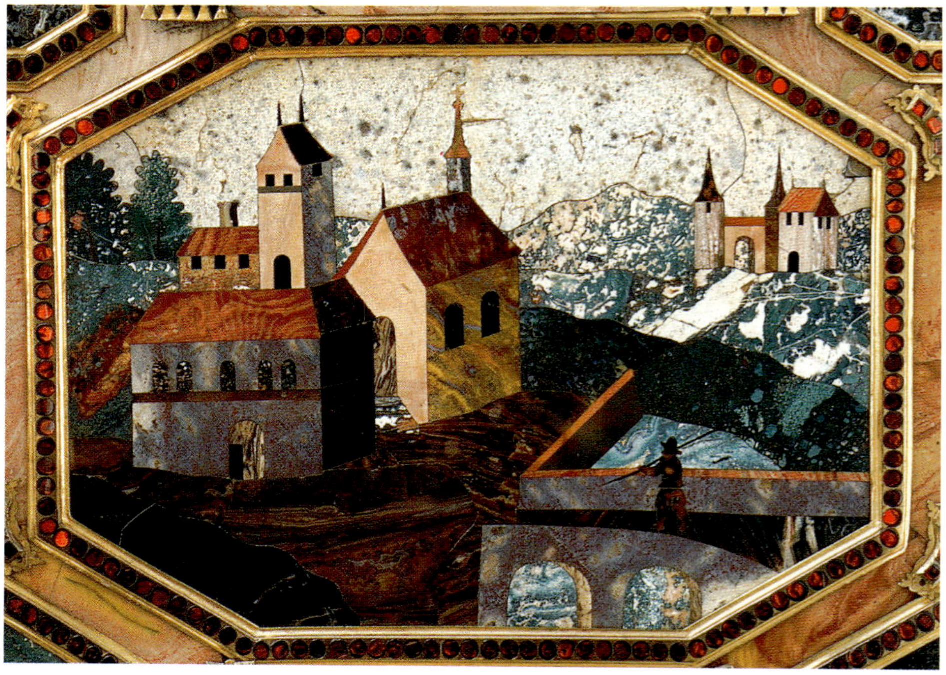

FIG. 4 Detail, Liechtenstein casket.

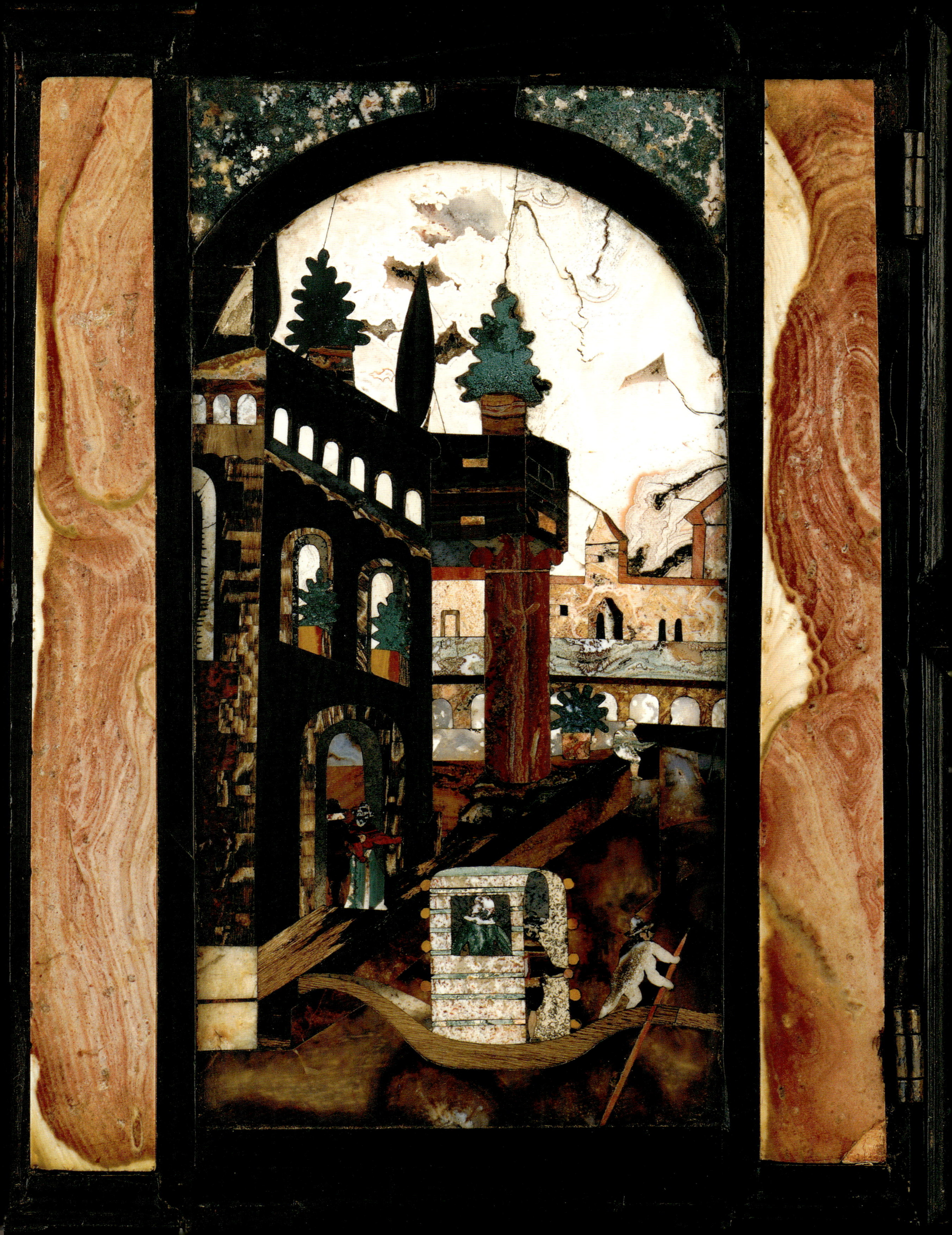

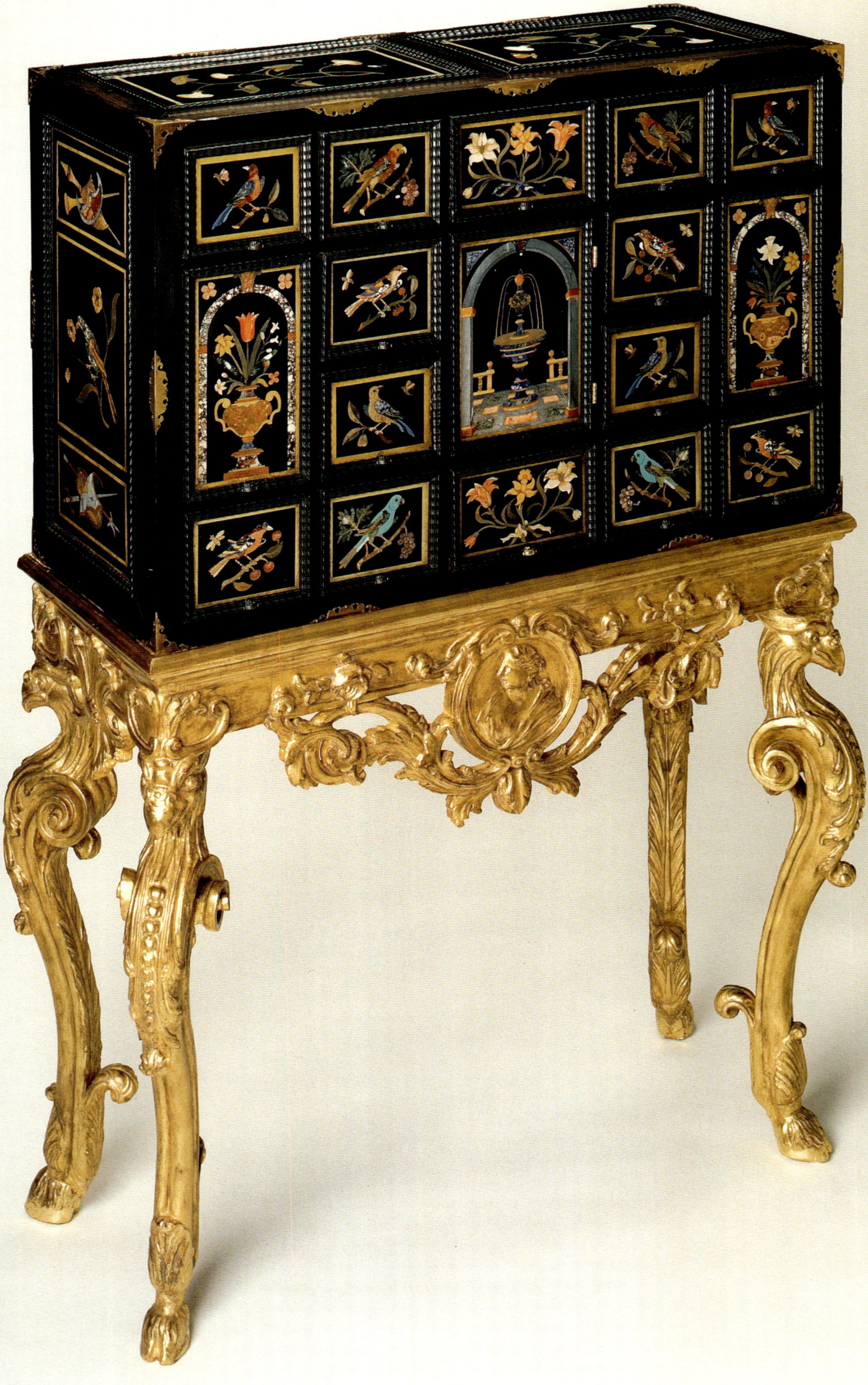

2. CABINET

Pietre dure: Florence, first half seventeenth century; cabinet: Northern Europe, mid-seventeenth century; stand: England, c. 1750
Pietre dure, ebonised wood and gilt base; cabinet: 57.5 × 89.5 × 35.6 cm (22⅝ x 35¼ × 14 in)
stand: 80 × 97.8 × 41.9 cm (31½ × 38½ × 16½ in)
1996.192 (MMII)

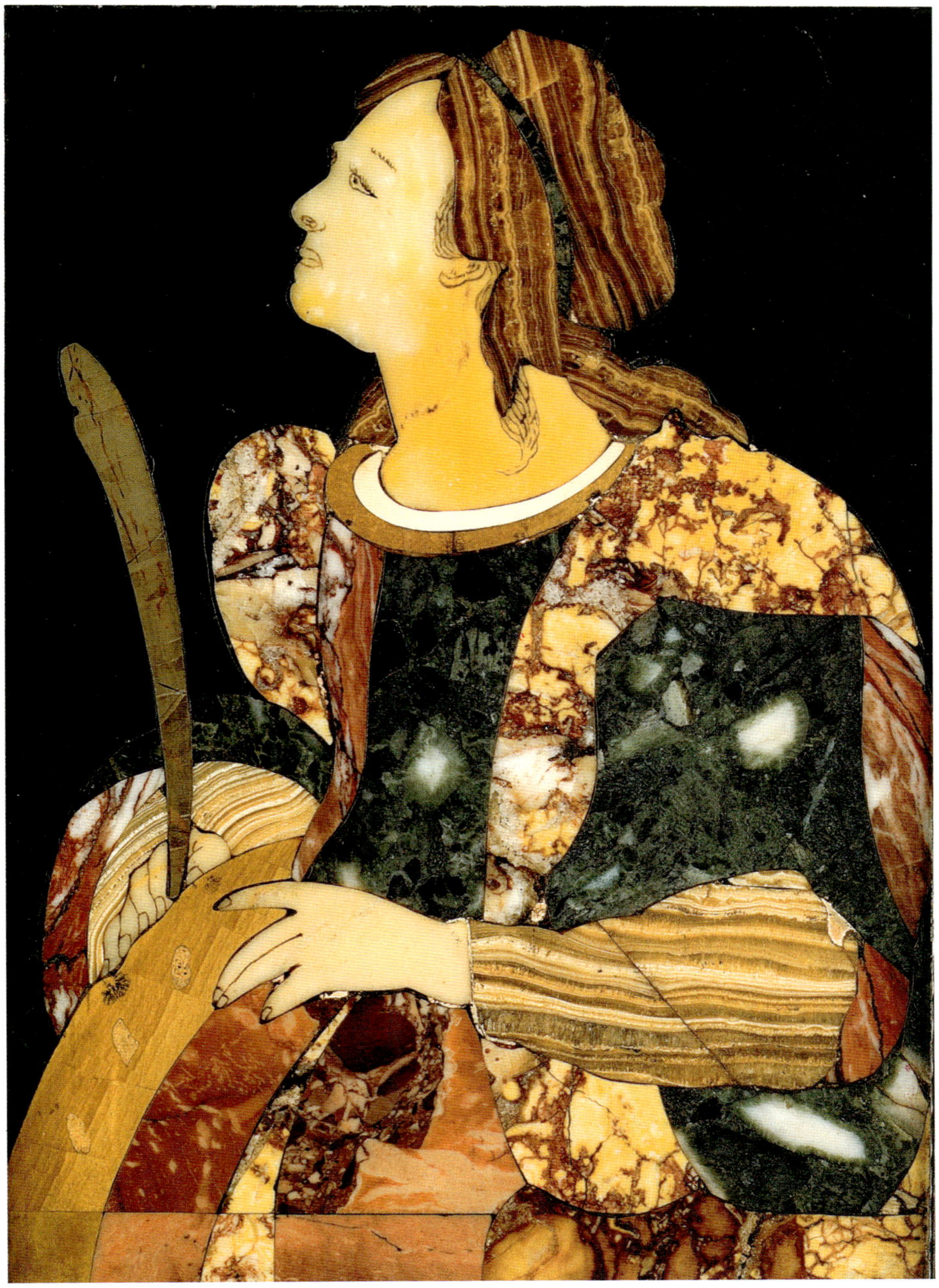

PROVENANCE: Sotheby's, sale, London, 25 July 1969, lot 105; Los Angeles County Museum of Art.

LITERATURE: Sherman 1971, no. 32; Avery and Emperatori 1975, no. 45; Hillier 1975, pl. A, p. 269; Sunset 1977, p. 71; González-Palacios 1977a, no. 4; González-Palacios and Röttgen 1982, no. 4.

EXHIBITIONS: Los Angeles, 1975; London, 1975; Los Angeles / Atlanta / San Antonio / Richmond / Seattle, 1977–79.

DESCRIPTION: A table cabinet made of softwood with ebony veneer and rippled moulding. The door in the centre of the façade is decorated with a *pietre dure* panel depicting a courtyard with a large arched entrance and a fountain in the middle. Inside the door is another *pietre dure* panel with a picture of a saint holding a martyr's palm. This door gives access to an interior section that can be pulled out, inside which there are two drawers edged in rippled moulding with black marble and *pietre dure* panels, decorated with sprigs of flowers.

The side wings of the cabinet have two drawers with vases of flowers inlaid on the outside. Each pair of the upper and lower *pietre dure* panels decorated with birds fronts a single drawer. The two panels on each side between the *pietre dure* with the fountain and the panel with flowers, each covers a whole drawer, as do the two plaques above and below the fountain decorated with three flowers tied with a ribbon. The cabinet is set on a stand of carved and gilded wood made in England about 1750.

The sides of the cabinet are faced with two large panels, each bearing three *pietre dure* mosaics, the centre one depicting a bird on a flowering branch, the upper and lower depicting trophies. The top has two further *pietre dure* panels with sprays of campanula. The *pietre dure* plaques contain various types of breccia and coloured marbles with an inlay of lapis lazuli, jasper, Sienese onyx, *verde d'Arno* and Albarese limestone. The edges and corners of the cabinet have gilt-bronze mounts. The birds in the lower corners resemble bramblings (*Fringilla montifringilla*), or Northern European finches; the parrots on the bottom row have ring necks like the rose-ringed parakeet (*Psittacula krameri*).[1]

COMMENTARY: This piece is constructed after the manner of the Flemish cabinetmakers of the mid-seventeenth century, who disseminated the style throughout the courts of Europe. It has certain similarities with a Flemish cabinet that has a view of the Villa della Petraia in the centre (Palazzo Vecchio, Florence), which was included in the inventory of goods left by Don Lorenzo de' Medici after his death in 1649.[2] The two panels set in the lid of the Gilbert Collection cabinet also occur in a cabinet formerly in the possession of the diarist John Evelyn (1620–1706),[3] and a cabinet with the Barberini coat-of-arms in the Metropolitan Museum of Art, New York.

Doubt has been cast by González-Palacios on the Florentine origins of the *pietre dure* panels, but they appear to be typical products of the Grand Ducal workshops in the first half of the seventeenth century. The fountain motif also appears on the Evelyn cabinet, which was made in Florence in 1645 by Domenico Benotti (fl. 1640–1653).[4] The military trophies on the sides, although belonging to the Roman tradition of mosaics from the second half of the sixteenth century, could also be of Florentine manufacture. Similar panoplies, made using a large amount of *pietre tenere*, can be seen on tabletops that are known to have been made in Florence in the first part of the seventeenth century. One dated 1615 and hailing from Florentine workshops bears witness to the fact that the craftsman Gualtieri Cecchi was paid for making a series of panels decorated with military trophies. The panels of the Gilbert Collection cabinet were probably acquired in Florence and mounted elsewhere in the Flemish style.

NOTES

1 Thanks to Kimball L. Garrett of the Los Angeles Museum of Natural History for identifying the bird species.

2 *Splendori di pietre dure* 1988, p. 148.

3 Boynton,1971, fig. 1.

4 Radcliffe and Thornton, 1978, pp 259-62.

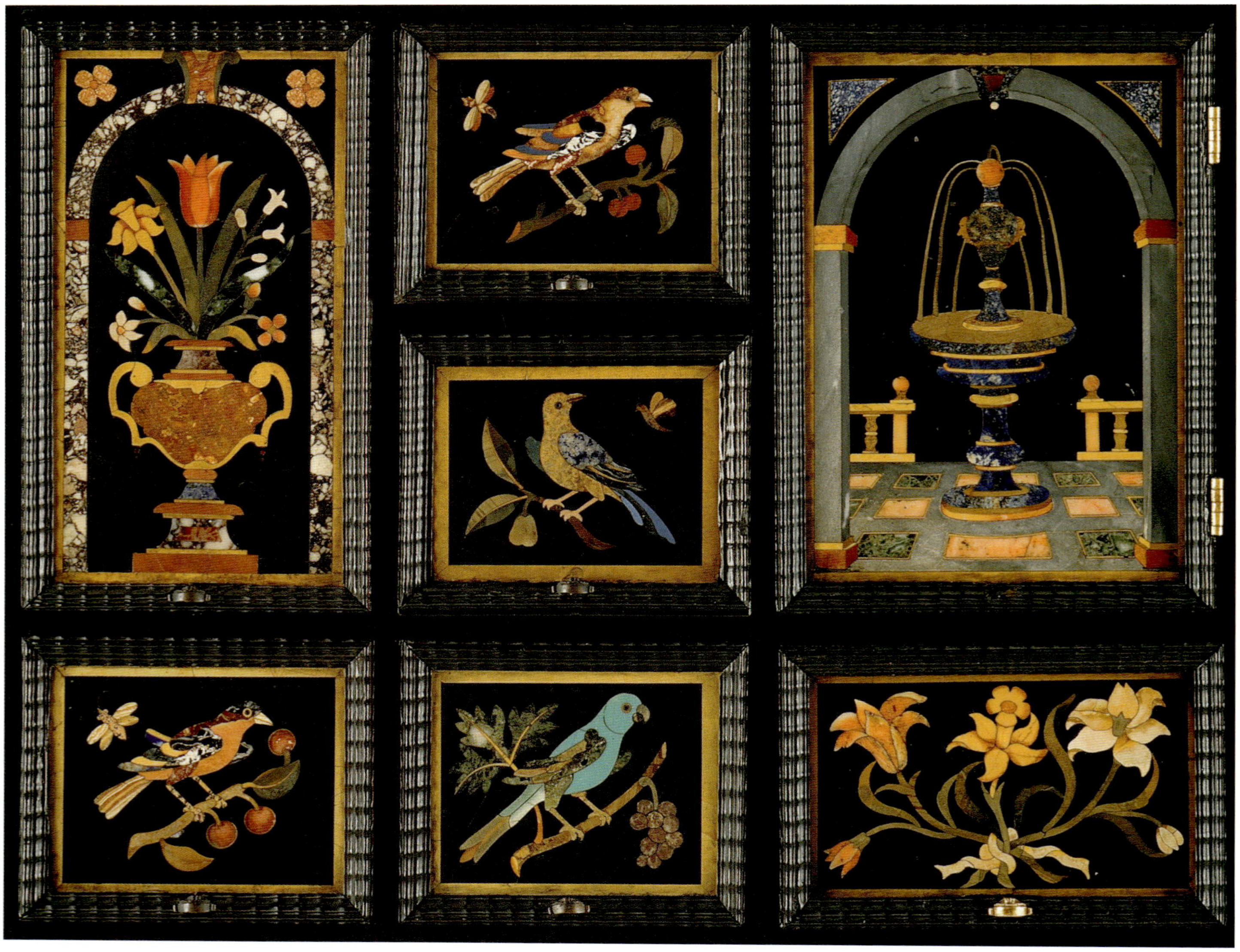

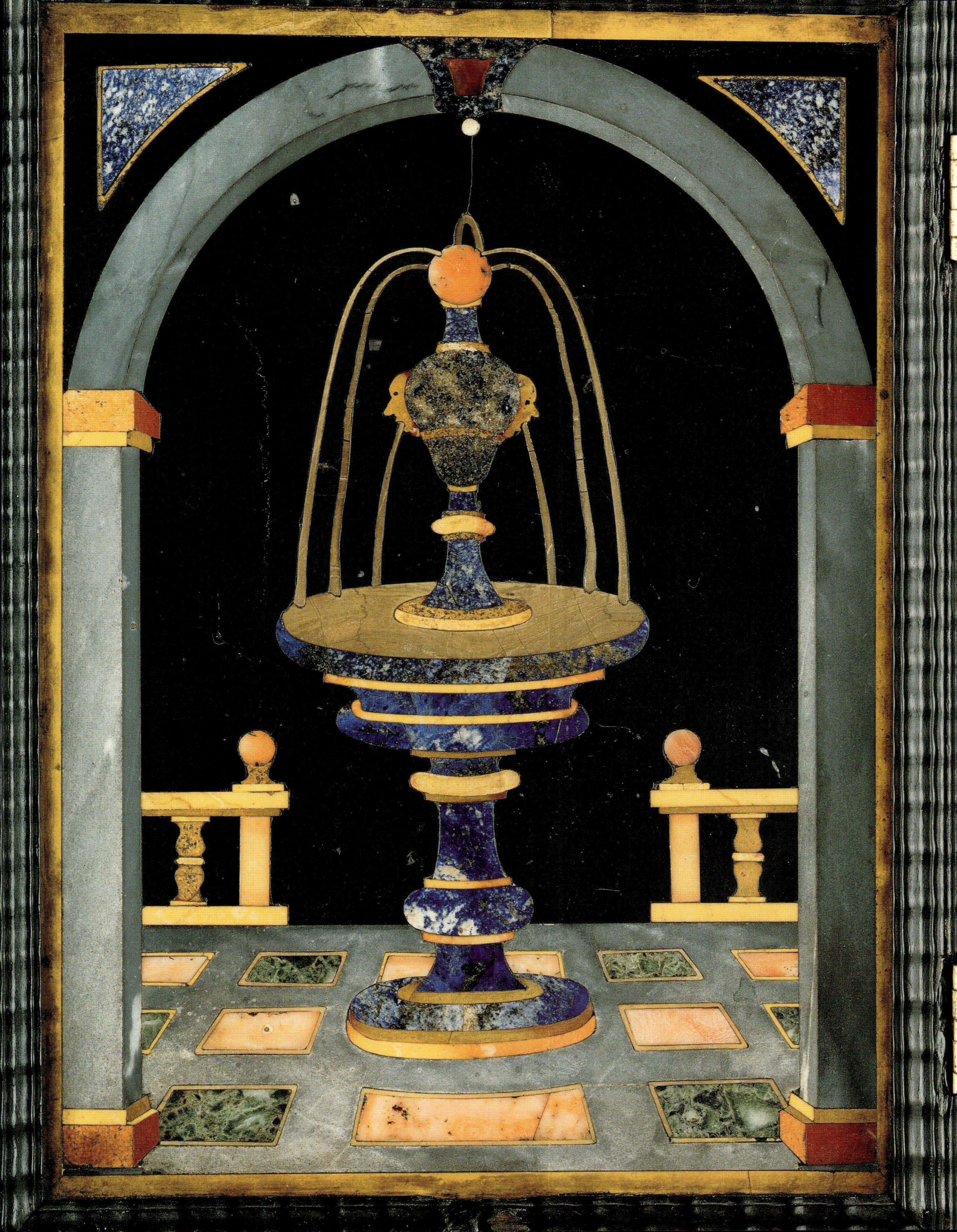

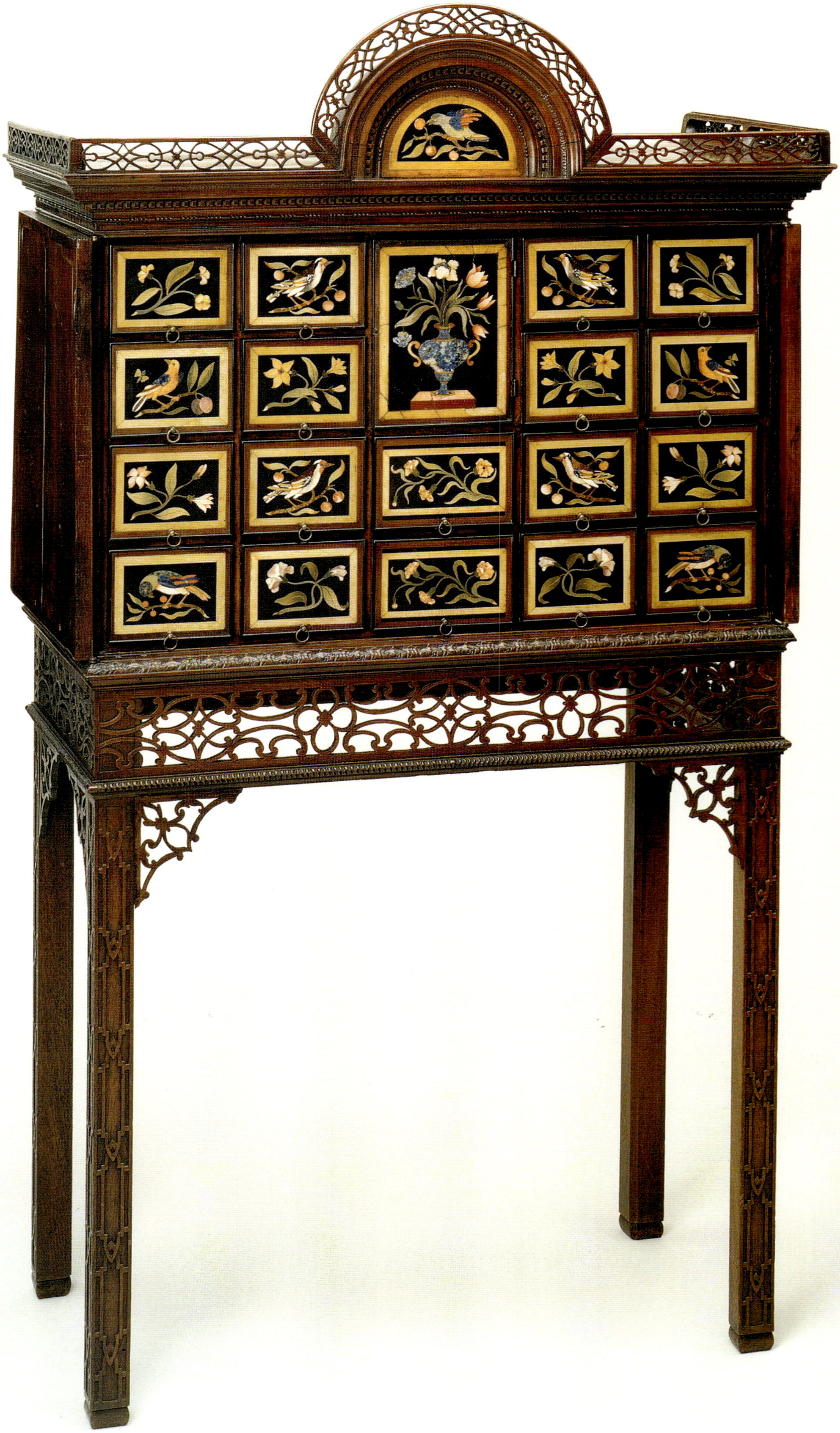

3. CABINET

Pietre dure: Florence, mid-seventeenth century; cabinet and stand: England, late eighteenth century
Mahogany, *pietre dure*, brass; cabinet: 71.1 × 86.8 × 42.1 cm (28 × 34 3/16 × 16 9/16 in); stand: 78.4 × 39.4 × 80.6 cm (30 7/8 × 15 1/2 × 31 3/4 in)
1996.263 (MM110)

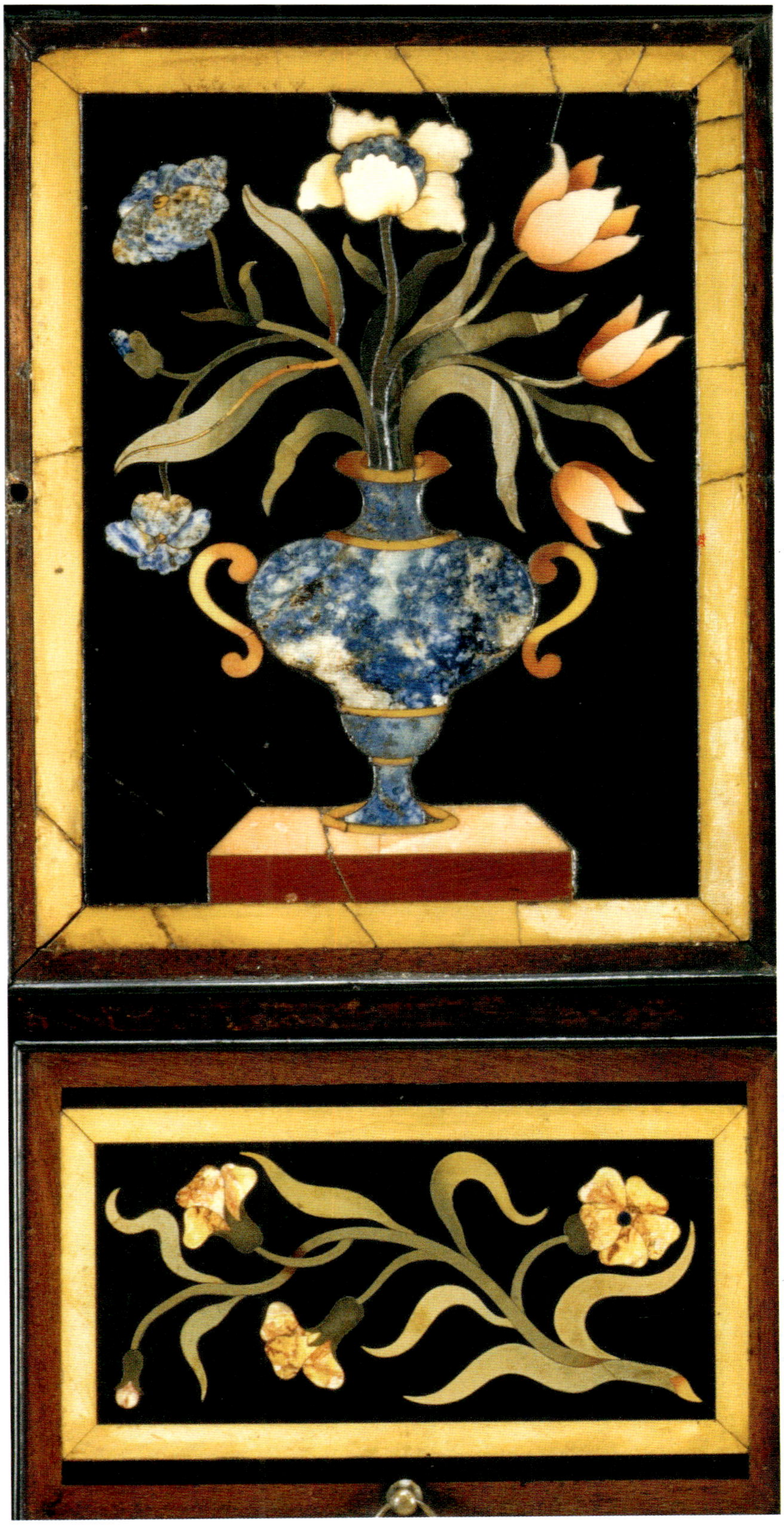

PROVENANCE: Thomas Alexander Fermor-Hesketh (third Baron Lempster), Easton Neston, Towcester, Northants, England; Richard Courtney, Ltd, London, 1971; Los Angeles County Museum of Art.

LITERATURE: *Connoisseur*, March 1971, p. 63; Avery and Emperatori 1975, no. 48; González-Palacios 1977a, no. 5; González-Palacios and Röttgen 1982, no. 5.

EXHIBITIONS: Los Angeles, 1975; London, 1975; Los Angeles / Atlanta / San Antonio / Richmond / Seattle, 1977–79.

DESCRIPTION: A cabinet in mahogany on a fretwork stand with carved feet. The upper part has two doors. The semicircular pediment has a fretwork gallery and a central *pietre dure* lunette. The eighteen drawers in the front are decorated with *pietre dure* panels of flowers and birds on a background of black marble edged with a yellow marble border.

COMMENTARY: *Pietre dure* plaques of this type were very common in Florentine baroque production. Similar naturalistic mosaics are on a cabinet of 1645 attributed to Domenico Benotti (fl. 1640–53). John Evelyn brought the nineteen plaques back from Florence and had a cabinet made in England for their display.[1] Another, with plaques similar to those of the Gilbert Collection cabinet was at Mallett and Sons (London, 1987) and was also attributed to Benotti. The latter cabinet also has plaques depicting the Piazza della Signoria and the Medici villa, La Petraia.[2]

NOTES
1 Boynton, 1971, fig. 1.
2 Mallett, 1987, p. 78

4. CABINET

Pietre dure and cabinet: Florence, Grand Ducal workshops, third quarter seventeenth century; stand: England, first half nineteenth century
Pietre dure, jasper, lapis lazuli, marble, ebony, marquetry of exotic woods, rosewood, brass, gilt bronze, gilt brass, silk; cabinet: 76.5 × 115.9 × 40.3 cm (30 1/8 × 45 5/8 × 15 7/8 in); stand: 80 × 129.5 × 42.5 cm (31 1/2 × 51 × 16 3/4 in)
1996.600 (MM112)

PROVENANCE: Daniel Finch, second Earl of Nottingham and seventh Earl of Winchelsea and Nottingham, c. 1700; Burley-on-the-Hill, Oakham, Rutland; anon., sale, Christie's, London, 25 November 1971, lot 91; Los Angeles County Museum of Art.

LITERATURE: Christie's *Review of the Season* 1972, p. 373; Avery and Emperatori 1975, no. 49; González-Palacios 1977, no. 3; Il Museo dell'Opificio 1978, no. P 292; González-Palacios and Röttgen 1982, no. 3.

EXHIBITIONS: Los Angeles, 1975, no. 30; London, 1975; Los Angeles, 1977.

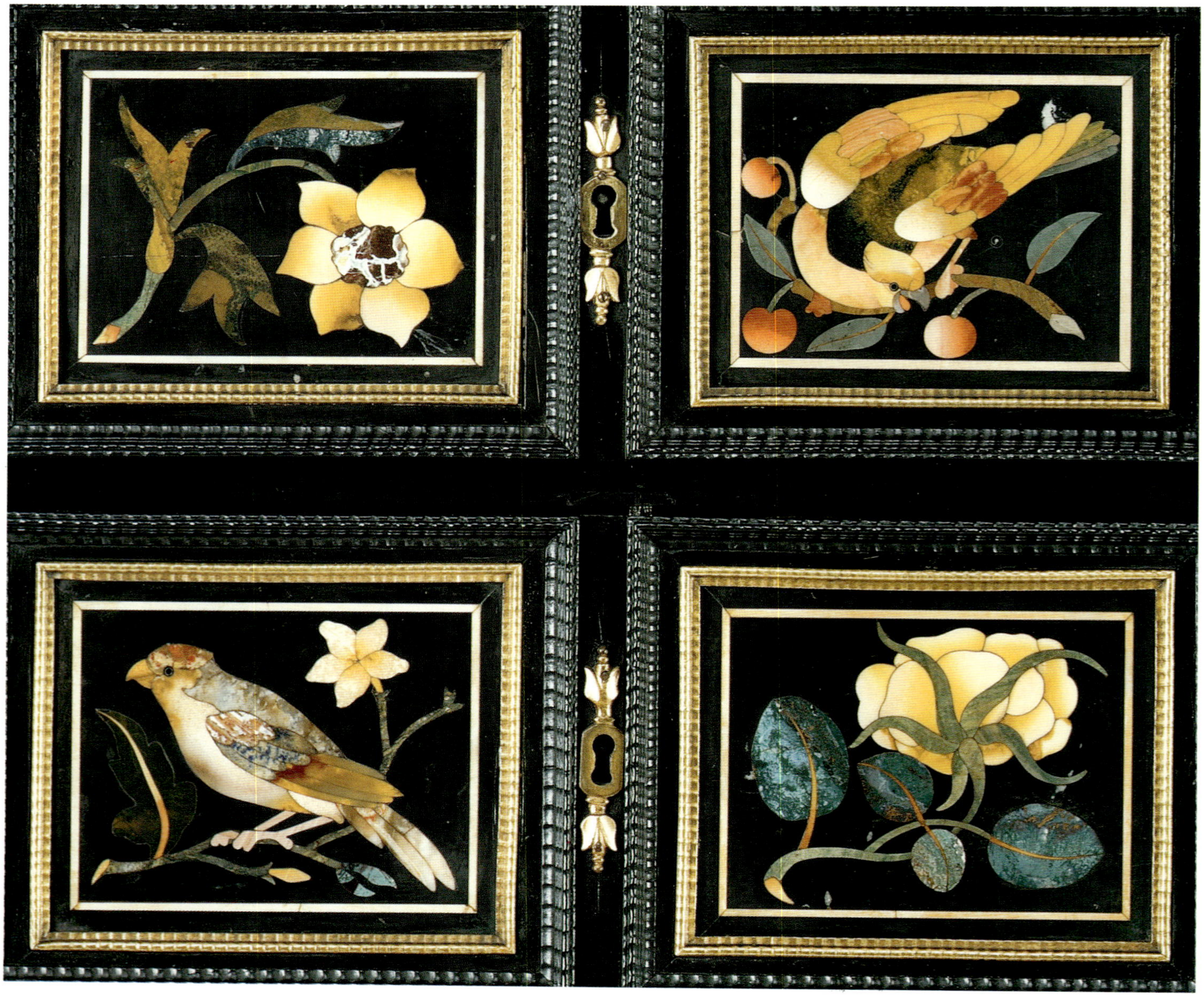

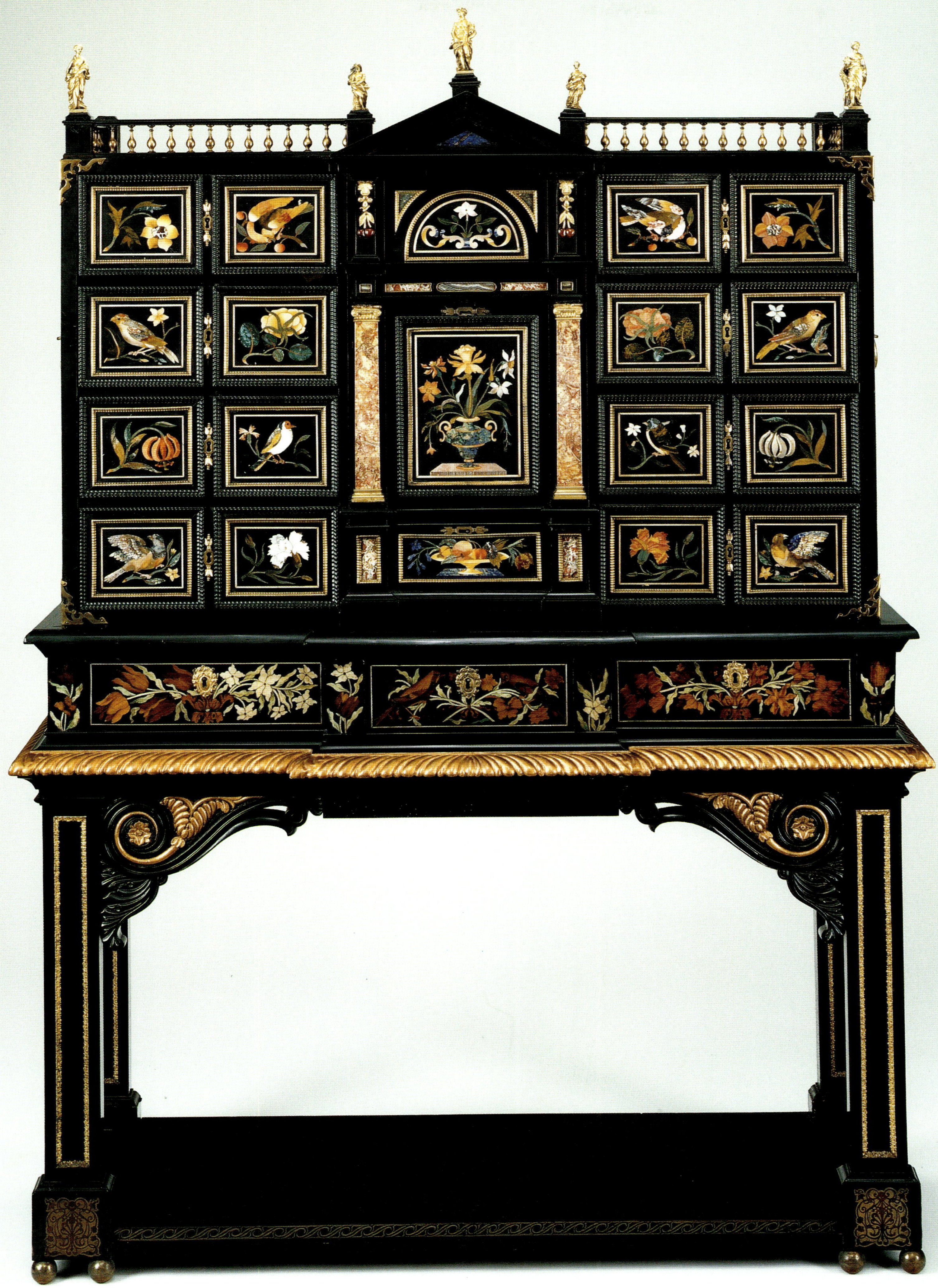

DESCRIPTION: A cabinet of ebony veneer with an architectural façade. The central door has a rippled frame and gilt-bronze inner border surrounding a *pietre dure* panel with a vase of flowers on a black marble background. This is flanked by two pilasters of *broccatello* marble with gilt-bronze Ionic capitals and bases. The door opens to reveal two inner doors faced with rosewood, surrounded by a fine ivory strip and outer ripple-moulded border. There are two rows of four drawers on either side of the central door, each faced with a *pietre dure* panel in a ripple-moulded frame, and with a central lock. These panels are largely made of *pietre dure*, depicting alternately flowers and birds perched on sprigs of flowers (roses, lilies and carnations). The panels opposite each other on either side are taken from the same design but use different stones.

The lower central panel is a drawer with a *pietre dure* depiction of a bowl of fruit and flowers. A border encrusted with agate and jasper separates the central part from the top storey, which has another drawer in the centre, faced with a lunette panel bearing a flower design in hardstone. The pediment consists of a moulded-ebony cornice with a tympanum inlaid with lapis lazuli. Along the top runs a balustrade of gilt bronze with a wooden pedestal at each corner. There are five gilt-bronze statuettes, two on each side and one on the pediment. Three of these are from the late eighteenth century (on the corners and the pediment) and represent from left to right, Spring, Autumn, and Summer. The two smaller statuettes flanking the pediment also represent Spring and Summer, and are fixed by means of a wooden dowel.

The bronze corner mounts are nineteenth-century in date, while the drawer handles are of the period. The nineteenth-century stand has three upper drawers faced in panels of wood marquetry; these have an inlaid ivory strip around naturalistic designs in the Dutch style, made in the same period as the cabinet. The drawer on the right contains five secret drawers, all with a padded and embroidered lining of yellow silk.

COMMENTARY: The cabinet has the same structural characteristics as the examples now in the Palazzo Vecchio in Florence.[1] In one of these can be found two panels with motifs of the genus *Lililum*, identical to the second panel from the top on either side of the Gilbert Collection cabinet and on one of the panels in a cabinet in the Musée de Strasbourg.[2] The bird and flower *pietre dure* panels of this cabinet are characteristic of the seventeenth-century plaques produced at the Grand Ducal workshops in Florence. This cabinet is cited by Giusti as being similar to the Opificio-produced plaques, a Uffizi cabinet, and one in the Hermitage.[3] At the Opificio in Florence is another, later, cabinet with a similar grouping of nineteen plaques.[4] Yet another plaque dated c. 1700 is in a cabinet of 1765 by Johann Melchior Kambli (fl. c. 1765) at the Sanssouci Neues Palais at Potsdam.[5]

Alvar González-Palacios discussed several comparable cabinets in the earlier catalogue of the Gilbert Collection. In addition, 25 similar plaques can be found on a pair of cabinets stamped *JOSEPH*, acquired by Louis XVI (r. 1774–92) at the Duke d'Aumont (d. 1782) Paris sale of 12 December 1782. Napoleon had a third cabinet made for this set of plaques by the *ebeniste*, Jacob Desmalter (1770–1841).[6] Cabinets with similar plaques were formerly at Warwick Castle, Kenwood, and in the Swaythling collection.[7]

Traditionally, this cabinet is said to have been brought from Italy by Daniel Finch (1647–1730), second Earl of Winchelsea and Nottingham c. 1700. He rebuilt Burley-on-the-Hill, inherited from his father in 1682, on a grand scale; its front compared to Bernini's colonnade at St. Peter's in Rome, which the Earl had seen on his Grand Tour of 1665–68.[8] While in Florence, his father wrote to him, 'want nothing that I can pay for which can be fit to divert you'.[9] It was perhaps on this tour that he purchased the Gilbert Collection cabinet.

NOTES

1 Baldini, Giusti, and Pampaloni Martelli 1979, figs. 144–45.
2 Ludman 1985.
3 Giusti, Mazzoni and Pampaloni Martelli 1978, p. 292; Efimova 1968, no. 9.
4 Giusti, Mazzoni and Pampaloni Martelli 1978, pl. 362, no. 436.
5 Kreisel 1970, no. 810.
6 *L'Estampille*, June 1987, no. 204, p. 28, figs. 18–19.
7 Christie's, London, 30 May 1968, lot 91; Christie's, London, 6 April 1978, lot 74; Christie's, London, 19 July 1962, lot 89.
8 *Dictionary of National Biography*, vol. VII, pp. 4–5.
9 Christopher Hussey, 'Burley-on-the-Hill: Parts I & II', *Country Life*, 10 February 1923, pp. 178–85; 17 February 1923, pp. 210–17; p. 231.

5. CABINET

Pietre dure: Florence, late seventeenth century; cabinet and stand: England, late eighteenth century
Pietre dure, *pietre tenere*, ebonised oak, mahogany, brass, gilt metal; cabinet: 65.1 × 76.5 × 41.9 cm (25⅝ × 30⅛ × 16½ in);
stand: 82.6 × 81.3 × 41.9 cm (32½ × 32 × 16½ in)
1996.347 (MM282)

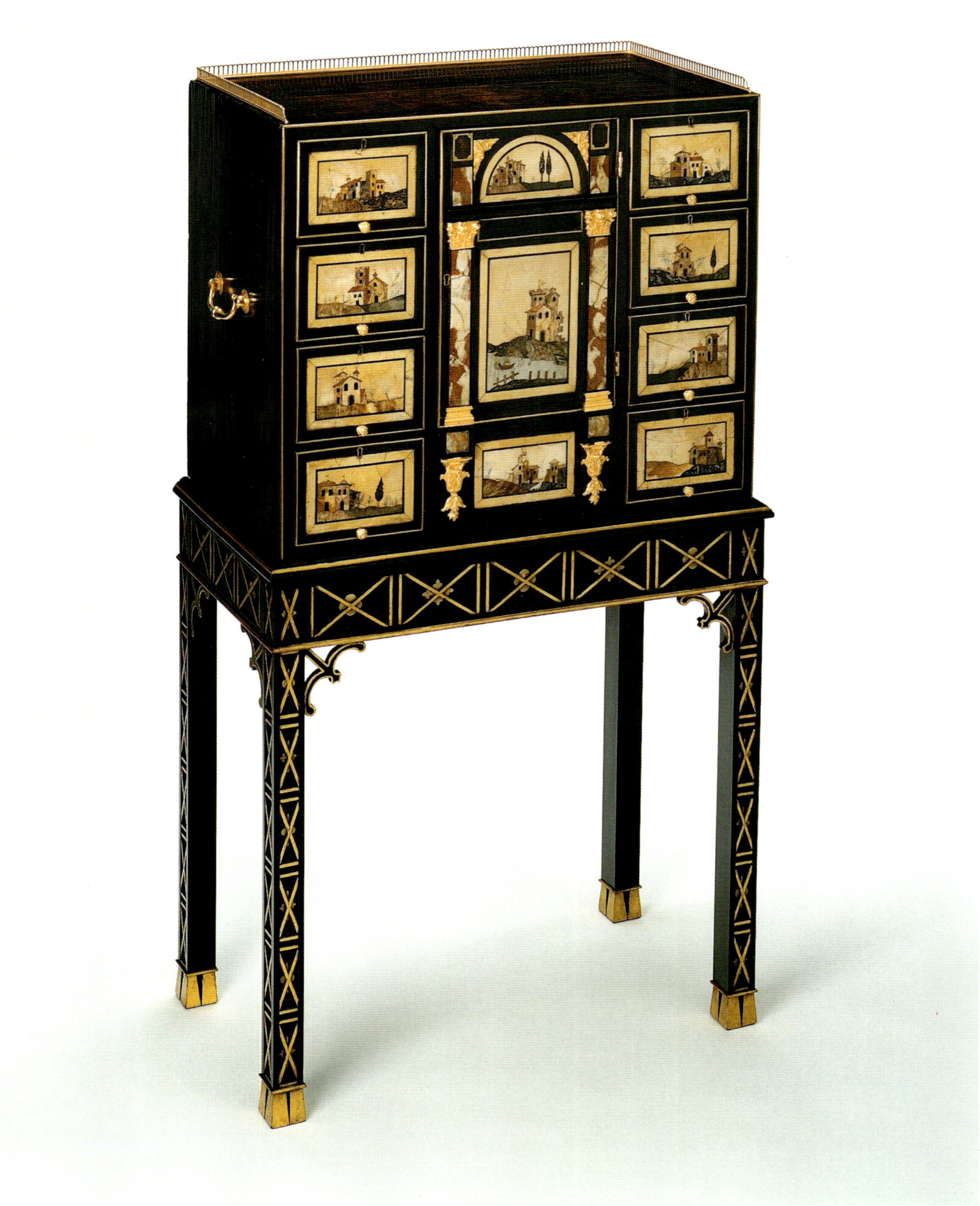

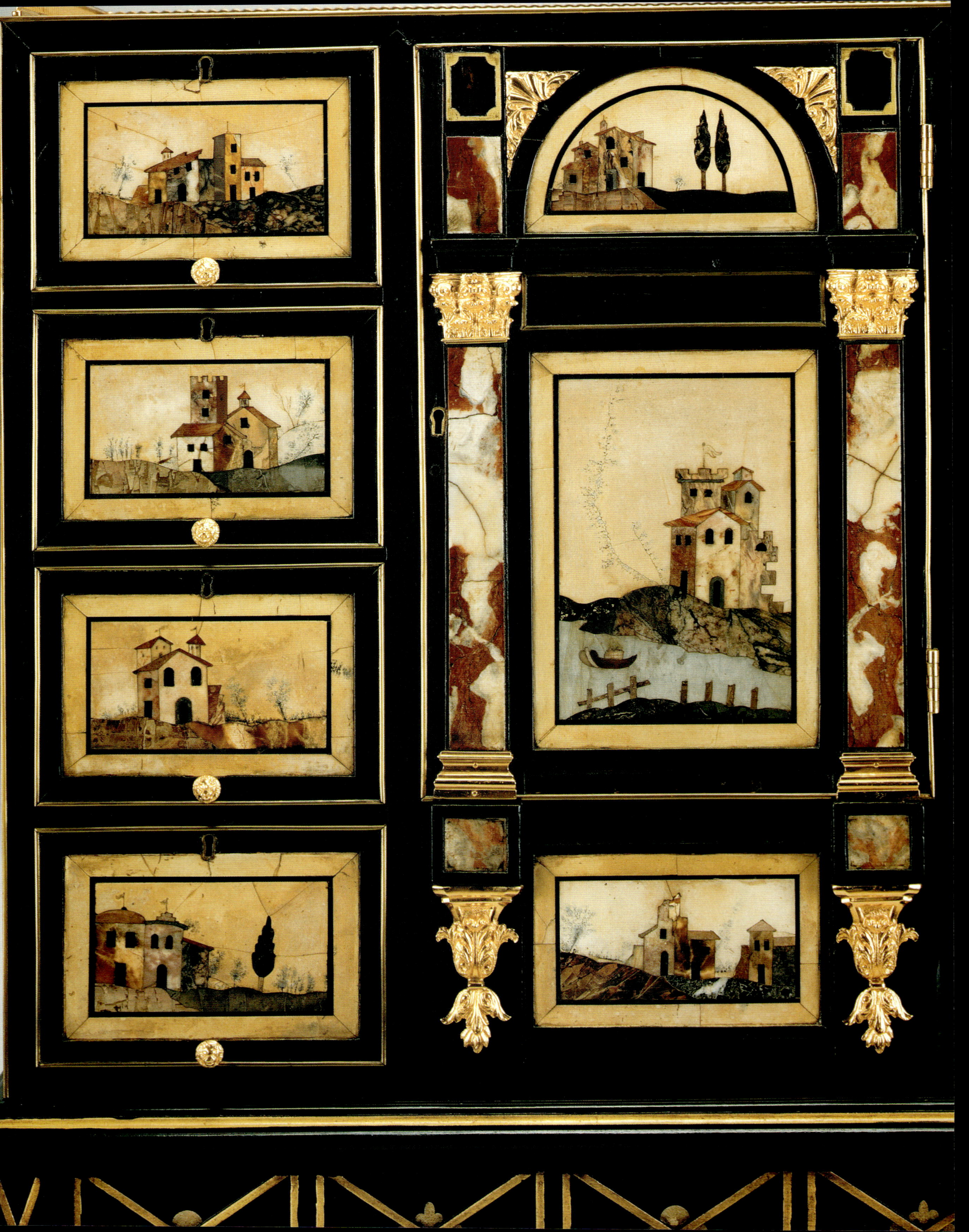

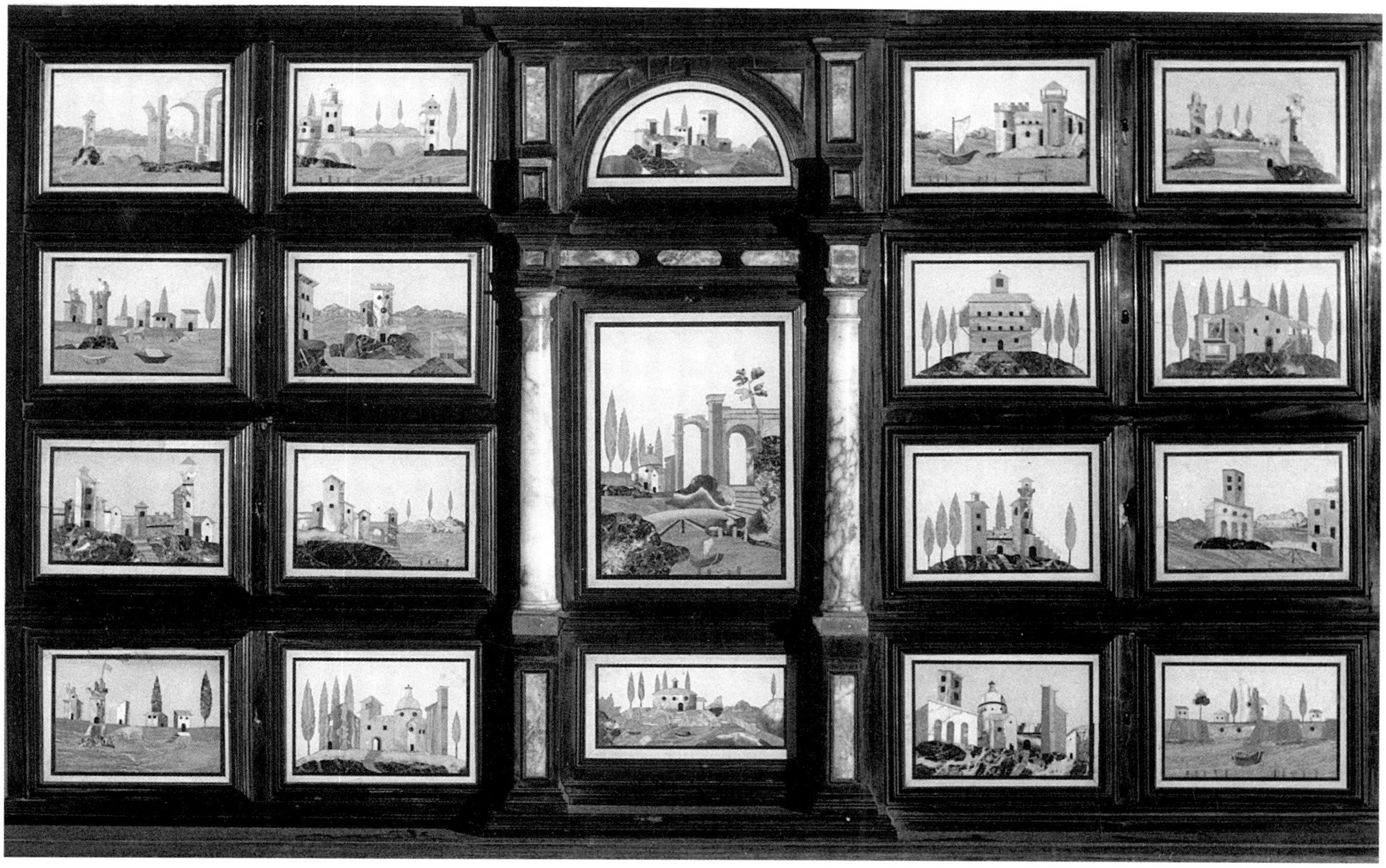

FIG. 5 Detail of cabinet formerly at Villa Poggio Imperiale.

PROVENANCE: Partridge Fine Arts, London, 1985.

EXHIBITION: Los Angeles, 1991.

DESCRIPTION: A cabinet with eleven *pietre dure* and *pietre tenere* mosaic panels on the front, with Tuscan landscape views on a background of Albarese limestone.

COMMENTARY: This cabinet was made in England in the late eighteenth century and is typical of the furniture inspired by the taste of travellers who, during their Grand Tour of Italy, bought Florentine mosaic work in the Grand Ducal workshops and had it set in made-to-measure cabinets on their return. The landscape panels are linked to those on a cabinet documented as being in the Villa del Poggio Imperiale after 1691 (fig 5).[1] They demonstrate the interest in landscape subjects in the Grand Ducal workshops during the late seventeenth century. Similar types of panels can be found on early eighteenth-century German furniture. Examples include cabinets from Ambras Castle,[2] Braunschweig and a desk in the castle at Wiesentheid.[3]

NOTES

1 Baldini, Giusti, and Pampaloni Martelli 1979, fig. 164.
2 Kunsthistorisches Museum 1987, p. 33.
3 Kreisel 1970, fig. 186.

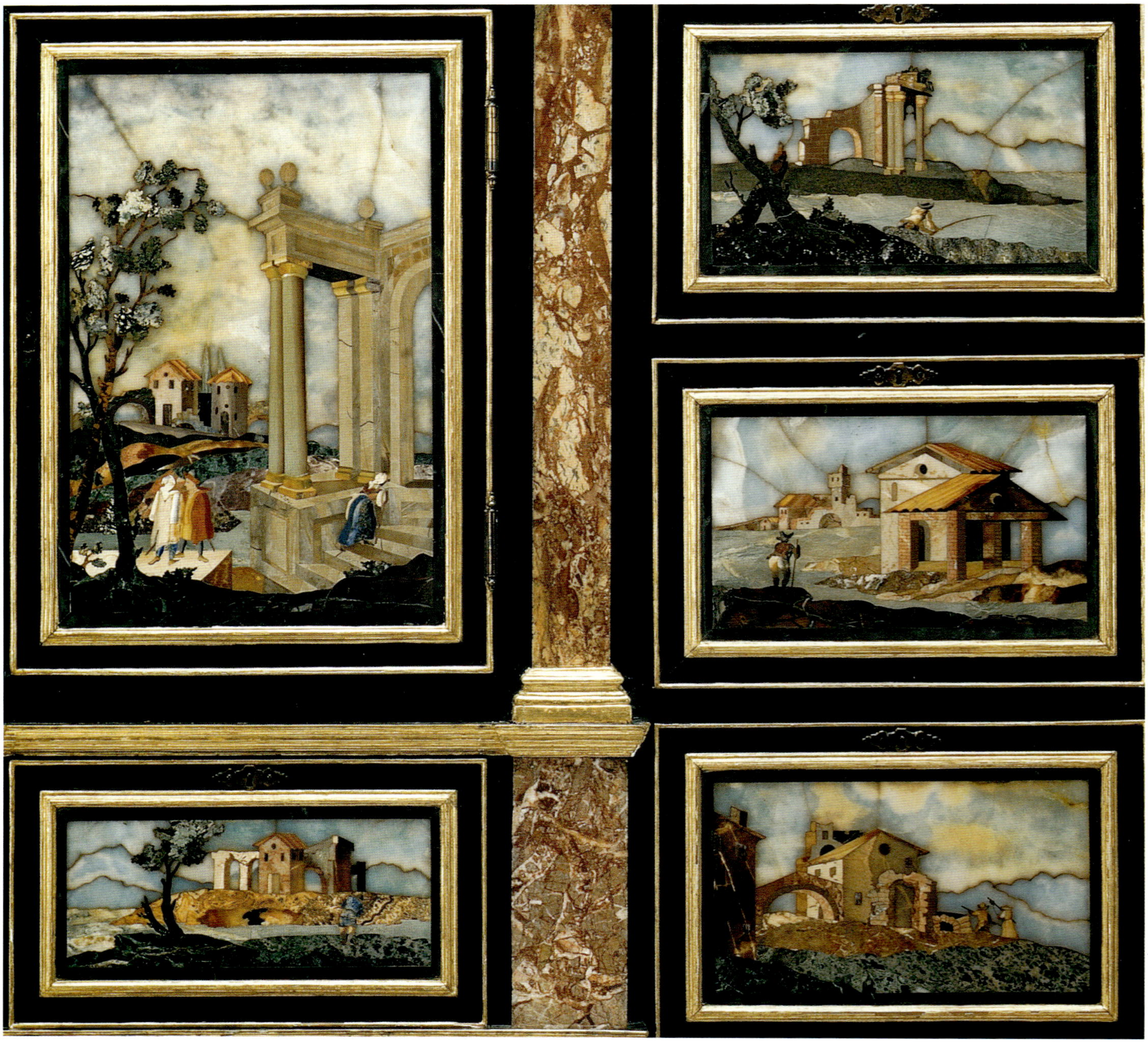

6. CABINET

Pietre dure: Florence, Grand Ducal workshops, early eighteenth century; cabinet: England, late eighteenth century; stand: England, late nineteenth century
Pietre dure, *broccatello* marble, ebonised and gilt wood; cabinet: 122.2 × 127.6 × 60.6 cm (48 1/8 × 50 1/4 × 23 7/8 in); stand: 92.1 × 127 × 59.7 cm (36 1/4 × 50 × 23 1/2 in)
1996.259 (MM30)

PROVENANCE: Graham Baron Ash, Wingfield Castle; Christie's, London, sale, London, 4 October 1967, p. 16, pl. 57; Mallett and Son, London, 1969.

LITERATURE: *Plaisir de France* 1969, p. 27; *Apollo* (advertisement), vol. 86, no. 10, October 1967, p. xvii; *Connaissance des Arts*, (advertisement), vol. 196, July 1968, p. 3; *Plaisir de France* 1969, fig. 8; Sherman 1971, no. 30; Avery and Emperatori 1975, no. 46; Hillier 1975, p. 270, fig. 1; *Los Angeles Herald Examiner* 1977, p. 18; Zucker 1977, p. 87; González-Palacios 1977a, no. 10; González-Palacios and Röttgen 1982, no. 10; Richardson 1985, p. 54; Irman

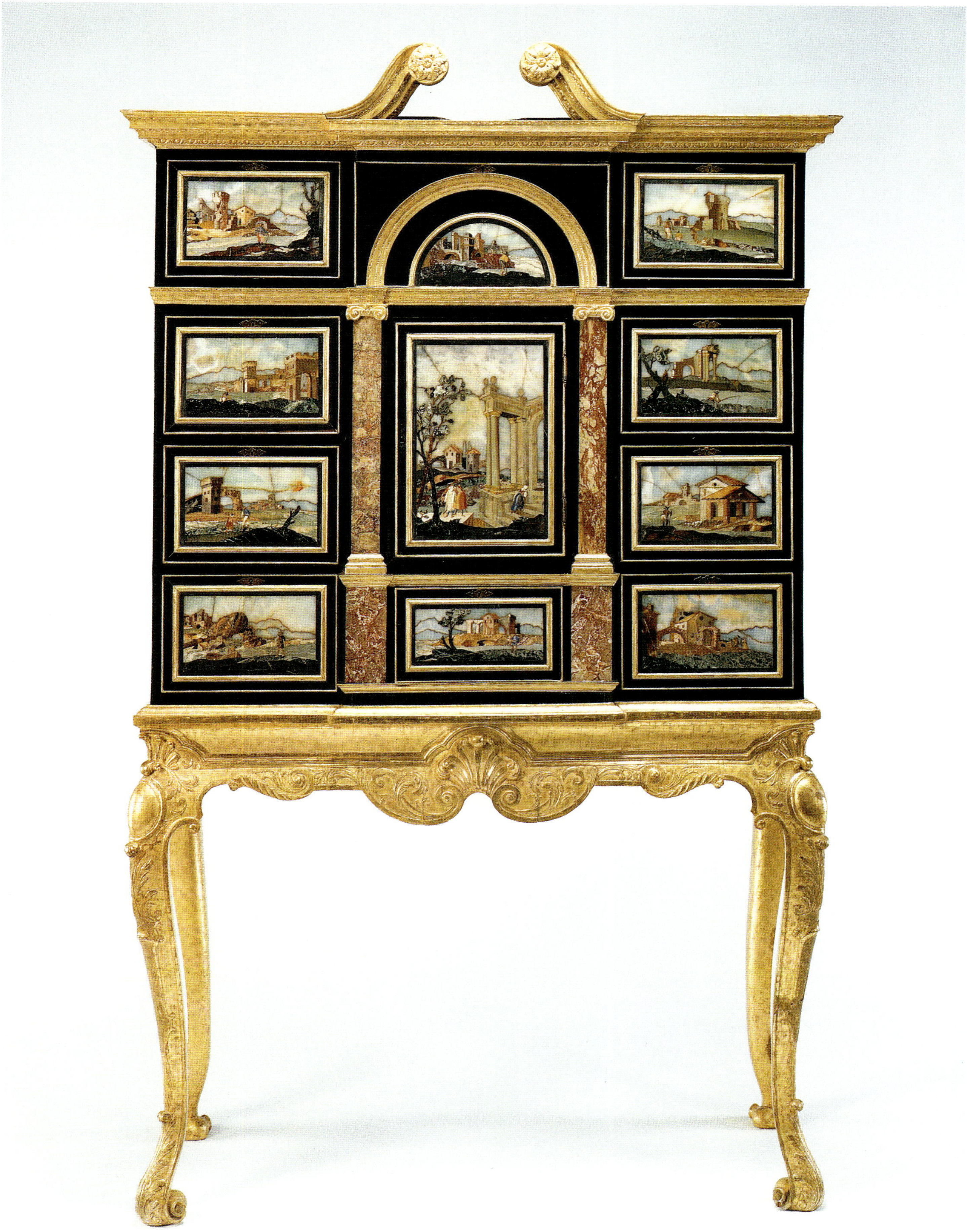

1986, ill. pp. 14–15; *Designers West* 1987, ill. p. 118.

EXHIBITIONS: Los Angeles, 1975; London, 1975; Los Angeles / Atlanta / San Antonio / Richmond / Seattle, 1977–79.

DESCRIPTION: A cabinet of ebonised wood, with cornices and pediment in carved and gilded wood. The door in the centre of the facade is faced with a *pietre dure* panel showing a landscape scene with ruins in the foreground. The central recess is flanked by two *broccatello* pilasters with a semicircular panel above, and a rectangular drawer below. To the left and right of this are two rows of four drawers, each with a landscape view in *pietre dure* on the front.

COMMENTARY: Landscapes with architectural ruins became popular in the Florentine workshops in the late seventeenth century. Some simple examples of these are found reused on another Gilbert Collection cabinet and casket (cat. nos. 5–6). The origins of these scenes go back to the taste of Grand Duke Cosimo II (r. 1609–20). His father, Ferdinand I (r. 1587–1609), a great patron of the arts, had previously commissioned the Flemish artist Giusto Utens (d. 1609) to depict views of the Medici residence.These were executed in a dozen lunettes of the Villa Artimino.[1]

Possibly the most magnificent existing example of the use of these plaques is a cabinet attributed to Domenico Cucci (c. 1635–1704), a gift to George IV from Sir Thomas Liddell (1797–1878), later first Earl Ravensworth. The cabinet is described in the history of Buckingham Palace as having been in the Green Room, 'of ebony and lapis lazuli with inlays of Florentine mosaic. There are twelve panels of Florentine mosaics. It is surmounted by six gilt bronze figures, and by a timepiece with a dial of lapis lazuli in the centre'.[2]

Alvar González-Palacios has cited similar Florentine plaques in several locations:[3] the Florentine room of Schloss Favorite near Baden Baden; a cabinet at Fredericksbourg Castle in Denmark; a cabinet probably made for Grand Duchess Vittoria delle Rovere, wife of Ferdinand II (r. 1620–70) at the Pitti Palace in Florence; a French commode;[4] and a Robert Adam (1728–92) cabinet of 1771 at the Victoria and Albert Museum.[5] Many other plaques of this type are still at the Museo dell'Opificio in Florence.[6]

NOTES

1 Giusti 1989, p. 50.

2 Clifford Smith, *The Complete History of Buckingham Palace*, London, 1931, p. 140; Avis Berman, 'East Side Renaissance', *Architectural Digest*, vol. 48, no. 12, November 1991, pp. 176–183, (ill. pp. 176–77).

3 González-Palacios and Röttgen 1982, no. 10. A Weisweiller commode is also cited, but it has marine landscapes.

4 Peter Thornton and William Reider, 'Pierre Langlois, Ebeniste', *Connoisseur*, vol. 179, no. 720, February 1972, pp. 105–112. (ill. p. 107, fig. 5).

5 Harris 1973, no. 41.

6 Giusti, Massoni, and Pampaloni Martelli 1978, figs. 50–55.

7. CASKET

Pietre Dure: Florence, late seventeenth to early eighteenth century; casket: Florence, second half nineteenth century
Pietre dure, *pietre tenere*, coloured marble, gilt bronze, mahogany, 21.6 × 29.2 × 22.2 cm ($8\frac{1}{2} \times 11\frac{1}{2} \times 8\frac{3}{4}$ in)
1996.202 (MM106)

PROVENANCE: The Honourable Mrs. Stuart; William Redford, London, 1972; Los Angeles County Museum of Art.

LITERATURE: Avery and Emperatori 1975, no. 118; González-Palacios and Röttgen 1982, no. 105.

EXHIBITIONS: Los Angeles, 1975; London, 1975; Los Angeles, 1977.

DESCRIPTION: A casket of wood with ebony veneer, on gilt-bronze bun feet. The sides and lid are set with five mosaic panels of landscape views in *pietre tenere* on a background of Albarese limestone. The edges are framed with gilt bronze, the corners reinforced with floral mounts in the same material. The landscape effects are achieved by the use of slices of stone with a wood grain, the natural markings giving the impression of vegetation. A paper label inside states that this casket belonged to *the Hon'ble Mrs. Stuart.*

COMMENTARY: Like those on cat. no. 5, the *pietre dure* plaques on this casket are typical of the burgeoning late seventeenth-century taste for landscapes.

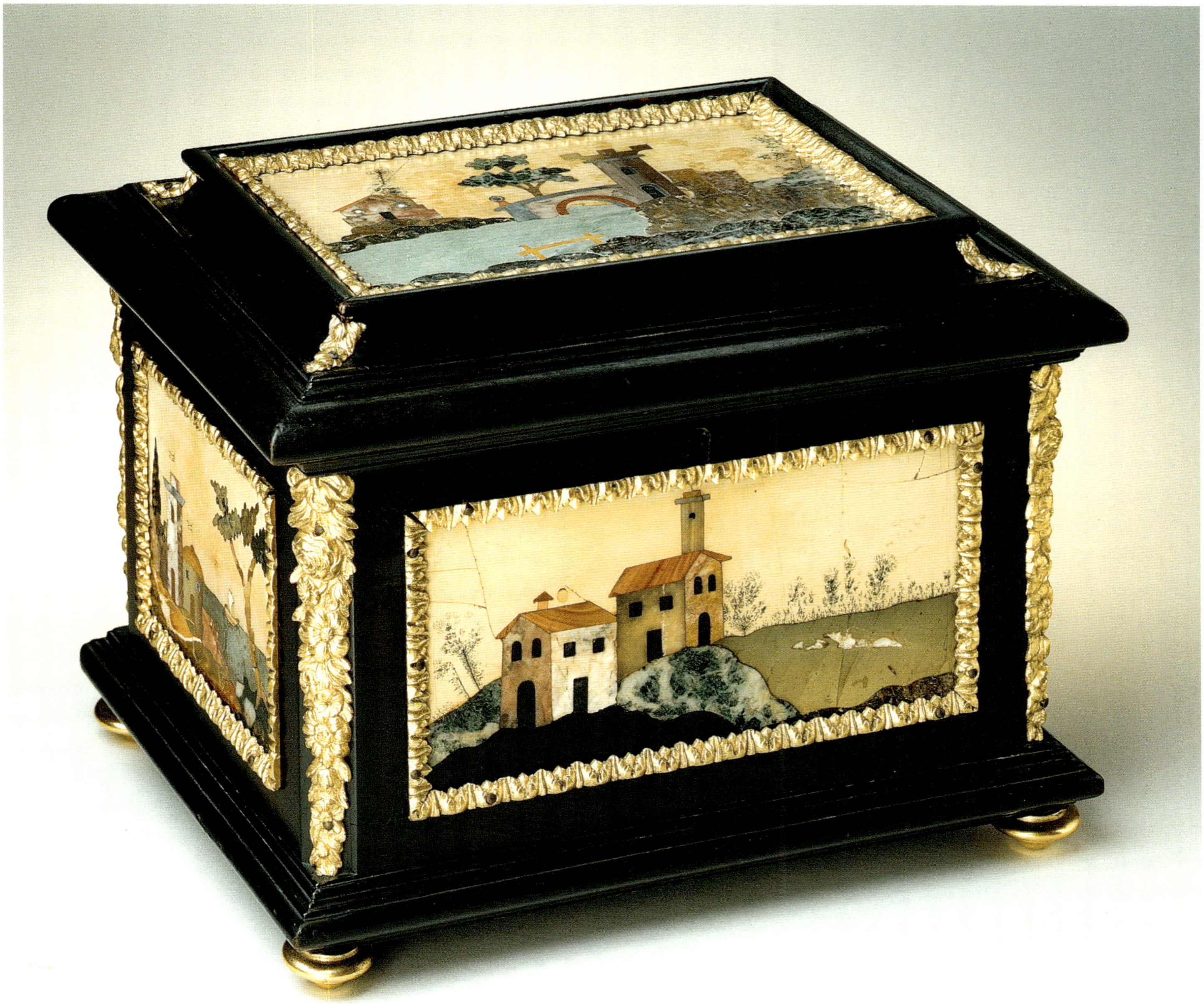

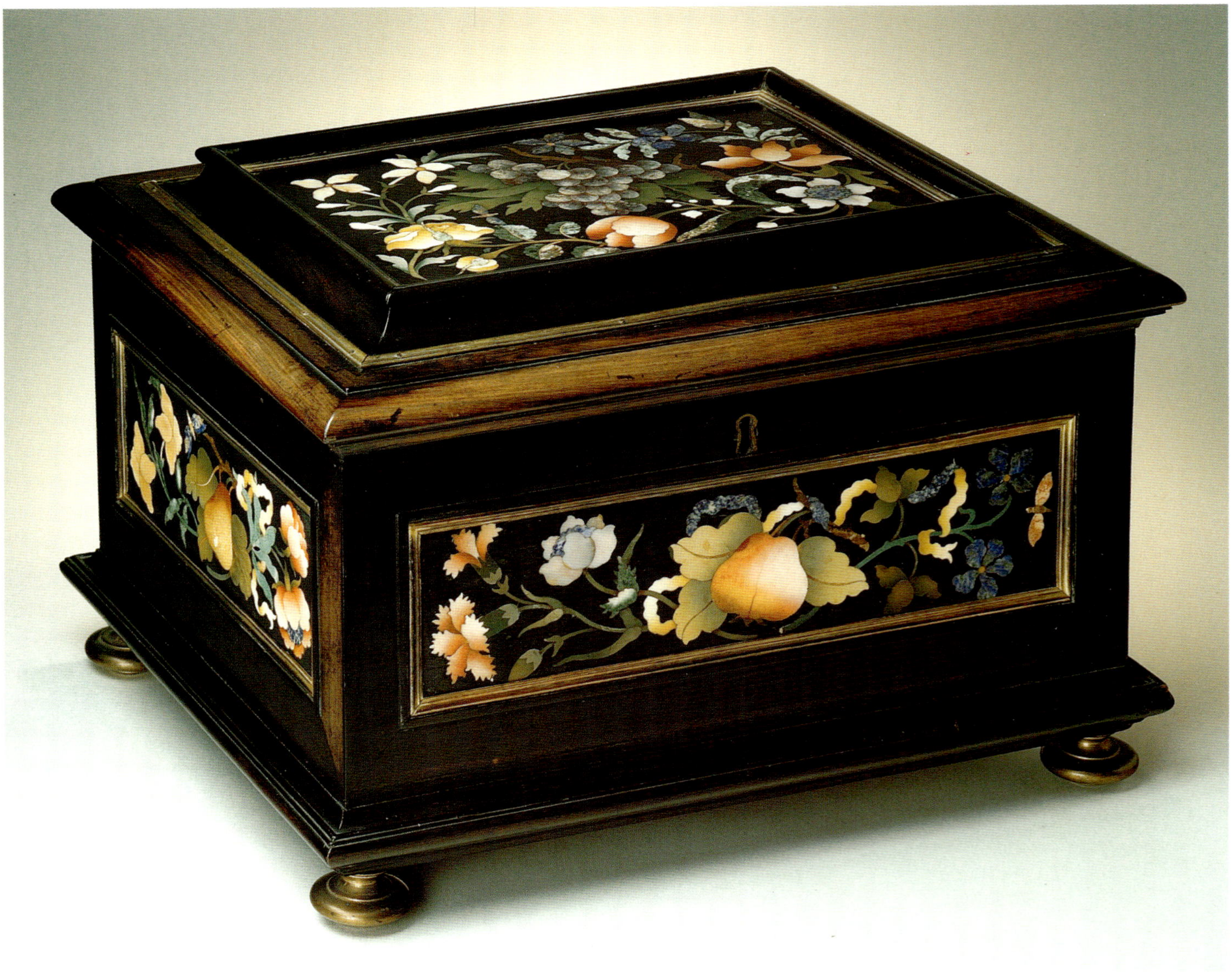

8. CASKET

Pietre dure: Florence, first half eighteenth century; casket: possibly Florence, late nineteenth century
Pietre dure, chalcedony, lapis lazuli, agate, marble, gilt bronze, mahogany, 26.7 × 39.4 × 31.1 cm (10½ × 15½ × 12¼ in)
1996.198 (MM25)

PROVENANCE: A. Cook, London, 1969; Los Angeles County Museum of Art.

LITERATURE: Avery and Emperatori 1975, no. 117; González-Palacios and Röttgen 1982, no. 106.

EXHIBITIONS: Los Angeles, 1975; London, 1975; Los Angeles, 1977.

DESCRIPTION: A mahogany casket set with five hardstone panels edged with gilt bronze on the sides and lid, standing on four bun feet in gilt bronze. The four panels on the front, back and sides are decorated with sprigs of flowers, fruit, and insects interlaced with a fluttering ribbon. The stones used are *verde d'Arno*, gabbro, agate, chalcedony, and lapis lazuli on a black marble background. The panel on top is larger; in the centre of the composition is a bunch of amethyst grapes.

COMMENTARY: The casket is of late nineteenth-century construction. The *pietre dure* panels, from the first half of the eighteenth century, can be compared in terms of their subject matter to various early eighteenth-century panels in the Museo dell'Opificio in Florence.[1]

NOTE

1 Giusti, Mazzoni and Pampaloni Martelli 1978, figs. 137–41.

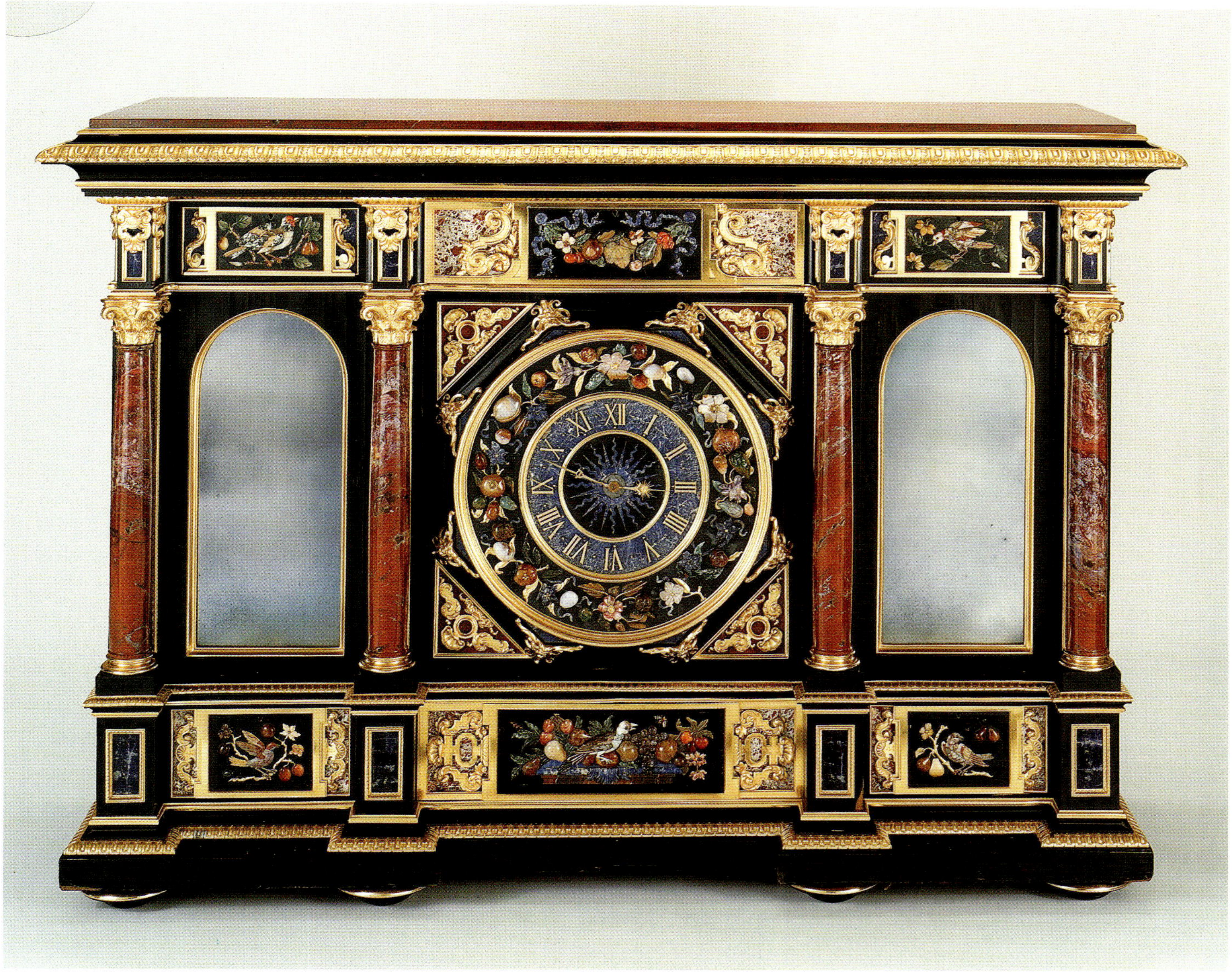

9. CABINET WITH CLOCK

Mosaics: France, Gobelins workshops, second half seventeenth century;
cabinet: London, Robert Hume (active 1804–40), 1824
Ebony, gilt bronze, *pietre dure*, jasper, lapis lazuli, agate, black marble, red Verona marble, and mirrors
115.6 × 165.1 × 55.9 cm (45½ × 65 × 22 in)
1996.361 (FA42)

PROVENANCE: Alexander Hamilton Douglas, tenth Duke of Hamilton, Hamilton Palace, Lanarkshire, by descent to the twelfth Duke of Hamilton; Christie's, Hamilton Palace sale, 26 June 1882, lot 520; Hugh Lupus Grosvenor, Duke of Westminster; Christie's Wateringbury Place sale, 31 May 1978, lot 311; Partridge, London, 1978.

LITERATURE: Gere 1989, pl. 88; Freyberger 1991, figs. 1, 5–6.

DESCRIPTION: Cabinet with three doors in an architectural form. The lower part has three drawers with relief mosaic panels in *pietre dure* on a background of black marble set into gilt-bronze frames. The central panel is larger than the other two and is decorated with an image of a bird pecking a bunch of grapes. The two side panels have pictures of birds perched on springs of fruit and flowers. The middle section has four monolithic columns of Sicilian jasper with Corinthian capitals and bases of gilt bronze. The doors to either side bear mirrors edged in gilt bronze. The central door is almost entirely filled by the large dial of a clock. At the centre of the clock is a circular plaque of black marble inlaid with a sunburst of lapis lazuli. Outside this is another band of lapis lazuli with applied numerals in gilt bronze. An outer border of black marble bears a garland of fruit and flowers in *pietre dure* relief. The whole is set into an octagonal ebonised frame applied with gilt-bronze mounts and lapis lazuli at each angle. The moulded cornice around the top has a border of gilt bronze; the top is made of red Verona marble. The pedestals on the lower and upper sections and the drawers on the upper side portions are faced with panels of lapis lazuli; the two central and side drawers below are faced with agate. The interior parts on either side are lined with red fabric and bear the marks of two shelves.

COMMENTARY: The six panels on the lower and upper cornices were made according to the relief mosaic technique developed in Florence under the influence of Giovanni Battista Foggini; this technique spread to the Gobelins factory in France when Florentine mosaicists went to work there. Apart from the two large cabinets designed by Domenico Cucci (Alnwick Castle, Northumberland), few pieces in *pietre dure* from the time of Louis XIV have survived. During the reigns of Louis XV (r. 1715–74) and Louis XVI (r. 1774–92), and later during the nineteenth-century eclectic period, some of the products of the Gobelins workshop were dismantled and the mosaics reused on more 'modern' pieces. Analysis of these dismantled pieces of furniture, now scattered all over the world, with the aid of a few pieces of documentary evidence, can help in the reconstruction of the history of the Gobelins production. In the case of this cabinet, the six panels with naturalistic motifs of fruit, flowers, and birds bear a clear relationship with a series of mosaics illustrated on a design for a cabinet by the Parisian antiquarian Philippe François Julliot (1735–1835). The mosaic of the bird pecking the grapes in the lower central section is practically identical to the mosaics in Julliot's design, which in turn is linked to two similar mosaics reused in a pair of cabinets by Adam Weisweiler (c. 1750–active until 1809) in the Royal Palace, Stockholm. The panel with the garland of fruit in the upper central section recalls two panels reused on a pair of cabinets by Weisweiler in the Wallace Collection, London. The clock in the centre framed with a garland of fruit and flowers does not match the other panels; it appears to be of later date and may have been commissioned in Florence by Robert Hume to complete the stone mosaic ornamentations of the cabinet he had designed. Documents recently discovered in the Hamilton archives (Freyberger 1991) refer to mosaic items procured by Hume in 1822 for the clock cabinet, which evidently was at an advanced stage of construction by this time. An earlier list of requirements, drawn up for Hume by the Duke of Hamilton in 1820, also mentions a clock in *pietre dure*, but no relationship with this clock cabinet is mentioned. The completion of this piece was announced by Hume in a letter to the Duke on 16 December 1824 (Freyberger 1991, p. 11).

The workmanship of the *pietre dure* on the clock differs significantly from the skilful artistry of the other relief mosaic panels. Its outer border contains various embellishments in inlaid lapis lazuli; the garland of fruit and flowers, in agate and various types of jasper, is created from single elements, carved in relief and attached to the background with gilt-bronze pins or fixed to the gilt-bronze stems. The two side panels in the lower section seem partly to be contemporary with the upper reliefs with the two birds; the insertion of the gilt-bronze branches, however, and the metal pins in the flower suggest more recent restoration.

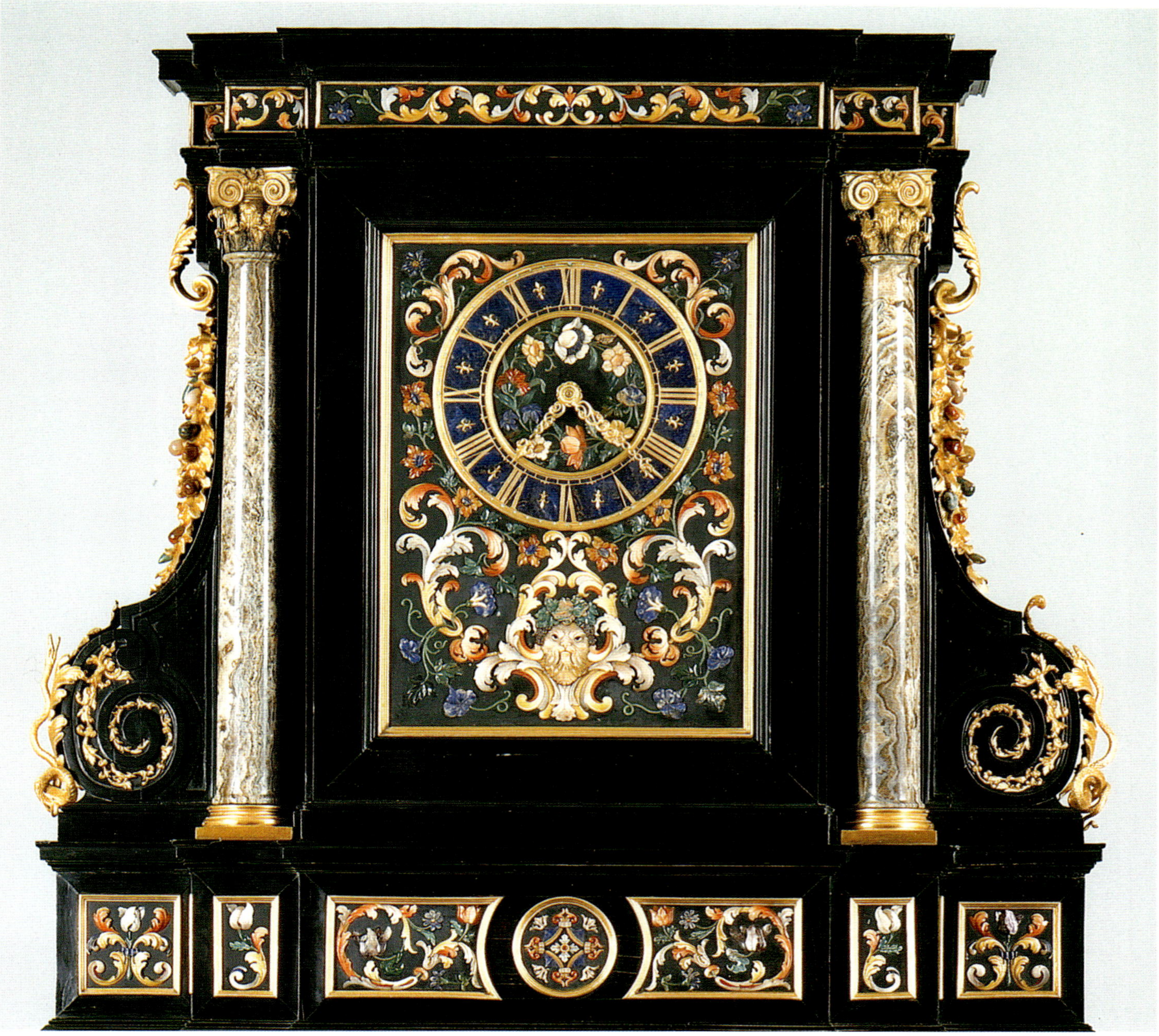

10. CABINET AND CLOCK

Upper section: Giovanni Battista Foggini, Grand Ducal workshops, Florence, 1652–1725; *pietre dure*, ebony, gilt bronze, brass; clock movement: Johannes Hittorff, Bonn, 1704, 94.6 × 101.6 × 21.6 cm (37¼ × 40 × 8½ in)
lower section: Florence, nineteenth century (central panel, Florence, c. 1700)
Pietre dure, mother-of-pearl, gilt bronze, ebonised wood, 98.1 × 130.8 × 45.7 cm (38⅝ × 51½ × 18 in)
1996.604 (MM137)

PROVENANCE: Anna Maria Luisa, Electress Palatine, Düsseldorf; Robert Staynor Holford; Sir George Lindsay Holford, Dorchester House, England; Christie's, sale, London, 13–14 July 1927, lot 81; Petite Musée, Montreal, Canada, 1974.

LITERATURE: Lankheit 1962, pp. 321–22, nos. 596, 603; *American Horologist* 1975, pp. 44; González-Palacios 1977b, figs. 1, 3, 4; *Lapidary Journal* 1977, p. 200; Hagans 1977, p. 31; Wilson 1980, p. 100; González-Palacios and Röttgen 1982, nos. 7–8; Irman 1986, p. 13; González-Palacios 1986, vol. 1, pp. 44–46, vol. 2, figs. 99–101.

EXHIBITION: Los Angeles, 1977.

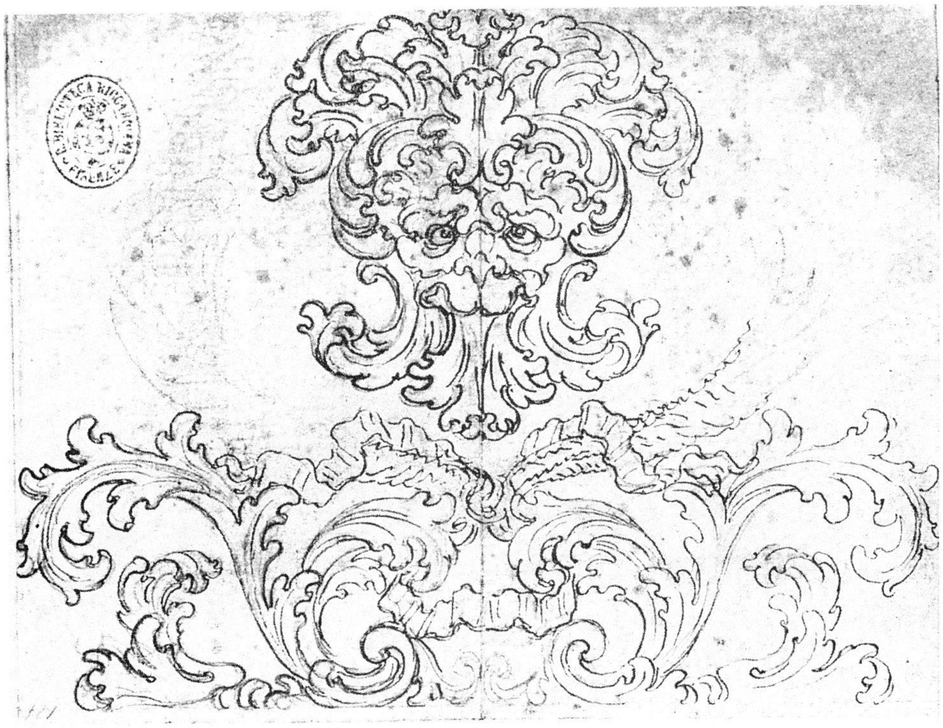

FIG. 6 Drawing from Foggini's journal of sketches.

DESCRIPTION: The cabinet is of ebonised wood with a projecting middle section and a high, moulded plinth. The façade has three doors: a central one with a recessed *pietre dure* panel, and two smaller side doors with narrow bands of gilt bronze and large gilt-bronze mounts with grotesque masks, flowers and *pietre dure* insertions. A pair of gilt-bronze and *pietre dure* mounts with a central rosette embellish the spaces between the three doors on the façade. The gilt-bronze borders, above and below, repeat the motif of grotesque masks and scrollwork. The bronze feet are bun shaped; the mounts on the lower corners are in the shape of acanthus leaves.

The upper, ebony section is of an architectural form with a clock in the centre. On the front of its base are a row of seven *pietre dure* panels framed in gilt bronze. The upper section has elaborate carved volutes mounted with gilt bronze on either side; the projecting central section is flanked by two columns of agate with Corinthian capitals and gilt-bronze bases. The central door bears a *pietre dure* panel in relief, depicting a grotesque face within scrolling acanthus and convolvulus of lapis lazuli, all on a background of black marble. Mounted on this is a clock with a lapis lazuli dial, the central portion inlaid with flowers. The interior is lined with silk and bears the monogram *AMEP*, for Anna Maria Electress Palatine, embroidered in gold thread and surmounted by the coronet of the palatinate. The frieze is decorated with small *pietre dure* panels of scrolls and flowers. On the sides are *pietre dure* depictions of fruit and gilt-bronze garlands.

COMMENTARY: The clock was made for the daughter of Cosimo III (r. 1670–1723), Anna Maria Luisa de' Medici (1667–1743), who was married in 1691 to the Elector Palatine, Johann Wilhelm von der Pfalz (r. 1690–1716). When the Elector died, Anna Maria returned to Florence, taking with her nearly all the *pietre dure* objects her father had given to her. Cosimo III had declared her successor to the throne after their brother, Prince Gian Gastone, but the death of Louis XIV in 1715 led to the quadruple alliance of Austria, England, France and Holland, which in 1718 excluded Anna Maria, in favour of Don Carlos of Spain. Protesting, the ageing Cosimo gradually put affairs of state into the hands of Anna Maria who, with far greater leadership skill than her brothers, proved her mastery in both foreign and domestic affairs until Cosimo's death in 1723, whereupon control passed to his son. For the next fourteen years, Anna Maria, immensely wealthy in her own right, retired from her dissolute brother's court to live in splendid seclusion and devote her time to charity. Sole possessor of one of the greatest art collections in the world, she stipulated that the family treasures should never leave Florence and should always be available for the public benefit of all nations. She thus secured the city's artistic heritage and future prosperity.

Published documents from the State Archives in Florence have been cited by Alvar González-Palacios establishing that this clock was made in the Grand Ducal workshops from 1704 to 1705 by two of the greatest artists of the time: Leonardo Van der Vinne (fl. 1662–1713) and Giovanni Battista Foggini (1652–1725). The relief *pietre dure* ornamentation of the clock is typical of the designs issuing

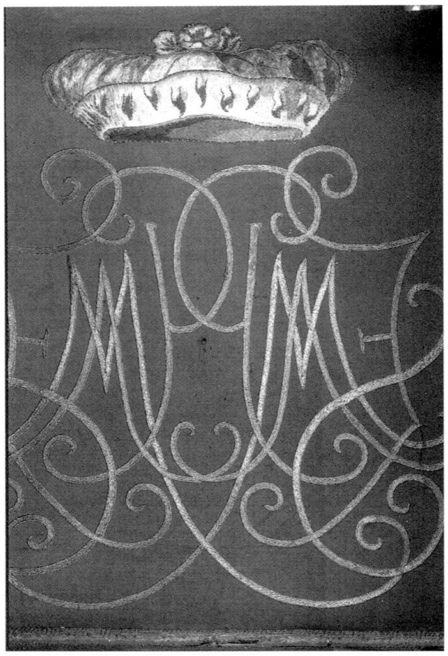

Medici monogram inside clock cabinet.

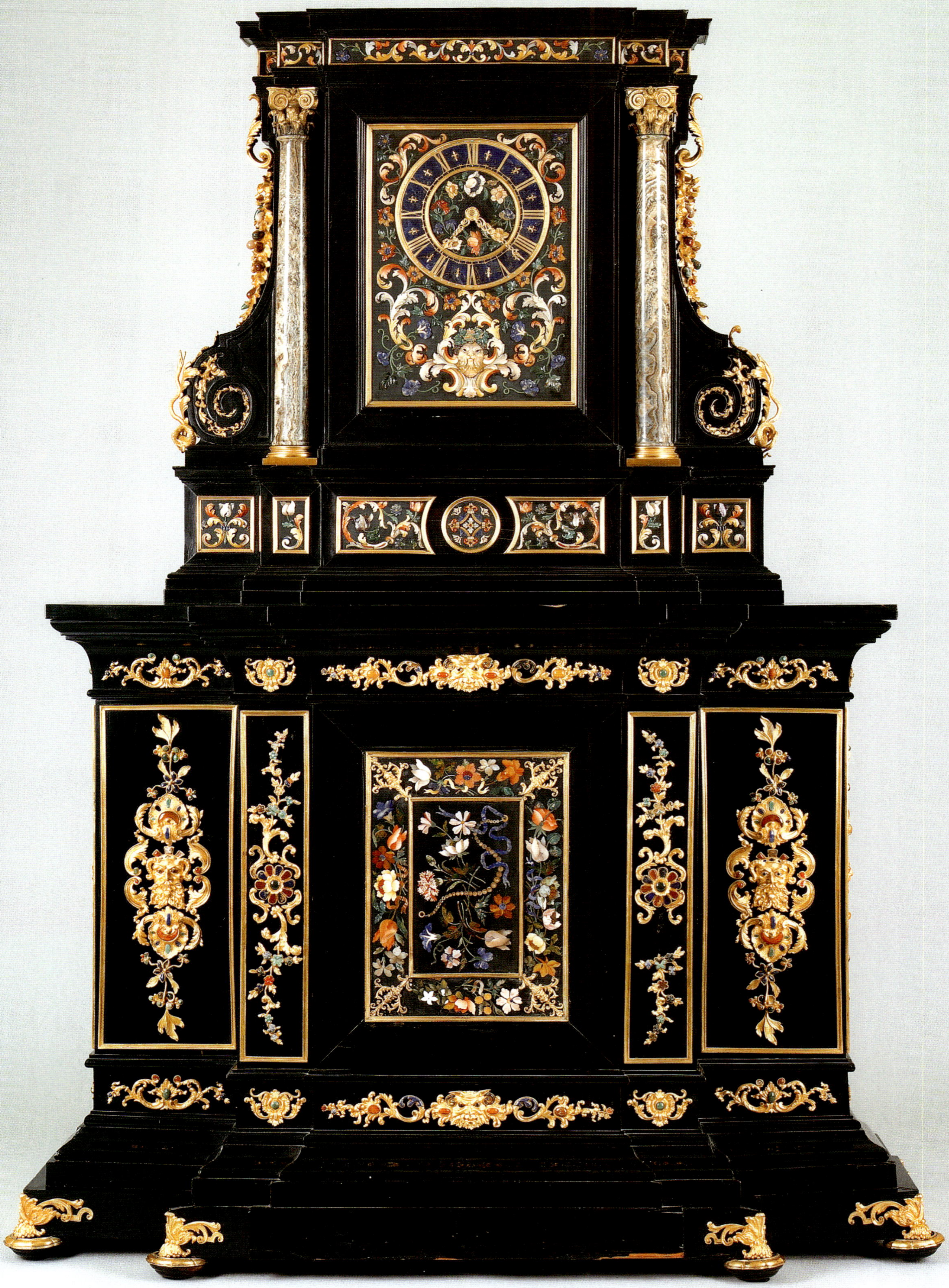

from the Grand Ducal workshops under Foggini's direction; these were committed to paper in Foggini's journal of sketches and drawings (fig. 6, G.D.S.U., Florence; Monaci 1977). The garlands of fruit on the sides, with their foliage in gilt bronze, are some of Foggini's favorite embellishments, appearing regularly on borders, table legs, and cabinets, including the cabinet originally made for the Electress Palatine's clock (Museo degli Argenti, Florence). The grotesque mask is a delicate example of stone mosaic work and is identical to one of the sketches in Foggini's notebook (Monaci 1977, p. 92, figs. 73-74). Similar designs can be found on items in the Museo dell'Opificio, which suggests that this was a standard pattern used regularly by mosaic workers at the end of the seventeeth century and the beginning of the eighteenth century.

González-Palacios also names Aurelio Vestri as agate carver, Giorgi as bronzier, and Tofani as maker of the clock face. Similar clocks are in Rome (Bulgari Collection), and in Munich.[1] The original clock movement, by Ignatius Hugford, or Huggeford, an Englishman (fl. 1658–98),[2] has been replaced with a clock signed *Johannes Hittorff a Bonn* (1757–1836).

The Gilbert Collection clock was not among the objects taken back to Florence by the electress. After a period of unknown ownership, it was purchased by Robert Staynor Holford (1808–92), whom at a young age inherited two great homes, a million pounds, and a fabulous art collection from his uncle. He was 'a dilletante of the best type: scholarly, imaginative, and with a high sense of the duties of a patron to artists and posterity'.[3] Holford bought the Gilbert Collection clock for his home, Dorchester House on Park Lane, which was designed by Lewis Vulliamy (1791–1871) after Villa Farnesina in Rome and built in 1857–59. It was declared by Beresford Chancellor 'without hyperbole ... the finest private dwelling in London', and was appointed with great Italian paintings, furniture and works of art.[4]

The lower cabinet, upon which the clock rests, is typical of the nineteenth-century cabinets inspired by eighteenth-century French furniture, and was probably built about the time Holford was furnishing Dorchester House. The central door bears a *pietre dure* panel made in Florence at the same time as the clock. The original purpose of this panel, attributable (thanks to the flower design) to the workshop directed by Foggini, is difficult to guess. The elegant string of pearls interlaced with the flowers and the blue lapis lazuli ribbon was a favorite motif of Foggini, who used it in the centre of his splendid table at the Pitti Palace.[5]

The *tromp l'oeil* necklace motif appeared in the Florentine workshops in the mid-seventeenth century on a celebrated table made in 1658 for Cardinal Antonio Barberini (1608–71), recently described by González-Palacios.[6] Filippo Baldinucci describes the table, mentioning 'the pearl necklace, so realistic that it deceives the eye and the hand too of anyone who touches it'.[7] The motif was used on other objects besides tabletops. One of the few known examples, a tray (c. 1745) in the Hofburg, Vienna, has the same motif in a floral composition. Trays mounted in silver gilt are documented in 1746, when the silversmith Gaetano Rabbuiati was commissioned to execute the mounts.[8] Two others have been noted, one in the saleroom, the other in the Landesmuseum, Kassel.[9]

The Gilbert Collection panel may possibly also have been intended as a tray. The size of the panel, too small for a tabletop, and the fact that the necklace is intended to be viewed from the side, giving the optical illusion of pearls lying on a flat surface, indicate that it was not originally meant for a cabinet. Its outline was obviously altered to adapt it to the requirements of the cabinet it now adorns. The nineteenth-century gilt-bronze masks on the corners cover the pieces of stone originally put in to disguise the joints. The bunch of flowers in the lower central panel has undergone extensive alteration, including the total reworking of the branch with leaves and the white flower.

NOTES

1 González-Palacios 1969, p. 58, fig. 1; González-Palacios 1986, vol. 1, pp. 45–46.
2 He is cited as Hugford by John Fleming in 'The Hugfords of Florence', *Connoisseur*, Oct 1995, pp. 106–10; but as Huggeford in the *Clockmaker's Company Collection*, Clutton & Daniels, 1975, p. 16.
3 Christopher Hussey, 'Dorchester House' Parts I & II, *Country Life*, 5 May 1928, pp. 646–653; 12 May 1928, pp. 684–90.
4 Sykes 1985. p. 291.
5 Baldini, Guisti, and Pampaloni Martelli 1979, p. 270, figs. 63–64.
6 González-Palacios 1993, vol. I, pp. 404–406, vol. II, no. 69.
7 Baldinucci 1846, vol. 3, p. 221.
8 *Splendori di pietre dure* 1988, p. 194, no. 53.
9 González-Palacios 1982b, pp. 58–59.

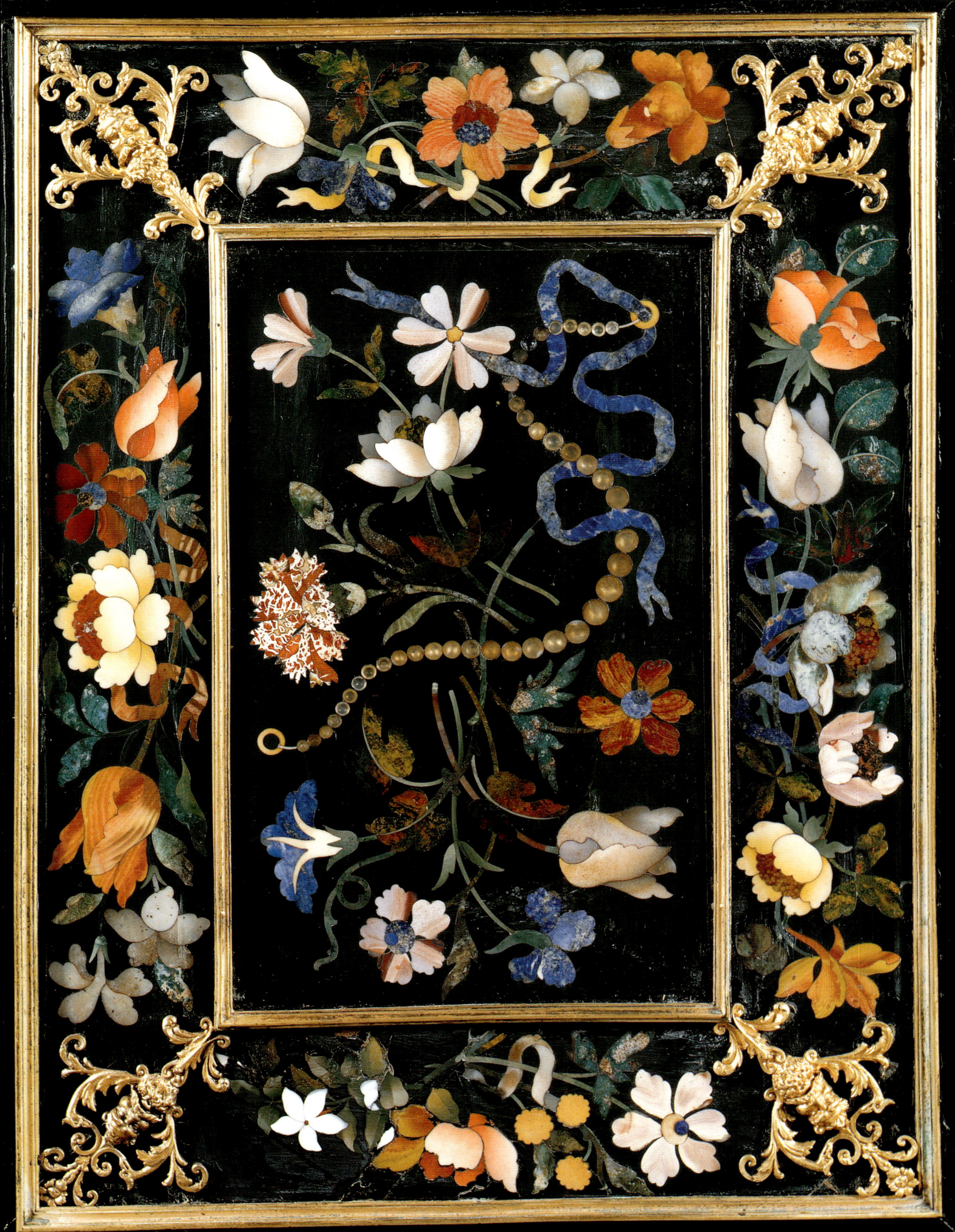

11. CABINET CLOCK

Augsburg, first quarter eighteenth century
Wood, tortoiseshell, silver, silver gilt, lacquer, micromosaic, mother-of-pearl, glass, mirror, *pietre dure*, oil on copper, garnets, turquoise, brilliants, painted porcelain, ivory, enamel, brass, 114.3 × 67.9 × 49.8 cm (45 × 26¾ × 19⅝ in)
1996.631 (MM264)

PROVENANCE: Fifth Earl of Rosebery, Mentmore Towers sale, Sotheby's, 20 May 1977, lot 1053; Ronald A. Lee, London, 1977.

LITERATURE: Sotheby's *Art at Auction* 1976–7, p. 17; *Town and Country*, vol. 133, no. 4989, May 1979, p. 123; *Connaissance des Arts*, October 1996, p. 85.

DESCRIPTION: A cabinet clock of architectural form in three sections: a base with shaped borders and volutes at the corners; a central body; and a top storey with a lantern. The cabinet is faced in tortoiseshell, with borders and Corinthian columns at each corner of silver gilt. Set into the front and back of the base are two *pietre dure* panels, the front one depicting a peach and flowers, the back a geometric design. The iconography of the whole is a combination of mythological images and oriental scenes. Chinoiserie panels, inlaid mother-of-pearl, ivory, enamel and brass are set around the base and upper storey. The front of the upper storey bears a large mother-of-pearl plaque inlaid with Chinoiserie motifs and relief designs in silver gilt. Small silver statuettes of Buddha adorn the volutes at the base, the centre of the upper storey, and the pediment of the lantern. Figures from classical mythology appear on the sides of the cabinet.

The front panel is faced with silver gilt and applied with plates of chased and pierced silver and silver-gilt scrolls and cartouches. Four medallions of mother-of-pearl adorn the sides, the two upper ones bearing profiles of the heads of emperors, the two below depicting Cupid and Bacchus and Cupid and Venus. At the top of the façade, a silver plate is engraved with a picture of the sun and the inscription DIES SOLIS (the day of the sun). Between this and the clock is a mother-of-pearl plaque engraved with the sun's face. The clock dial is mother-of-pearl, the numbers consisting of strips of brass inlaid with cut garnets. Between the inner and outer dials is a band of brass set with cabachon turquoise. The hands are inlaid with micromosaic in a floral design. Two small, classically draped figures of embossed silver symbolising Night and Day decorate the arch of the façade, one sleeping, the other looking up to the sky. Two other classical figures on the pediment of the upper storey stand on either side of the Buddha; one is holding the circle of the zodiac.

On the front of the base is a red-velvet-lined drawer containing a tiny Meissen tea service from 1720 consisting of nine pieces: a teapot and cover, sugar box and cover, four tea bowls and three saucers. The service (see detail illustration, p. 59) is painted with gilt Chinoiserie figural scenes in the style of Johann Friedrich Böttger (1682–1718), the inventor of European hard-paste porcelain. The front of the drawer is decorated with an inlay of brass, hardstone, ivory, mother-of-pearl and silver, depicting a Chinese figure astride a rhinoceros. Below this is another drawer faced with similar materials depicting two oriental figures in a boat. The drawer contains a removable, square, silver-gilt inkwell and pounce pot, and has two rectangular compartments, probably intended to hold pens and keys. There are six keys, one large and five small.

On the right-hand side of the base, a niche holds a silver statuette of Hercules; above this are two small drawers, and above them a niche with walls inlaid with mother-of-pearl and mirror tiles. On the back wall is a slab of gilt-bronze, incised and with an engraved background. Above this, a band bears the inscription APOLLO DEUS ARTIUM (Apollo God of the Arts). A portrait of Apollo cut from a sheet of silver decorates the niche on the top storey with a silver term on either side.

The left-hand side of the clock is treated in similar fashion, with different gods in the niches: Jove below and Mercury above, with the inscription MERCURIUS LEGATUS DEORUM (Mercury Messenger of the Gods). The door at the back bears a miniature oil on copper depicting Mercury and Venus garlanded with flowers. It is set within a cartouche-shaped frame of engraved and incised silver in the manner of Andreas Thelot (Augsburg 1655–1734). Inside the door, a mirror is engraved with a portrait of Diana. The door gives access to two small drawers and the movement of a clock, protected by a glass door engraved with festoons and a cupid. On the upper storey of the back are two inlaid Chinese figures between niches with flat, silver-winged cherubs carrying bows and arrows.

The clock mechanism has a calendar movement and is quarter striking.

COMMENTARY: Augsburg and Nuremberg were the most important centres during the golden age of clock-making from the mid-seventeenth to mid-eighteenth centuries. Housed in extravagantly luxurious and elaborate cases, these rare and costly objects were created through the collaboration of independent masters with a variety of skills, organised by tradesmen, who in turn

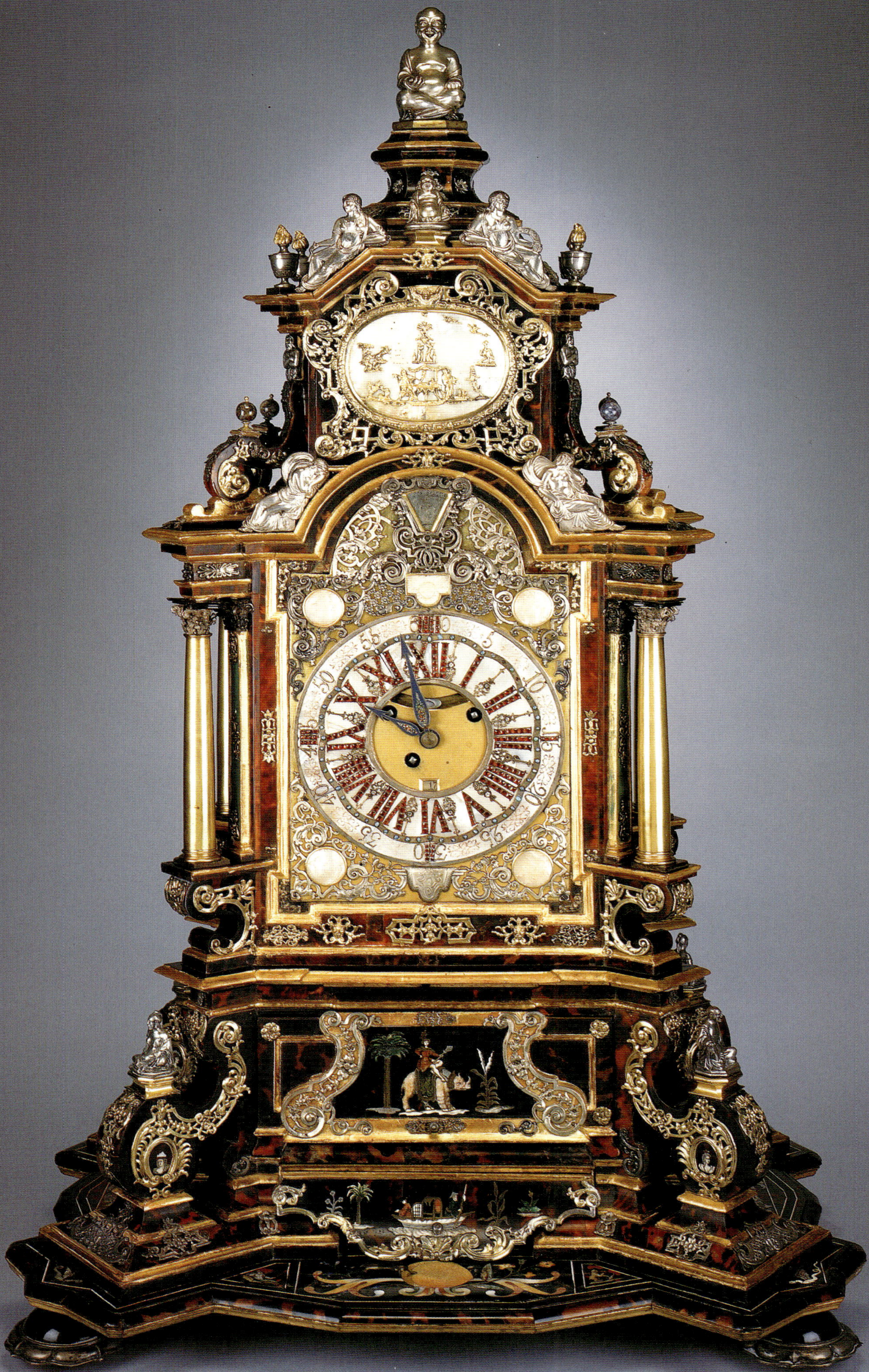

provided financing and took commissions from important patrons.

Like most of these, the Gilbert Collection clock was almost certainly made for royalty or nobility. Certain of its characteristics have linked it with the Count of Schönborn at Pommersfelden. The Indian rhinoceros on the drawer front is a composite type derived from Philippe Galle's 1586 engraving of the Madrid rhinoceros, which was among a set of drawings reputedly made for Rudolf II of Prague (r. 1575–1612), and from a famous engraving of a rhino by Albrecht Dürer (1471–1528).[1] Chinoiserie scenes with a rhino like that on the Gilbert Collection clock are found on at least three other objects of the period that are linked with Pommersfelden. A woodcut of the Dürer rhinoceros and Augsburg altar clock of 1710 similar to the Gilbert Collection clock were in the Kunstkammer at Schloss Pommersfelden. A rhinoceros of the same type is found on a boulle tabletop made in Augsburg c. 1712–15 (Badisches Landesmuseum, Karlsruhe) and on an Augsburg writing desk, also c. 1712–15. A figure astride a rhinoceros like that on the Gilbert Collection clock is found on another writing desk formerly at Pommersfelden (Bamberg), dated c. 1720 and inlaid with the Schönborn coat-of-arms.[2] It is noted in an inventory of 1759 as having come from Augsburg.[3] A set of panels dating to the first quarter of the eighteenth century and with the same type of boulle marquetry and tortoiseshell as the Gilbert Collection rhino were on sale in 1996.[4] Each of these bore the crest of the Schönborn family. They depict a dromedary and figures, an elephant carrying the Emperor of China, a pagoda with the Emperor of China, a party scene, the Empress of China in a pagoda, and two Jesuits.

The Schönborn family goes back to the thirteenth century, and the members of one of three existing lines, the Schönfeld-Wiesentheid, still live at

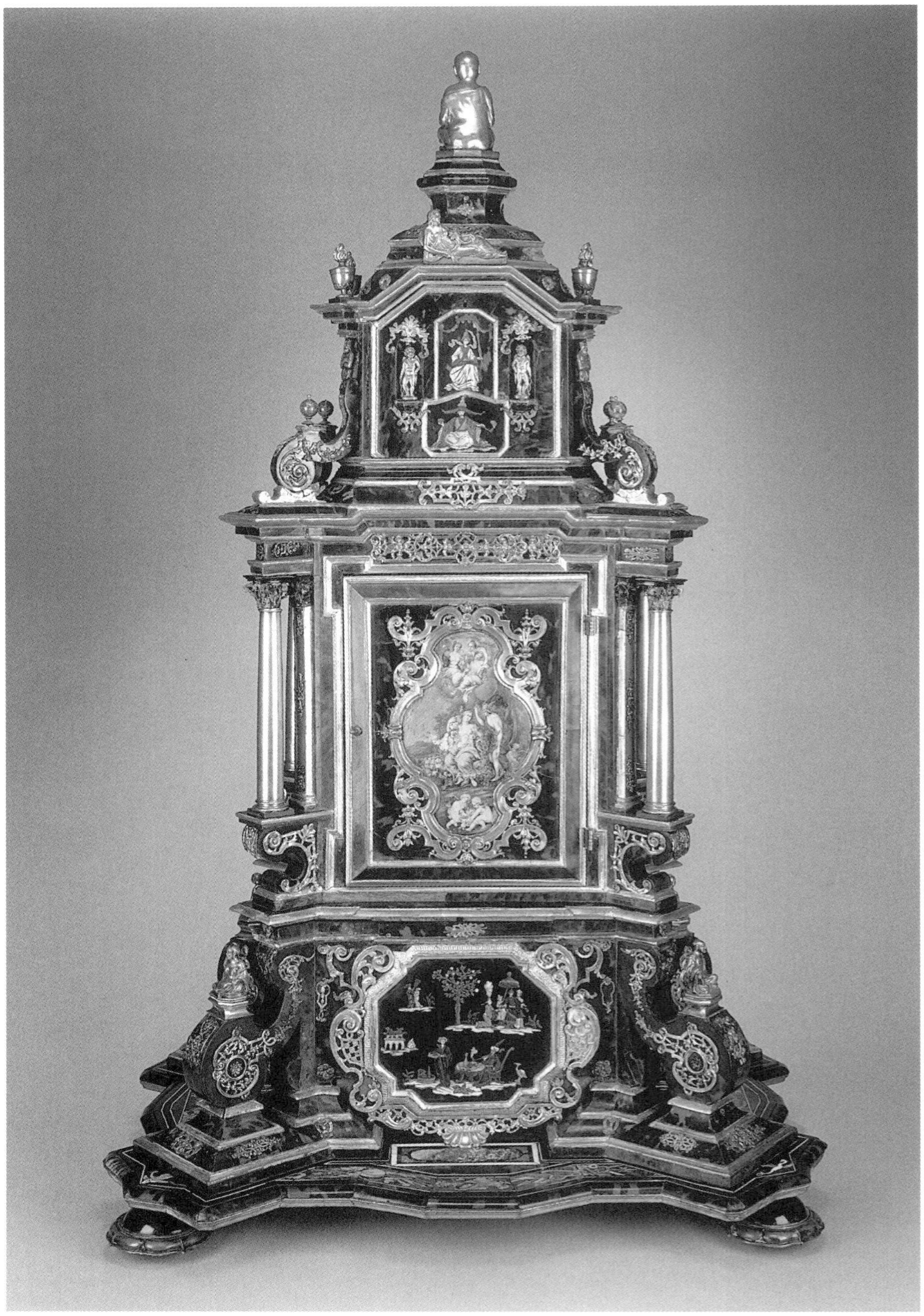

Pommersfelden. In 1701 the head of the family, Prince Lothar Franz (1655–1709), was given a gift of 100,000 *thalers* by the Habsburg rulers for the express purpose of building Pommersfelden to glorify them and their chancellor. Passionately involved in planning Schloss Pommersfelden and filling it with art treasures, the Count collaborated with Jacob Lucas von Hildebrandt (1668–1745) and Fischer von Erlach 1656–1723) on its design.[5] Its building period, 1711–18, coincides with the date of the Gilbert Collection clock. It is tempting to speculate that the clock was made as a part of Pommersfelden's vast artistic programme.

This Gilbert Collection clock is also associated with a rare group of similar Augsburg clocks, most unsigned and dating between 1690 and 1710.[6] One example with silver mounts attributed to Thelot, and which originally held a toilet set, can be found at the Maximilian Museum

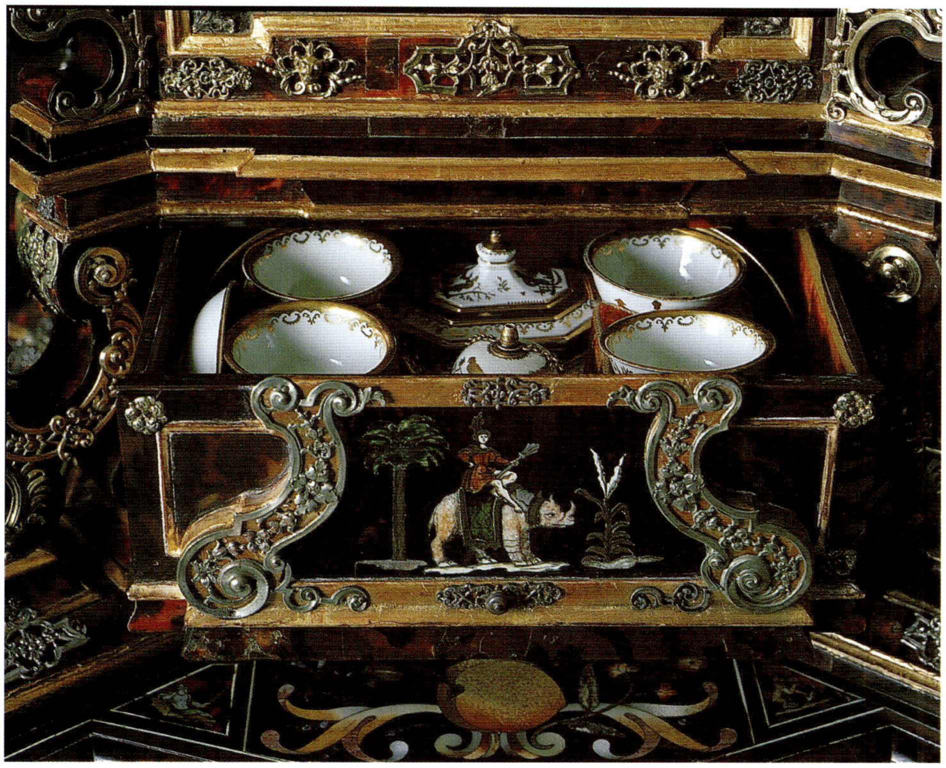

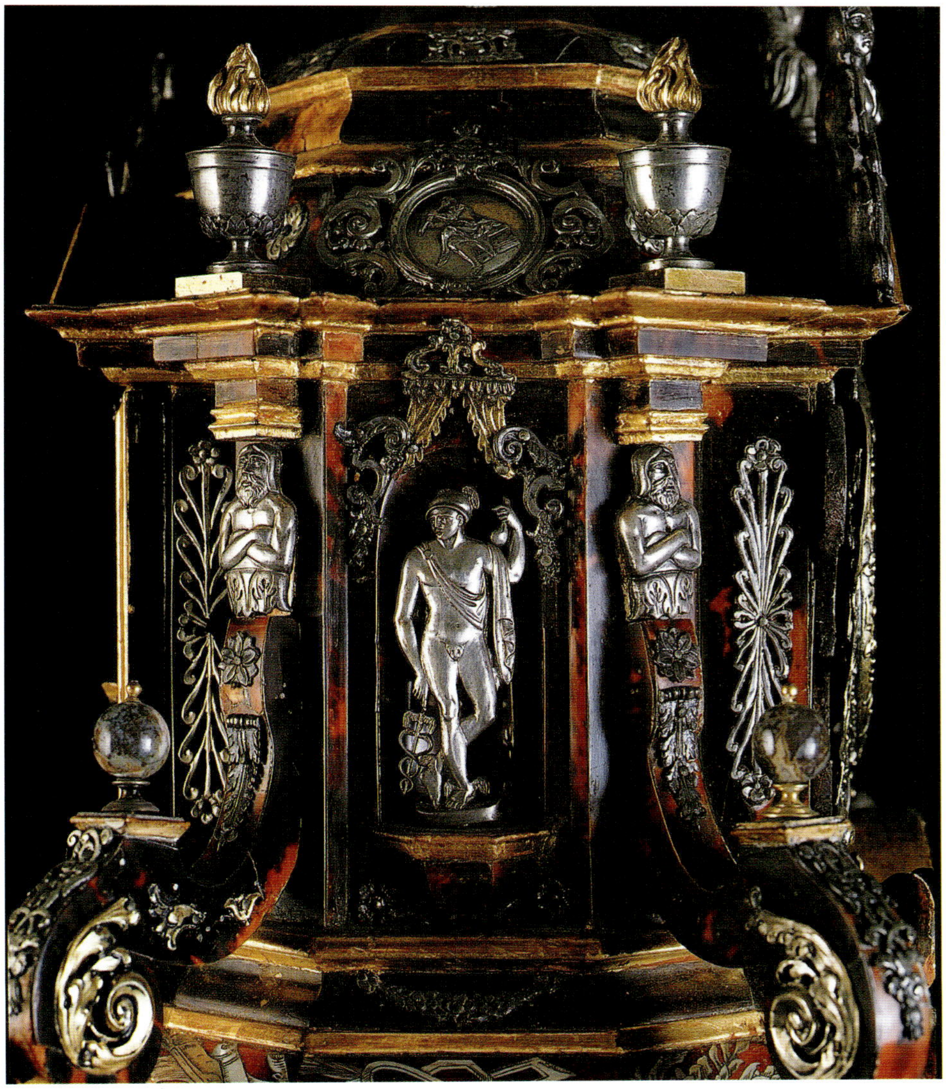

in Augsburg. Another at Schloss Charlottenburg, Berlin, has silver panels marked by Thelot. The Victoria and Albert Museum also has a clock with silver mounts by Thelot, which holds a gold-mounted toilet set by the Augsburg goldsmith Elias Adam (fl. c. 1669–1745). Other variations are a clock in Brunswick at the Herzog Anton Ulrich Museum; a famous clock with an astrolabic dial and movement signed by Joseph Schöner at the Württembergisches Landesmuseum in Stuttgart; a clock at the Schlossmuseum in Gotha with movement by David Haas; an unsigned example at the Regensburg Museum; four clocks in Rosenborg Palace, Copenhagen (one of these signed by Georg Braun) and another in a private collection in Milwaukee.[7]

Archibald Philip Primrose (1847–1929), fifth Earl of Rosebery, had a successful career in politics, becoming Prime Minister in 1894–5. In 1878, he married Hannah Rothschild (d. 1890), the daughter of Baron Mayer Amschel de Rothschild (1818–74), heiress to Mentmore and £12 million. The estate was expanded to magnificent porportions and furnished with works of art. In his introduction to the Mentmore sale catalogue, Sir Francis Watson quotes Lady Eastlake, 'I do not believe that the Medici were ever so lodged at the height of their glory'.[8]

NOTES

1 T. H. Clarke, *The Rhinoceros from Dürer to Stubbs 1515–1799*, Sotheby's Publications, London, 1986, p. 120, fig. 92.
2 *Bayern-Kunst und Kultur*, Munich, 1972, no. 1379, p. 188, pl. 29.
3 Thanks to Dr. Katherina Bott.
4 Sotheby's, London, 14 June, 1996, lot 14, *Sotheby's Preview*, July 1996, p. 16.
5 Hofmann 1968.
6 Thanks for Sebastian Whitestone of Bobinet for bringing these to my attention.
7 Maurice 1976a, figs. 704, 720; Seling 1980, vol. 2, no. 1077; Alfieri 1986, no. 120; Kunstgewerbemuseum 1989, no. 142.
8 Mentmore, sale, Sotheby's, 18–27 May 1977, introduction.

12. MUSICAL CLOCK

Workshop of Giuseppe Valadier (Rome 1762–1839), Rome, c. 1785–95; clock mechanism: Paris, J. Robert and Sons, c. 1795
Marble, *pietre dure*, gilt bronze, clock mechanism, 106.7 × 61 × 108.3 cm (42 × 24 × 42½ in)
(TU142)

PROVENANCE: Marshall Antiques, Los Angeles, 1981.

DESCRIPTION: A musical clock with a single-fusee, cam-actuated roller, playing nine separate tunes on a ten-bell carillon, and with a silk-thread-suspended pendulum. The Grand Sonnerie is signed *J. Robert et Fils, a la Chaux de Fonds, Paris.* The case holds a Swiss movement, which strikes the hours and the quarters and shows the days of the month. The white enamel dial has Roman numerals for the hours, enclosed by outer and inner bands of Arabic numerals for the seconds and the days of the month. The carved, arch-shaped, white marble case is mounted with gilt-bronze figures and animals after the antique. It rests on four gilt-bronze supports in the form of 'Termini' lionesses; at the centre, above a panel of hippogryphs and rosettes, sits a recumbent lion. The dial has a laurel-leaf frame and in the spandrels below are two small sphinxes and foliage. The arch above the dial is supported by four 'Villa Albani' caryatids; above the arch rest two figures of slaves beside a pair of garlanded rams' heads and a central panel with the motto *S.P.Q.R.* The slaves are chained to two further figures of lionesses seated on top of the clock, flanking the crowning figure of Minerva who holds an orb and a spear. The borders of the clock are set with bands of stiff-leafed foliage and beading.

COMMENTARY: The multifaceted activities of the dynasty of Roman goldsmiths and founders – Andrea Valadier (1695–1759), his son Luigi (1726–85) and grandson Giuseppe (1762–1839) are well documented.[1] That both Luigi Valadier and his son made clock cases was first proposed by Alvar González-Palacios, who correctly attributed to the workshop three multi-coloured marble and bronze clocks.[2] The identification of the corpus of Valadier workshop drawings in Faenza and London,[3] where there are more than 30 designs for clock cases, and the numerous references to clocks in the *Registro*, the inventory of his workshop made by Giuseppe Valadier in 1810, have confirmed these activities.

The drawings in Faenza and London are by both Luigi and Giuseppe Valadier, as well as other studio draughtsmen, ranging in style and date from the late Roman rococo of the 1760s through the Empire styles of the early nineteenth century. None specifically relates to the present clock, though there are many similar features.

The three published clocks mentioned above can all be dated to the 1780s. Since Luigi Valadier did not die until 1785 (he committed suicide), it is possible that he was involved in their design and construction, or that the work was that of his son. However, a clock made for the Villa Borghese is certainly by Luigi,[4] while a later example in the Rothschild Collection at Waddesdon Manor is by Giuseppe.[5] To these should be added two further clocks, one on the Italian art market,[6] another in a private collection in England. The Gilbert Collection clock makes a notable addition to this group of seven. The arched shape develops directly from the three clocks published by González-Palacios. The design of those was inspired by the entrance of the Pio Clementine Museum in the Vatican (the portico was completed in 1773), which is flanked by two Egyptian athletes (from the Villa Adriana in Tivoli), replaced in the design of the Gilbert Collection clock with caryatids derived from the renowned ancient marble figures in Villa Albani.

As with the two caryatids, the gilt bronzes that decorate the clock are typical of the repertoire of Grand Tour subjects after the antique made in several Roman foundries of the late eighteenth century.[7] However, the exact models found here are all repeated elsewhere in various products of the Valadier workshop and, indeed, many of them relate directly to those used in one of the most important Valadier commissions, the mounting of the collection of cameos for Pope Pius VI's Sacred and Profane Museum in the Vatican. From 1779, Luigi Valadier made numerous inventive and highly decorative mounts and frames, for the museum, ornamented with gilt bronze, silver, enamel, marble and hardstones. This work, continued by Giuseppe Valadier after his father's death, went on until 1797, when, by the terms of the Treaty of Tolentino, the entire collection of the museum was removed to Paris. Several of the mounted cameos still exist and are now in the Louvre, where they were the subject of a recent exhibition.[8]

The lionesses on the Gilbert Collection clock are copied from the antique prototypes formerly on the fountain of Termini (now in the Vatican) and are found on the base of the frame for the Carpegna cameo of *The Triumph of Bacchus*, completed in 1780 by Luigi Valadier for the museum[9] and were later regularly used as bases for *desserts* and clocks from the workshop.

The two bronze slaves derive from the group of six seated around the base of the mount for the cameo of Augustus, completed by Luigi Valadier at the beginning of 1785.[10] The seated figure of Minerva is a replica of the

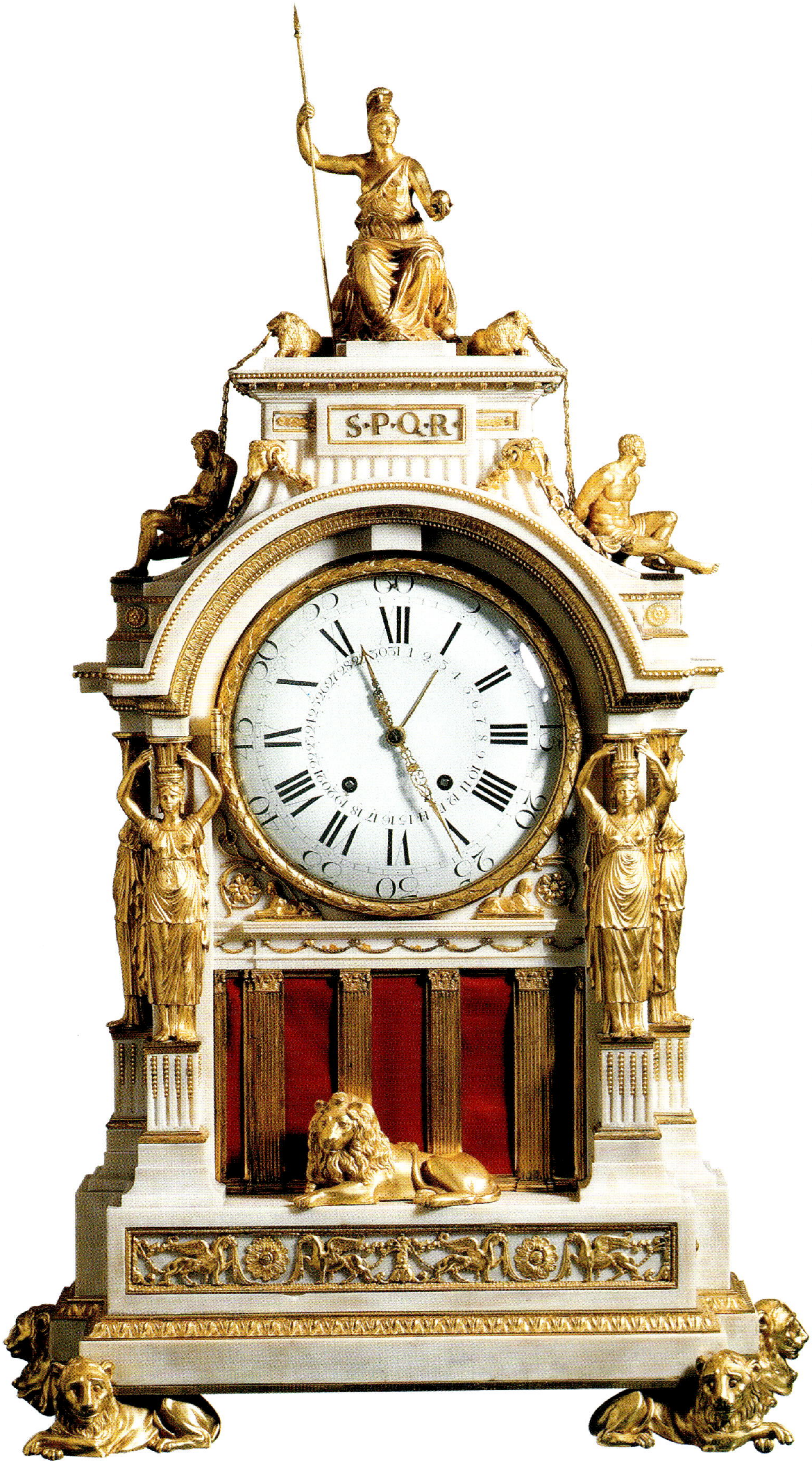

antique porphyry figure placed in front of the Capitol in Rome, popularly called *La Dea Roma*. A reduction of it, reproduced in porphyry and other stones, was also made for the museum, carved by Giacinto Frey (1761–1824) and completed in the workshop by Giuseppe Valadier in 1786.[11] All these antique models are amongst those found in the Valadier *Registro* of 1810.

The movements of all eight clocks are varied: Italian (Roman), Swiss and French. It is possible that some have been changed or adapted, but it would in any case seem unlikely that the mechanisms were produced by the Valadiers. However, the enamel dials on all the clocks are remarkably similar and it is probable that they were indeed made in the Via del Babuino workshop.[12]

NOTES
1 *Luigi Valadier au Louvre*, 1994–95.
2 González-Palacios 1984, pp. 129–36.
3 *Valadier, Three Generations…* 1991; *Valadier, Sacro e Profano* 1991.
4 González-Palacios 1993, p. 226, fig. 460.
5 Valeriani 1991–92.
6 Finarte, Milan, 16–17 May 1984, lot 213.
7 The Righetti and Zoffoli workshops, for example, produced similar bronzes.
8 *Luigi Valadier au Louvre*, 1994–95.
9 Ibid., no. 2, pp. 55–59.
10 Ibid., no. 5, pp. 84–87.
11 Ibid., no. 6, pp. 100–107.
12 Thanks to John Winter for kindly providing information on this clock.

13. CLOCK

Case: Italy, Giacomo Raffaelli (1753–1836), 1804; clock: Paris, Abraham-Louis Breguet (1747–1823)
Pietre dure, amethyst, lapis lazuli, malachite, labradorite, jasper, agate, marble, micromosaic, gilt bronze, clock movement,
90.2 × 51.1 × 20.6 cm (35½ × 20⅛ × 8⅛ in)
1996.624 (MM243)

PROVENANCE: By tradition, Pope Pius VII to Napoleon Bonaparte, Paris; Empress Josephine, Malmaison; probably Eugene Beauharnais, first Duke of Leuchtenberg; probably Josephine Beauharnais, Queen of Sweden and thence by descent; Sir Alexander Kleinwort, London; H. Burton Jones; A. Gifford-Scott; Sotheby's, sale, London, 15 June 1973, lot 33; John Partridge, London 1976.

LITERATURE: *American Horologist* 1975, vol. 44, ill., p. 44; González-Palacios 1976, p. 42; González-Palacios 1977a, no. 29; *Lapidary Journal* 1977, p. 198; Zucker 1977, p. 84; González-Palacios 1976, pp. 33–48, fig. 34 B; Hagans 1977, ill., p. 30; *Town and Country* 1979, p. 123; *View* 1978, p, 27; González-Palacios 1981, p. 20; González-Palacios and Röttgen 1982, no. 29; González-Palacios 1982a, p. 20; González-Palacios 1984, vol. 1, p. 143, pl. 24, vol. 2, p. 135, fig. 296.

DESCRIPTION: A clock mounted on top of a triumphal arch of red and white antique marble. The façade has four agate pilasters with Corinthian capitals and bases of gilt bronze. Between the pilasters are four panels of lapis lazuli and two of micromosaic bearing military trophies. The vault of the arch is faced with red marble caissons decorated with gilt-bronze rosettes. On the interior and exterior sides of the pilasters are panels of jasper and lapis lazuli framed in gilt-bronze beading and edged in red antique marble. The colonnade on the front consists of four amethyst columns with Corinthian capitals and gilt-bronze bases; the cornice and top are of red antique marble; the frieze is white marble decorated with ox skulls of gilt bronze. The top part of the clock consists of a marble block on a granite base, edged with red antique marble, with pilasters of jasper and panels of lapis lazuli. At the centre, the clock dial is surmounted by a trophy of arms in gilt bronze with a winged Victory on one side and Fame on the other, plus an eagle and cockerel on the corners. At the centre of the arch is a statuette of Mars in gilt bronze on a stone base. The marble structure is signed on the back GIACOMO RAFAELLI / FECE ANNO 1804. The clock has a calender hand and engine-turned surround, quarter-striking movement numbered *304* and stamped IPCR, and outside rack striking. Upon the upper clock face are the words BREGUET / A PARIS.[1]

COMMENTARY: In his entry on this clock in the 1982 catalogue of the Gilbert Collection, Alvar González-Palacios wrote:

> This masterpiece of neoclassic design and workmanship, signed and dated by the foremost mosaicist in Rome, Giacomo Raffaelli, in 1804, was presented by Pope Pius VII to Napoleon Bonaparte. Made of marbles, agate, jasper, lapis lazuli, amethyst, a stone of great rarity called labrador, and other rare stones, the clock is a subtle allegory appropriate to the recipient of the papal gift: a triumphal arch dedicated to Mars whose statuette is seen in the middle of the arch and whose sacred animals – the cock, the vulture, and a wolf and dog now removed – were originally represented at the top. The ancient Roman trophies in mosaic to the right and left of Mars and the bronze trophy flanked by two Victories that crown the work enhance it as an exquisite piece of political adulation.[2]

This clock and a marble fireplace were among the gifts chosen by Antonio Canova (1757–1822) to be taken to Paris by Pius VII, who had been asked to preside over Napoleon's consecration and coronation as Emperor. When the ceremony took place, Napoleon unexpectedly took the crown from the Pope's hands and placed it on his head himself; he then turned and did the same for Josephine. Eventually, by tradition, the clock found its way to Malmaison, one of the luxurious residences the Emperor had acquired for Josephine before their marriage was dissolved due to her failure to produce an heir. It is listed (together with some other Gilbert Collection objects) in her death inventory of 1814.[3]

A similar, but less elaborate, arch of 1801 by Raffaelli is at the Hermitage.[4] It has no upper storey, clock, nor gilt-bronze figures. The figures on the Gilbert Collection clock are of great virtuosity, and González-Palacios suggests they may have been made in Raffaelli's workshop in the Via S. Sebastianello.

The maker of the clock movement was Abraham-Louis Breguet, a genius in the history of European horology. Sent by his stepfather to study watchmaking at the College Mazarin in Versailles when he was fifteen, he displayed an extraordinary talent that brought him to the attention of royal clients. By 1775, he had opened his own shop in Paris at quai d'Horlogue, where he dedicated himself to perfecting complex and costly instruments like the self-winding watch, a speciality that earned him international renown and many patrons.

Because Sir Alexander Kleinwort (1858–1935) is reputed to have received this clock 'in acknowledgement of financial advice' from one of the descendants of Charles XIV of Sweden, Sotheby's Kleinwort sale

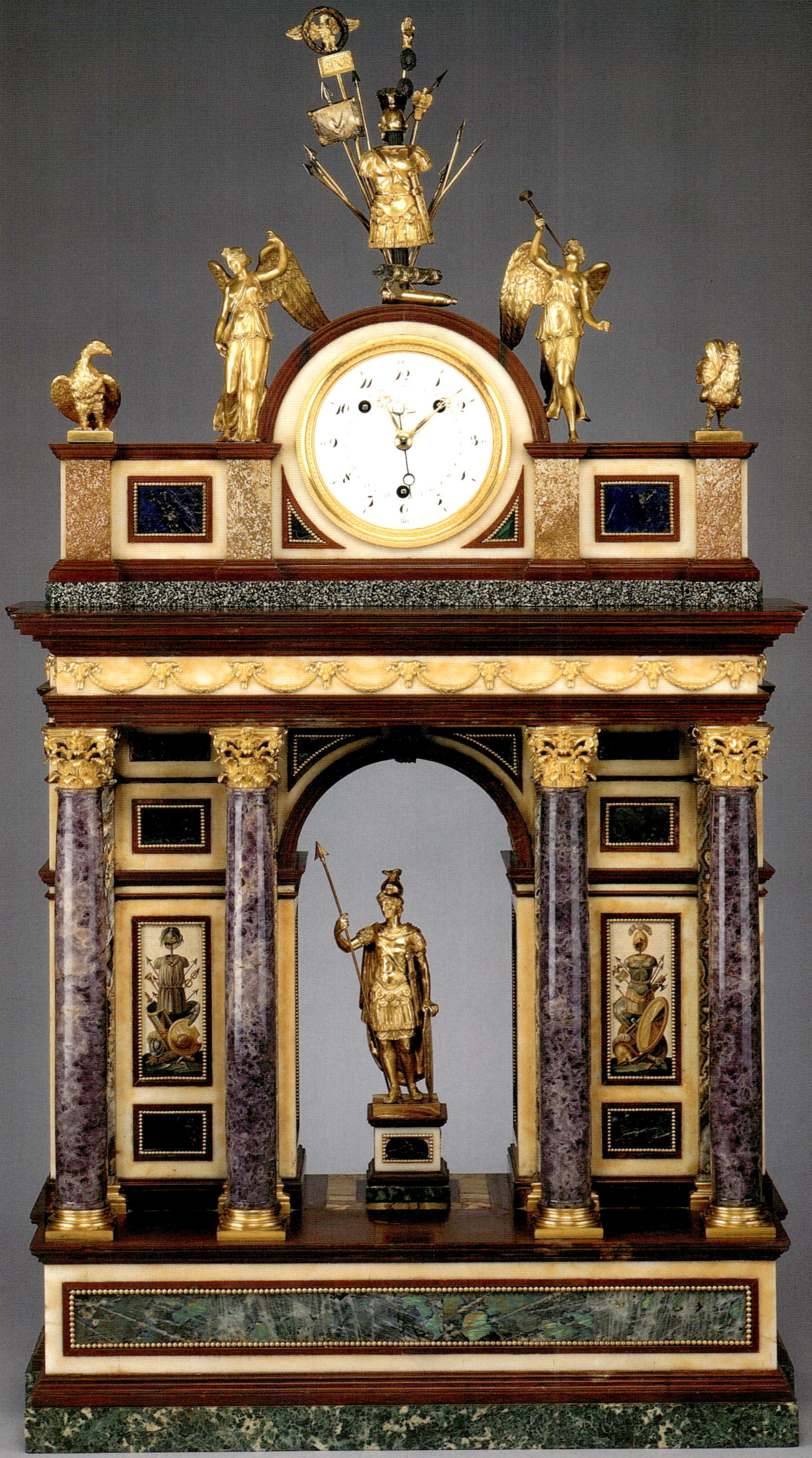

catalogue made the erroneous statement that Napoleon had given the clock to the future King of Sweden. He was 'said to have presented the clock to Marshal Bernadotte, later King of Sweden as Charles XIV (r. 1818–44), one of whose descendants gave it to Sir Alexander Kleinwort in acknowledgement of financial advice'.[5] As González-Palacios pointed out, this would have been impossible because it was in Josephine's inventory in 1814. Bernadotte moved to Sweden several years before this, was made heir apparent to the throne in 1810, and in 1814 became Charles XIV, John, King of Sweden and Norway. Swedish royal archives of Charles XIV and the estate inventory of his consort, Queen Desiree (r. 1818–44), show no record of the clock.[6]

Since the clock is listed in Josephine's 1814 death inventory, it seems reasonable to speculate that it might have come to Sweden by another route, namely through Josephine's son (and Napoleon's adopted son), Eugene Beauharnais, Duke of Leuchtenberg (1781–1824). Eugene owned various objects from his parents' collections. A hardstone and mosaic table by Belloni (1772–1863) with an eagle in a medallion and the letters NR was acquired by the Hermitage from the Leuchtenberg collection.[7] A Raffaelli centrepiece (Villa Carlotta) of 1804 also belonged to the Duke.[8] Eugene's daughter Josephine (1807–76), married in 1823 Bernadotte's son, Oscar I, the future king of Sweden, (r. 1844–59), becoming Queen Josephine of Sweden.

NOTES

1 Thanks to Sebastian Whitestone of Bobinet for information on the movement.
2 González-Palacios and Röttgen 1982, p. 116.
3 Grandjean 1964, p. 197.
4 Efimova 1968, no. 52.
5 Sotheby's, 15 June 1973, lot 34.
6 Thanks to Karyn Frykholm of the Royal Collection, Stockholm; to Jehanne Wake, biographer of the Kleinworts.
7 Efimova 1968, no. 76.
8 González-Palacios 1984, vol. 1, pl. XXIII, p. 143; vol. 2, pp. 134–35.

14. CLOCK

Pietre dure: Florence, second quarter nineteenth century;
case: England or France, c. 1850
Pietre dure, jasper, lapis lazuli, coloured marble, gilt bronze, ebony and ebonised wood, enamel, clock movement, 100 × 52 × 25.1 cm (39 3/8 × 20 1/2 × 9 7/8 in)
1996.859 (MM295)

PROVENANCE: Sotheby's London, 3 March 1995, lot 192.

DESCRIPTION: A mantel clock with an ebonised wood case. The front and sides are inlaid with hardstone-mosaic panels in jasper, lapis lazuli and coloured marble, set in a background of black Belgian marble depicting birds, butterflies, and branches of fruit. The borders of the case are outlined in gilt bronze, a frieze of acanthus foliage and ovolo moulding. The base and the upper part of the case bear two masks; a pair of terms of Hercules support the cornice. The top is surmounted by a parcel-gilt bronze group of two fighting dogs. The gilt-bronze dial is set with white enamel plaques with blue Roman numerals. The case rests on four boars'-head feet.

COMMENTARY: This clock is a typical example of the nineteenth-century revival of the decorative style of the French *ébeniste*, André-Charles Boulle (1624–1732). The overall ensemble of gilt-bronze mounts is similar to a cabinet in the same materials.[1] The two fighting dogs and the boars'-head feet are derived from the animal bronzes of nineteenth-century French sculptors.[2] They were in widespread serial production for use on decorative furnishings; examples could be seen in the international exhibitions in Paris and London from the mid-to-late nineteenth century.

The boars'-head castings are virtually identical to those on a pedestal for sculptures manufactured by Palmer and C. Brighton and exhibited at the Great Exhibition in London in 1851. The model for these castings was made by Benedetto San Giovanni (1781–1852).[3] The sculptor, who trained in Italy and then settled in London in 1827, exhibited at the Royal Academy until 1847, showing figures and groups of animals and various other naturalistic and genre subjects.[4] At the Crystal Palace Exhibition he displayed a bronze group with dogs attacking a stag in the same style as the group on this clock.[5]

The hardstone plaques that decorate the case, typical mid-nineteenth century products of the Florentine workshops, are in the taste of the baroque manufactures of the Grand Ducal workshops. Similar plaques are often found in French and English cabinetry of the 1800s, as exemplified by a pair of works in the Gilbert Collection (cat. no. 16).

NOTES

1 Payne 1981, p. 71.
2 Horswell 1971.
3 Crystal Palace 1851, p. 97.
4 Makay 1977, p. 33.
5 Crystal Palace 1851, p. 106.

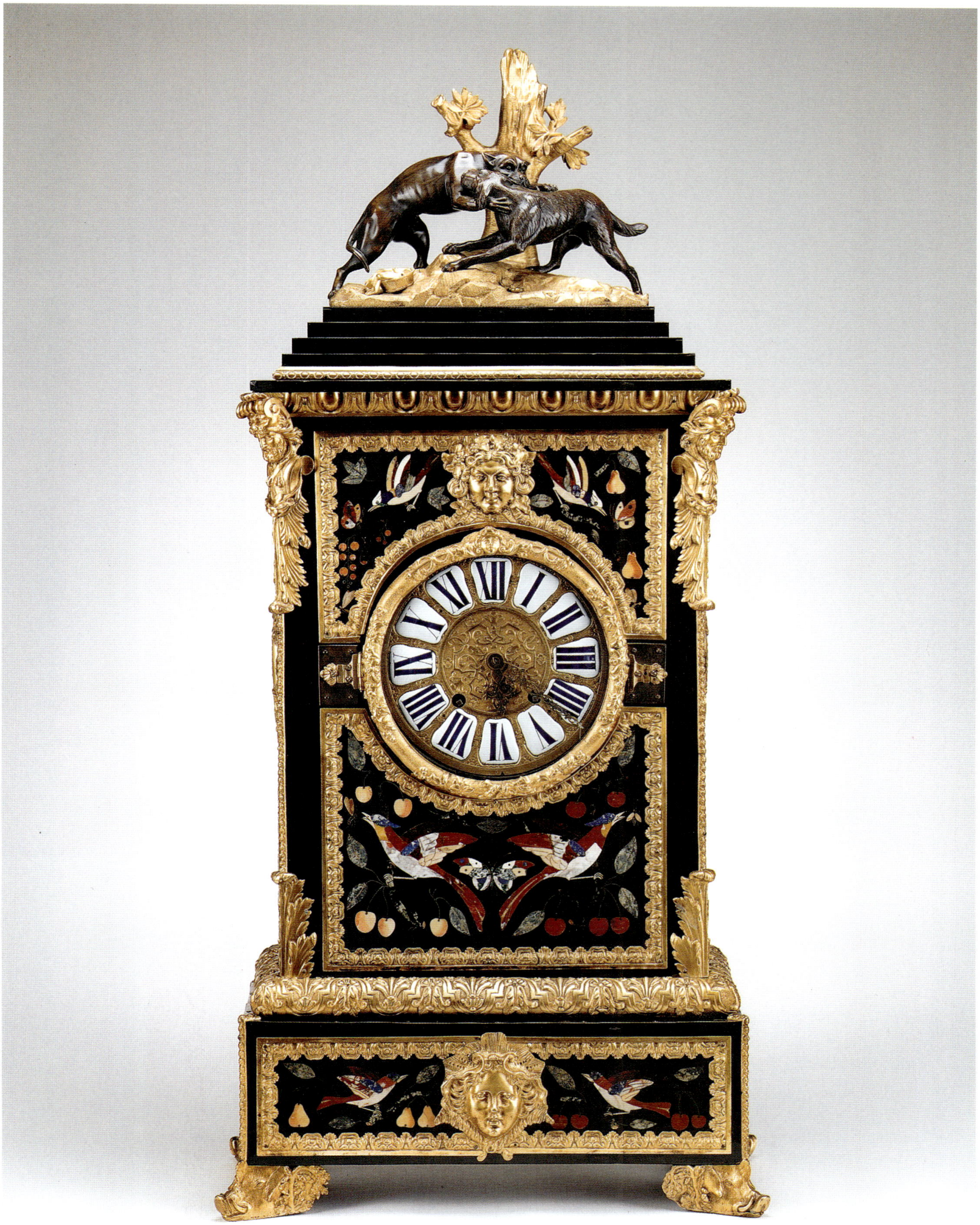

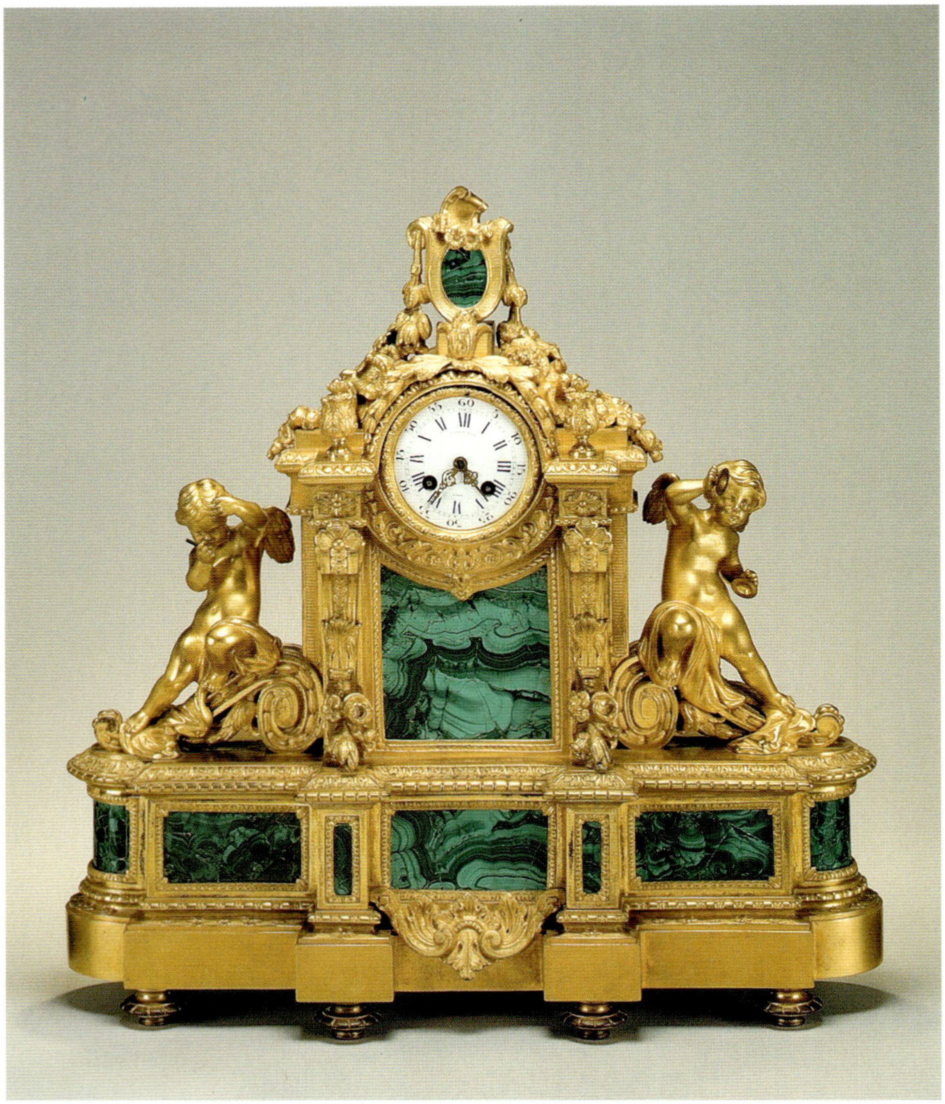

15. CLOCK

Paris, mid-nineteenth century
Malachite, gilt bronze, 50.8 × 50.8 × 17.1 cm (20 × 20 × 6¾ in)
(TU51a)

PROVENANCE: Krex, New York, 1968.

DESCRIPTION: A clock with bronze base and mosaic panels of malachite. The raised central part, panelled in malachite, bears a richly decorated bronzed structure with drawers. There is scrollwork on the base and top and a set of urn-shaped terminals. Two bronze statuettes of cherubs are at the sides. An inscription on the face reads: RAINGO FRES A PARIS.

COMMENTARY: The elaborate bronze structure of this clock echoes the ornamentation of the Renaissance and baroque periods. It exemplifies the taste for *objets d'ameublement* represented at the international exhibitions of the mid-nineteenth century.

16. PAIR OF CABINETS

Pietre dure: Florence, mid-nineteenth century; cabinets: France, mid-nineteenth century
Pietre dure, *pietre tenere*, marble, ebonised wood, gilt bronze, 122 × 94 × 46 cm (48 × 36 × 18 in)
1996.602-603 (MM116AB)

PROVENANCE: Walter Fradin, New York, 1973.

DESCRIPTION: A pair of cabinets of ebonised wood with gilt-bronze mounts. Five panels on the doors (four in the corners and one oval panel in the centre) bear naturalistic motifs of flowers and birds in *pietre dure* and *pietre tenere* on a black marble background.

COMMENTARY: Although executed in the seventeenth-century manner, these mosaic panels were in fact produced in the Florentine workshops in the mid-nineteenth century. This style of cabinet was popular in France at the time of Napoleon III (r. 1852–70), when furniture in the Louis XVI style was all the rage, largely owing to Empress Eugenie's passion for anything connected with Marie-Antoinette.

A pair of cabinets stamped by Beaufort Jeune (fl. c. 1836) similar to these examples, appeared at auction in 1989.[1] Another unsigned, but with a bronze pediment identical to the one on these cabinets was sold at the Drouot in Paris.[2] A very close example won a gold medal at the *Esposizione Universale Fiorentina* in 1855.[3] All of these pieces are connected to a single model designed by Georges Marie Paul Vital and Bonifacio Monbro.[4]

NOTES
1 Christie's London, 16 February, lot 93.
2 22 December 1989, lot 119.
3 Payne 1981, fig. 487.
4 Ledoux-Lebard 1984, p. 494.

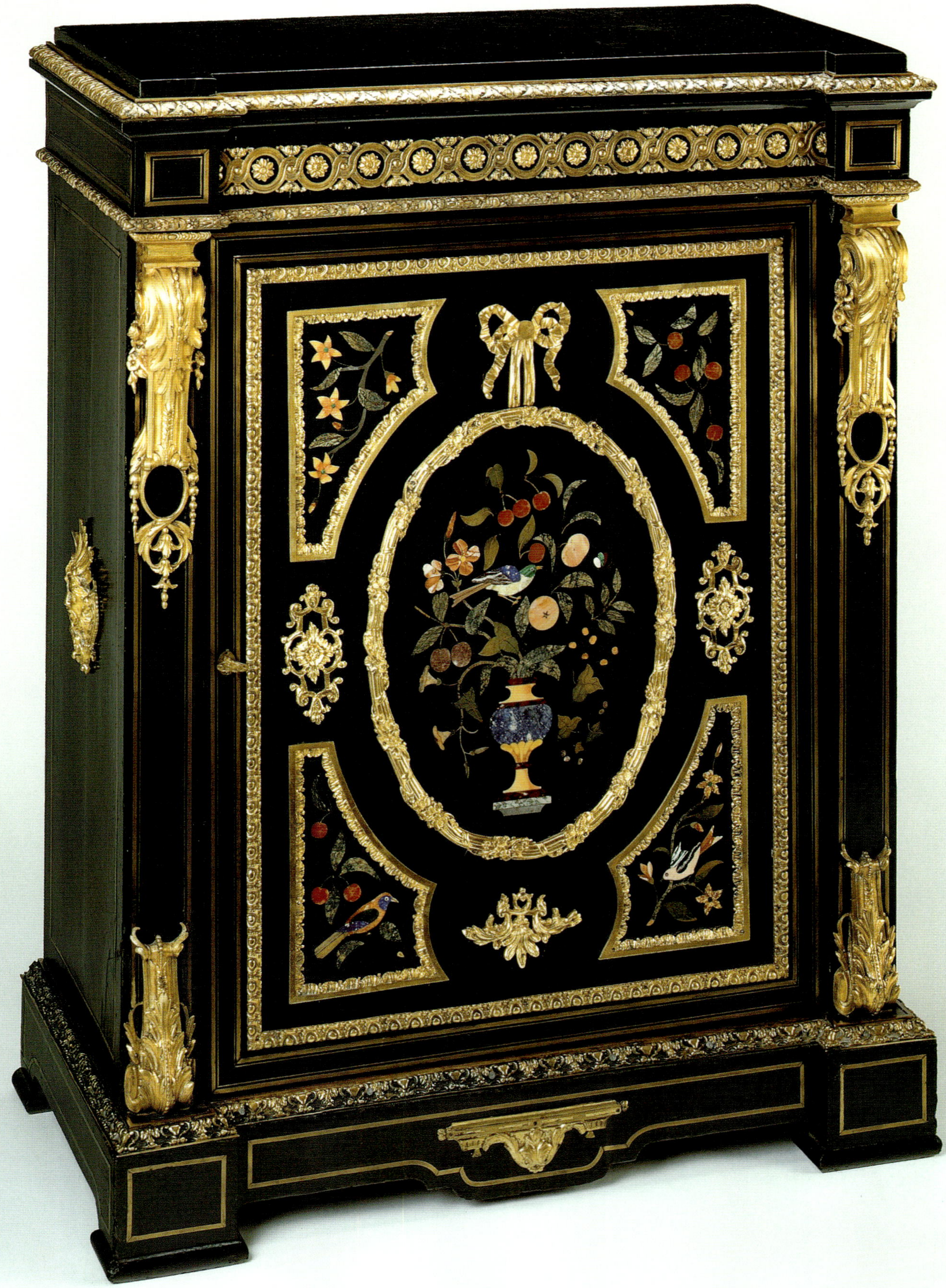

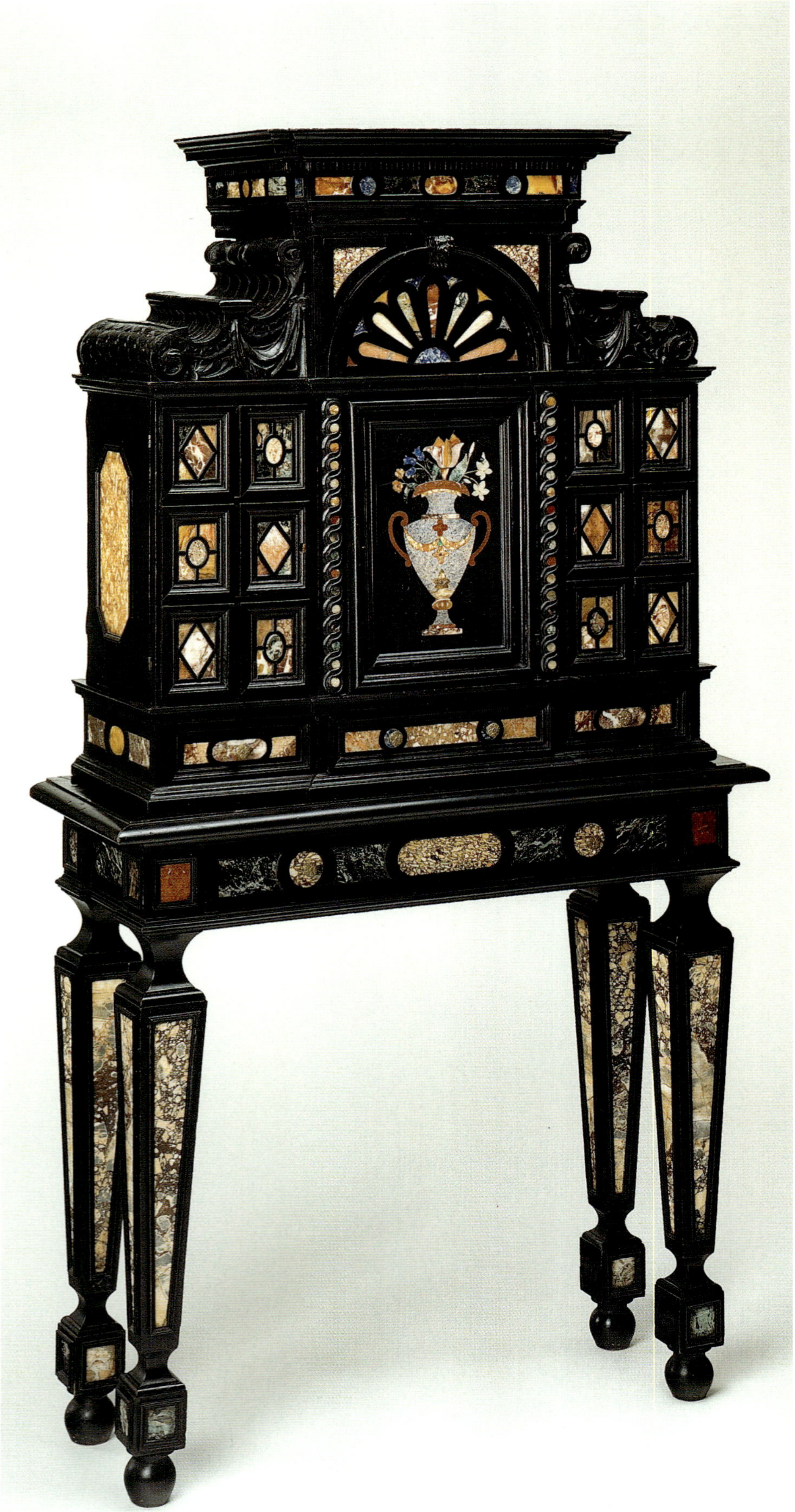

17. CABINET

Pietre dure: Italy, possibly Rome or Naples, late nineteenth century; cabinet: Italy, second half nineteenth century; stand: South Italy, late nineteenth century
Pietre dure, marble, coloured breccia marble, ebonised walnut; cabinet: 86 × 81.9 × 29.8 cm (33 7/8 × 32 1/4 × 11 3/4 in); stand: 86.4 × 92.7 × 34.9 cm (34 × 36 1/2 × 13 3/4 in)
1996.220 (MM60)

PROVENANCE: Old World Imports, Los Angeles, 1968.

LITERATURE: Sherman 1971, pl. XXV, p. 50.

EXHIBITION: Los Angeles, 1977.

DESCRIPTION: The cabinet is made of ebonised walnut. Both the lower and upper parts are encrusted with marble and coloured breccia. The joints between the stones are covered with strips of wood, and all the panels are framed in moulded wood. The vase inlaid in the central door, although inspired by seventeenth-century prototypes from the Grand Ducal workshops, obeys none of the rules, gives no visual clues as to its volume, and, in addition, is placed on its black marble background without a horizontal surface to stand on and without any spatial references.

COMMENTARY: The origin of this cabinet is uncertain, but the use of marble and breccia from Rome and southern Italy suggests that it is from Rome or Naples. The design of the stand is typical of the late nineteenth century.

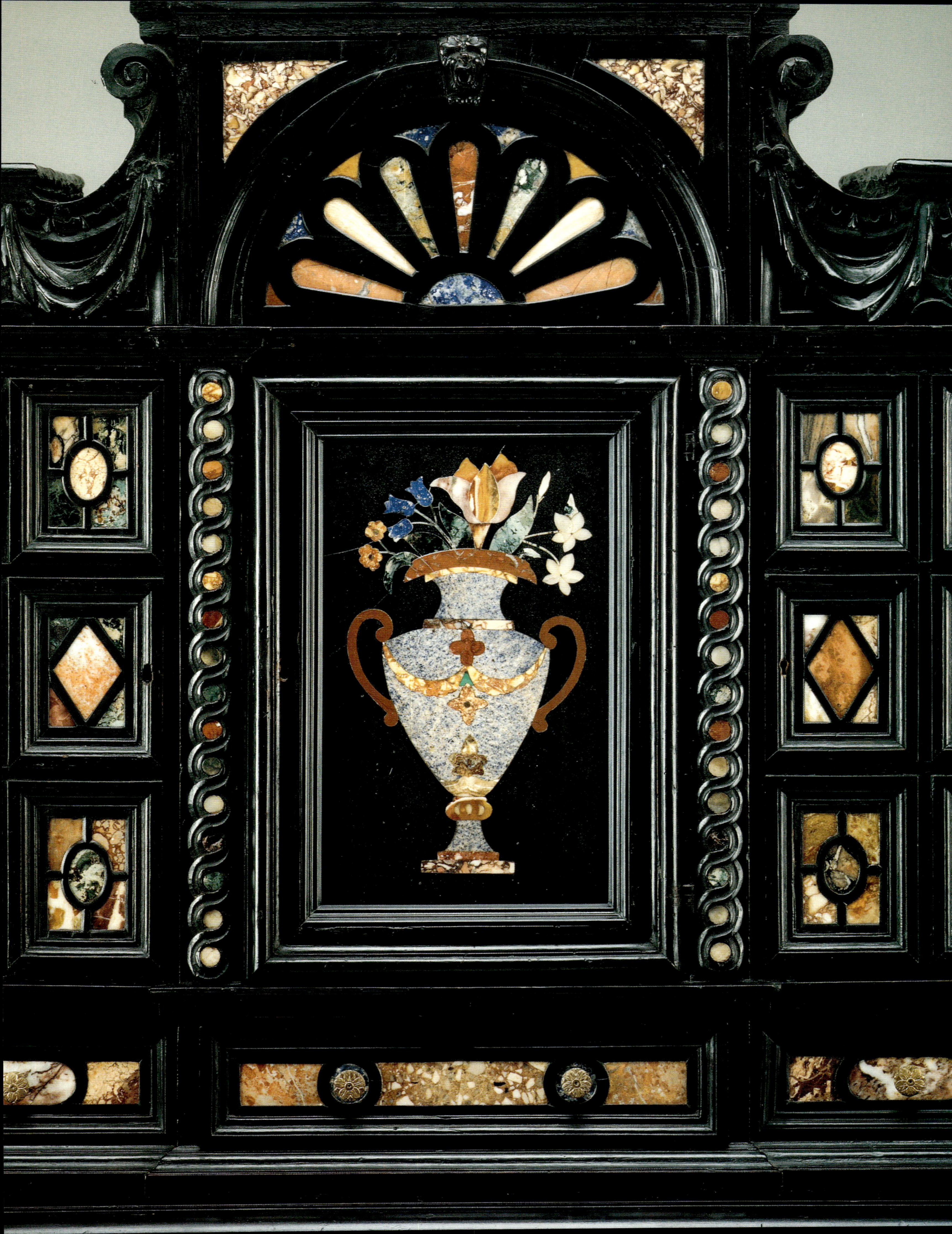

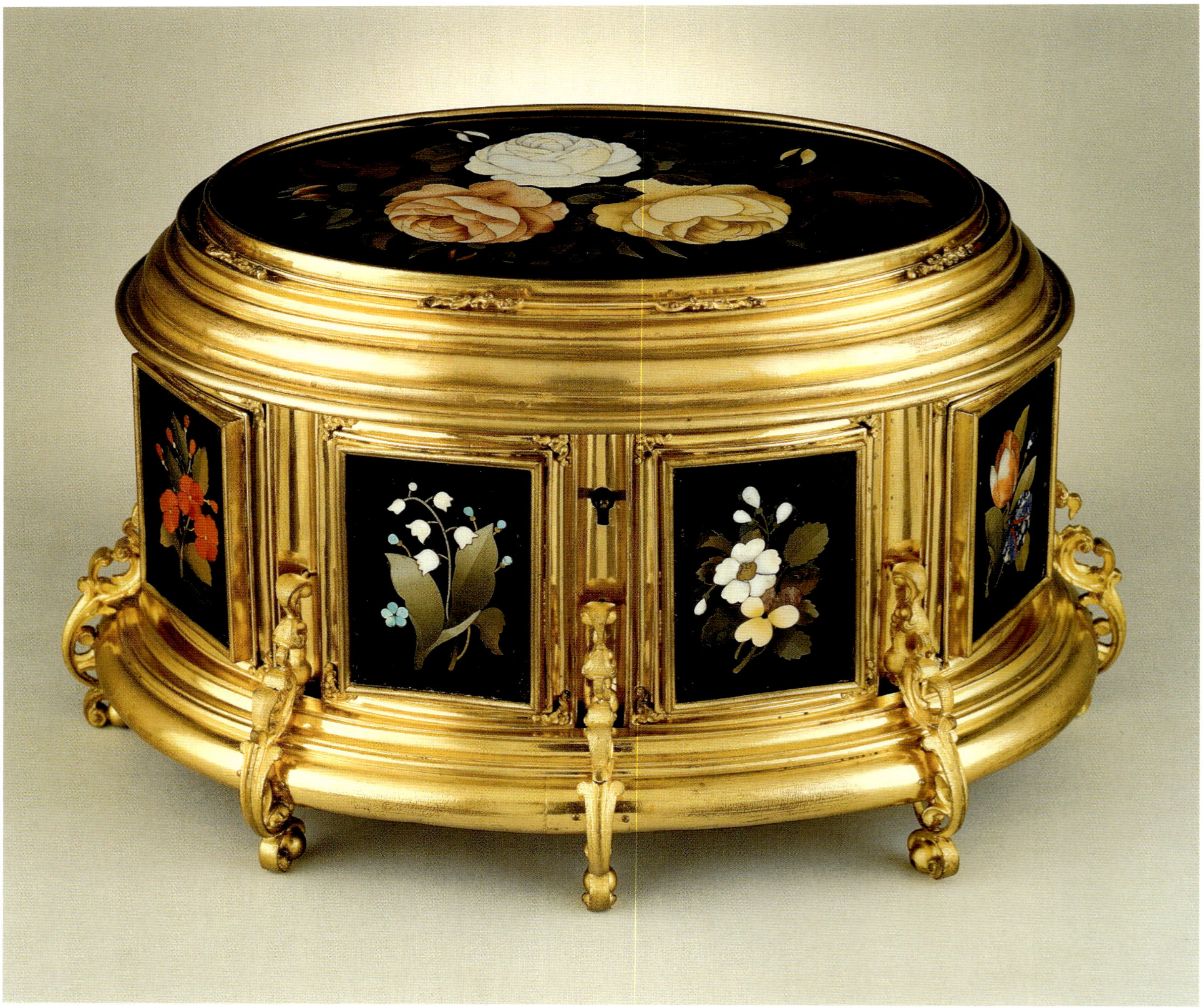

18. CASKET

Florence, late nineteenth century
Pietre dure, *pietre tenere*, gilt brass, silk, 16.2 × 23.5 × 30.5 cm (6 3/8 × 9 1/4 × 12 in)
1996.309 (MM202)

PROVENANCE: Sotheby's, sale, Los Angeles, 5 May 1975, lot 41.

EXHIBITION: Los Angeles, 1977.

DESCRIPTION: An oval casket made of gilt brass. The sides are applied with eight black marble panels mounted on a fretwork; the panels are inlaid with sprigs of flowers in *pietre dure* and *pietre tenere*. An oval plaque with inlaid roses constitues the lid; the inside is lined with white watered silk.

COMMENTARY: This casket is a typical example of the output of Florentine private workshops in the late nineteenth century. Similar metal caskets were made in the Ugolini workshop and can still be seen today in the firm's collection. A jewel box of gilt metal with an oval lid with coloured marble flowers on a black Belgian marble ground and sides set with similar smaller panels inlaid with different kinds of flowers was sold at Sotheby's, London, 6 November 1992, lot 172.

Tables

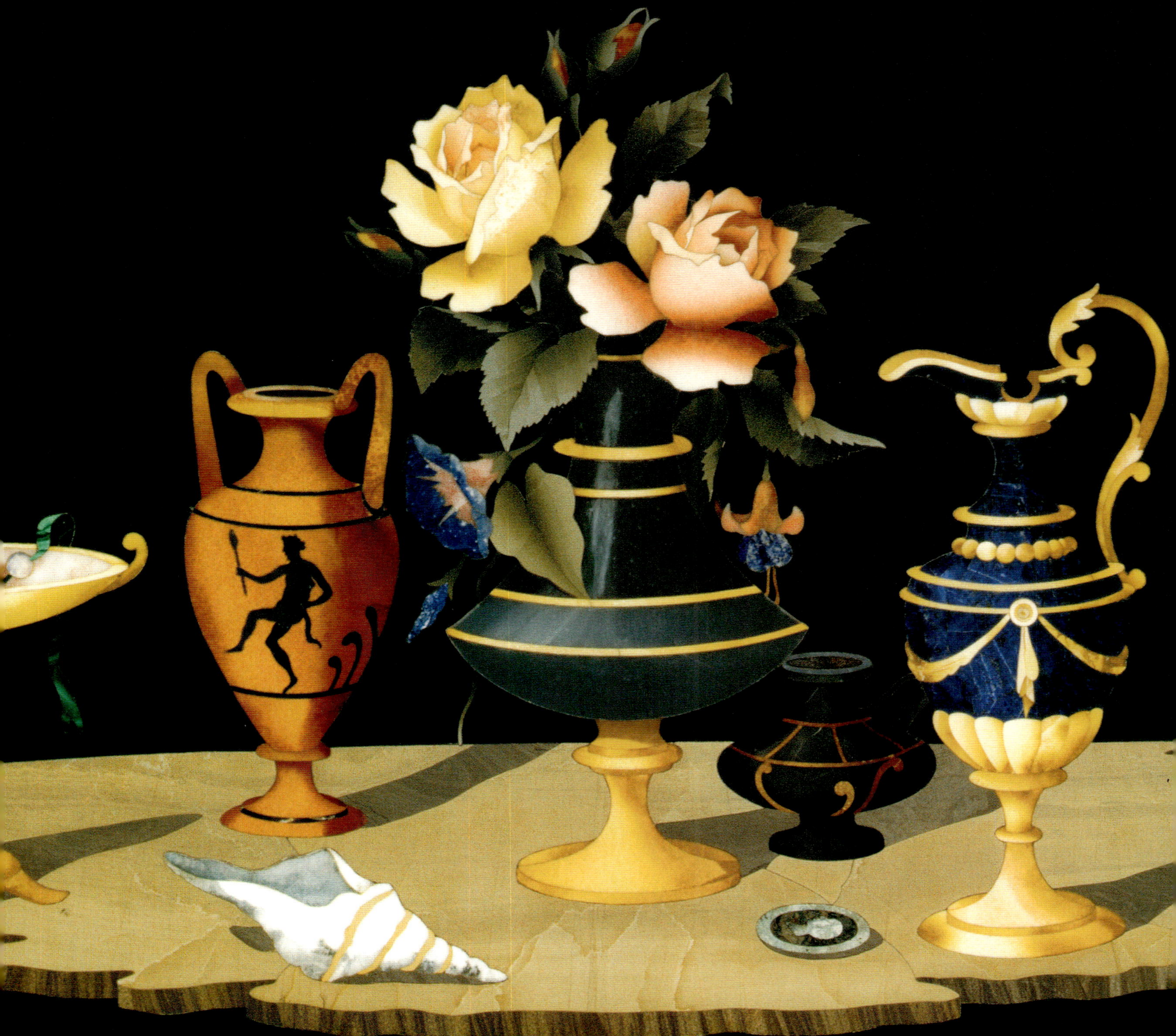

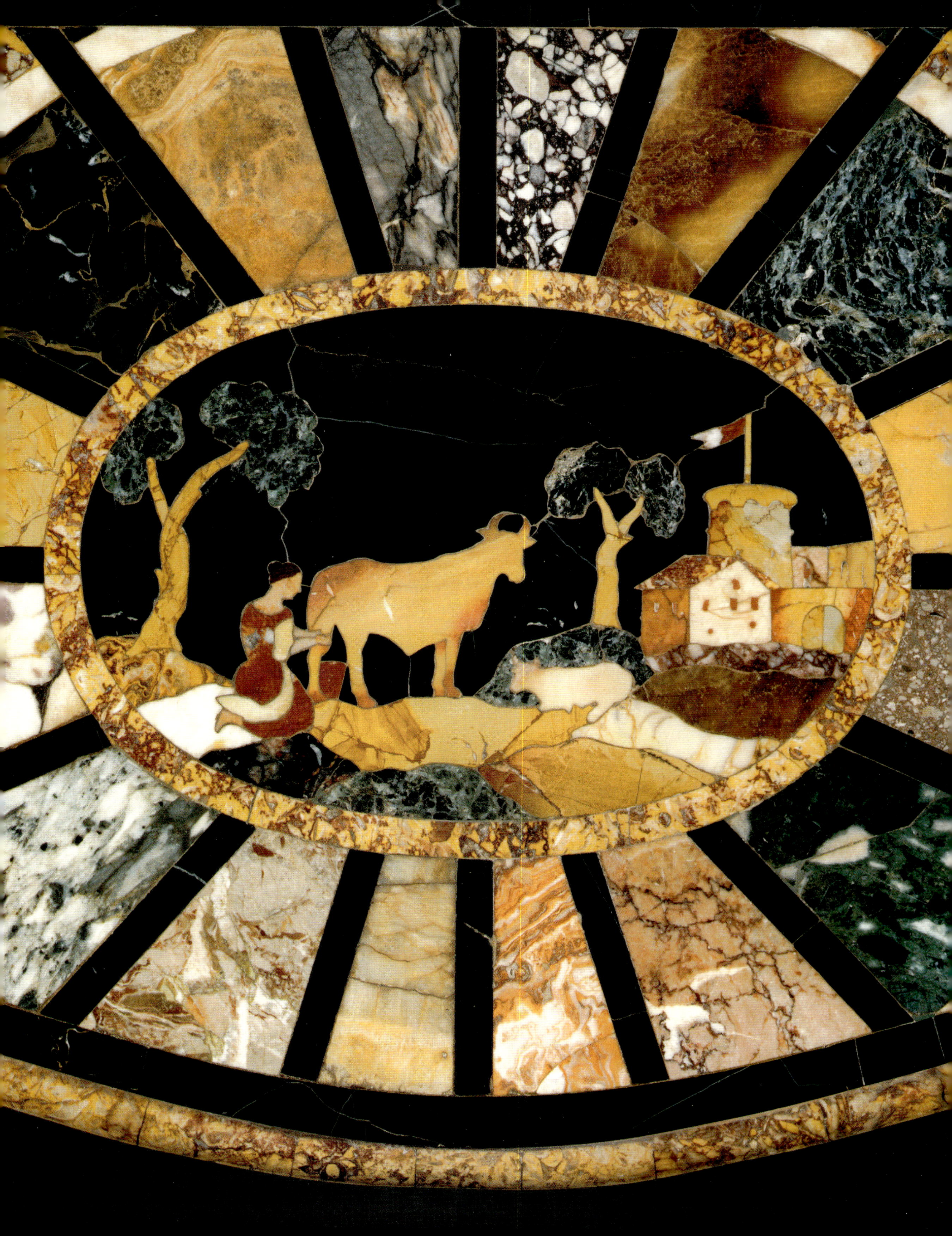

TABLES

In a letter to the Duke of Ferrara, written in Milan on 14 December 1575, Tomaso Zerbinati proposes the purchase of an octagonal table made of ebony edged with gold, 'of exquisite design', inlaid with stones of different types, including lapis lazuli, agate, carnelian, and oriental jasper. In Zerbinati's opinion the table was 'for its beauty, opulence and craftsmanship worthy of any Great Prince', and it was being offered for sale at the price of twelve thousand *scudi*.[1] A few months later, on 11 June 1576, Gasparo Visconti sent a letter, also from Milan, to the Grand Duke Francesco I de' Medici telling him about an exceptionally beautiful table that he had found on his return to Lombardy, also suggesting that the Duke purchase it:

> The table in question is round and could comfortably seat eight people; it is covered all over with mosaic of the finest oriental stones, expertly put together. The stones are all separated by a gold thread. I promise your Highness that it is such a remarkable piece that if it had to be remade, only the boldest craftsman would agree to fashion another like it, and I don't know how many years would be required to complete it. As for the price, they have told me that they would send it to a reputable jeweller for an estimate.

These letters provide valuable information about the characteristics of the inlaid furniture being produced in Milan in the second half of the sixteenth century. Judging by the description, and by comparison with one of the few extant pieces of Milanese furniture of the period, the technique employed consisted of setting individual geometrically shaped panels of hardstone into a frame of wood or a block of stone; each panel was then outlined with a metal thread (often gilt silver) and disposed according to a symmetrical plan. This technique is commonly known as *lavori di gioie*.

Some years earlier, Giorgio Vasari mentioned similar jewel work in a passage frequently quoted by scholars in relation to one of the first *pietre dure* craftsmen in Florence, Bernardino di Porfirio: 'He recently completed, to a design by Vasari, a unique table inlaid all over with oriental alabaster; it contains large pieces of jasper, heliotrope, carnelian, lapis, and agate, with other precious gemstones to the value of twenty thousand *scudi*'.[3] Francesco used artists from Milan to establish the stone workshop in the Casino di San Marco in Florence, and it would be justifiable to imagine that they brought with them the gem-cutting techniques for vase making and also the art of stone-inlay work for decorating furniture that had been fashionable in their home town at the time.

The type of lapidary mosaic produced in Rome can be distinguished from the jewel work of Milan or Florence by its archaeological character; a great deal of antique marble from excavations was used, and the techniques employed for setting the stones derive from the *opus sectile* (mosaic work) of ancient Rome. A Roman tabletop in the Gilbert Collection, which dates from the second half of the sixteenth century, is one of the most typical examples of the work of the Roman workshops (cat. no. 19). The large central stone is characteristic: this feature usually consists of a slab of antique

Previous page
Detail of cat. no. 36

Opposite
Detail of cat. no. 28

marble from an excavated site, surrounded by a frame inlaid with cartouches and shields combined in different ways. The decorative effect is heightened by the combination of silicic stones and *pietre dure* of different colours.

The work of artists such as Vasari, Giovanni Antonio Dosio (1535–1609), and Giacomo Vignola (1507–73) stands out among the very large number of objects produced in Rome at this time.[4] Additional examples became famous because they belonged to well-known people, like the table owned by Cardinal Richelieu (Galerie d'Apollon, Louvre, Paris). Of others, only a mention or appreciation in contemporary documents survives, like the tables described by Bartolomeo Ammanati (1511–92) as belonging to the residence of Pope Julius II (r. 1550–55) in Villa Giulia in Rome. In a letter written in 1555 to his Paduan patron, Marco Mantova Benavides, Ammanati describes the internal arrangements: 'In the middle of these rooms there are two large marble tables, seventeen spans long and six wide, with mixed marble borders; their feet are ornamented with mixed marble, as are the tops. Each table has three feet to support its length, and they are rare and wonderful items'. Later, he mentions marble tables in two other rooms.[5]

The first efforts made to update the repertory of lapidary ornamentation by adopting elements from the natural world fit neatly into the scientific interests of the first Grand Duke of Florence, who gave great encouragement to the collection and classification of plants, botanical illustration and the publication of books on botanical subjects, and to the study of other branches of the natural sciences. On the initiative of Cosimo I de' Medici, the botanist Luca Ghini, from Imola, established botanical gardens in Pisa and Florence between 1544 and 1545. Here, plants collected from all over Italy, and as many exotic species as it was possible to track down abroad, were cultivated. It was in this context, in 1583, that one of the most important botanical books was published: *De Plantis Libri XVI*, edited by Andrea Cesalpino, a pupil of Ghini who worked in Pisa for many years. The volume was dedicated to Francesco I. The studies conducted in Florence reflected the strong interest in botany that was widespread throughout Europe at the time and occasioned the publication of a large number of books at the end of the sixteenth century. Such a production of written works gave rise to the need for plates illustrating the species described.

The Bolognese naturalist Ulisse Aldrovandi had close relationships with the court in Florence and applied to the Grand Duke when he needed information about plants or animals, or drawings of them, while he was compiling his great works of natural history. During the reign of Francesco, the court painter, Jacopo Ligozzi, from Verona, put together a collection of 146 scientific illustrations,[6] which constitute the finest examples from the late sixteenth century. These scientific interests gave rise to certain innovations in the field of ornamentation, as can be seen in a table from the Gilbert Collection (cat. no. 20).

A more curious and rare feature of Florentine mosaic work was the use of burlesque and caricature ornamentation.[7] This style of mosaic decoration occurs sporadically on pieces that are difficult to date accurately, for example, a small neoclassical cabinet in the Royal Collection that is

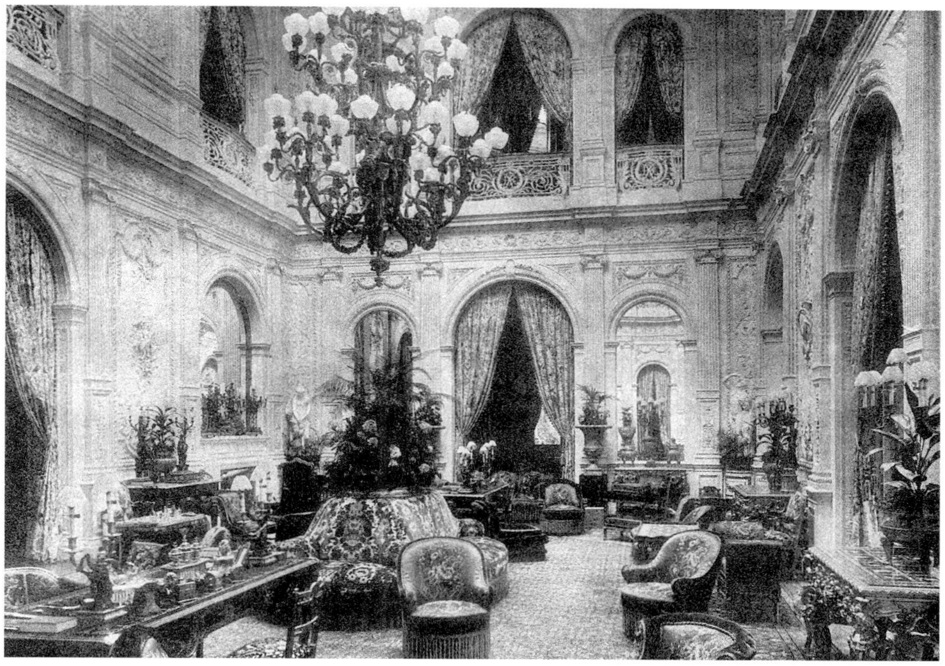

FIG. 7. The saloon at Halton House, Buckinghamshire, with the Rothschild table (cat. no. 23) at bottom right.
Photo courtesy National Monument Record

decorated with panels in Florentine mosaic of differing periods. Two of the panels bear portraits taken from drawings by Baccio del Bianco (1604–50) and from engravings from the series of hunchbacks published by Jacques Callot (1592–1635) in 1616. A tabletop now in Versailles combines zoomorphic panels and comic portraits, also derived from Callot. Additionally, he provided inspiration for the panels of a table in a private collection in New York and a panel in Kassel.[8] To these items, examined in the essay cited above, can be added a table in the collection in Schloss Ambras made of panels depicting subjects typical of the Florentine workshops, such as vases of flowers, fruit, and birds, interspersed with four plates bearing pictures of hunchbacks, also taken from Callot's series of engravings,[9] and a table in the Gilbert Collection (fig 7; cat. no. 23).

In the second half of the eighteenth century, when scientific and archaeological inquiry were at their height, a new endeavour was disseminated from Rome: the identification and collection of antique marbles. Libraries of stone samples were built up, the ornamental and didactic value of the different marbles going hand in hand. This interest influenced the decoration of tabletops. Nicola Minelli, who had a workshop in Campo Vaccino in Rome, was among the stonemasons selling marble samples.[10] An example of this kind of work can be seen in the portrait of Marchesa Gentili Boccapaduli painted in 1777 by Laurent Pecheux; she is depicted standing in her natural history cabinet beside a marble sample table.[11] A pair of sample tables with marble slabs cut in a rhomboid shape ordered by Prince Marc'Antonio Borghese during the alterations to the Villa Pinciana in 1782[12] are very similar to the examples in the Gilbert Collection (cat. no. 38). All of these tables exemplify what was surely Rome's most typical product during the last decades of the eighteenth century and the first decade of the nineteenth century. Such works were particularly popular with visitors from abroad.

In connection with the enthusiasm for science and archaeology that was widespread in the early nineteenth century, the name of Francesco Sibilio, the celebrated Roman dealer, stoneworker and collector, is of great interest. He was known in the field of archaeology because, as a collector, he had identified various kinds of stones that were so rare that the scholar Francesco Belli named them after him in his catalogue of the collection of stones used during the classical period, published in Rome in 1842. These included 'Sibilio's grey porphyry' and 'Sibilio's red lumachella'.[13]

In the mid-nineteenth century, floral themes were particularly popular in Florentine production and with the buying public at the great exhibitions at which the Opificio was represented increasingly sporadically. One of the most important patrons at this time was Ludwig of Bavaria for whom, in 1876, a very special rectangular table was made. Here, a central garland of lilies in a background of lapis lazuli surrounds Ludwig's coat-of-arms, held up by allegorical figures rendered in micromosaic (Schloss Linderhof, Bavaria; González-Palacios 1982b, p. 59). When the direction of the Opificio passed to Edoardo Marchionni, floral themes combined with fruit, birds, and neoclassical motifs remained popular. Magnolias, poppies, and azaleas were Marchionni's favourite flowers, and his mature style displayed a generous personal touch, elegant draftsmanship, and an unmistakeable penchant for faded, almost indistinct, colours. This can be seen in the table acquired in 1879 by the banker Sebastiano Fenzi for a client, William Boyd, of whom Marchionni did a likeness.[14] While the Opificio was going through an irreversible decline, the private studios that had emerged in Florence and used ornamental schemes typical of the Opificio, though seldom matching its quality of technique, design and materials (such as the shell they often used in their roses), were finding a foothold commercially. The workshop of Giovanni Ugolini, which opened in Via dei Fossi in 1868, was making a name for above-average quality, exemplified by the porphyry table with a still life in the centre inspired by the work of Antonio Cioci (fig. 10).

NOTES

1 Quoted in Campori 1879, p. 6.
2 The letter was transcribed by Zobi in 1853, p. 152, but no archive reference is given.
3 Tuena 1990, pp. 142–44.
4 Raggio 1960; Morrogh 1985, figs. 37–38, 66–67; Tuena 1988; González-Palacios 1993, vol. 1, pp. 380–86.
5 Tuena 1988, pp. 54–59.
6 Bacci and Forlani Tempesti 1961.
7 González-Palacios 1993, vol. 1, pp. 409–13.
8 González-Palacios 1993, vol. 2, figs. 730–40.
9 Sammlungen Schloss Ambras, Mobel; Kunsthistorisches Museum 1987, p. 28, no. 18.
10 Ficoroni 1744, pp. 189–90.
11 González-Palacios 1991a, p. 141, no. 60.
12 Galleria Borghese, Rome; Della Pergola 1971, p. 44.
13 Gnoli 1971, p. 105.
14 Giusti, Mazzoni, and Pampaloni Martelli 1978, p. 280, no. 28.

Opposite
Detail of cat. no. 34

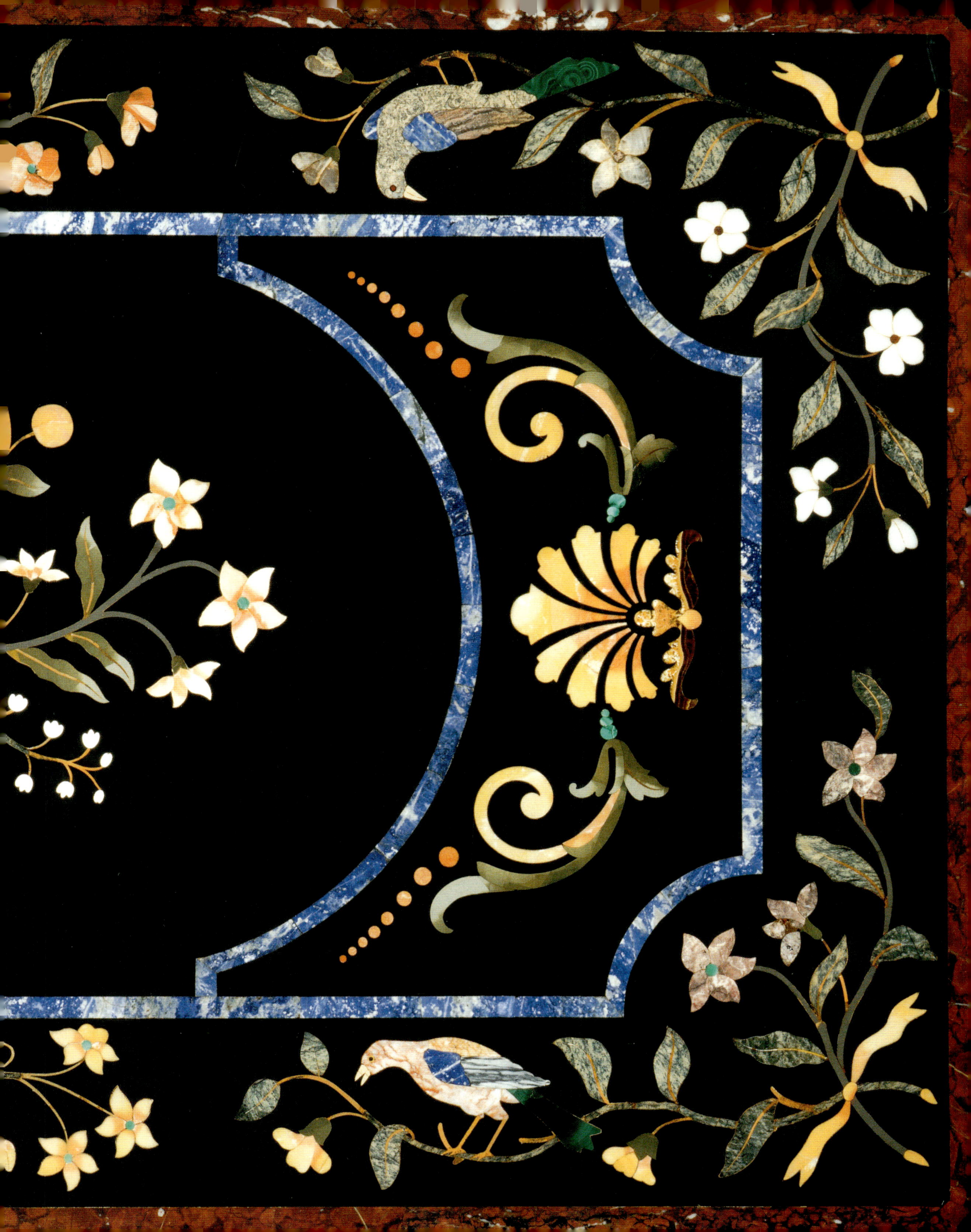

19. TABLE

Top: Rome, late sixteenth century; base: France, 1880–90
Marble, *pietre dure* and fruitwood, 96.8 × 174.6 × 115.6 cm (38 1/8 × 68 3/4 × 45 1/2 in)
1996.240 (MM90)

PROVENANCE: The Right Honorable the Lord Margadale of Islay; Christie's, sale, Fonthill House, Tisbury, Wiltshire, 1 November 1971, lot 30; Los Angeles County Museum of Art.

EXHIBITIONS: Los Angeles, 1975; Los Angeles, 1977.

DESCRIPTION: A rectangular tabletop, the central panel consisting of fragments of black and white antique marble of archaeological origin. The centre is edged with a wave pattern in yellow and old rose. The outer border is made of *broccatello* and bears a series of cartouches, with shields at each corner and arabesque patterns of black marble, *fior di pesco* (peach blossom), onyx, lapis lazuli, alabaster, and yellow antique marble, all edged by white marble. The outer rim of the tabletop is of *verde antico* marble.

COMMENTARY: The slab of Aquitanian marble (also called 'black and white antique' or, in French, *grand antique*) in the centre of the table comes from a cave in the Aubert region of the Pyrenees, nicknamed 'the cave of forgetfulness'. This was exploited until the end of the nineteenth century, but is now abandoned. The marble was highly prized in Roman times and can frequently be seen in buildings of the late Justinian period. By the eighteenth century, Aquitanian marble was already so scarce that each section cost 20 *zecchini*, as Ficorini records.[1] Close study of a number of tables that are stylistically similar to the Gilbert Collection piece suggest that the elaborate inlaid borders were merely a frame designed to show off the central panel to best advantage. The attention of the customers ordering and purchasing these tables was focused almost exclusively on the piece of antique marble in the middle, prized for its antiquity and size.

A tabletop closely related to the Gilbert Collection table in its large central panel and border design is a sixteenth-century Roman example, formerly in the collection of Cardinal Richelieu (1585–1642) and now at the Louvre.[2] The British Museum also owns an example of this genre.[3] Another superlative marble slab is on a table from the Farnese Palace, now at the Metropolitan Museum of Art. Formerly at Hamilton Palace, it was probably acquired by the Duke of Hamilton, who lived in Rome and Naples for some time and had a passion for collecting marbles and hardstones such as this and those in the Gilbert Collection clock cabinet (cat. no. 9).[4] Charlecote Park boasts the Borghese table, whose sixteenth-century top was purchased for Fonthill Abbey by William Beckford.[5]

The fruitwood base is an example of a late nineteenth-century French reinterpretation of a Louis XIV table.

NOTES

1 Ficorini, 1744, pp. 187–88. For information about Aquitanian marble see Gnoli 1971, pp. 193–98.
2 Tuena 1988, 54–69.
3 Rossi 1954, pl. LXIX.
4 Raggio 1960, p. 219.
5 Wainwright 1989, p. 218.

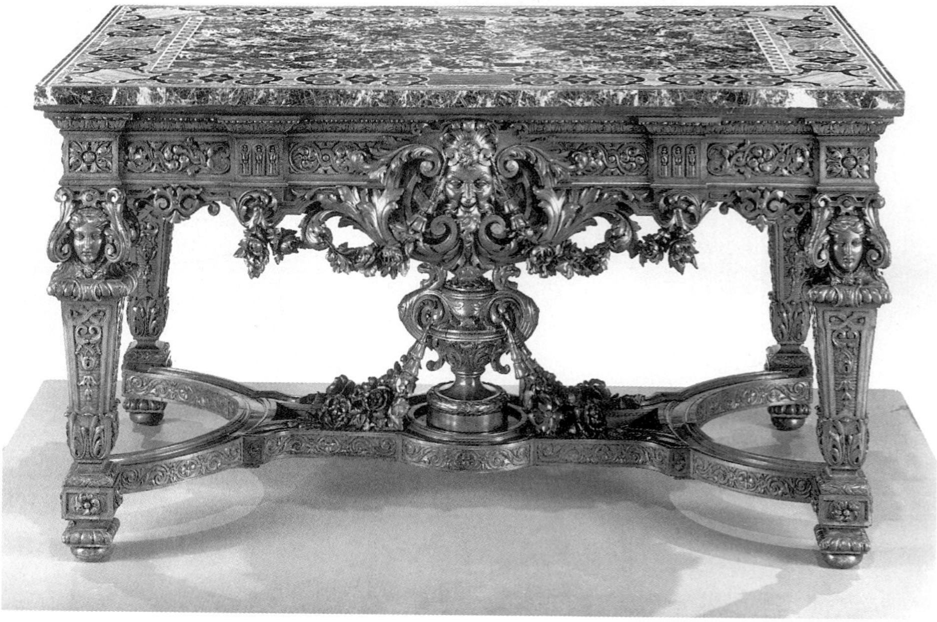

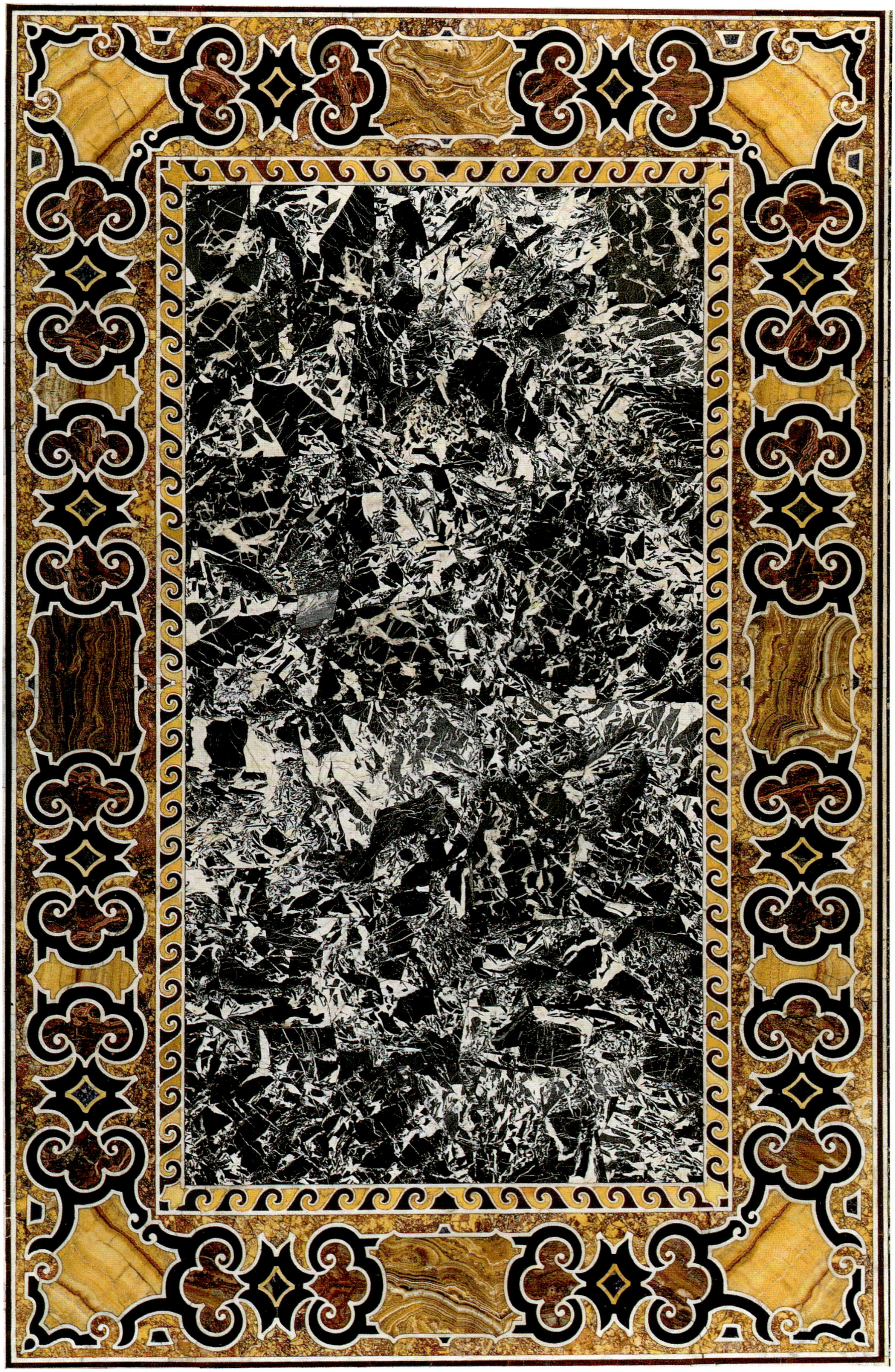

20. TABLETOP

Florence, mid-seventeenth century
Pietre dure, *pietre tenere*, marble, breccia, 58.1 × 117.8 cm (22⅞ × 46⅜ in)
1996.286 (MM141)

PROVENANCE: Unknown; purchased, 1959.

LITERATURE: Sherman 1971, no. 28; Hillier 1975, p. 271, fig. 6; González-Palacios 1977a, no. 6; González-Palacios and Röttgen 1982, no. 6.

EXHIBITIONS: Los Angeles / Atlanta / San Antonio / Richmond / Seattle, 1977–79.

DESCRIPTION: A tabletop of black marble inlaid with a central cartouche of *pietre tenere*, edged in yellow and red antique marble with a surround of *broccatello* and *verde antico* marble, materials that were widely used in the Grand Ducal workshops in the seventeenth century. Depicted inside the cartouche is a parrot perched on a cherry branch. The background contains four large branches of fruit and flowers: pear, jasmine, orange, and berries, with foliage in *verde d'Arno*. Above and below the edges of the cartouche are single flowers: anemone, hyacinth and narcissus.[1]

COMMENTARY: *Pietre dure* compositions illustrating various types of floral foliage derive from the Florentine tradition started by Jacopo Ligozzi (1547–1632). As early as 1577, he was creating drawings admired by Francesco I (1541–87), and by the end of his career he was court painter and superintendent of galleries for Ferdinand II (1610–70). His paintings were admired for their scientific accuracy, which appealed to the late Renaissance fascination with the natural world. A tabletop by Ligozzi at the Museo degli Argenti with flowering branches and a central parrot is typical of this genre.[2] Three additional tables with compositions are at the Hermitage, St. Petersburg.[3] A later tabletop made about the same time as

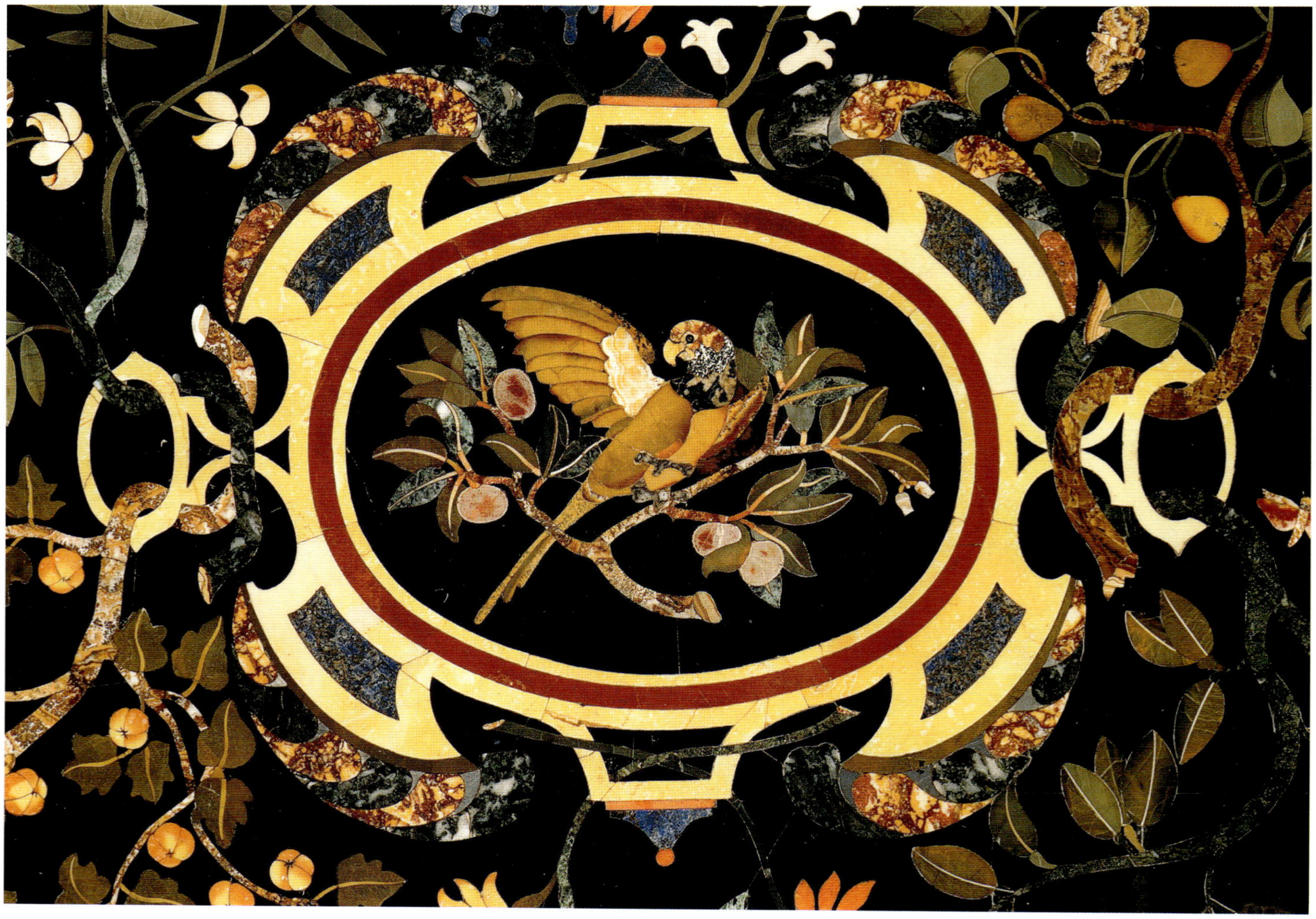

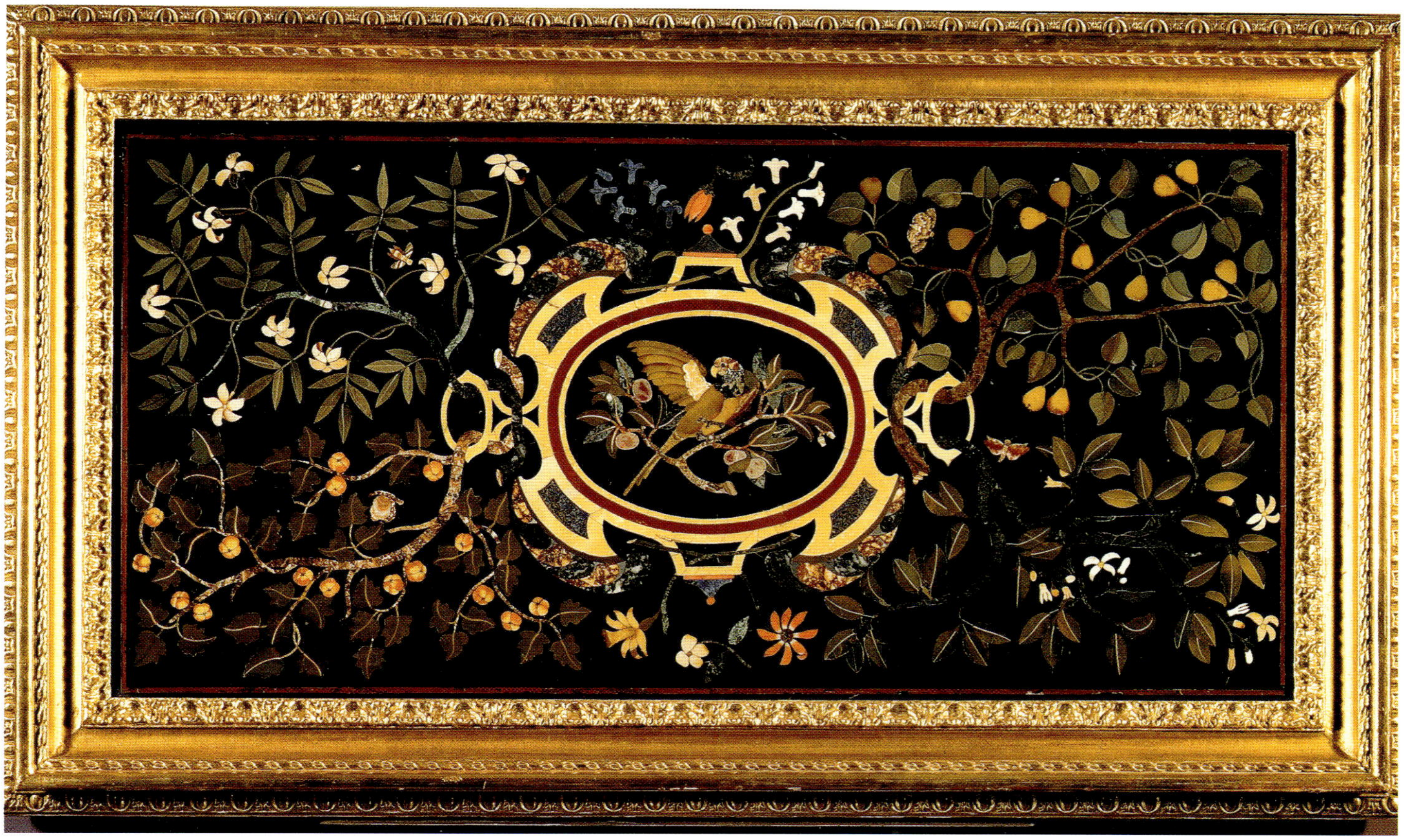

the Gilbert Collection table had the same motifs with the added coats-of-arms of Robert Paston (1631–83), first Earl of Yarmouth.[4] The Gilbert Collection table has been linked to the front of an altar in the church of Santo Stefano in Venice; the altar is almost certainly attributable to the Corbarelli workshop.[5] The inscription in capital letters beneath the altar (GIOVANNI FERRO P. MDCLVII), probably refers to the person who commissioned the work, rather than to the mosaicist.

NOTES

1 Thanks to Robert Gustafson of the Los Angeles Museum of Natural History for his help in identifying these species.
2 Giusti 1989, fig. 8.
3 Efimova 1968, nos. 9, 10, 12.
4 Christie's, London, 9 March, 1992, lot 119.
5 González-Palacios 1977a, no. 6, and González-Palacios and Röttgen 1982, no 6.

21. TABLE

Pietre dure: Possibly France, second half seventeenth century
Top: South Germany or Austria, early eighteenth century; base: European, probably nineteenth century
Pietre dure, mother-of-pearl, tortoiseshell, brass, gilt brass, wood, 80.3 × 73.7 × 50 cm (31⅝ × 29 × 20 in)
1996.605 (MM138)

PROVENANCE: Edmond de Rothschild; Alfred de Rothschild; Miss Davidson; Frank Partridge Ltd, London, 1969.

LITERATURE: Davis 1884, vol. 2, no. 111; González-Palacios 1977a, no. 14; González-Palacios and Röttgen 1982, no. 14.

EXHIBITION: Los Angeles, 1977.

DESCRIPTION: The table is described in Charles Davis' 1884 inventory of Alfred de Rothschild's collection:

> A Louis XIV Boule [sic] table. This table is inlaid with coloured metals and mother-of-pearl representing terminal figures, masks, and birds. On the top is an oval plaque of engraved mother-of-pearl and metal, with a bacchanalian group in the centre. The plaque in coloured marble on the front of the table represents a bird and some flowers ... the back of the table is similarly ornamented. The ends are decorated with figures supporting crowns. The legs are square, tapering and fluted, and are joined by cross rails which support a square mosaic plaque.[1]

COMMENTARY: A combination of styles and types of inlay is common in German mosaic tables of the first half of the seventeenth century. From Augsburg, for example, came the table that was originally the stand for a lost

Pomeranian cabinet, inlaid with a variety of woods, with arabesque patterns in ivory intarsia, painted panels of stone, and *pietre dure* mosaics (1610–16, Kunstgewerbemuseum, Berlin).[2] Also from Augsburg is a table inlaid in ivory, gold, silver, bronze and *pietre dure* mosaic panels, made by Georg Hertel and Lucas Kilian in 1626 (Schatzkammer der Residenz, Munich).[3] French taste, as represented by the elegant intarsia work in the style of André-Charles Boulle (1624–1732), quickly found a place within the tradition of hardstone decoration.

At the end of the seventeenth century, the leading German centres for the production of Boulle-style furniture were Kunwelhau, where H. D. Sommer, a pupil of the French master craftsman, ran a furniture workshop from 1666 to 1684, and Augsburg, where the cabinetmaker Johann Georg Esser (1652–1727) specialised in this kind of inlay work. A table in the Rezidenzmuseum, Munich, signed by Esser and dated 1680, is related to the Gilbert Collection table.[4] The Munich tabletop is rectangular in shape and has a series of mosaic panels on a black marble background. The central and largest oval panel bears an image of Diana, the medallions around it depicting flowers and birds. The outer borders have metallic intarsia work, with two vases of flowers at either side and a pair of peacocks facing each other. The outside edge is decorated with a frieze of scrollwork, grotesque masks, mother-of-pearl putti, and ducks appearing through garlands of acanthus leaves. The same ornamental language, although rather simplified, is on the frieze around the Gilbert Collection tabletop. Mother-of-pearl masks and ducks peep out from between the bands of brass foliage, suggesting a link with the activities of Esser. The shape of the Gilbert Collection tabletop belongs to the early eighteenth century, although it is later than the one from Munich.

The ornamentation of the hardstone panels on the Gilbert Collection table bears no connection with seventeenth-century Florentine naturalistic designs, in which birds are usually depicted on a branch. The birds on the Gilbert Collection table are in a landscape on the ground, pecking at something in a basket. The Esser table in Munich has the same type of landscape, as do one or two unmounted panels in the Liechtenstein collection that have been tentatively linked to the Prague workshops of the early seventeenth century.[5] This taste spread to the Gobelins workshop in France. Panels similar to the ones on the Gilbert Collection table can be found on two French tabletops of 1684–1700 in the Palais de Compiegne.[6]

NOTES

1 Davis 1884, no. 111.
2 Kunstgewerbemuseum 1989, no. 137.
3 Kreisel 1968, p. 169, pl. 6.
4 Kreisel 1968, pp. 263, 279, pls. 577–78, 619.
5 Liechtenstein 1985, pp. 54–55, no. 31–33.
6 González-Palacios 1993, vol. 2, figs. 14–15.

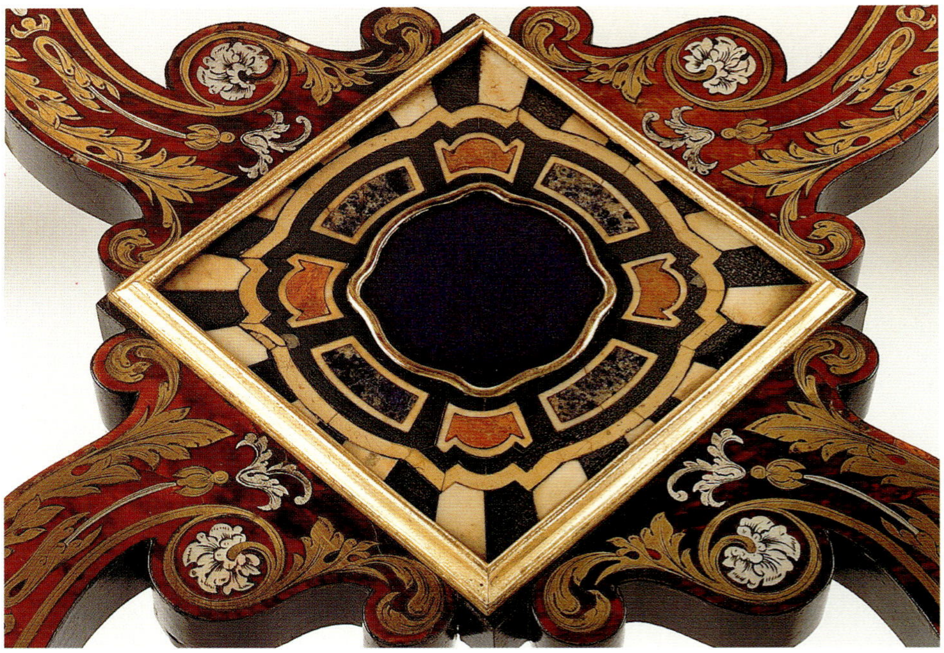

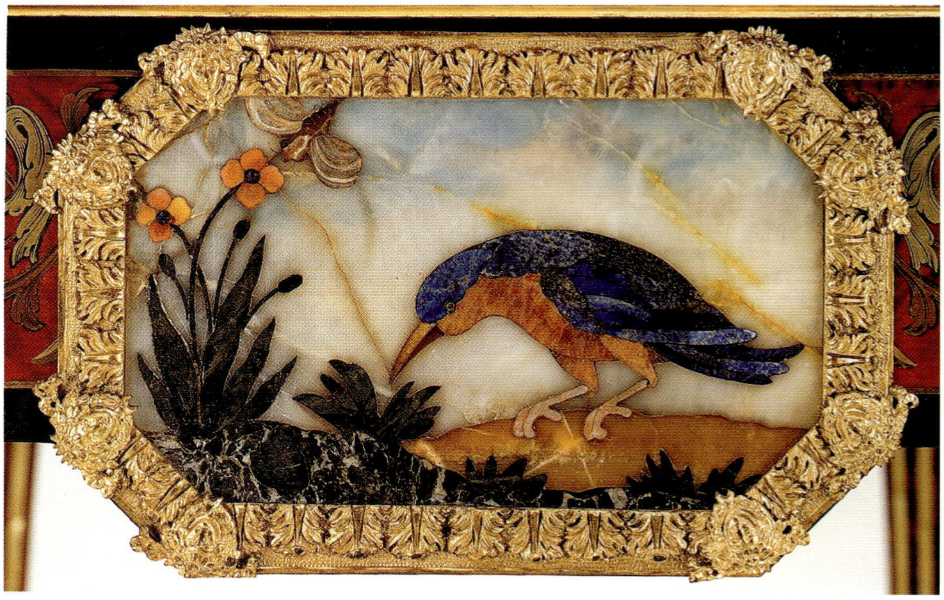

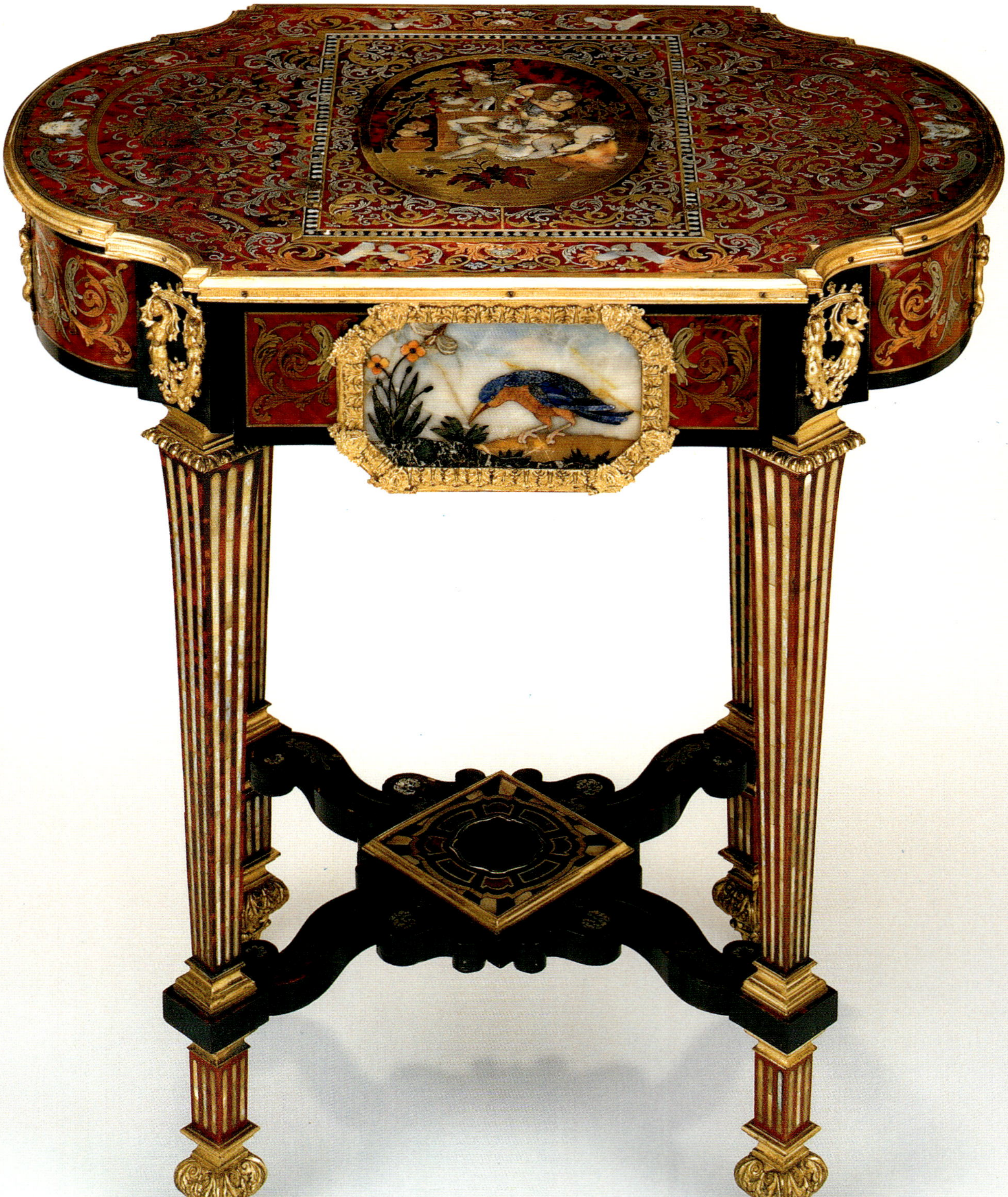

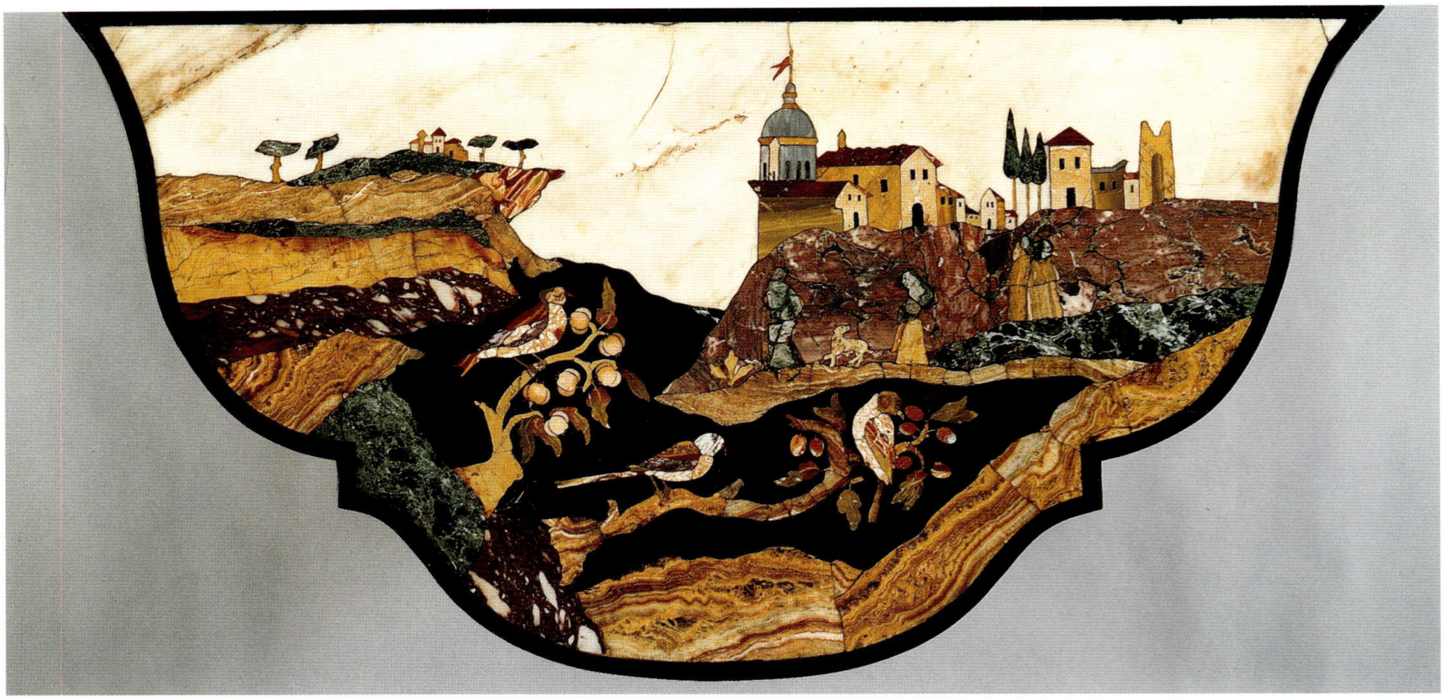

22. CONSOLE TABLE WITH LANDSCAPES

Italy, probably Naples, c. 1750
Marble, gilt wood, 90.2 × 118.7 × 53.3 cm (35½ × 46¾ × 21 in)
1996.252 (MM103)

PROVENANCE: Christian Dior; A. F. Drysdale, London, 1972.

EXHIBITION: Los Angeles, 1991.

DESCRIPTION: A console table inlaid with a *pietre tenere* mosaic depicting a simplified landscape. The broad background of different stones creates patches of contrasting colour.

COMMENTARY: On both technical and artistic grounds, this work can be compared with a table inlaid in polychrome marble in the Palazzo Reale in Caserta. [1] These pieces are considered typical products of the Neapolitan marble workshops in the second half of the eighteenth century. A similar landscape can also be seen on the top of a console table in the castle at Potsdam, dating from c. 1765.[2]

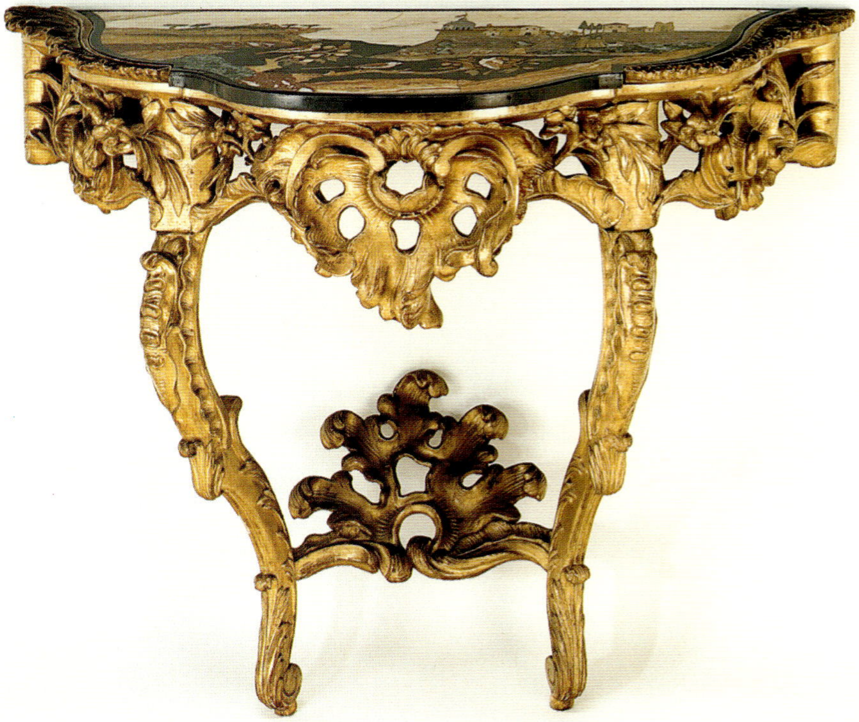

NOTES
1 *The Golden Age of Naples* 1981, p. 360, no. 117.
2 Nicht 1980, p. 29, no. 40.

23. TABLE

Panels: Florence, c. 1775–85; marble border: probably Rome, c. 1775–85; base: Italy, second quarter nineteenth century
Pietre dure, *pietre tenere*, marble, gilt wood, 86.4 × 119.1 × 65.4 cm (34 × 46⅞ × 25¾ in)
1996.317 (MM213)

PROVENANCE: Edmond de Rothschild; Alfred de Rothschild; Christie's, London, sale, 3 July 1975, lot 63; Frank Partridge Ltd., London, 1975; Los Angeles County Museum of Art.

LITERATURE: Davis 1884, vol. 2, no. 236; González-Palacios 1977a, no. 16; González-Palacios and Röttgen 1982, no. 16; González-Palacios 1993, vol. 1, p. 199.

EXHIBITIONS: London, 1975; Los Angeles / Atlanta / San Antonio / Richmond / Seattle, 1977–79.

DESCRIPTION: A table consisting of a green antique marble top with a Greek key border of yellow and red marble on a black background. Fourteen mosaic panels in *pietre dure* and *pietre tenere* on a black background are decorated with grotesque figures.

COMMENTARY: This table and its pair (Hanisee Gabriel 2000, cat. no. 3) stood in the glass-domed saloon of Halton House, Buckinghamshire. In the preface to his catalogue of 1884, Alfred de Rothschild remarked, 'The principal objects, and those which, needless to say, I most prize, I inherited from my dearly beloved father, and, in addition to the great pleasure which they afford me, they

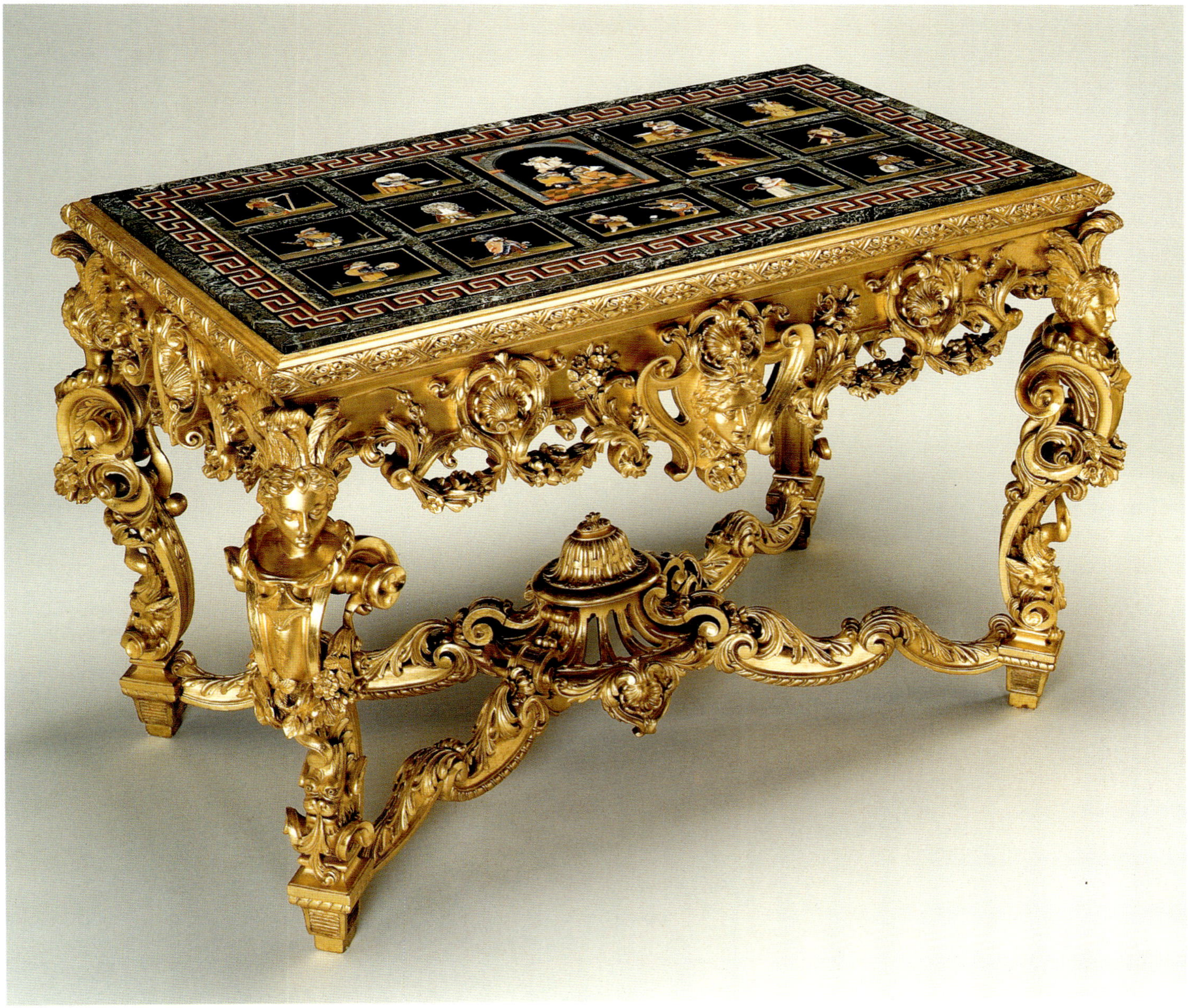

constantly remind me of his most perfect judgements and good taste.'[1] The depiction of dwarfs in hardstone are taken from designs by Baccio di Bianco (1604–54) and Jacques Callot (1592/3–1635).[2] Similar panels are found on furniture at Charlecote Park, Marlborough House and Versailles.[3]

The panels of plaques representing dwarfs were originally said by González-Palacios to have the 'stylistic characteristics of works made in the Opificio during the second half of the eighteenth century'. He goes on to compare their sizes and technique to other panels made in that period.[4] More recently, he has attributed them to the first half of the seventeenth century.[5] As Giusti has pointed out, most of the seventeenth-century plaques with this subject matter are set in eighteenth- and nineteenth-century furniture.[6] However, eight plaques of this type can be found on a table dated 1640 at Charlecote Park and previously in the collection of William Beckford at Fonthill Abbey.[7] A cabinet (unpublished) at Marlborough House also has such panels, as does a tabletop at Versailles.[8]

The style and arrangement of the mosaic panels suggest that the series was designed to decorate the front of a cabinet. The subject matter of dwarfs is after drawings by Baccio del Bianco (1604–54) and from etchings by Jacques Callot (1592/3–1635). Del Bianco worked extensively for the Medicis, designing all manner of objects in diverse media, and organising spectacles. Callot's book, *Varie Figure Gobbi*, published in 1616, shows a sixteenth-century travelling troupe of performing dwarfs who were at the court of Cosimo II (r. 1609–1621) at the same time as Callot.

The old woman with a cauldron, the drinker and the lady with the fan are direct transcriptions from a drawing by del Bianco (fig. 8), now in the Uffizi.[9] The mandolin player in the lower central panel comes from a series of engravings of hunchbacks by Callot, printed in 1616 (fig. 9). González-Palacios has identified sources for four of the panels on the Gilbert Collection table. The bottom central panel with the lute and bagpipe players is a reverse image from Callot's series of hunchbacks. The left centre, top right and bottom right are after drawings of gluttons by Bianco, now in the Gabinetto dei Disegni in Florence.[10]

NOTES

1 Davis, 1884, introduction, unpaginated.
2 González-Palacios and Röttgen, 1982, no. 16.
3 Giusti, 1992, p. 103; Wainright, 1985, pp. 507–8.
4 González-Palacios and Röttgen 1982, no. 16.
5 González-Palacios 1993, vol. 1, pp. 409–12.
6 Giusti 1992, figs. 26, 205, pp. 201–3.
7 Wainright 1985, pp. 507–8.
8 Giusti 1992, p. 103; González-Palacios and Röttgen, 1982, no. 16.
9 G.D.S.U., no. 3295F)
10 González-Palacios and Röttgen 1982, no. 16.

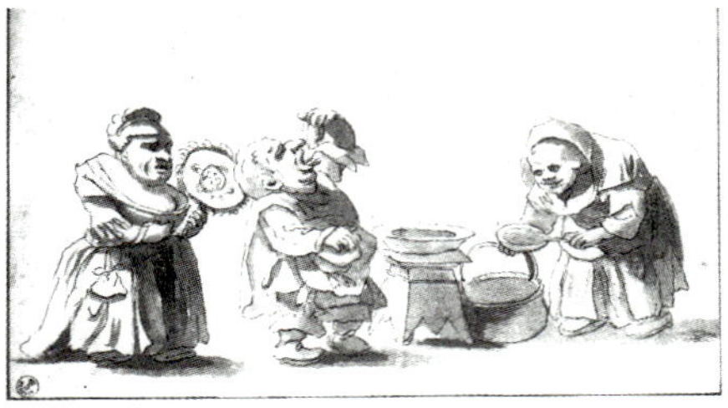

FIG. 8 Baccio del Bianco dwarfs.

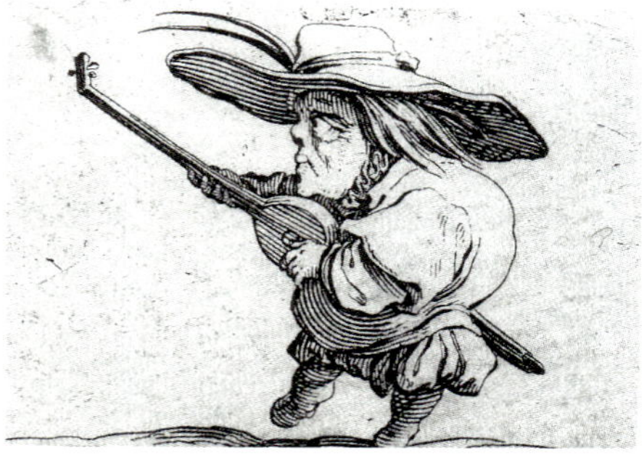

FIG. 9 Jacques Callot, dwarf from *Varie Figure Gobbi*.

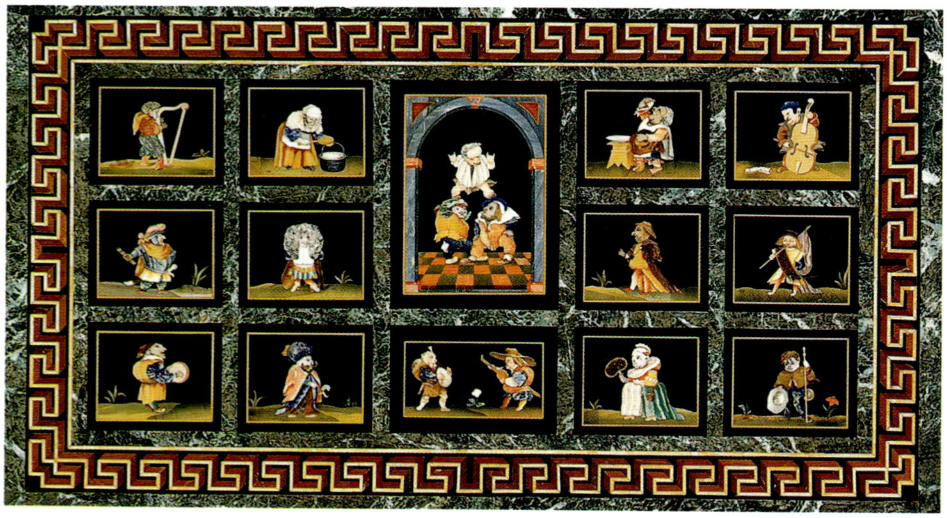

Detail of cat. no. 23

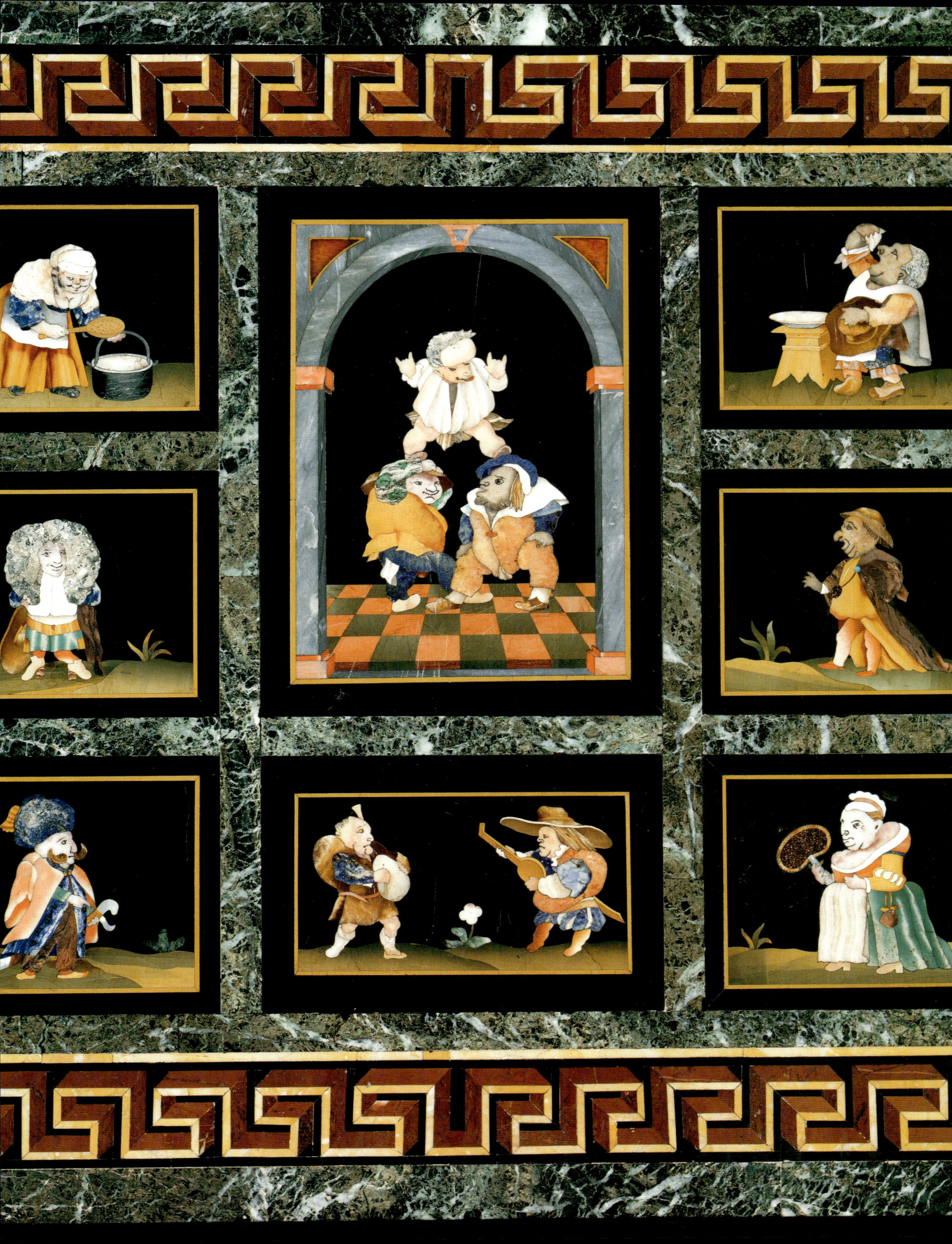

24. GUERDION TABLE

Rome, attributed to Francesco Sibilio, (fl. first half nineteenth century)
Green and white marble, green and red porphyry, gilt bronze, mahogany, 83.8 × 69.8 cm (33 × 27½ in)
1996.608 (MM152)

PROVENANCE: Charles J. Winston, New York, 1974; Los Angeles County Museum of Art.

DESCRIPTION: A circular marble table-top with design of concentric bands inlaid with geometrical patterns, with a complex star motif in the centre. The green and white marble and green and red porphyry presumably came from excavations and is inlaid using red, blue and yellow vitreous grout. The base has three gilt-bronze legs in the shape of swans, with lion's-paw feet resting on a shaped triangular mahogany and gilt-bronze plinth.

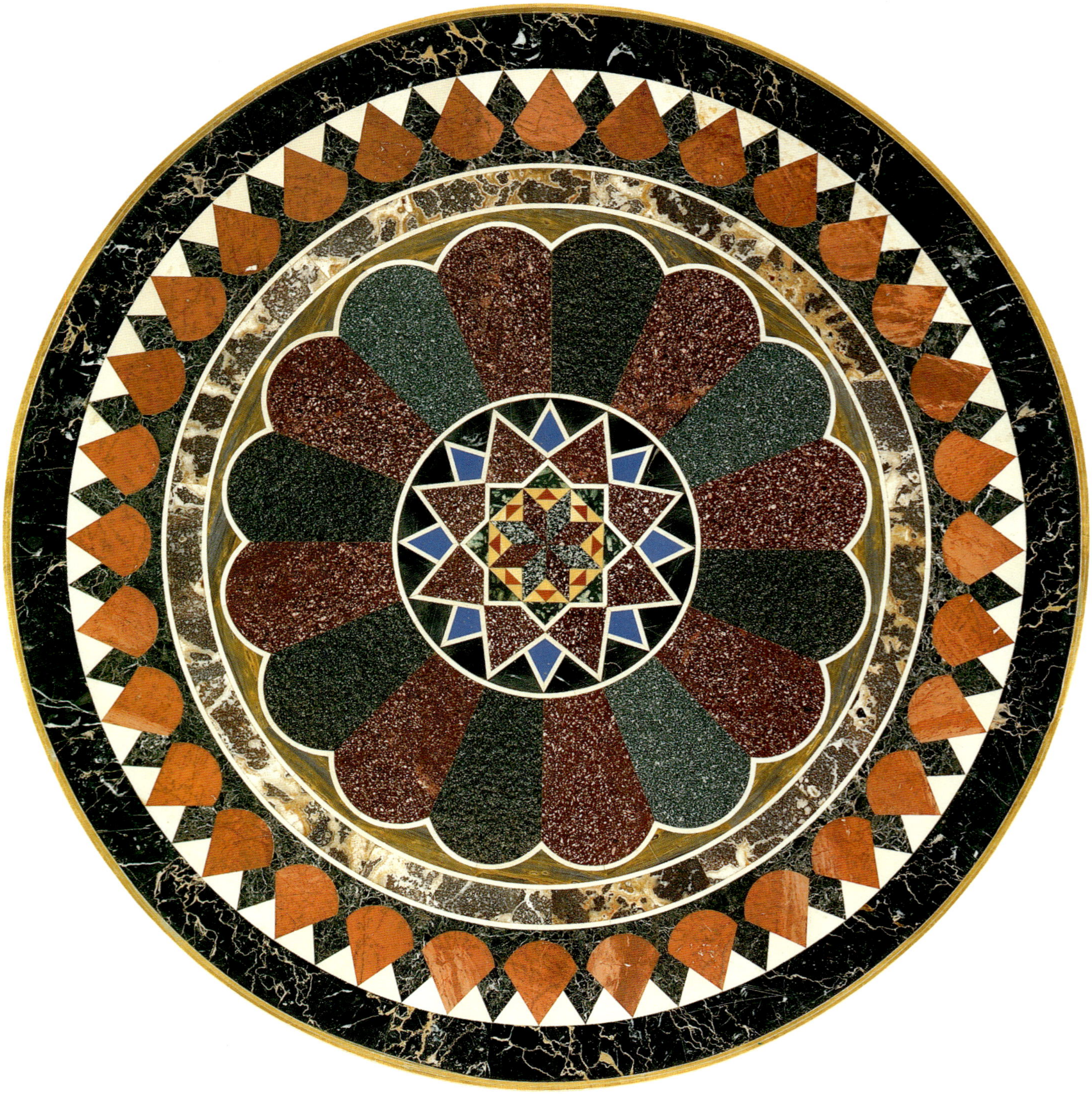

COMMENTARY: The stone on this table was inlaid according to the method and design of the stone craftsman Francesco Sibilio, who was active in Rome during the first half of the nineteenth century. Sibilio's great passion for the ancient world, combined with his extraordinary imagination, encouraged him to make mosaics of hitherto untried combinations of materials. The designs he invented are a surprising mixture of classical and medieval themes.

González-Palacios was responsible for the discovery of two small, circular panels, signed and dated 1823 and 1824 by Sibilio.[1] The most striking feature of these two tabletops is the classical/medieval effect achieved by the use of small, intersecting geometric shapes, sometimes combined with successions of triangles in a radial scheme; bands of concentric borders with lance-shaped motifs, and scalloped friezes encircling a rosette or mask. The most revolutionary aspect of Sibilio's work is the combination of different materials: porphyry and serpentine, marbles and coloured-glass paste, which is fragile and difficult to combine with stones of different degrees of hardness in mosaic. This table should be added to the meagre collection of works hitherto attributed to Sibilio (based on similarities in design and the combination of stones and vitreous paste). Two other small round tables with marble and breccia mosaic tops and geometric designs, similar to this work, were sold at auction.[2]

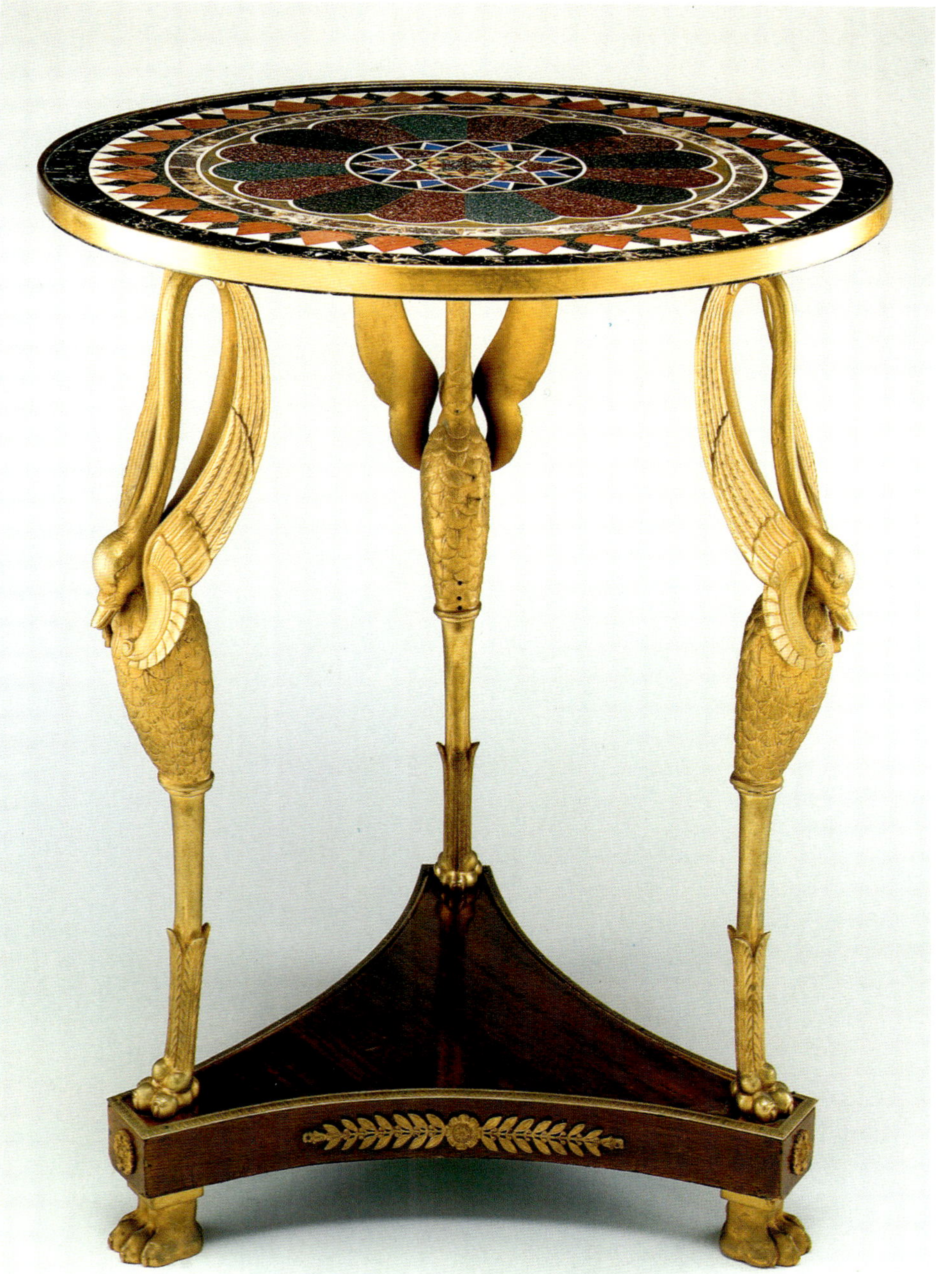

NOTES

1 González-Palacios 1991a, pp. 187, 209.

2 Christie's, London, 8 June 1989, lot 145; 23 November 1989, lot 203.

25. TABLE

Top: Rome, mid-nineteenth century; base: possibly England, first half nineteenth century
Marble, gilt wood, 87.6 × 81.3 cm (34½ × 32 in)
1996.303 (MM179)

PROVENANCE: Mallett, London, 1974.

EXHIBITION: Los Angeles, 1991.

DESCRIPTION: A table with a top consisting of a circular block of breccia. The central black marble medallion is inlaid with the Paxton coat-of-arms and motto, PRO FIDE REGE ET LEGE. The outside border has alternate panels of grey breccia and panels of black marble inlaid with shell motifs in the eighteenth-century style. The stand consists of three one-legged lions of carved, gilded wood.

COMMENTARY: This unusual table shares similarities with one sold at Sotheby's, London, on 7 November 1986. The design of the stand is copied from classical marble supports and popular at the end of the eighteenth and first half of the nineteenth centuries.

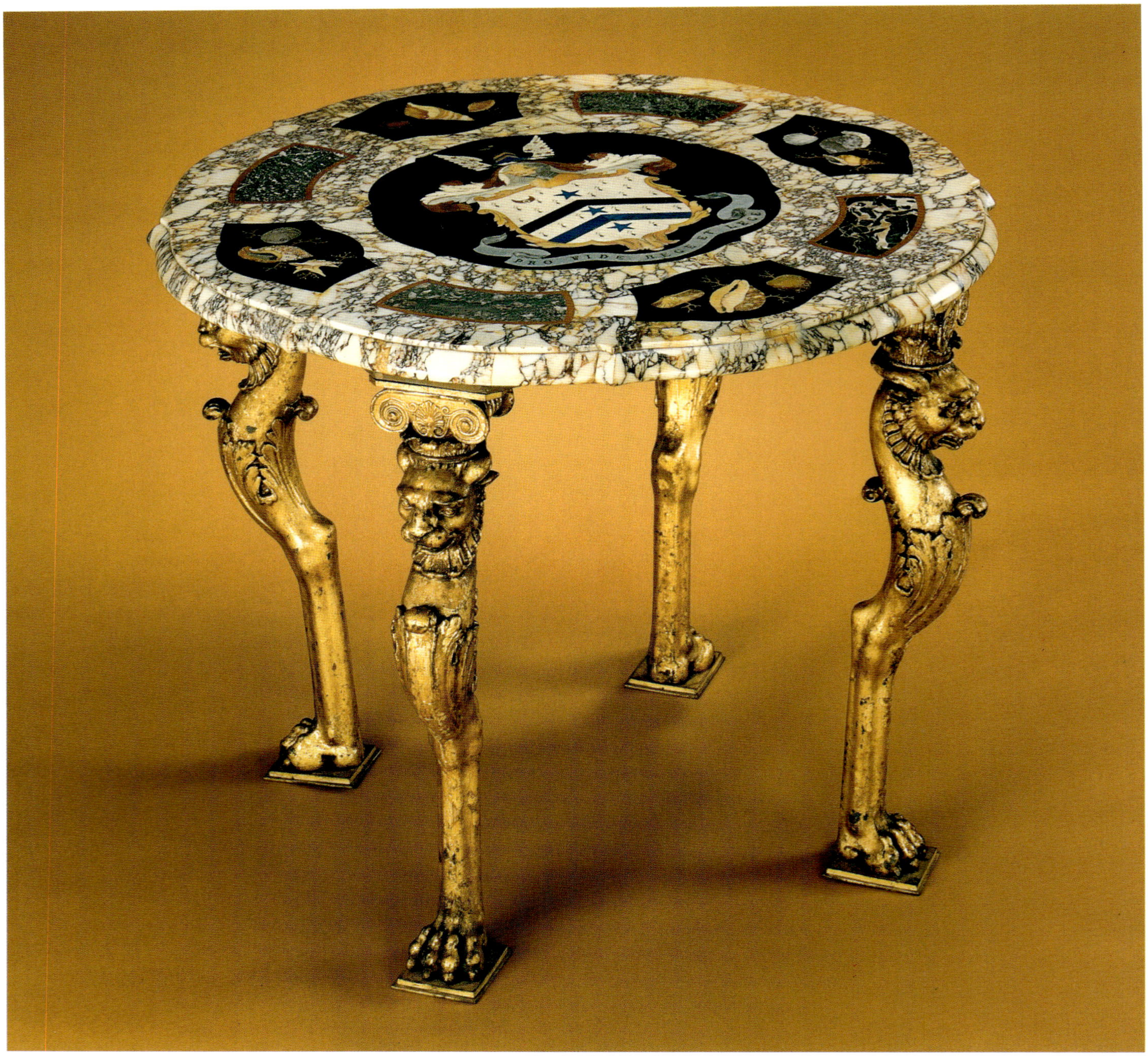

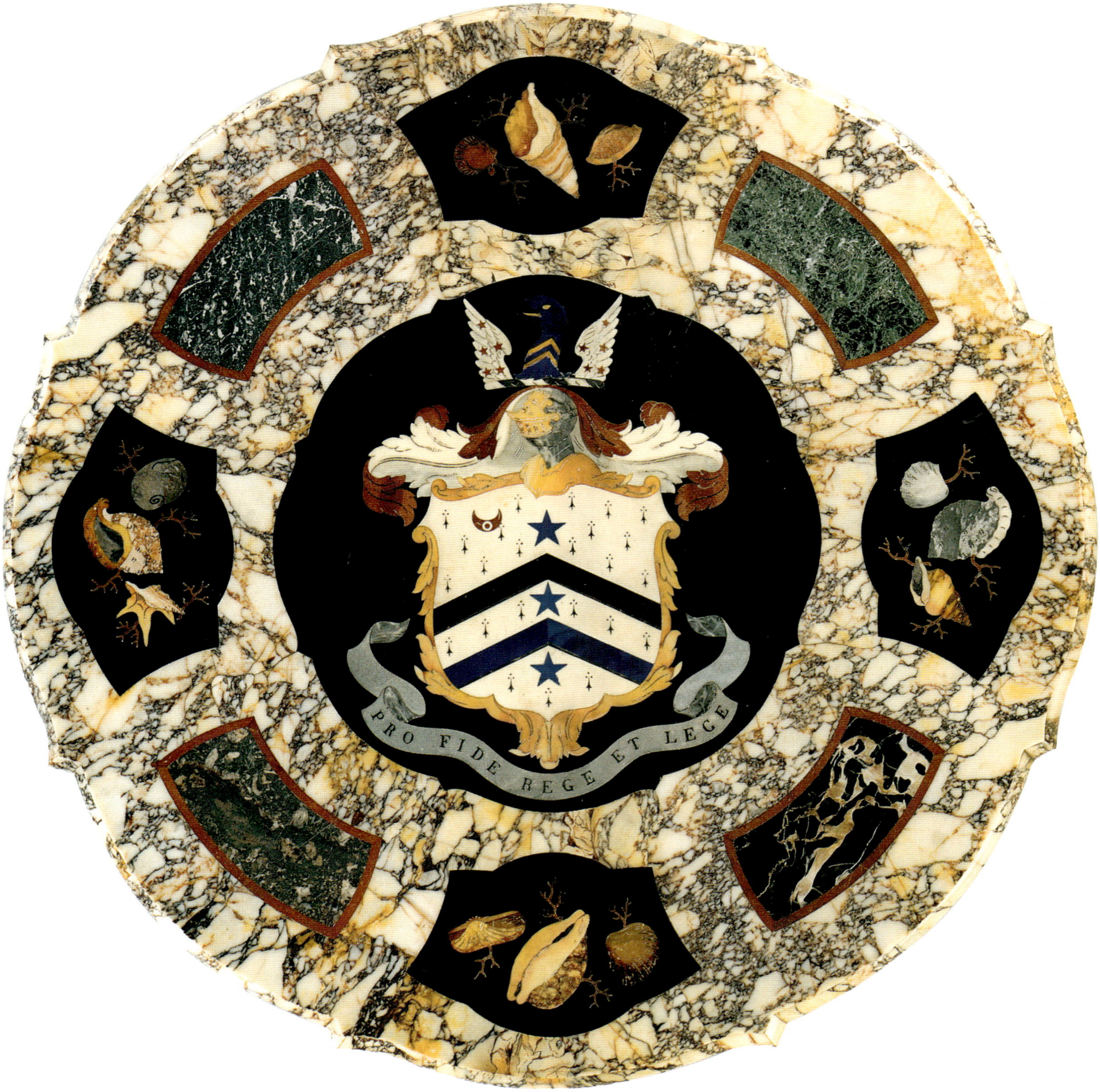
PRO FIDE REGE ET LEGE

26. TABLE

Top: Rome, second half nineteenth century; base: possibly England, mid-nineteenth century
Marble, coloured breccia, walnut, 74.3 × 70.5 cm (29¼ × 27¾ in)
1996.613 (MM195)

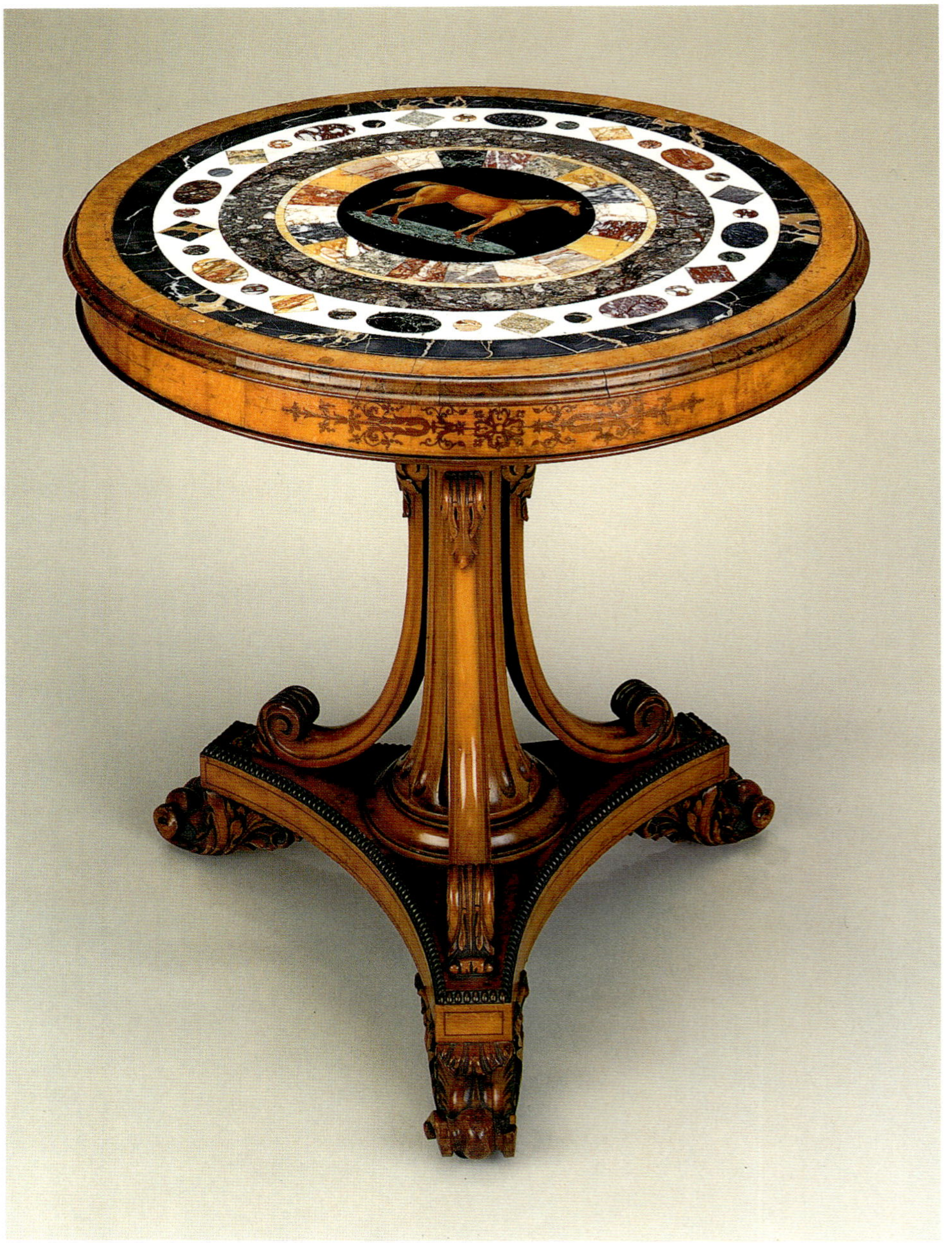

PROVENANCE: Sotheby's, Belgravia, 22 January 1975, lot 126.

DESCRIPTION: A circular tabletop inlaid with concentric bands of coloured marble. The white bands contain a series of panels in different kinds of breccia. On the central, black marble medallion is depicted a brown horse carved from a single piece of jasper, standing in right profile; the details of the body are sculpted and emphasised with black ink. The hardstone tabletop is framed in a wooden surround and supported on a carved-wood pedestal base.

COMMENTARY: This table exemplifies Roman mosaic work of the mid-nineteenth century, in which geometric tabletops bearing a variety of ancient marble specimens were often combined with a central, figurative motif. A tabletop similar to this one, but with a 'Greek' profile in the central medallion, is signed and dated *Soldaini 1868* (Private collection, Florence). The Gilbert Collection mosaic is framed in a wooden surround and supported on a carved wooden base in the English taste. The horse motif also recalls English rather than Roman style and may indicate that the piece was commissioned by an English visitor to Rome. A Sicilian or Maltese *pietre dure* top, inlaid with a similar central gesso composition of a horse on a black ground, was sold from the collection of the Hazelrigg Family at Noseley Hall, Leicestershire.[1]

NOTE

1 Sotheby's, London, 28–29 September 1998, lot 154.

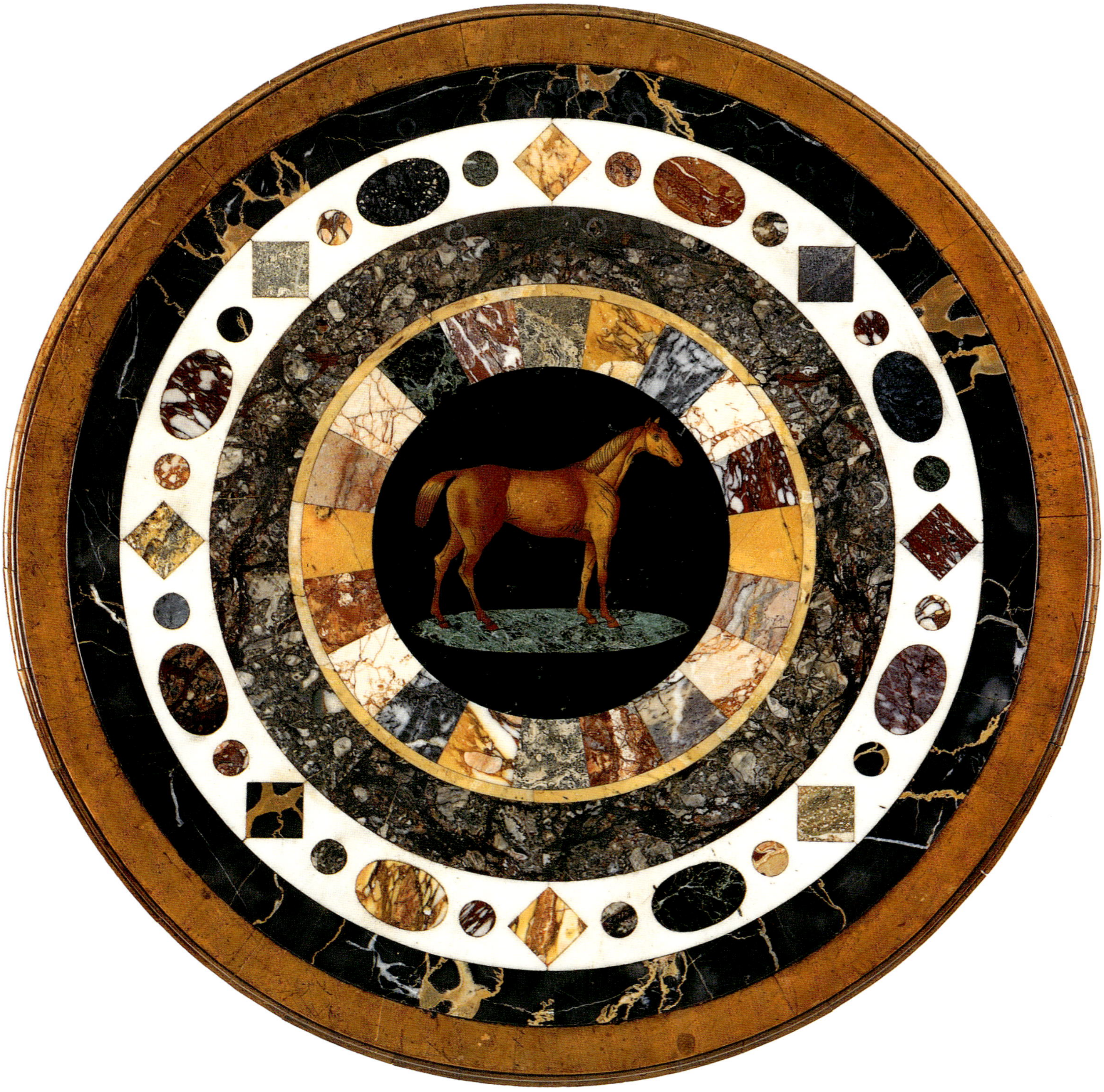

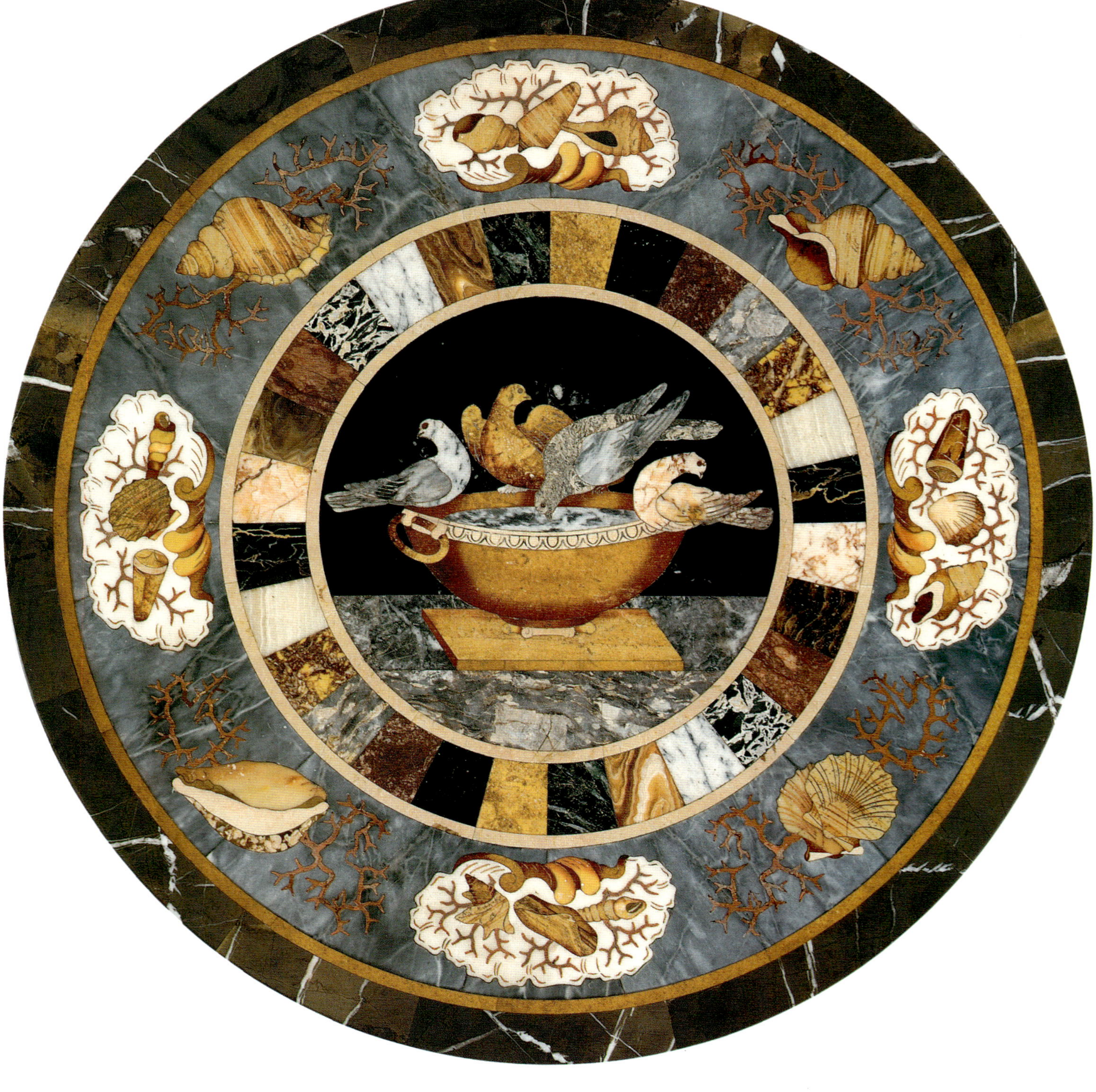

27. TABLE

Rome: second half nineteenth century
Marble, gilt wood, 87.6 × 81.3 cm (34½ × 32 in)
1996.195 (MM19)

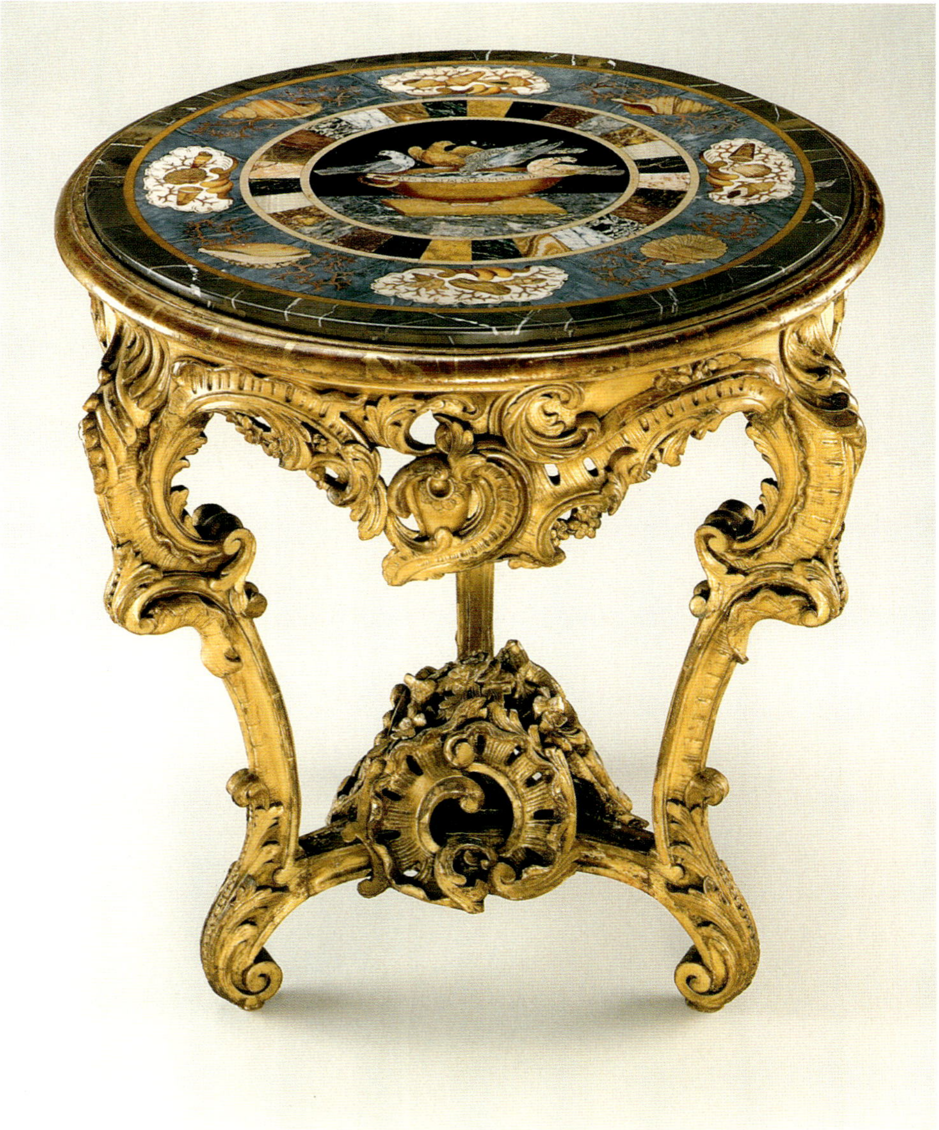

PROVENANCE: Nestle, Inc, New York, 1969.

LITERATURE: Sherman 1971, no. 18; Avery and Emperatori 1975, no. 32.

EXHIBITIONS: Los Angeles, 1975; London, 1975; Los Angeles, 1977.

DESCRIPTION: A tabletop composition consisting of concentric bands of marble specimens. The outer border is of grey marble, with a series of inlaid shell designs of white marble and onyx and branches of coral made of a paste similar to *scagliola*. The middle band consists of coloured panels of various kinds of marble, including *broccatello*, porphyry, onyx, antique black marble, and Aquitanian black and white marble. The central medallion is inlaid with a motif derived from antiquity: the Capitoline Doves.

COMMENTARY: The imagery on this tabletop is taken from a celebrated Roman mosaic (Capitoline Museum, Rome) discovered in 1737 during the excavation by Cardinal Giuseppe Alessandro Furietti (1685–1764) of the Emperor Hadrian's villa near Rome. Furietti considered the mosaic to be the masterpiece of Sosus mentioned by Pliny the Elder, but other scholars regard it as a copy of the original made for Hadrian.[1] The subject of doves was widely used in Rome as a prototype for micromosaics but was less frequently employed for marble *commesso* work.

NOTE
1 Plinio 1988, book 26; Furietti 1752; Bocconi 1930, p. 101, no. 13a.

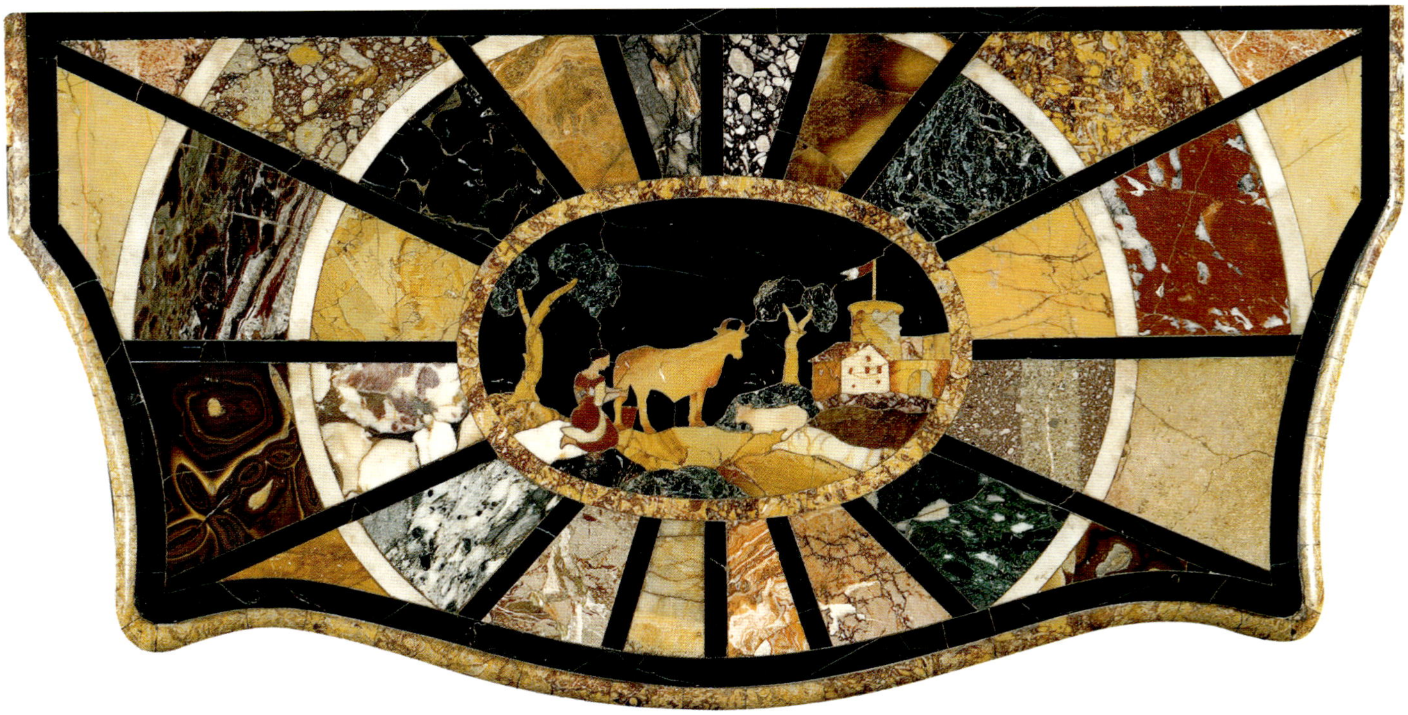

28. CONSOLE TABLETOP

Possibly Rome, second half nineteenth century
Marble, 83.8 × 58.4 cm (33 × 23 in)
1996.264 (MM113)

PROVENANCE: Alberto di Castro, Rome, 1972.

LITERATURE: Avery and Emperatori 1975, no. 40.

EXHIBITION: London 1975

DESCRIPTION: A tabletop with central medallion inlaid with a scene of a woman milking a cow in a landscape near a country village. It is surrounded by a sunburst divided with strips of black marble that intersect with the white marble bands encircling the medallion. The geometric network thus created has inlaid pieces of coloured breccia and marble, interspersed with the black and white.

COMMENTARY: This tabletop appears to have been designed as a specimen. A sunburst design would fit better into a circle than a rectangle, and it is possible that it was cut from a circular tabletop.

The types of stone used, and the specimen format, are characteristic of the output of a Rome workshop in the latter half of the nineteenth century. A rectangular table with a similar sunburst and circular design is listed among the effects of the Palazzo Visconti di Brighano, Gere d'Adda (Algranti-Semenzato; sale, 21–23 May 1998).

29. TABLE

Top: Florence, late nineteenth century; base: Italy, second half nineteenth century
Pietre dure, black marble, gilt bronze, wood, 73 × 60 cm (28¾ × 23⅝ in)
1996.201 (MM29)

PROVENANCE: Maurice Sigal, New York, 1969.

EXHIBITION: Los Angeles, 1977.

DESCRIPTION: A round tabletop of black Belgian marble inlaid with a still life in *pietre dure* of a vase of flowers, some cherries, a bunch of grapes with leaves, a pomegranate and a pumpkin.

The late nineteenth-century gilt-bronze stand is a tripod in the French style of c. 1770.

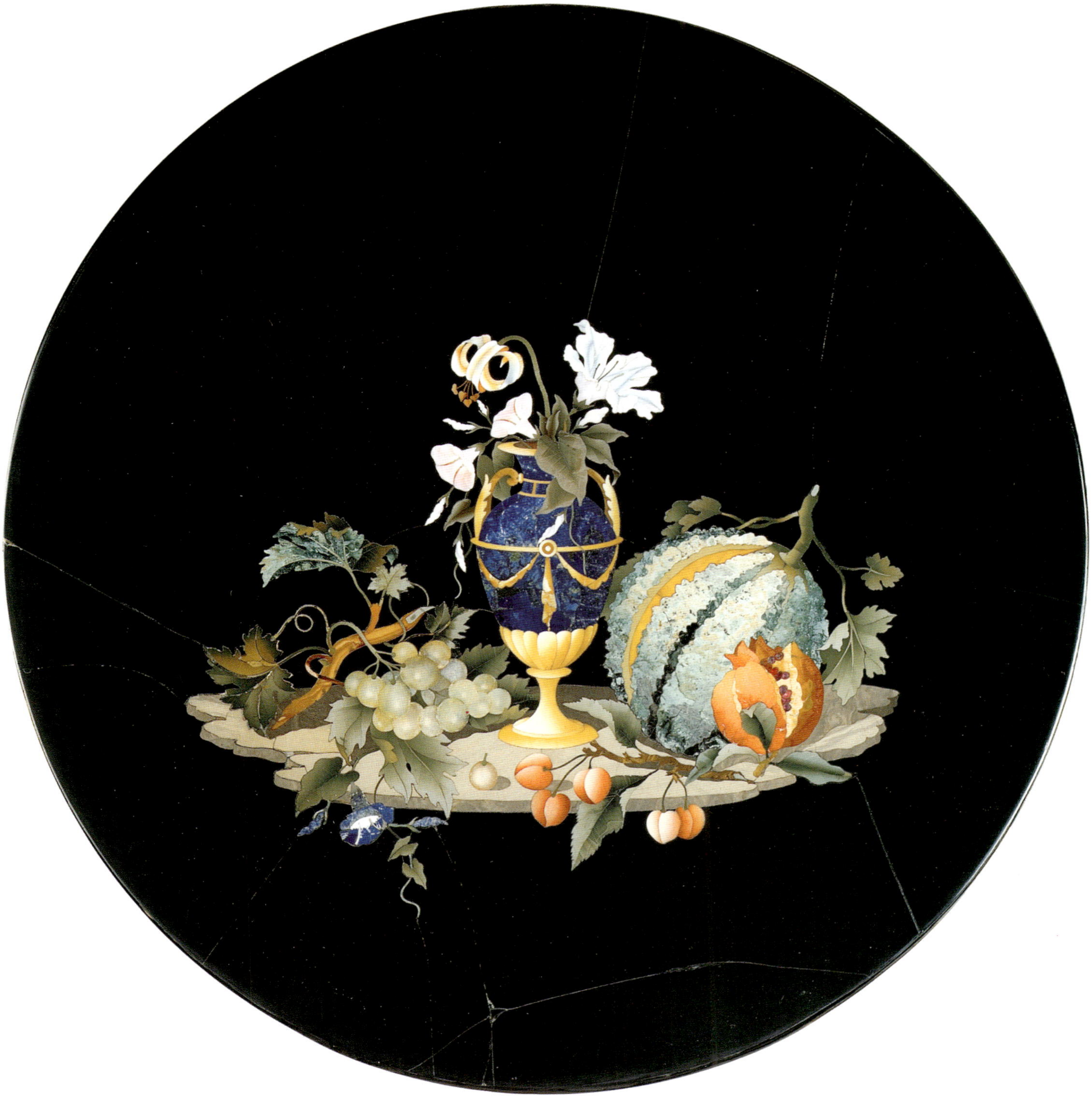

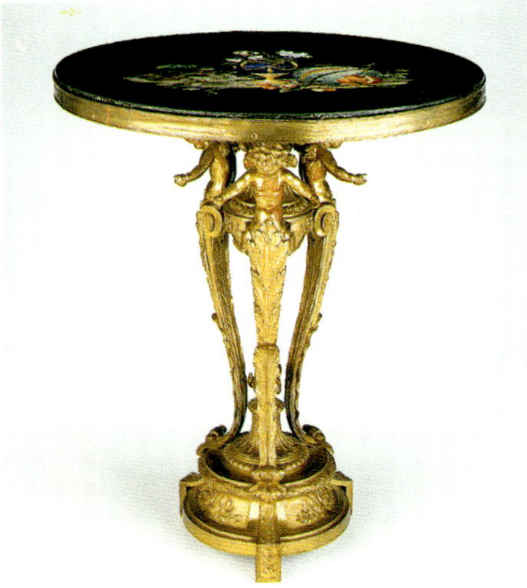

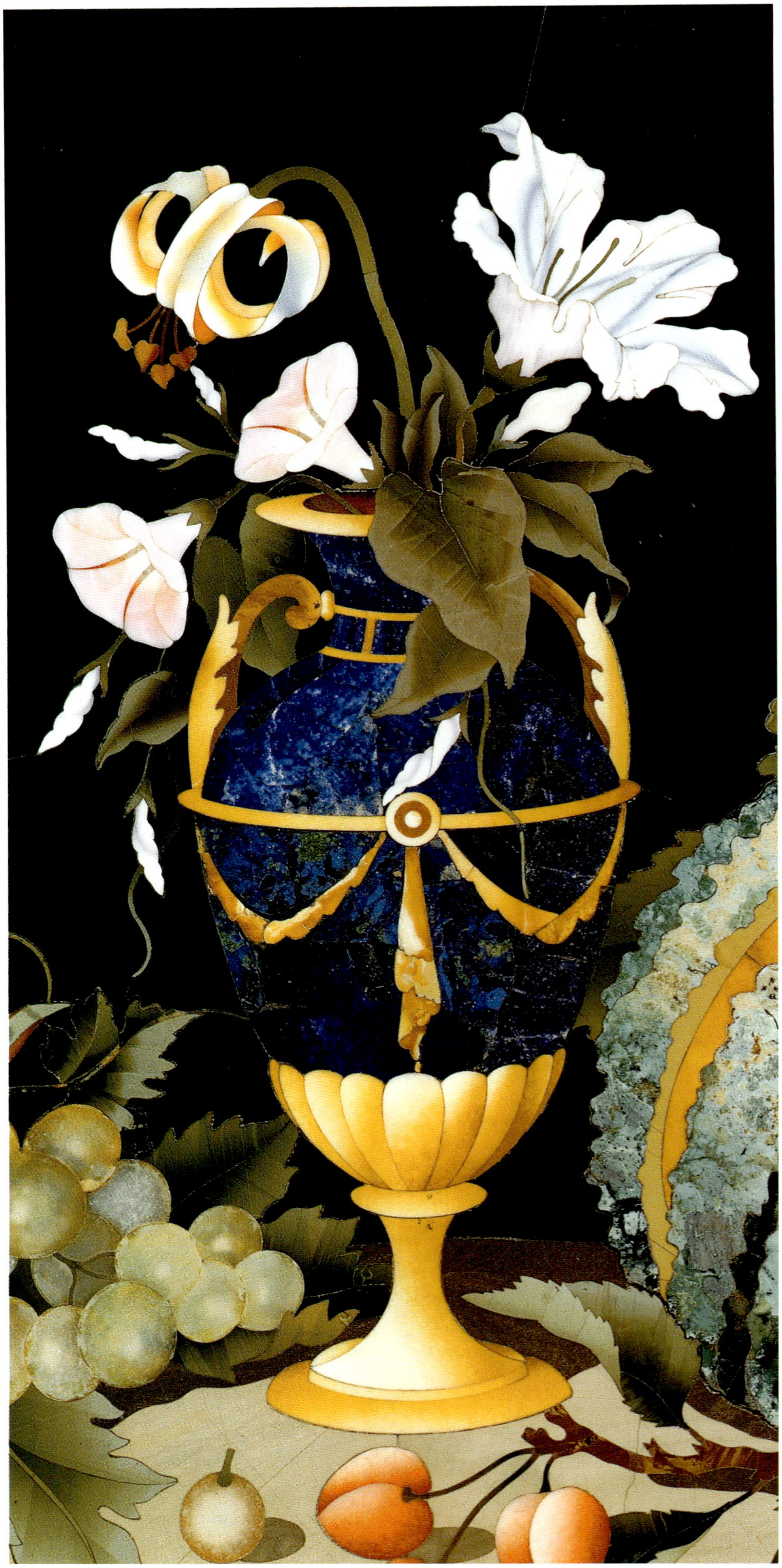

COMMENTARY: This tabletop is signed on the back F. SCAPPINI, FIRENZE. Nothing is known about him or his activity. The tabletop uses the classic black marble background, the composition being inlaid in a slab of Albarese limestone. The stones used include jasper, *verde d'Arno*, and lapis lazuli. The variegated effect of the chalcedony used for the grapes is particularly effective.

Still lifes depicting fruit were amongst the recurrent themes of late nineteenth-century mosaic design in Florence. Fruit designs were especially popular in the 1880s; various unmounted panels with plums, pears, grapes, cherries, lemons, etc. can be seen in the Museo dell'Opificio.[1] A still-life plaque signed by Bosi of Florence with the medallion from the Exhibition of the Industry of All Nations, New York, 1853, is inlaid *pietre dure* with a goldfinch, melon, grapes, pomegranate, and lemon.[2]

NOTES

1 Giusti, Mazzoni, and Pampaloni Martelli 1978, figs. 198–206.

2 Sotheby's, London, 16 March, 1990, lot 41.

30 TABLE

France, c. 1840
Malachite, gilt bronze, walnut, 80 × 105.4 × 121.9 cm (31½ x 41½ x 48 in)
(FA50)

PROVENANCE: Ferdinand Philippe, Duke of Orleans (1810–42); David Orgell, Los Angeles, 1981.

DESCRIPTION: A quadrangular centre table with projections at the corners and four pairs of tapering legs. The surface is faced with malachite. Around the tabletop is a rich decorative gilt-bronze frieze of high-relief decoration consisting of volutes enclosing a variety of animals: a panther, wolf, eagle, vulture, owl, and pelican. At the front and back, the frieze has a central design of four cherubs surrounding a winged female figure playing the viol. At each angle is a shield flanked by two sirens; the French royal crown surmounts the shield. In the shields the monogram FP is intertwined with an O, for Ferdinand Philippe, Duke of Orleans (1810–42), son of Louis Philippe (r. 1830–48), King of France.

COMMENTARY: Malachite is a carbonate of copper, with a low hardness value (3.5–4). Its name is derived from the Greek, malache (mallow) and it was used in classical times (for some of the columns in the temple of Diana at Ephesus, for example, later removed to Hagia Sophia in Constantinople). However, malachite was scarcely known in European workshops in the sixteenth and seventeenth centuries. It came back into fashion at the end of the eighteenth century following the discovery of great malachite deposits in the central Urals during prospecting promoted by Tsarina Catherine II.

In the second half of the eighteenth century the rich mineral reserves of the Russian mountains also yielded many different varieties of porphyry and jasper, agate and aventurine, used in the production of decorative objects like vases, candle-holders, clocks etc.

The exploitation and transportation of these minerals was set up with considerable financial support from Imperial funds, and specialist factories were established to process the stones: Peterhof, Ekaterinburg and Kolyyan. Many private workshops were established at the same time in St. Petersburg, the most celebrated of these being the one belonging to the Demidoff family, owners of a large number of mineral concessions in the Urals.[1] Prince Demidoff commissioned a temple whose cupola was supported by eight malachite mosaic and gilt bronze columns. In 1833 he presented it to Tsar Nicholas I.[2]

The relative softness of malachite, compared with other stones meant that it was generally extracted in smallish blocks and therefore could not be worked in large monolithic pieces. On the occasions when monumental blocks could be extracted, they would be full of holes. In order for these to be used (as in the case of the columns in the cathedral of St. Isaac in St. Petersburg), the empty spaces had to be filled with fragments of the same material. The Russian stoneworkers invented a special mosaic technique that allowed them to compensate for the natural faults in the malachite. The stone was cut into small pieces and these would be reassembled to form attractive patterns, laid on a base of wood or metal. Any space remaining between the mosaic pieces would then be filled in with a grout made of fragments of malachite and a green cement. In this way, furnishings and ornamental objects could be created, as well as architectural accessories such as columns or chimney-pieces.

The passion for malachite received a new impetus in the second decade of the nineteenth century when, between 1810 and 1814, further deposits of the stone were discovered, allowing it to be used in enormous quantity. Its employment was also encouraged in the mid-nineteenth century by advances in processing techniques made by L. Leopold Joffrian. In 1840, he perfected a machine with arms that rotated at great speed, which was able to slice the stone extremely finely along the veins without breaking it.

The greatest triumph of malachite construction was in the cathedral of St. Isaac in St. Petersburg, reconstructed at the behest of Alexander III between 1819 and 1858 by the French architect Auguste Montferrand. Its gigantic iconostasis is flanked by vast columns of lapis lazuli and malachite.

This triumph was endorsed by the architect Alexander Bryullov, who was responsible for the decoration of the malachite room in the Winter Palace in St. Petersburg; the walls are panelled in malachite, with monumental columns. The chimney-piece and tables, candelabra and other furnishings are all made in malachite combined with gilt bronze.

The taste for malachite began to spread throughout Europe, thanks particularly to the opulent gifts sent from Russia to potentates and crowned heads all over Europe. Alexander I (1801–25) presented Napoleon with an important series of pieces in malachite mounted in bronze, designed for the Grand Cabinet de l'Empereur in the Grand Trianon at Versailles. In the centre of the room was a large malachite vessel supported by three herms with lions' paws; in the corners malachite columns bore candle holders. A cabinet by Jacob Desmalter in ebony and gilt bronze supports two slender malachite amphorae on a surface of the same stone.

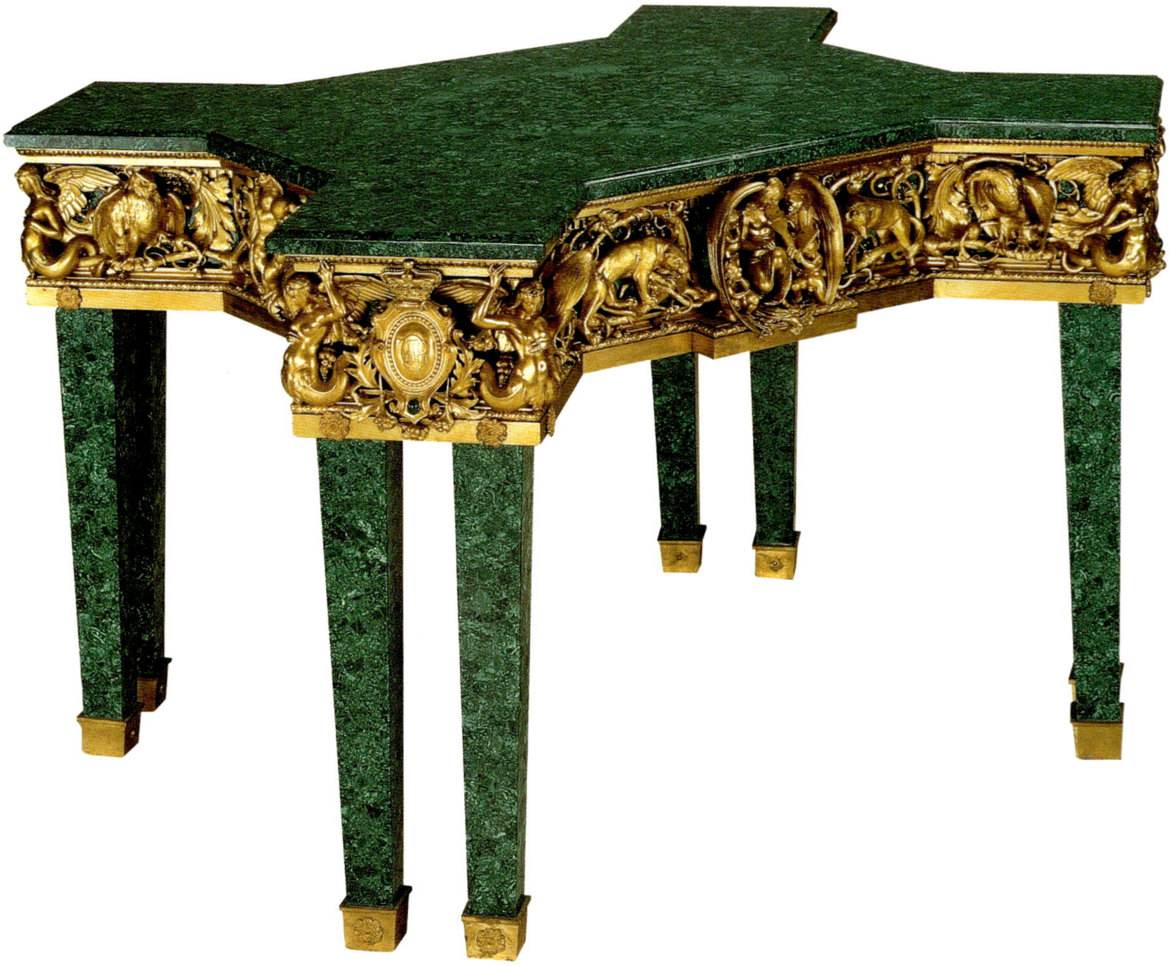

The use of malachite in room furnishings (later known as malachite rooms) became instantly fashionable all over Europe. The deep green of the stone, combined with the burnished glow of gilt bronze, created a contrast of colour and tone that fitted the Empire style to perfection. In the Paris workshop of Pierre Philippe Thomire (1751–1843) the marriage of gilt bronze and malachite became a trademark and was used in small decorative items as well as in monumental tables, vases, candleholders, or bases like the ones in the Gilbert Collection (TU10AB, 11AB, 108AB, 141AB). In 1819, the Thomire workshop made an imposing rectangular table, richly mounted on bronze legs, for Prince Nicholas Demidoff, Russian envoy in Tuscany. It was presented to Grand Duke Leopold II in 1829.[3] Between 1804 and 1809, Thomire created an even more sumptuous round table supported by four bronze winged chimeras and a centrepiece held up by dancing bronze nymphs with a statue of Zephyr in the centre. It was sent to the Villa Demidoff in Florence after the marriage of Mathilde Bonaparte, daughter of Jerome, to the Prince Anatol Demidoff.[4] This table was conspicuous even in the villa in San Donato, where malachite had been used with no regard for cost.

When the contents of the Florentine villa were auctioned in 1880, various works by the French bronzesmith were sold, as well as a collection of later works, probably produced in the Prince's factory in St. Petersburg. The catalogue lists two large urns of the same material, mounted in bronze and nearly two metres in height, with a diameter of a metre and a half; three Regency-style vases, presented at the Exposition Universelle in 1878; two candleholders with nine branches in the rococo style, 120 centimetres high; a wall clock mounted in gilt bronze and silver gilt; a large stoup supported by three herms with female bodies, also executed by Thomire; two large console tables on carved wooden bases taken from two antique tables in the Palazzo Capponi in Florence; two round vessels with gilt-bronze pedestals engraved with acanthus leaves. In the so-called 'mosaic room', the walls were lined with blue silk and decorated with Florentine mosaic and Roman micromosaic and there was an impressive display of objects in malachite: a clock and two candleholders by Thomire in bronze, with relief *pietre dure* mosaics and malachite; a block of natural malachite; an oval vase cut from a single block, with gilt-bronze handles in the shape of serpents; four replicas of the famous

Medici vase with handles and bas-reliefs in gilt bronze; eight large eight-branched candlesticks made by Thomire for Jerome Bonaparte's residence in the German town of Kassel and evidently returned to the Demidoff collection in the same circumstances as the table quoted above. In the Grand Canova Gallery was the opulent rococo malachite doorway, and three replicas of the Medici vase, and in the *salon d'honneur* the malachite fireplace with the three medallions in Florentine mosaic now in the Museo Stibbert in Florence.[5]

Following its triumphant success during the Empire, malachite continued to be used for furnishings and ornaments throughout the nineteenth century. Even during the decades that followed, it was chosen for architectural features like the great chimney-piece formerly in the throne room of the Italian Embassy in St. Petersburg.[6]

NOTES

1 On the Russian gemstone factories, see Chenevière 1988, pp. 259–282.
2 See M. di Grecia, Palazzi Imperiali Russi, Milan, 1992, p. 147.
3 In the Palazzo Pitti, Florence. See Giusti 1992, pl. III.
4 In the Museo Stibbert, Florence. See Giusti 1992, pl. 110.
5 Palais de San Donato 1880, p. 7, nos. 28, 29; p. 24, nos. 76, 77; p. 28, nos. 92, 94; p. 29, no. 96; p.73, no. 290; p. 77, no. 303; p.78, nos. 309, 311; p.236, no. 940; p. 253, nos. 1018, 1019, p. 479.
6 In the Museo dell'Opificio delle pietre dure. See Il Museo dell'Opificio 1978, p. 315, pl. 370.

31. TABLE

France, 1850/60
Malachite, gilt bronze, wood, 71.1 × 5.5 cm (28 × 22¼ in)
(MM14)

PROVENANCE: Nestle, Inc, New York, 1967.

DESCRIPTION: Circular table with a top of malachite on a wooden support, surrounded by a gallery of gilt-bronze volutes, acanthus leaves and rosettes. The lower part has a baluster of malachite with three scroll-shaped, gilt-bronze terminal figures, each bearing the bust of a cherub with butterfly wings and holding a bird. The base is of malachite, with borders and mounts of gilt bronze and bun feet.

COMMENTARY: The shape of this table and the style of the gilt bronzes connect it to French production of the mid-nineteenth century, like that of a pair of cabinets in the Gilbert Collection (cat. no. 16). For further information see cat. no. 30.

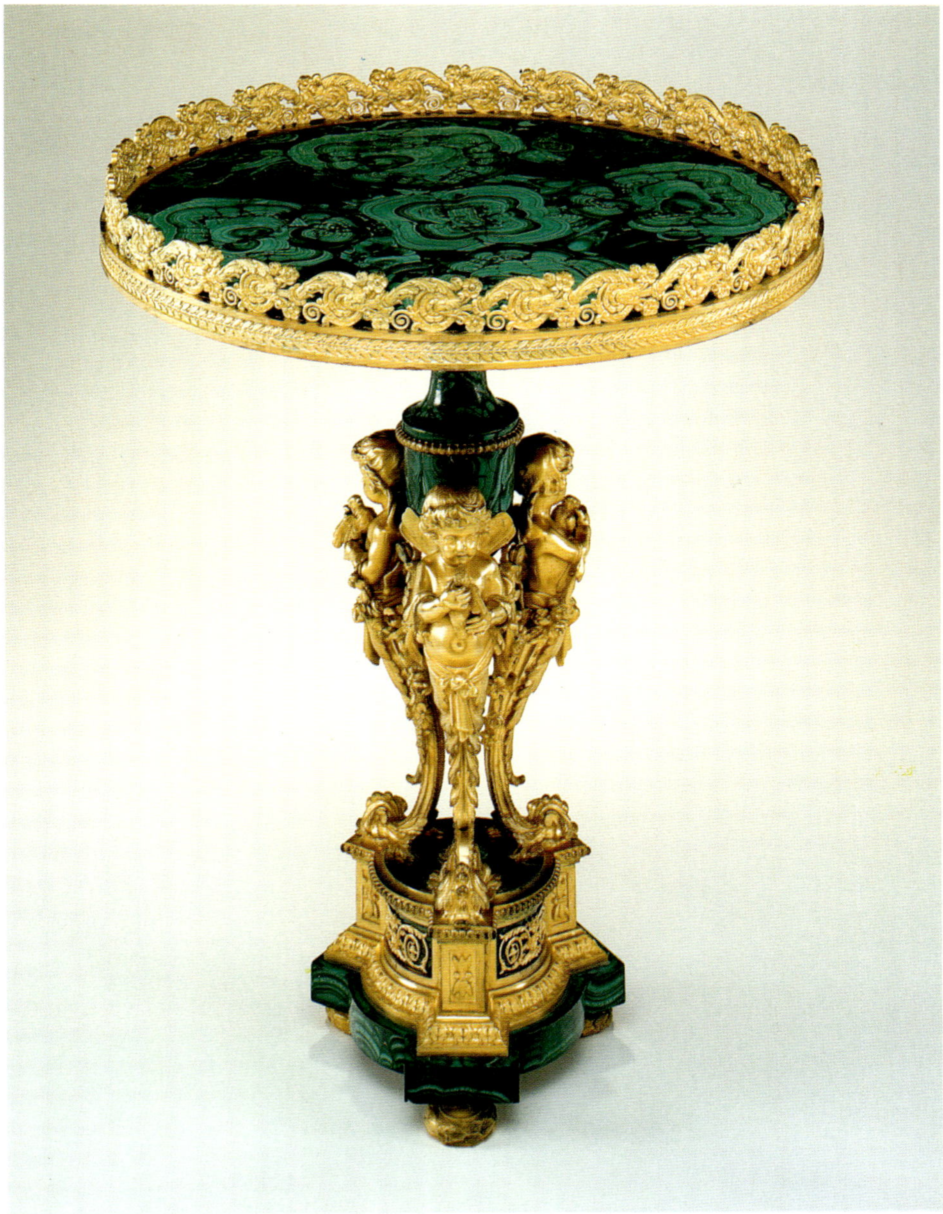

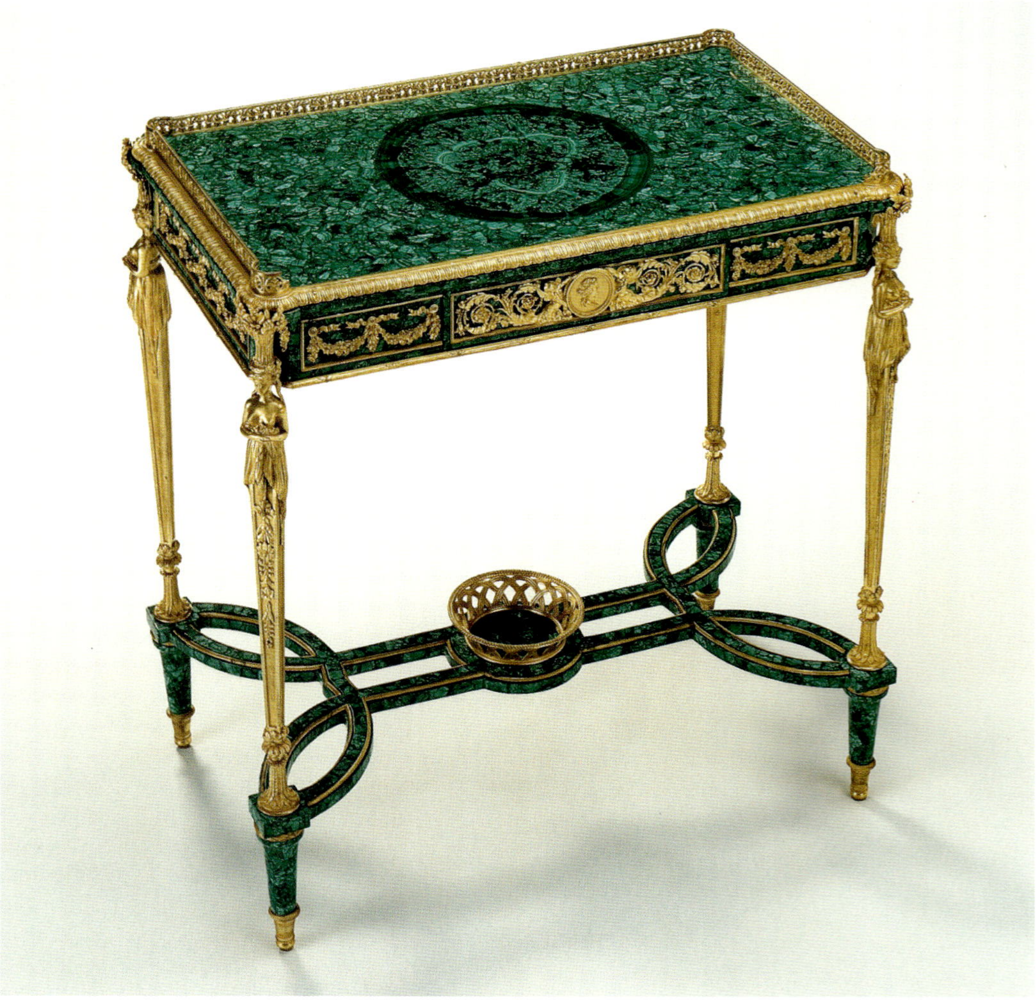

32. TABLE

France, third quarter nineteenth century
Malachite, gilt bronze, oak, 52.7 × 71.8 × 42.2 cm (20¾ × 28¼ × 16⅝ in)
(FA45)

PROVENANCE: David Orgell, Los Angeles, 1979.

DESCRIPTION: A rectangular table with a malachite top on a wooden support with a gilt-bronze gallery. The tabletop is supported by straight, tapering gilt-bronze legs with tops in the form of caryatids bearing baskets upon their heads. The gilt-bronze frieze around the top is applied with garlands. On the front is a bas-relief plaque, flanked by acanthus scrolls and tendrils, which covers the front of a drawer. The lower portion has a flat malachite stretcher with loop-shaped corners, the centre supporting a gilt-bronze basket.

COMMENTARY: The shape of this table, the supports, and the bronze detail are similar to those on a writing table veneered in ebony and Japanese lacquer in the Louvre. The Louvre table was made by Adam Weisweiler (1744–1820) in 1784 for the chateau of Marie Antoinette's (r. 1774–93), Saint-Cloud.[1] The Queen's writing desk was ordered from the *marchand mercier* Dominique Daguerre (fl. 1772–96), with whom the cabinetmaker frequently collaborated. Daguerre often provided Weisweiler with designs for furniture and bronze ornaments, as in the case of the desk made for Marie Antoinette. At the end of the nineteenth century there was a marked revival of interest in Weisweiler's work, especially in the Marie Antoinette writing desk. In 1865, it was acquired by Empress Eugenie (1826–1920), who kept it in the *Salon bleu* of the Tuileries, which she used as her audience chamber. Innumerable copies and new versions were made by Parisian cabinetmakers who specialised in copies of period furniture.[2]

NOTES

1 Pradère 1989, p. 389, no. 475.

2 Alcouffe, Dion Tennenbaum and Lefebure 1993, vol. 1, pp. 290, 292.

33. TABLE

Top: Livorno, F. Della Valle, c. 1850; base: Tuscany, attributed to Luigi Falcini (1794–1861) and Angiolo Falcini (1801–50), second quarter nineteenth century
Scagliola, ebony, marble, marquetry of various woods, mother-of-pearl, 85.1 × 133.7 × 81.6 cm (33½ × 52⅝ × 32⅛ in)
1996.308 (MM201)

PROVENANCE: South Audley Art Galleries, London, 1975; Los Angeles County Museum of Art.

LITERATURE: *Great Exhibition* 1851, p. 1,300; González-Palacios 1977a, no. 74; Wilson 1980, p. 100; González-Palacios and Röttgen 1982, no. 81; Massinelli 1993, pl. 337, p. 201; Scagliola l'arte della pietra di Luna, Rome, 1977, p. 46, pl. 31.

EXHIBITIONS: London, 1851; Los Angeles, 1977.

DESCRIPTION: Tabletop of *scagliola* with a black marble background, the outer border composed of naturalistic decoration of cornucopias with vine leaves and birds. The inner border of entwined plants surrounds a panel; in the centre are two European goldfinches sitting on the branch of a fruit tree. The stand is veneered with different woods and has a frieze around the perimeter, veneered with a motif similar to that on the outer circumference of the tabletop. Four legs join the tabletop to a lower panel, which rests on four tortoises of carved wood.

COMMENTARY: This table, signed F. DELLA VALLE, was shown at the Crystal Palace Exhibition in London in 1851 and is illustrated in the exhibition catalogue with the following description: 'A rectangular table in *scagliola*, with various ornaments, and entirely inlaid, in imitation of works of hard pebbles, executed in the exhibitors' Scagliola Works, in Leghorn'.[1]

Marquetry in floral designs using exotic, coloured woods and ivory was a specialisation brought to perfection in the seventeenth century by the French cabinetmaker, Pierre Gole

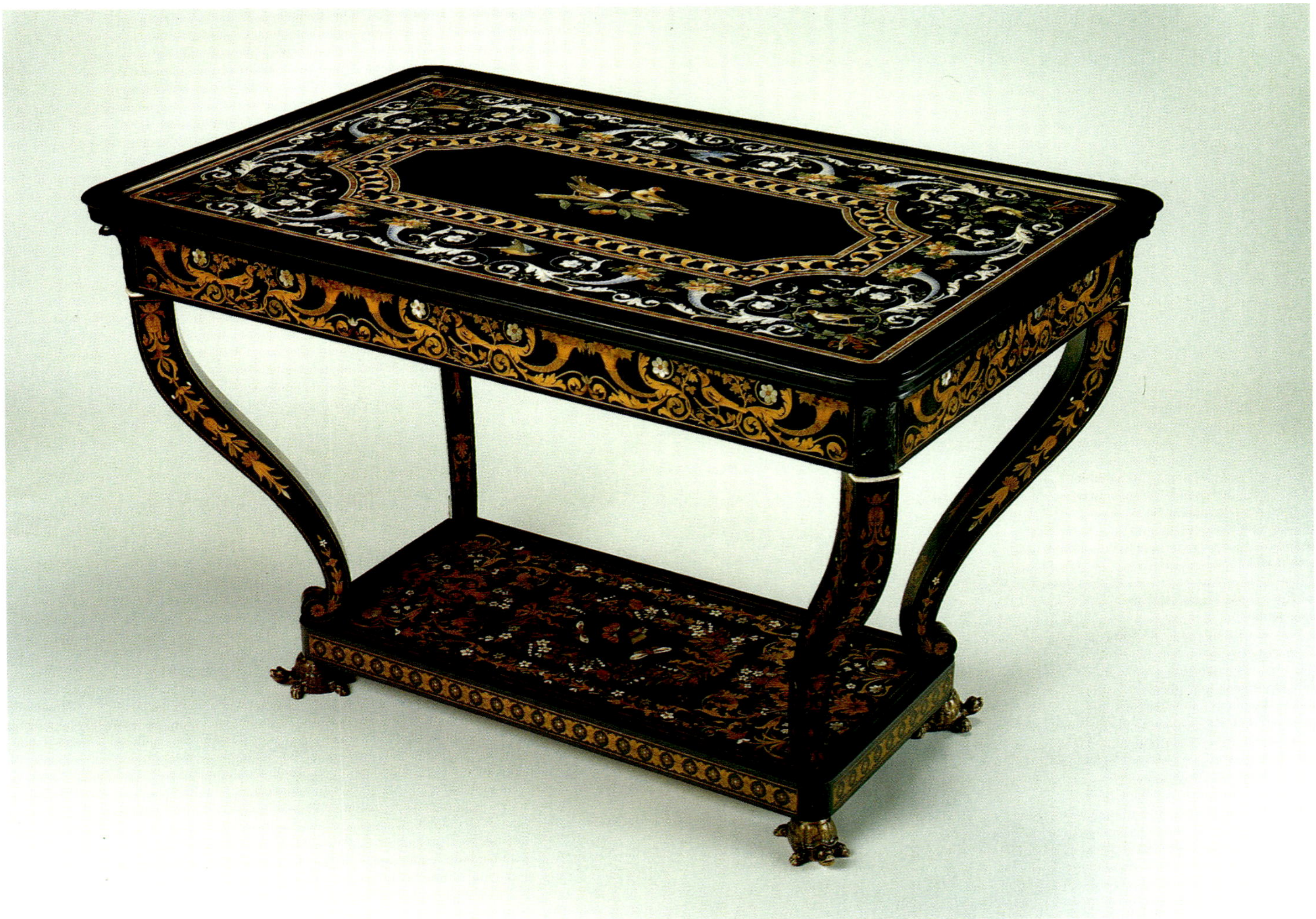

(c. 1620–1684), at the Gobelins, and Leonardo van der Vinne (fl. 1662–93) in Florence. *Scagliola* was also masterfully used in 1840 by Gioacchino Barberi for a tabletop with the Rothschilds' coat-of-arms at the centre.[2]

A revival of marquetry arose in the nineteenth century through Italians such as Raffaele Bucci (fl. c. 1862), Francesco Pucci (1817–86), and the Falcini brothers. An example of the Falcini's work appeared in the 1969 sale of Prince Demidoff's collection in the villa of Pratolino, Florence,[3] which included four tables comparable to the Gilbert Collection piece. As González-Palacios has mentioned, Luisa Bandera has convincingly shown that these are from the hand of the Falcini brothers.[4] A gouache by Fortune de Fournier (1798–1864) shows two of four tables by Falcini in the ballroom of the Villa Demidoff at San Donato, Florence, as early as 1841. Two of the Demidoff tables were purchased by the Superintendent of Fine Arts in Florence, and are now in the Pitti Palace.

A circular tabletop of simulated black marble, inset with a scene of St. Peter's Basilica and four rectangular vignettes of famous monuments signed *Della Valle*, was sold at auction.[5] Another *scagliola* tabletop, depicting Aurora after Guido Reni, came on the market[6] bearing a trade label, PETER DELLA VALLE & BROTHER / MANUFACTURERS AND PAINTERS OF SCAGLIOLA / NUM. 1473 PER PORTA CAPPUCCINI / LEGHORN. A third rectangular tabletop signed F. DEL LA VALLE and ordered with bird and foliage decoration similar to the Gilbert Collection table appeared at auction in 1983.[7] And, most recently, a Falcini table after a model by Van der Vin (d. 1713) came on the market in 1998.[8]

Gypsum, also called *pietra di luna* (moonstone) or *scagliola* in its finest version, is hydrated calcium sulphate, found in great quantity in the calcareous rocks around Modena. Because of its ductility, it is highly suitable for modelling. The following description by Guiseppe Pelli Bencivenni (1729–1808) provides a good overview of the material and its uses:

> *Scagliola* is made of a type of transparent calcareous stone which scientists follow Vallerio in classifying with the gessi, calling it selenite. It is, however, popularly known as *specchio d'asino* (asses' mirror), or dog's mirror. The gesso is ground to the finest powder and then made into a paste and smoothed; when it is dry and hard, designs can be carved in it and these then filled with the same material mixed with whatever colour suits the kind of work it is intended to imitate. When the final result is cleaned and polished, a solid, gleaming picture appears which shines as if covered with crystal ... It is not my business here to describe the many uses to which *scagliola* can be put, but if you consider that it can be used to imitate all different marbles and all the rarest stones, and from it can be composed pictures of animals, flowers, scenes from history, and views of landscape and buildings, then you will have some idea of the great esteem in which it is held.[9]

In the wake of the widespread European fashion for wood intarsia, inlaid ivory and showy *pietre dure* mosaics, *scagliola* became popular as a way of imitating inlaid stone mosaics, as in this table (see also cat. no. 119).

NOTES

1 Great Exhibition 1851, p. 337.
2 Lizzani 1970, fig.LXXX.
3 Sotheby's, 21–24 April 1969.
4 Bandera 1969, p. 66.
5 Christie's New York, 25 October, 1991, lot 144.
6 Christie's, New York, 24 April 1980, lot 135.
7 Sotheby's, New York, 12 November 1983, lot 37.
8 Sotheby's, London, 2 October 1998, lot 337.
9 Pelli Bencivenni 1779, vol. 2, pp. 436–41.

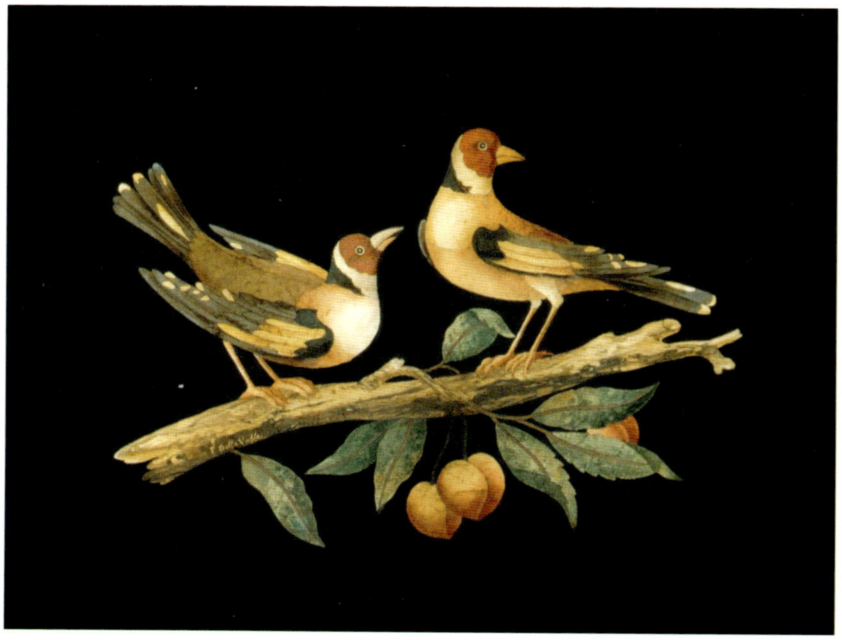

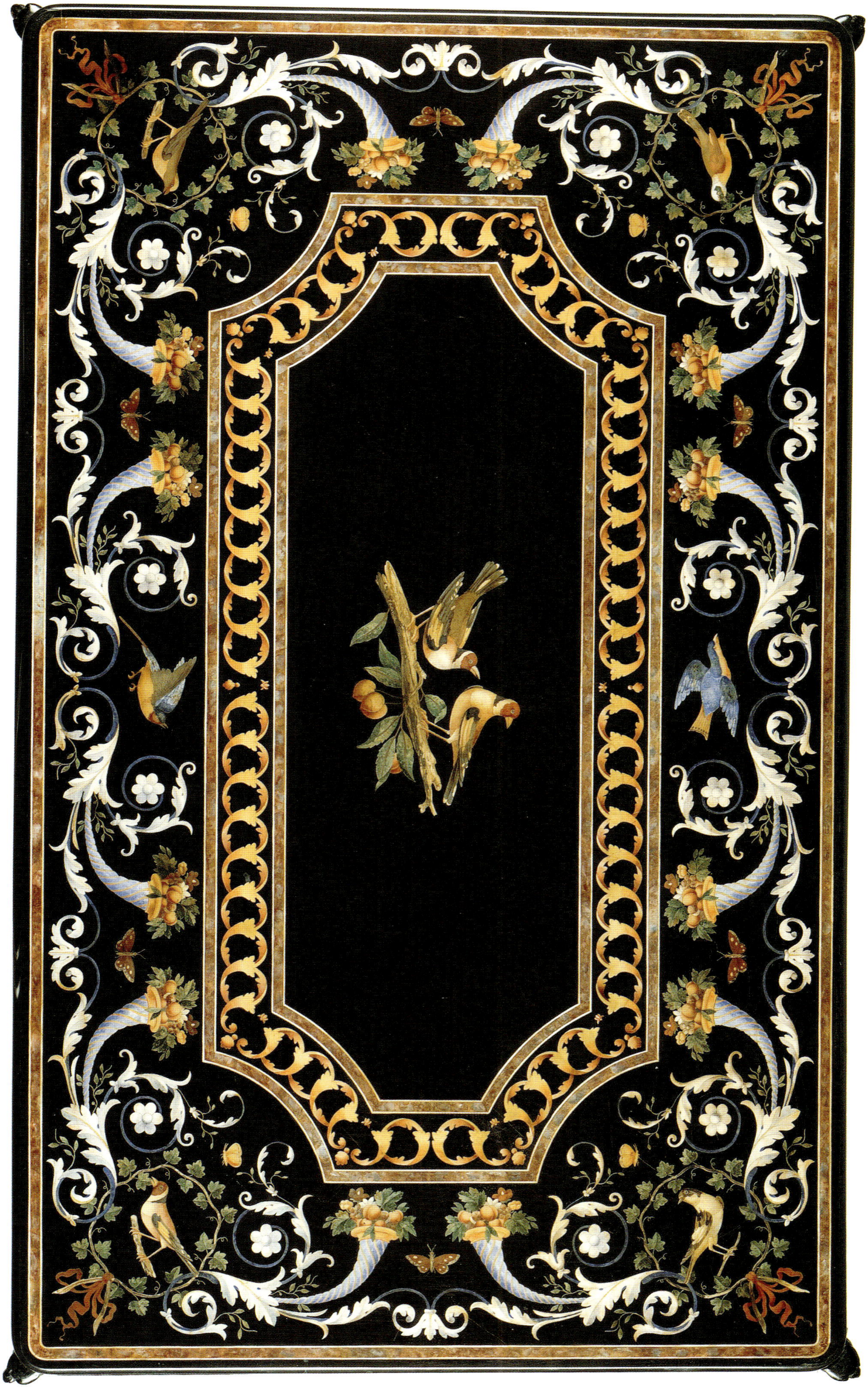

34. BUREAU PLAT

Pietre dure: possibly Florence, c. 1840–60; base: Paris, Beaufort Jeune, c. 1840–60
Pietre dure, marble, ebonised wood, wood marquetry, gilt bronze, 30 × 132 × 71.8 cm (3½ × 52 × 28¼₆ in)
1996.599 (MMIII)

PROVENANCE: Enzo Constantini, Rome, 1971.

DESCRIPTION: Bureau plat in the Louis XVI style, the rectangular body and legs composed of ebonised wood with gilt-bronze mounts. Each leg is surmounted by a gilt-bronze female bust, the sides and front of the desk inlaid with panels of *pietre dure* decorated with inlay of flowers and fruit. The central of the three front panels, all of which are decorated with raised-relief *pietre dure* leaves and flowers, is recessed between two gilt-bronze mounts in the form of bearded deities' heads. The top of the desk is of black marble, inlaid with coloured *pietre dure*, the large central decoration depicting fruit and flowers within a rectangular band of lapis lazuli, a further band of floral inlay, and an outer band of red marble.

COMMENTARY: Like cat. nos. 16 and 32, this table belongs to the wave of French furniture inspired by eighteenth-century models. The base is signed by the French cabinetmaker, Beaufort Jeune, whose workshop was at 56 rue Montorgueil in Paris in 1836. He is identified with the Befort [sic] Jeune who worked in Paris in the rue Neuve-Sainte-Gilles from 1844 until 1866. According to Denise Ledoux-Lebard, this cabinetmaker often misspelled his name when signing his works (e.g. 'Beffort' and 'Defort'), but was known as a specialist in furniture in the style of Boulle and in the use of bronze and hardstone.[1] A similar table was sold at Christies in 1988.[2]

NOTES
1 Ledoux-Lebard 1965, p. 29.
2 London, 29 September, lot 110.

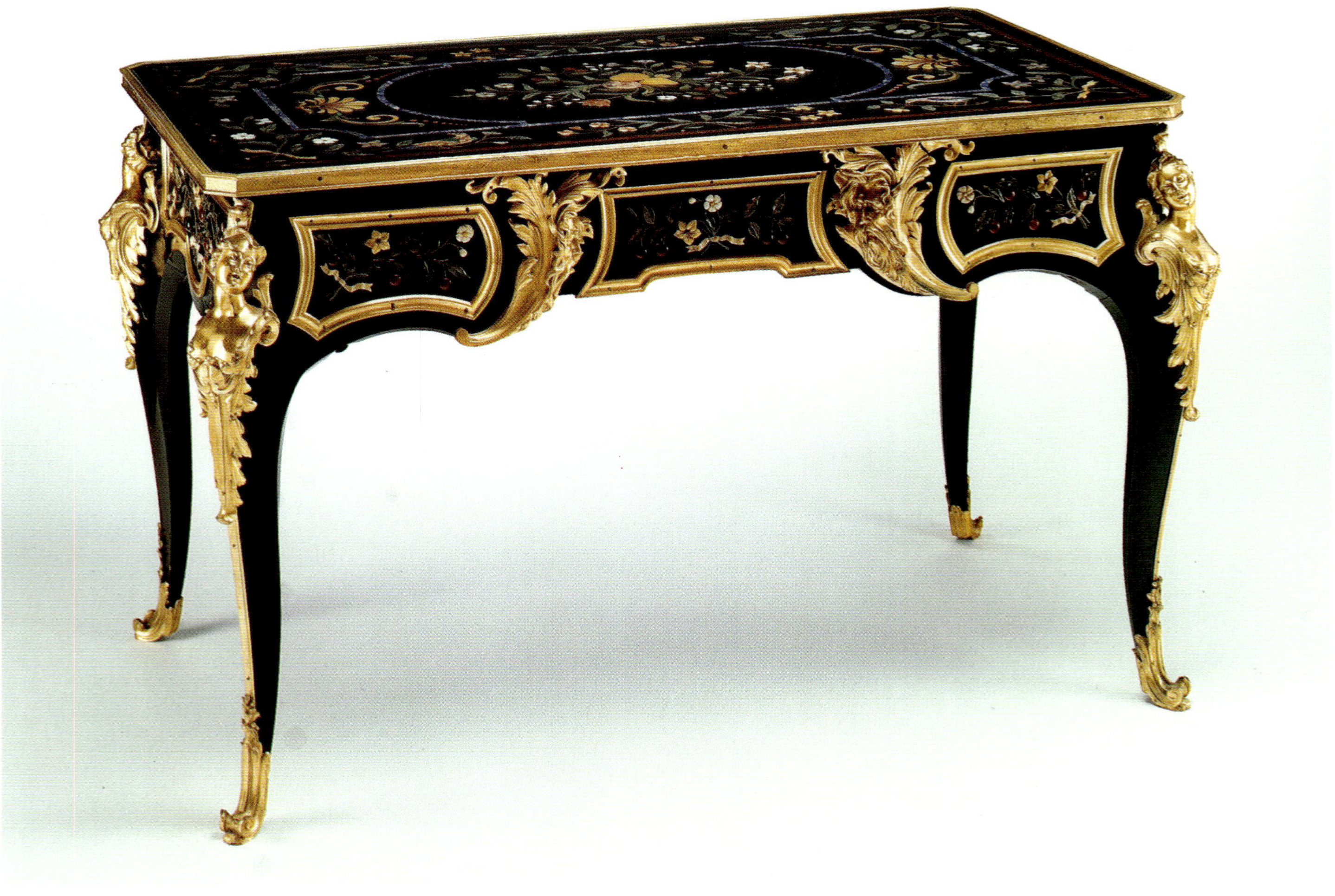

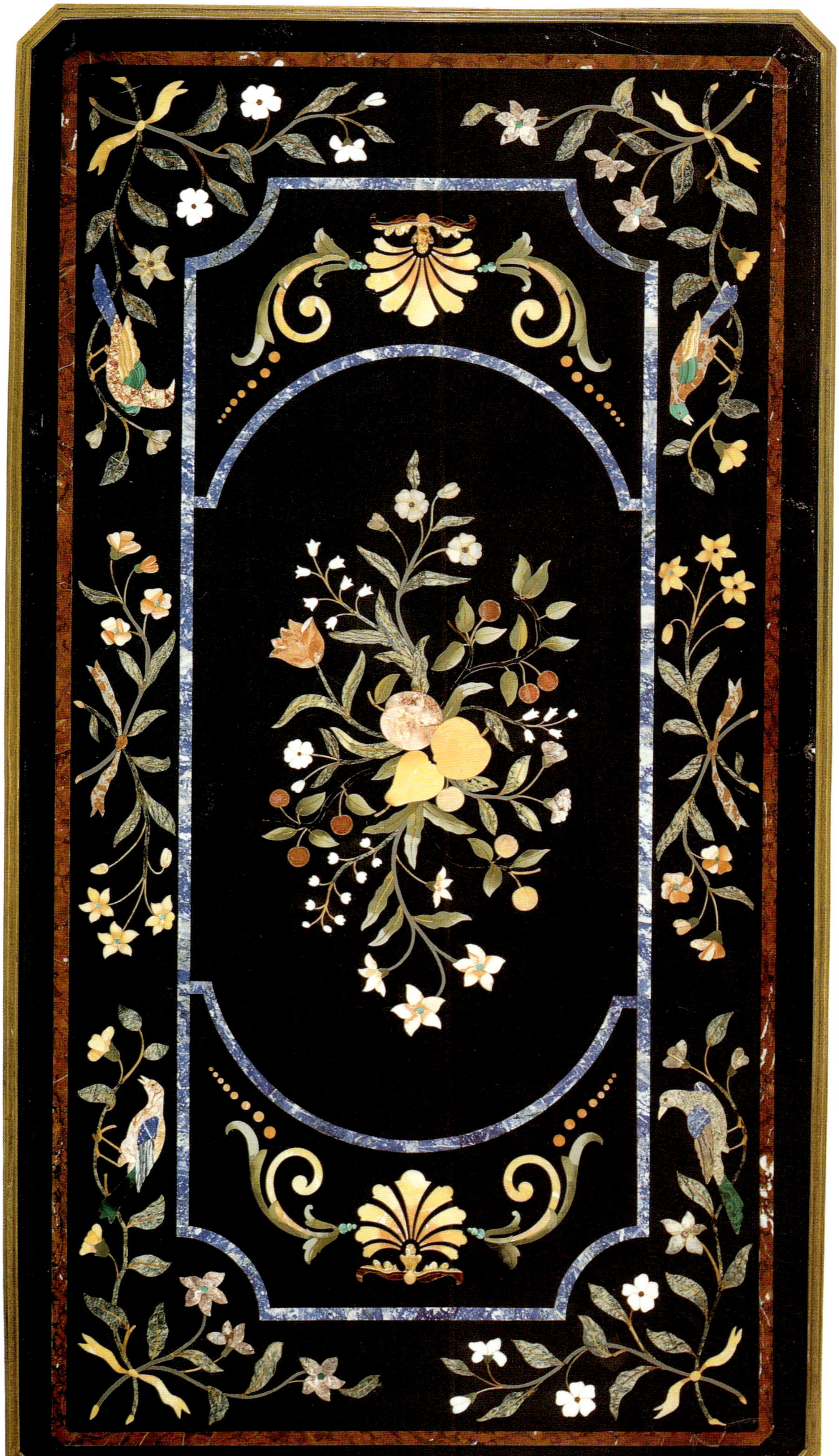

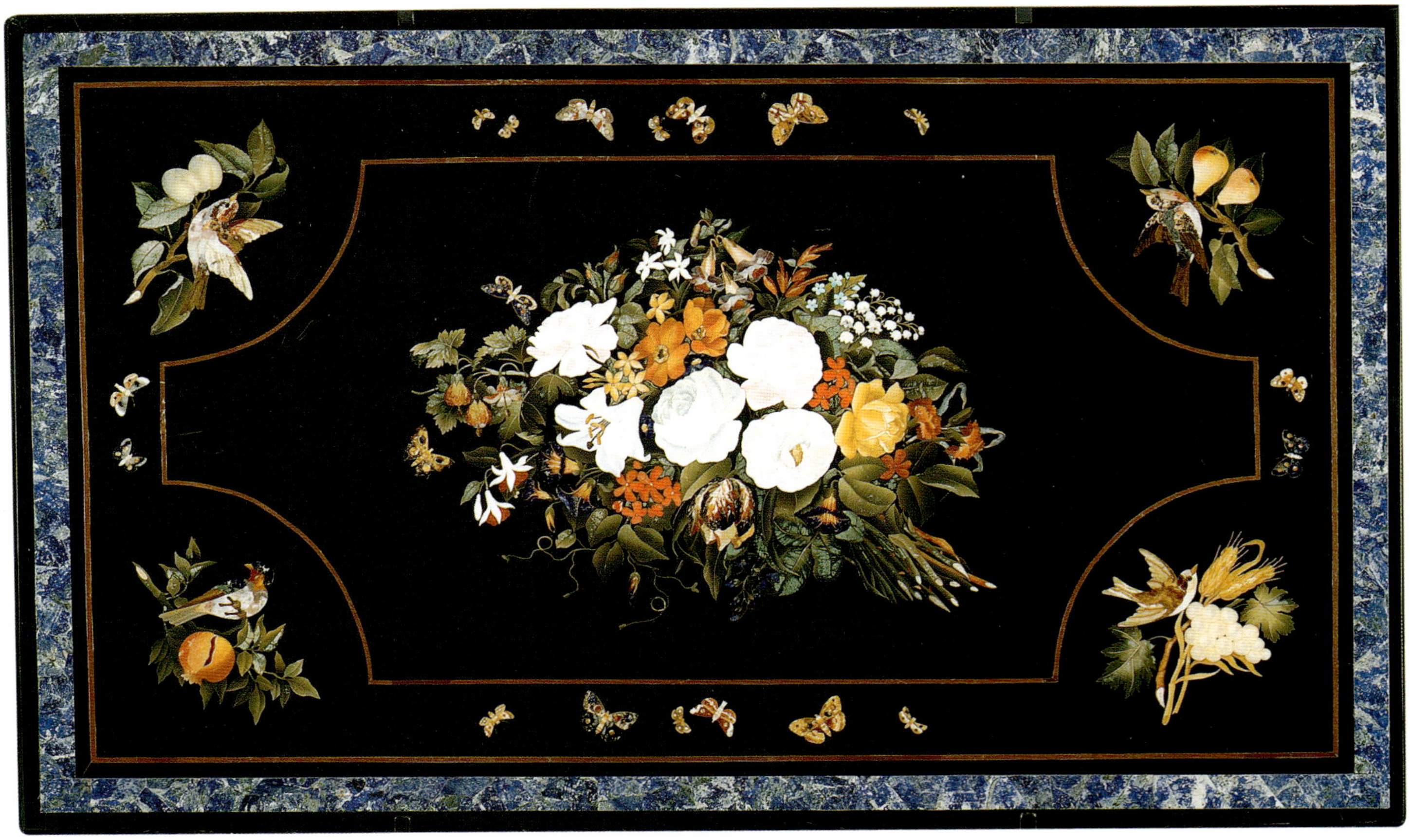

35. TABLETOP

Florence, c. 1860
Black marble, lapis lazuli, *pietre dure*, shell 115.5 × 68.6 cm (45½ × 27 in)
1996.241 (MM91)

PROVENANCE: Giorgio Rovelli, Rome, 1971; Los Angeles County Museum of Art.

LITERATURE: Avery and Emperatori 1975, no. 38.

EXHIBITIONS: Los Angeles, 1975; London, 1975; Los Angeles / Atlanta / San Antonio / Richmond / Seattle, 1977–79.

DESCRIPTION: Table with traditional black marble background embellished with an outer edge of lapis lazuli. The naturalistic motifs use large amounts of *verde d'Arno*, onyx, white marble, jasper, and chalcedony from Volterra. Some of the flowers are in lapis lazuli; two roses are made of shell, a material frequently used for flower petals.

COMMENTARY: This tabletop reinterprets in the nineteenth-century manner the naturalistic designs that evolved in the Grand Ducal workshops in the seventeenth century. There are two tabletops of this type in the Ugolini collection in Florence, one circular and one rectangular. Nineteenth-century photographs of the products of that workshop include many examples similar to the Gilbert Collection piece. Another Florentine workshop specialising in this type of table belonged to Piero Bazzanti, at Lungarno Corsini 12. A floral table by him, with the craftsman's label still attached to the base, was auctioned in 1990.

NOTE

1 Christie's, London, 29 November 1990, lot 97.

36. TABLE

Florence c. 1870
Pietre dure, gilt wood, 78.7 × 79.7 × 50.8 cm (31 × 31 3/8 × 20 in)
1996.325 (MM232)

PROVENANCE: Gwynby Antiques, Cleveland Heights, Ohio, 1975; Los Angeles County Museum of Art.

LITERATURE: González-Palacios and Röttgen 1982, no. 108; Irmas 1986, ill. p. 3.

EXHIBITIONS: Los Angeles / Atlanta / San Antonio / Richmond / Seattle, 1977–79.

DESCRIPTION: Rectangular tabletop of black marble inlaid with a *pietre dure* still life of a tazza containing a pearl necklace, a 'Greek' vase, a shell, a vase of flowers, a smaller vase, a Renaissance-style ewer, and a 'Roman' bronze lamp in the form of a bird. The composition rests on a background slab of Albarese limestone, which appears to float against the black ground. The gilt table base, heavily carved with Gothic motifs, is adjustable and can be tilted to show the top at an angle.

COMMENTARY: This tabletop demonstrates the interest in neoclassical themes in late nineteenth-century Florentine mosaic workshops. It was obviously inspired by the late eighteenth-century tabletops designed by Antonio Cioci, and represents a synthesis of the most popular motifs used by the court workshops: flowers, the *tromp l'oeil* pearl necklace, the shell, archaeological items, classical urns, and the bronze lamp (the *verde d'Arno* is used to particularly good effect to imitate the bronze of the lamp). The table can be compared with other typical products of the private workshops in Florence, such as the table in the Ugolini collection with an archaeological composition on a porphyry background (fig. 10). It can also be compared with examples that have appeared at auction, such as two tables formerly in the Lord Astor of Hever Collection[1] and a table

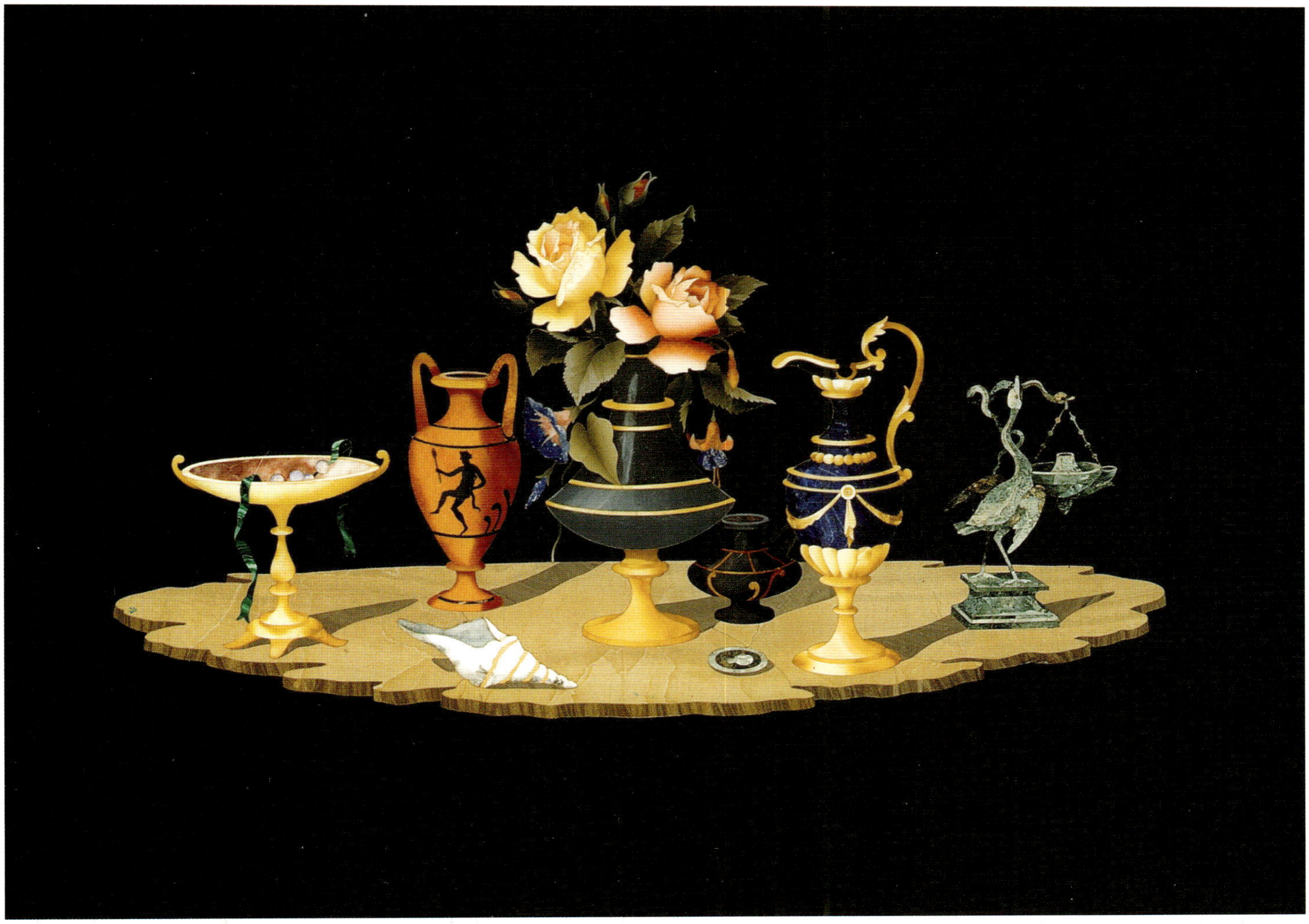

designed by Pasquale Orlandini dated 1873.[2]

These hardstone tabletops were often mounted in stands of neo-Gothic or neo-Renaissance style, decorated with opulent carved and gilded ornament. The top section was often on a hinge (as is the case with the Gilbert Collection table) so that it could be inclined, thereby becoming a work of art to be appreciated like a painting on an easel. The stand of the Gilbert Collection table represents a style that remained fashionable until the early years of the twentieth century, as evidenced by the photograph of the Ugolini pavilion in the Paris Exhibition of 1900 (fig. 1).

NOTES

1 Christie', London, 30 May 1963, lot 117.
2 Sotheby's, London, 4 November 1988, lot 180.

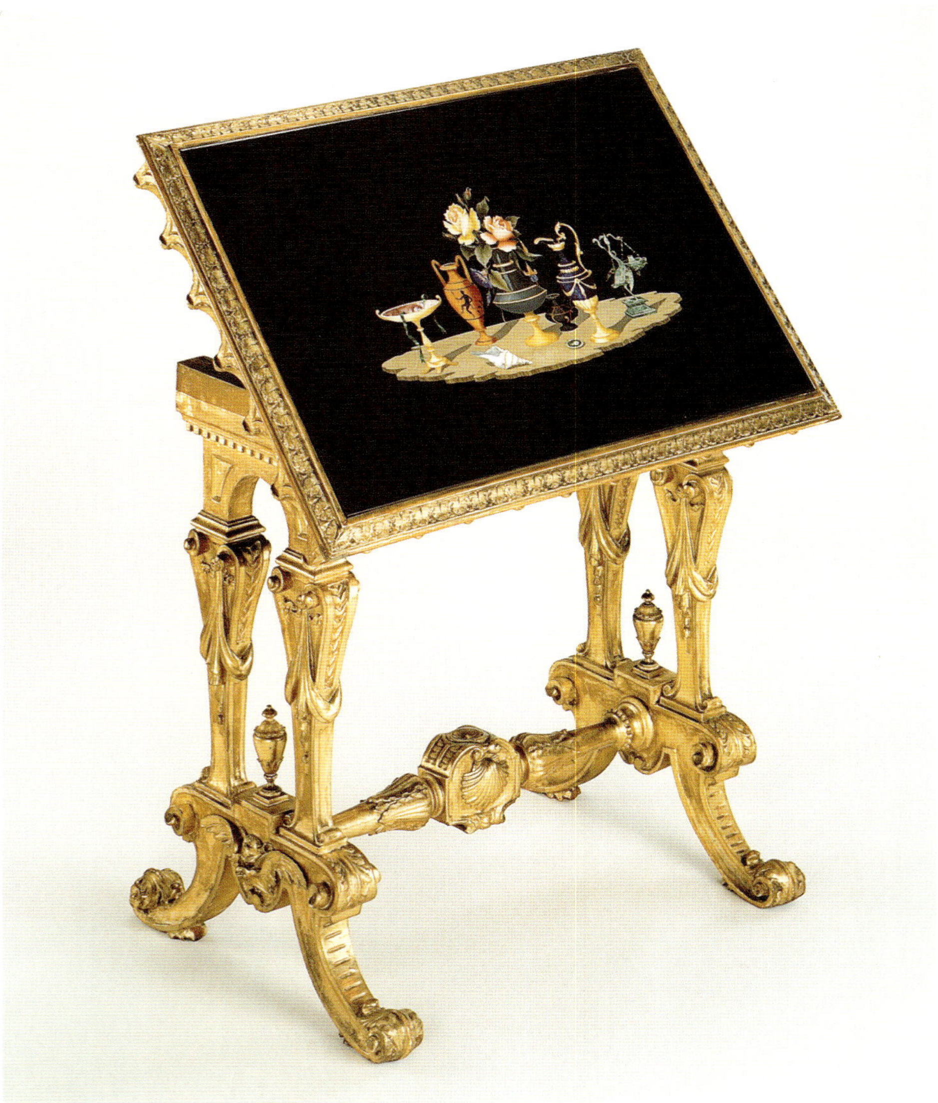

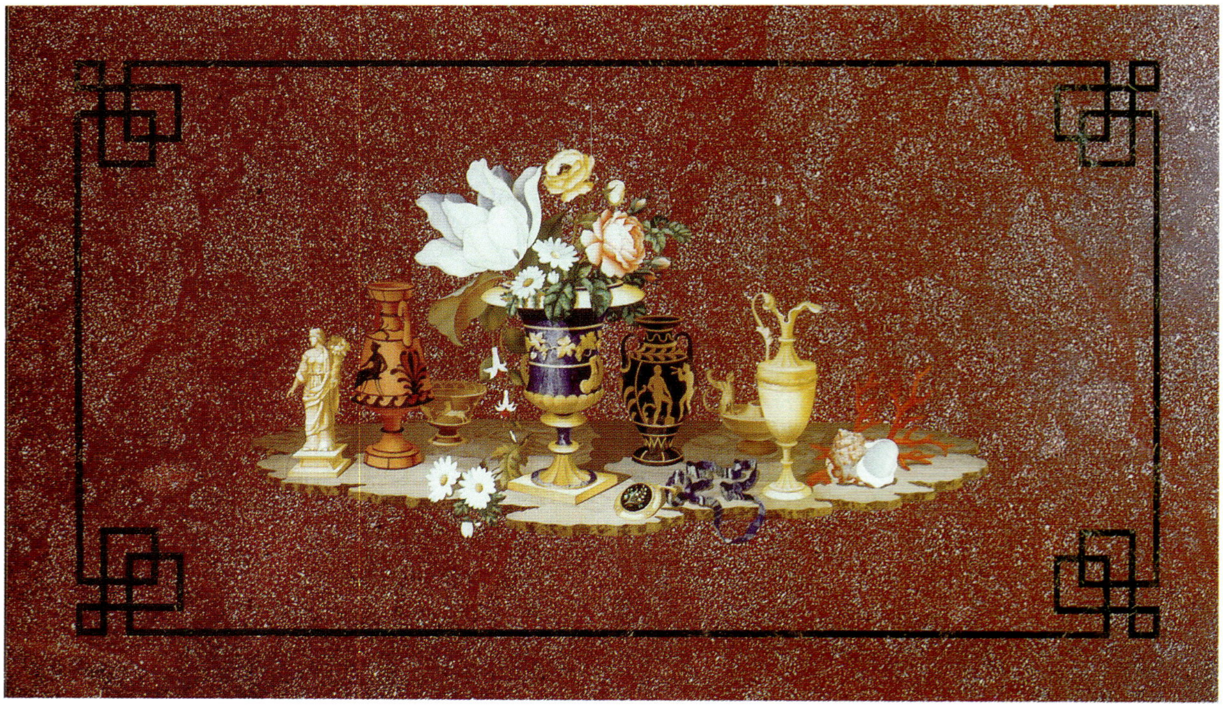

FIG 10 Tabletop in the Ugolini Collection, Florence.

37. TABLE

Top: Possibly Florence, third quarter nineteenth century; base: France, third quarter nineteenth century
Pietre dure, marble, malachite, ebonised wood, gilt bronze, 71.1 × 115.6 × 71.1 cm (28 × 45 × 28 in)
1996.311 (MM207)

PROVENANCE: Firestone and Parsons, Boston, 1975; Los Angeles County Museum of Art.

LITERATURE: González-Palacios 1977, no. 93; González-Palacios and Röttgen 1982, no. 104.

EXHIBITIONS: Los Angeles / Atlanta / San Antonio / Richmond / Seattle, 1977–79.

DESCRIPTION: A shaped oblong table in the Louis XVI style with a hardstone top depicting a parrot eating cherries within a central wreath of fruit and floral foliage. The top is further banded with malachite, floral vines, stylised leaves and an outer band of red marble. The sides of the top are applied with six hardstone panels with hardstone fruit and leaves in relief and gilt-bronze mounts in the centre. The base has a stretcher surmounted by a gilt-bronze urn.

COMMENTARY: This hardstone tabletop is a typical product of Florentine private workshops in the third quarter of the nineteenth century. The base is in a historicising style, inspired by eighteenth-century *ébénistes* such as Adam Weisweiler (1744–1820). As González-Palacios has observed, 'There were a vast number of furniture makers working in Paris in the late nineteenth century, and little is known about their individual styles and methods. In the absence of a maker's stamp, it is virtually impossible to attribute this table to one of them'.[1]

NOTE
1 González-Palacios and Röttgen 1982, p. 209.

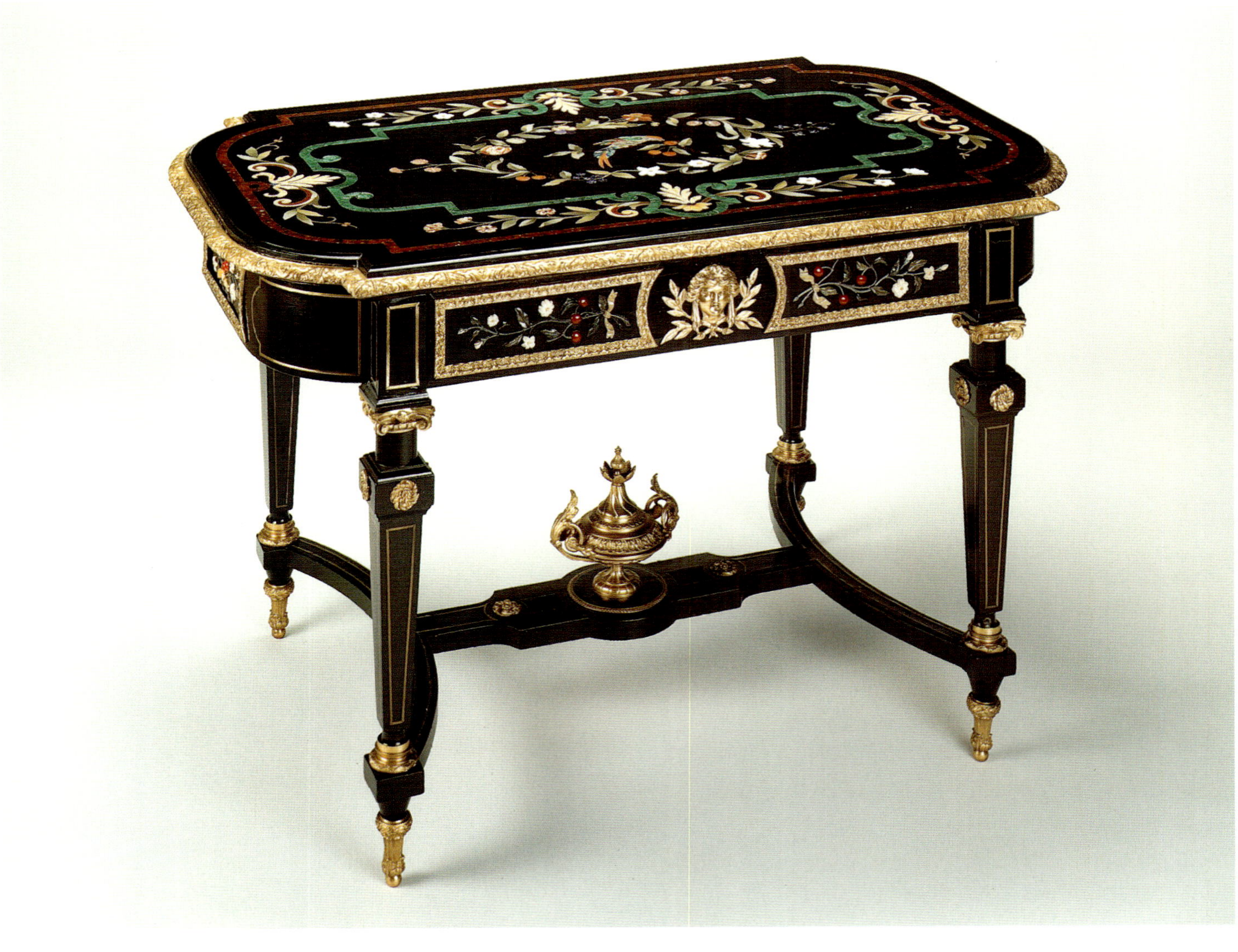

38. PAIR OF SPECIMEN TABLES

Tops: Rome, late nineteenth century; bases: England, late nineteenth century
Marble, gilt metal, gilt wood, 90.8 × 153.7 × 51.4 cm (35¾ × 60 × 20¼ in)
1996.266 (MM118AB)

PROVENANCE: Exton Park, Rutland; Crowther of Syon Lodge, London, 1971.

LITERATURE: Avery and Emperatori 1975, nos. 41–42.

EXHIBITIONS: Los Angeles, 1975; London, 1975; Los Angeles, 1977.

DESCRIPTION: A pair of rectangular specimen marble tabletops, each composed of 104 lozenge-shaped, and 34 triangular-shaped, pieces of marble, edged in a narrow band of black marble. These are framed by a solid surrounding band of pink and white marble known as *fior di pesco* (peach blossom). The bases are in the Adam style with six straight-fluted, carved legs of circular section supporting square plinths below a wide apron with fluted sections, carved urns over each leg, and a central carved reserve of a recumbent lion.

COMMENTARY: Tabletops such as these with specimens of Italian marbles were objects of special interest for collectors who wished to display their connoisseurship. Christopher Gilbert has described a pair of particular quality by Giacomo Raffaelli and Giuseppe Leonardi (Temple Newsam House), acquired in Rome by Sir Clifford Constable (1806–89) while on his honeymoon in 1827.[1] Like many of the best examples, these are accompanied by diagrams

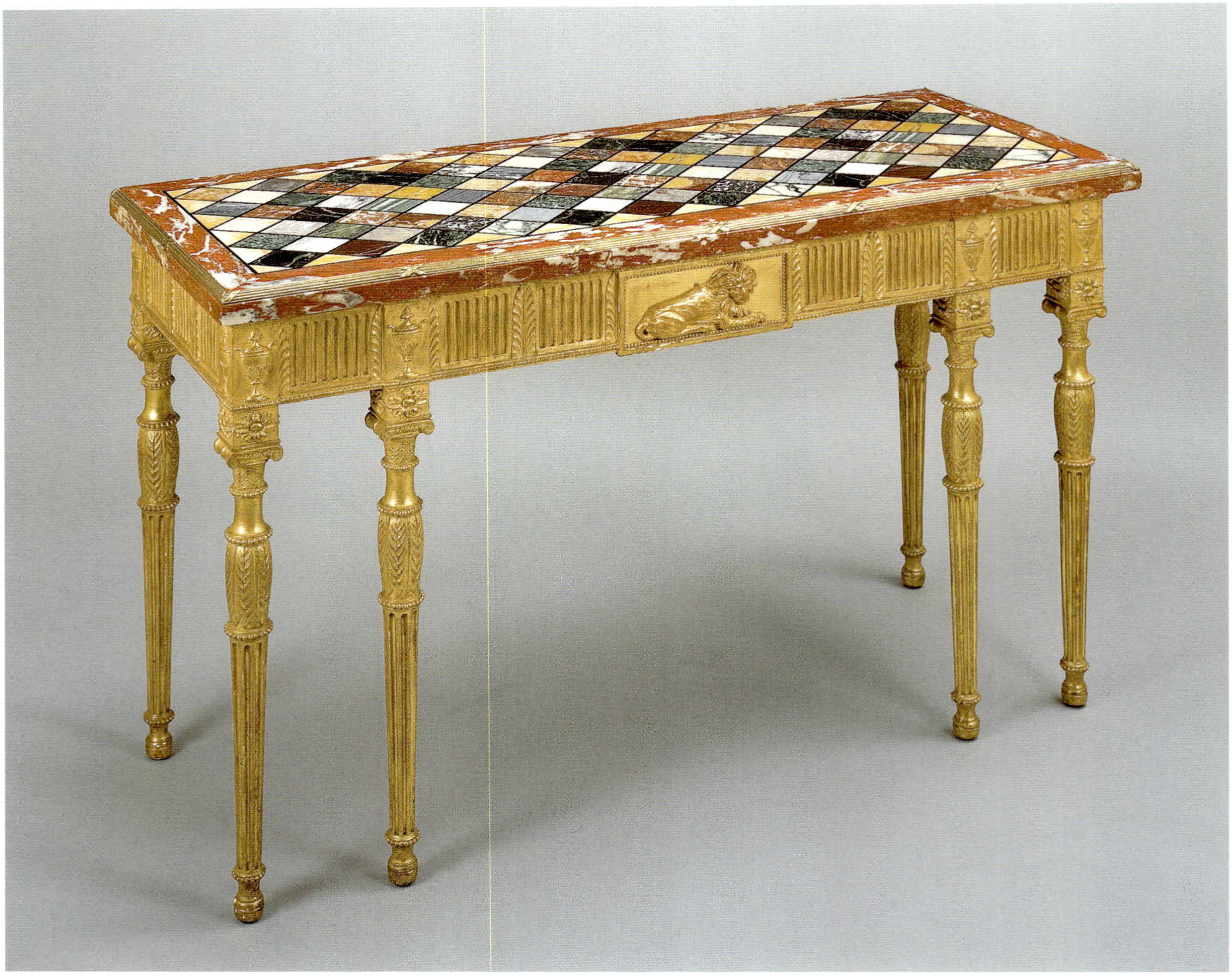

identifying each type of marble used.

Another pair of Neapolitan tabletops in the same collection, one with specimen marbles, was purchased earlier by the English antiquary, collector and patron, William Constable (1721–91) on his Grand Tour of 1769–71. He ordered frames for them from Thomas Chippendale (1718?–79) in 1778, illustrating the manner in which tourists brought home Italian tabletops to mount in English furniture. James Parker cites a sale of 18 November 1782, in which a table formerly in the collection of Madame de Pompadour (1721–64) is described as 'a top of Roman stones forming a complete collection, as rare as they are precious, of all the marbles in Italy, in compartments of regular lozenges'. Another table in the Kress Collection at the Metropolitan Museum of Art has a base by Ince and Mayhew made for the sixth Earl of Coventry, at Croom Court in about 1794.[2] Sir William Chambers (1726–96), the architect of Somerset House, designed a marquetry table incorporating specimen marbles, executed by John Linnell c. 1768–70.

The Gilbert Collection pieces are identical to a pair of side tables of 1775 in the Royal Collection, purchased by Queen Mary in 1931.[3] Another pair of superb specimen tables of 1765 with similar neoclassical bases are at Burghley.[4] A pair of late eighteenth-century examples with tops identical to the Gilbert Collection tables is at the Borghese Palace.[5]

NOTES

1 Thanks to Michela Biseo for bringing these to my attention and to Christopher Gilbert for offering further information. Christopher Gilbert, 'A pair of Roman Marble Centre Tables', *NACF Review* 1991, pp. 117–120.

2 James Parker, *Decorative Art from the Samuel H. Kress Collection at the New York Metropolitan Museum of Art*, New York, Phaidon Press 1964, pp. 41–42.

3 *Treasures from the Royal Collection* 1988, exhibition catalogue, The Queen's Gallery, Buckingham Palace, no. 97.

4 Treasure Houses of Great Britain, National Gallery, Washington D.C. 1985, no. 227.

5 Della Pergola 1971, pp. 44–45, figs. 24–25.

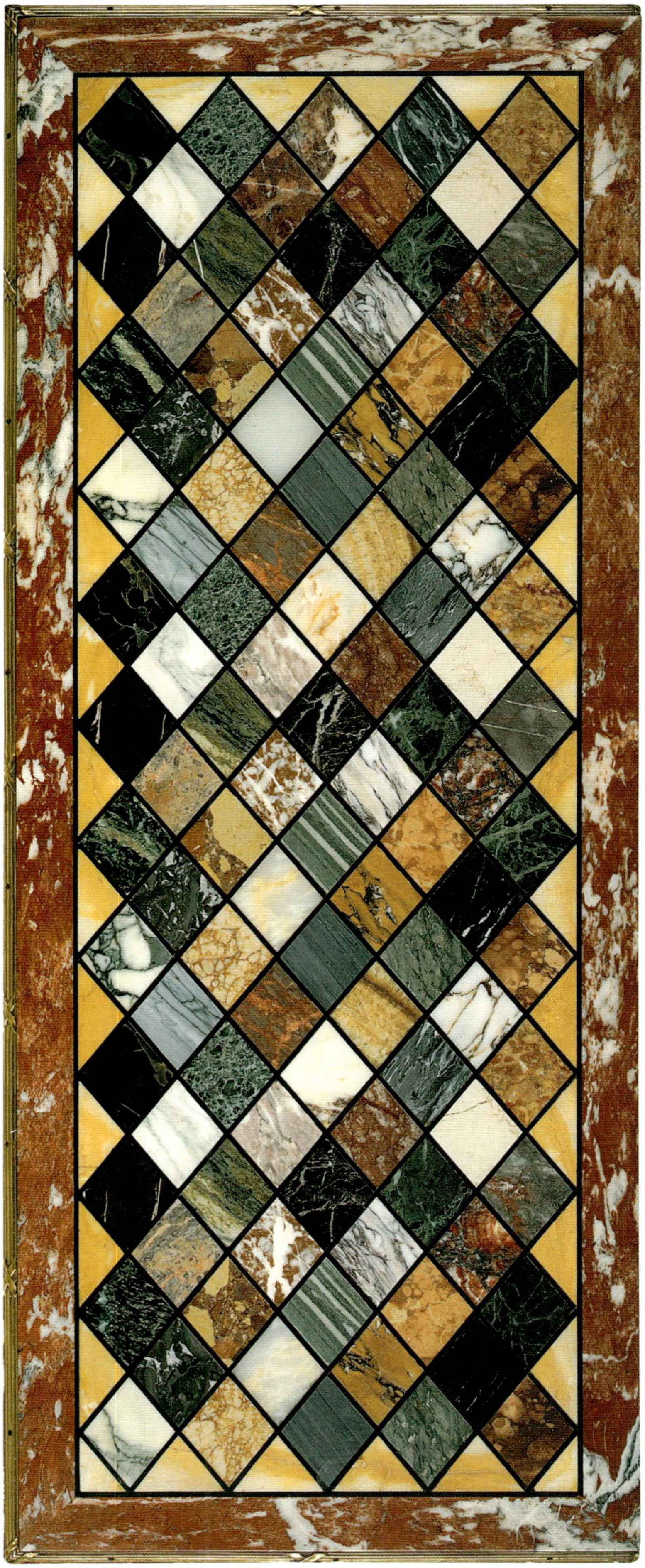

Ecclesiastical Objects

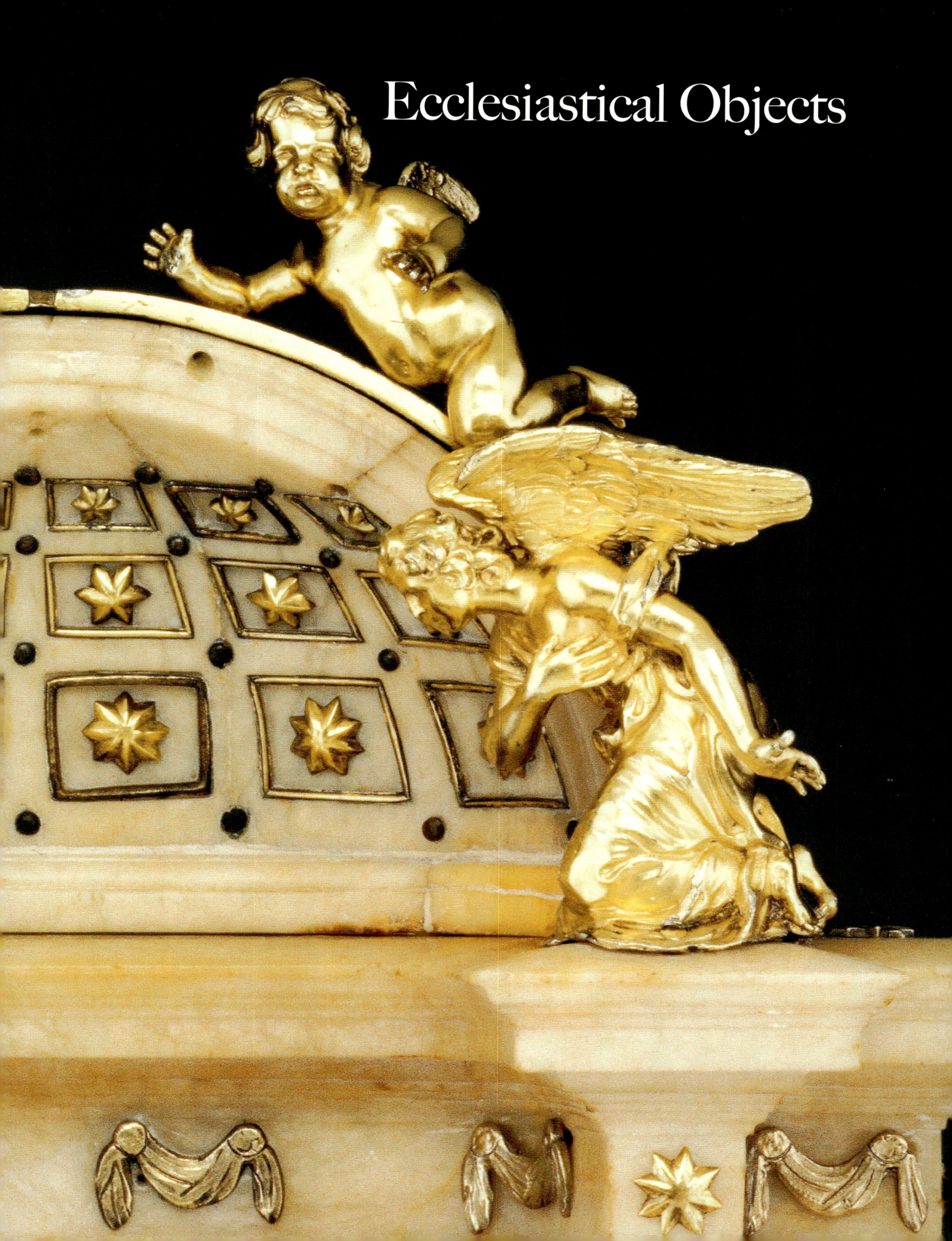

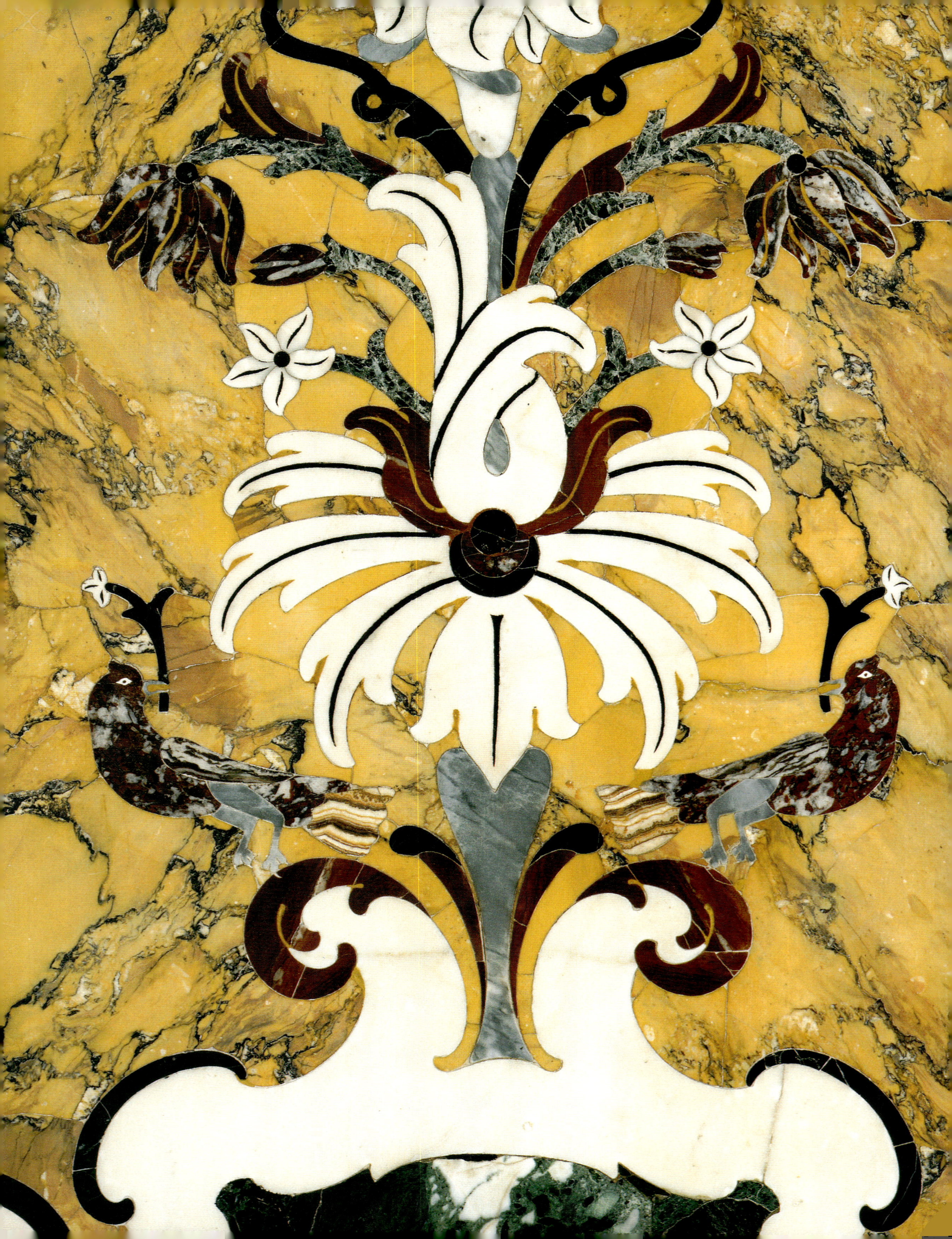

ECCLESIASTICAL OBJECTS

In addition to the use of hardstones for the decoration of cabinets, caskets, clocks, and tables, *pietre dure* was widely employed for ecclesiastical decoration. Floors, walls, steps, altars, tabernacles and the reliquaries of chapels, churches, and cathedrals were all subject to such treatment. In 1853 Antonio Zobi discussed the two oldest examples of ecclesiastical ornamentation executed in inlaid marble: the floor of the Duomo in Siena and the altars in the Certosa in Pavia.[1]

The construction of the paved floor in the Duomo, begun in the fourteenth century, was protracted until the mid-sixteenth century. It seems likely that Duccio di Boninsegna (c. 1255–1319) was employed there in 1310; 40 artists were at work on the floor, nearly all of them Sienese, between 1369 and 1547. The 56 panels of the paving contain a series of linked designs featuring coats-of-arms, allegorical figures, and scenes from the Old Testament executed in black, white, and coloured marble from the hills around Siena. The technique used was close to that of wood intarsia: the silhouettes of the figures were cut into different coloured pieces of marble, and the patches of colour thus obtained were softened by shading with an engraving tool (the engraved lines were etched as deep as required by the drawing).

Results closely resembling Florentine mosaic work were obtained in the mid-sixteenth century on the altar frontals in the Certosa. This work was begun in the early sixteenth century by Giovanni Battista Sacchi, a member of a family that ran an intarsia and mosaic workshop in the city until the eighteenth century. The mosaics in the Certosa display intricate floral designs executed in *pietre dure* and marble; the semiprecious stones most often used are lapis lazuli, oriental and German agate, and jasper from Sicily and Cyprus. Although Zobi emphasises more than once the technical uneveness and slight roughness of the work in Pavia compared with what was produced in Florence, it is undoubtedly true that when the Florentine workshop was being set up, these were the mosaics that the stoneworkers wanted to emulate. A payment made to Nicodemo Ferrucci (1574–1650) on 14 April 1597 shows that he was sent to the Certosa to measure and make drawings of the *pietre dure* ciborium and to colour the drawing.[2]

In Rome at this time, the taste in ecclesiastical decoration was quite different in spirit, the stoneworkers having access to large quantities of antique marble among the ruins of the imperial city. They used great slices of this to decorate their walls. In these early examples, handsome slabs of coloured marble were juxtaposed in such a way as to achieve rich decorative effects.[3] Mosaic decoration began in the final three decades of the century when papal commissions gave a great boost to church decoration, involving artists like Giacomo della Porta (1537–1602), Carlo Maderno (1556–1629), Domenico Fontana (1543–1607), and Giovanni Battista della Porta (c. 1542–1597). In the decorations they designed, mosaic panels are inserted around the edges of the panels of marble on walls, altars, and memorial slabs. *Pietre dure* techniques do not appear to have spread to the stone workshops of Rome, where

Previous page
Detail of cat. no. 48

Opposite
Detail of cat. no. 45

the decorative inlay was made; one possible reason for this absence is that semiprecious stones, more difficult to cut and inlay than marble, may have been the province of goldsmiths rather than of marble masons.

Very small-scale inlaid work, aiming at the gem-like refinement that was the fashion in Florence and Milan, can be found on the cornices of the chapel of San Filippo in Santa Maria in Vallicella, Rome, where Onorio Longhi and other Roman craftsmen were employed; the decorations were completed in 1600. Jasper, lapis lazuli, and mother-of-pearl are inlaid in a border of stylised flowers and panels; the untidy joints between the stones are covered with strips of gilded copper for which the goldsmith Bartolomeo de' Bardi received payment.[4] The enthusiasm aroused by this type of work is shown in a document dating from 1602, when Pope Clement VIII gave a certain Giacomo Antonio Cremona permission 'to introduce to Rome the art of making inlaid work of all kinds from gem stones such as agate, [lapis] lazuli, jasper, and rock crystal'.[5] This would appear to refer to one of the few craftsmen to bring to Rome the skill of cutting *pietre dure*, classified as 'gem stones' (the term had been in use in Milan and Florence for several decades by this time).

The taste for marble facings in ecclesiastical decoration was also widespread in Tuscany during the second half of the sixteenth century. In Siena, the architect and sculptor Flaminio del Turco (d. 1634), whose activity is documented from 1581, used local marble and alabaster from the quarry in Castelnuovo dell' Abate in his altar decorations, adding inlaid semiprecious stones. Halfway through the seventeenth century there were more than 70 altars decorated like this in the region of Siena, 'rich with gems, beautifully designed and executed with consummate skill'.[6] The most important work in this field was being done in Florence, however, first of all by Giovanni Antonio Dosio. His sojourns in Rome (1549–63, 1566–75, 1578–82) meant that the fashion for marble wall facings in family chapels was brought to Florence. Dosio's style was perfectly suited to the taste of the Florentine collector, Niccolò Gaddi, and their collaboration marked an important stage in the development of coloured marble church decoration. The Gaddi chapel in Santa Maria Novella (1575–78) was completed, and the decoration of the Niccolini chapel in Santa Croce was begun in 1582.[7] By the 1570s, echoes of schemes being carried out in Rome were making themselves heard in Florence in undertakings like the Cavalcanti chapel in San Spirito, completed in 1562. The Roman training of Giovanni Caccini (1556–1613) should not be overlooked, as he was influential in introducing to Florence the Roman use of *specchiature* (wall facings) in costly types of marble within the internal architectural construction of ecclesiastical buildings. The ciborium of the church of San Spirito and the oratory of San Sebastian, attached to the church of the Santissima Annunziata, show the direct influence of Rome.

The most ambitious scheme of all was Vasari's grandiose plan (1563–64) for the Cappella dei Principi, the Medici mausoleum in San Lorenzo. It was so ambitious, in fact, that the interior *pietre dure* decoration, begun in 1613, dragged on until the early years of the twentieth century. Without reviewing the complex series of events surrounding the construction and decoration of the chapel and the ciborium, already the subject of close study,[8] it might be worthwhile to mention how, after Vasari's initial involvement in the planning stages, followed by Bernardo Buontalenti's intervention, the whole architectural and ornamental scheme was subject to direct interference from Don Giovanni de' Medici (1567–1621), assisted by the architect Matteo Nigetti (1580–1649). Later, Nigetti became the sole interpreter of the wishes of Don Giovanni and of Ferdinand I.

When the building of the chapel was finished, the *pietre dure* decoration of the interior began, using a great number and variety of semiprecious stones, in particular the violet-coloured jasper of Barga. The grandiloquent style and opulence of the materials were already causing a stir among visitors, whose response to the chapel was so overwhelmingly enthusiastic that it was considered one of the wonders of the world. Work proceeded slowly as the century wore on; in 1650 Giovanni Battista Balatri succeeded his uncle Matteo Nigetti as chief architect, then in 1673 the responsibility passed to Pier Maria Baldi and in 1695 to Giovanni Battista Foggini. The architects worked alongside a whole series of *pietre dure* craftsmen who were preparing the mosaic work for the walls and the elaborate tabernacle in the Grand Ducal workshops. Because the tabernacle was not finished, it was not installed in the chapel but remained in the Galleria degli Uffizi until the end of the eighteenth century, when it was dismantled. The costly ornamentation, including columns in agate and rock crystal, statuettes in three-dimensional mosaic, mosaic panels, and the structure itself, were all dispersed to different places to be put to different uses.[9]

The decorative work carried out on the Medici chapel inevitably influenced taste in ecclesiastical decoration in the seventeenth century. The recurrent decorative themes used in the craft workshops involved in altar decorations were generally based on inlaid plant motifs and coats-of-arms; *pietre tenere* was used on a background of white Carrara marble. In the more routine schemes, decoration was limited to the facing of the walls with slabs of different coloured marble or the application of panels with inlaid cartouches to the top few steps of the altar.

The panels in the Gilbert Collection (cat. no. 41) may have been intended to face the steps of an altar. Their cartouches recall the late sixteenth-century panels in the Caetani chapel in Santa Pudenziana in Rome, but the combination of flat and relief mosaic and the inexpert technique of the central rosettes and of the palmettes bordering the cartouches may indicate that these belong to a less opulent Neapolitan tradition and derive from the fashion set by Cosimo Fanzago (1591–1678). Other fragments of ecclesiastical ornamentation in the Gilbert Collection – the two facings for pilaster strips in coloured marble mosaic (cat. no. 45) and the two pairs of balustrades (cat. nos. 46–47) – belong to the same background.

Studies of the work of Fanzago have increased during the last few years. He moved from Clusone (Bergamo) to Naples in 1608 and began working as a sculptor in the workshop of his brother-in-law, Angelo Laudi, who was Tuscan. His prolonged labours in the Certosa di San Martino, where he succeeded Giovan Giacomo di Conforto in 1631, probably laid the foundations for his particular style of ornamentation. This, and the way in which he organised his workshop, earned him his reputation as a 'versatile entrepreneur'. [10] The style of stone inlay work that had developed in Naples thanks to the influence of Tuscan master craftsmen now, under Fanzago, began to acquire a local style of ornamentation that would survive until the rococo period. He succeeded in abandoning the dense floral schemes in use at the time by the Neapolitan marble workers, which were often derived from fabric designs. Having absorbed the Roman taste for marble wall facing, Fanzago devised a style of inlay for the architectural mouldings consisting of opulent plant patterns, with extended and somewhat simplified tendrils and rosettes that were particularly suitable for reproduction, in series if need be. The balustrades leading up to the altar, which in Rome and Florence followed the classical pattern of a sequence of three-dimensional elements turned to look like vases, were transformed by Fanzago with great slabs of marble bearing a patchwork of shapes in different marbles, as for instance in the high altar in the church of Santa Maria delle Anime del Purgatorio in Naples.[11] The large number of marble masons who were apprenticed to Fanzago or trained in the workshops of the monastery of San Martino spread the taste for decoration in the style of Fanzago in Naples and in the Campania. The resulting schemes reiterated the same themes over and over again, until the first decades of the eighteenth century, but they conferred an unmistakable character on Neapolitan ecclesiastical ornamentation between the baroque and rococo periods.[12]

NOTES

1 Zobi 1853, pp. 145–60.
2 Ibid., p.195.
3 Di Castro, Peccolo and Gazzaniga 1994.
4 Tuena 1989, fig. 29.
5 González-Palacios 1988a, p. 46.
6 Ugurgeri Azzolini 1640, p. 392; for a biography of the artist, see Franchina 1990, pp. 321–23.
7 On Dosio's activity in Florence, see Morrogh 1985.
8 Baldini, Giusti and Pampaloni Martelli 1979; *Splendori di pietre dure* 1988, pp. 62–73.
9 Przyborowski 1982; *Splendori di pietre dure* 1988, pp. 108–35.
10 Cantone 1969, p. 227.
11 *Civiltà del 600 a Napoli* 1984, p. 289.
12 On the activity of Fanzago, see Causa 1967; Cantone 1969; Madruga 1975; Boesel 1978; Pane 1984.

39. TABERNACLE

Rome, mid-seventeenth century
Agate, alabaster, jasper, lapis lazuli, gilt bronze, gilt copper, 55.9 × 27.3 × 14 cm (22 × 10¾ × 5½ in)
1996.285 (MM140)

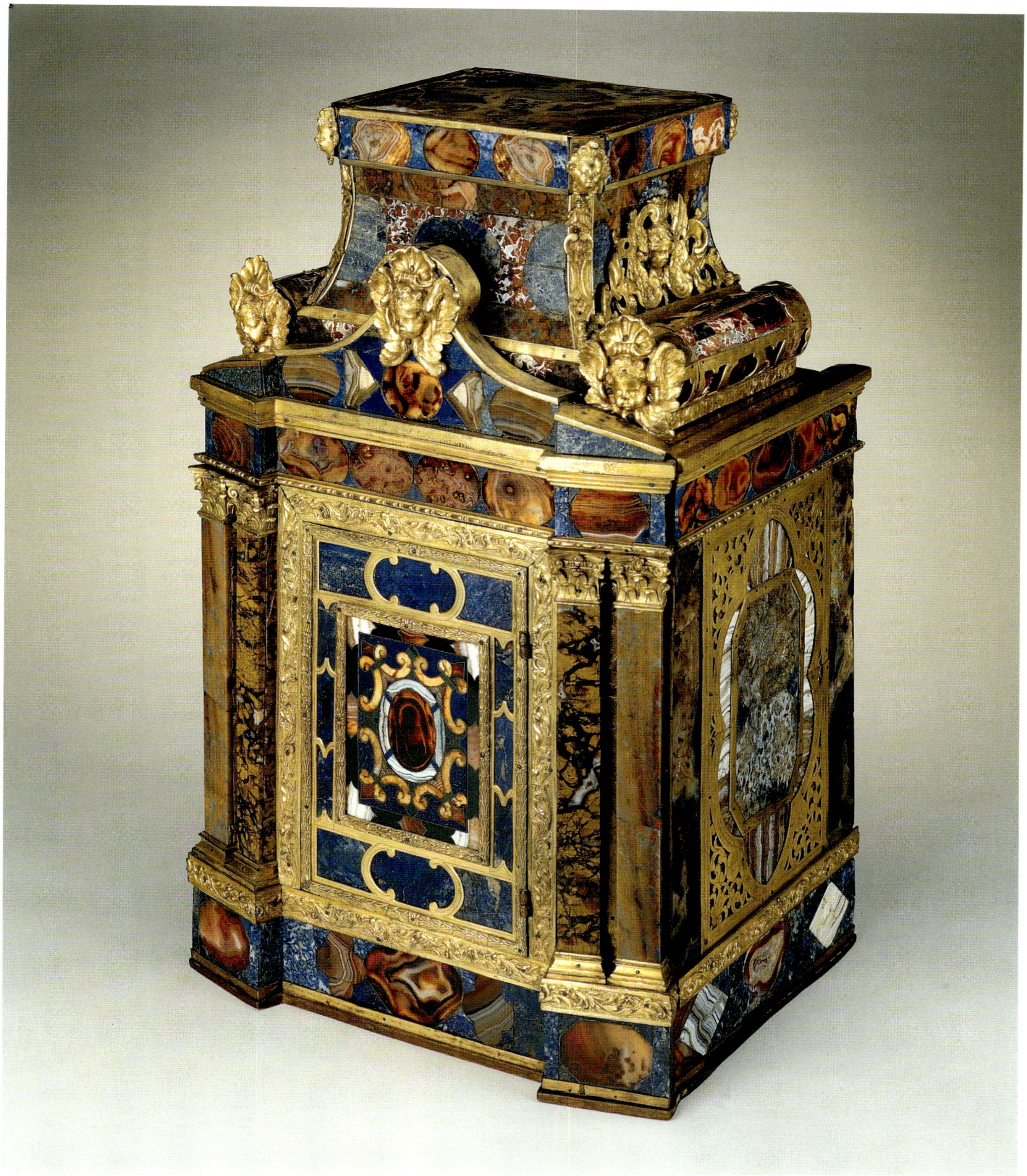

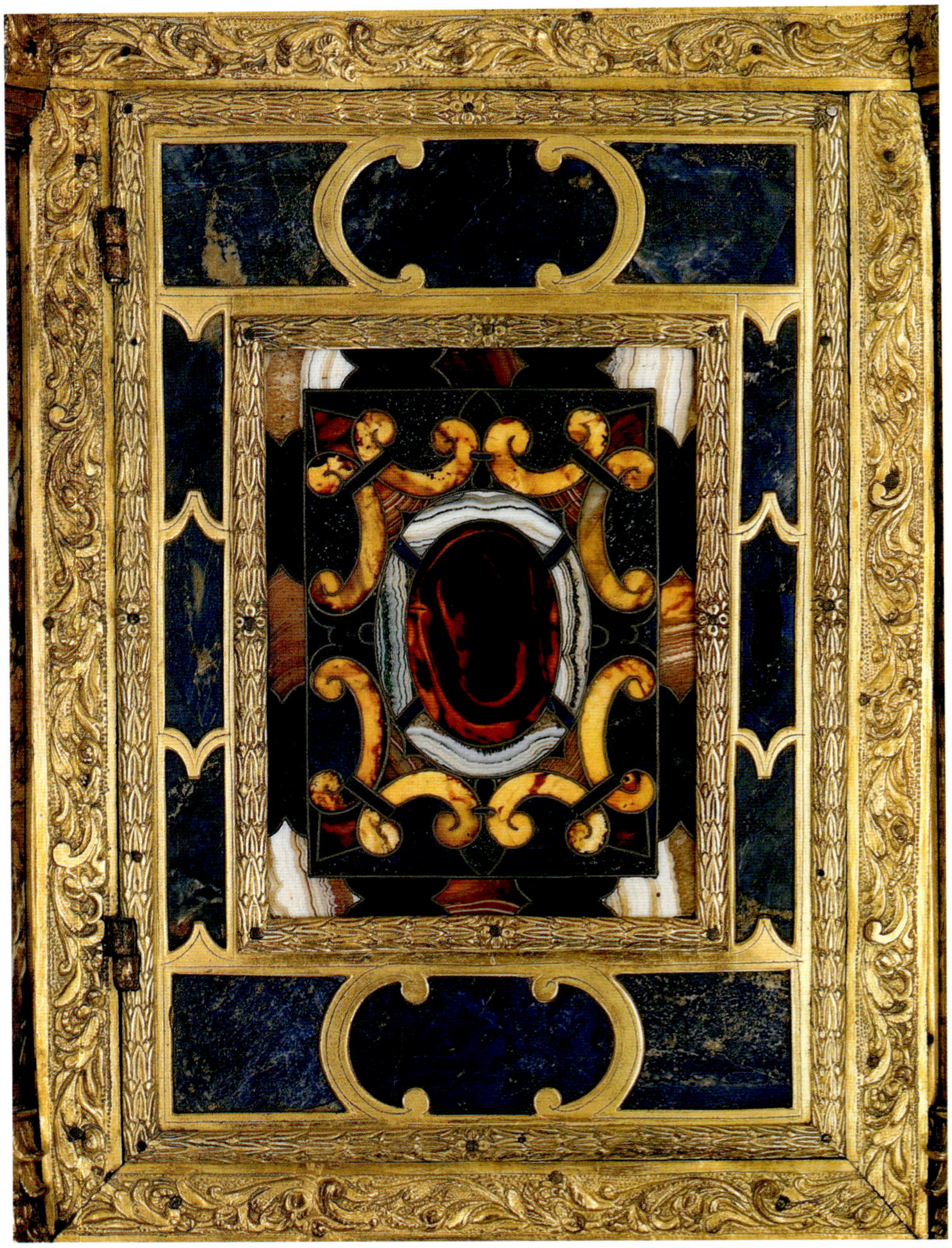

PROVENANCE: Alberto di Castro, Rome, 1972.

LITERATURE: González-Palacios 1977a, no. 9; González-Palacios and Röttgen 1982, no. 9.

EXHIBITIONS: Los Angeles / Atlanta / San Antonio / Richmond / Seattle, 1977–79.

DESCRIPTION: A wooden tabernacle with a square base, two projecting wings on either side of the central door, and a pediment above the cornice. The flat lid bears a movable element, presumably designed as a stand for a chalice. It is faced with lapis lazuli, agate, and jasper and mounted with gilt bronze, with a rectangular base and concave walls. The walls of the tabernacle are completely covered by panels of stone with gilt-bronze mounts. The top and base have borders of lapis lazuli inlaid with oval, quatrefoil, and lozenge shapes in agate and chalcedony. The façade has coupled pilasters made of jasper with gilt-bronze Corinthian capitals and bases. The opening in the façade is outlined by a gilt-bronze border chased with a frieze of acanthus leaves like the one applied above the lower band of lapis lazuli. The doorway has a gilt-bronze border with a lotus-flower motif. The joints in the lapis lazuli border are concealed by strips of bronze. A lotus-flower border like the one on the door outlines the central panel, which contains an oval panel of chalcedony, bordered by pairs of scrolls, also of chalcedony, joined with bloodstone links, the remainder filled with lapis lazuli. The walls are flanked by two vertical bands of agate; in the centre is a rectangular plate of fretted copper gilt with a lobed inner profile, which frames a sheet of onyx overlaid with a rectangular copper-gilt framework. Inside this are two pieces of alabaster, one on top of the other, with canted corners filled with triangular pieces of lapis lazuli.

COMMENTARY: The slightly blurred joints between the oval inlays in the lower and upper borders suggest that originally all the pieces were outlined with metal or wooden strips, after the fashion prevalent in Rome in the first half of the seventeenth century. Strips like this can be found on the stone intarsia in the reliquary of the Pallavicini Collection, Rome, where the inlay on the border strongly resembles that on the Gilbert Collection tabernacle.[1]

NOTE

1 *Splendori di pietre dure* 1988, p. 144.

40. PANEL

Naples, second half seventeenth century
Coloured marble, breccia, mother-of-pearl, 45.1 × 130.8 cm (17¾ × 51½ in)
(MM74)

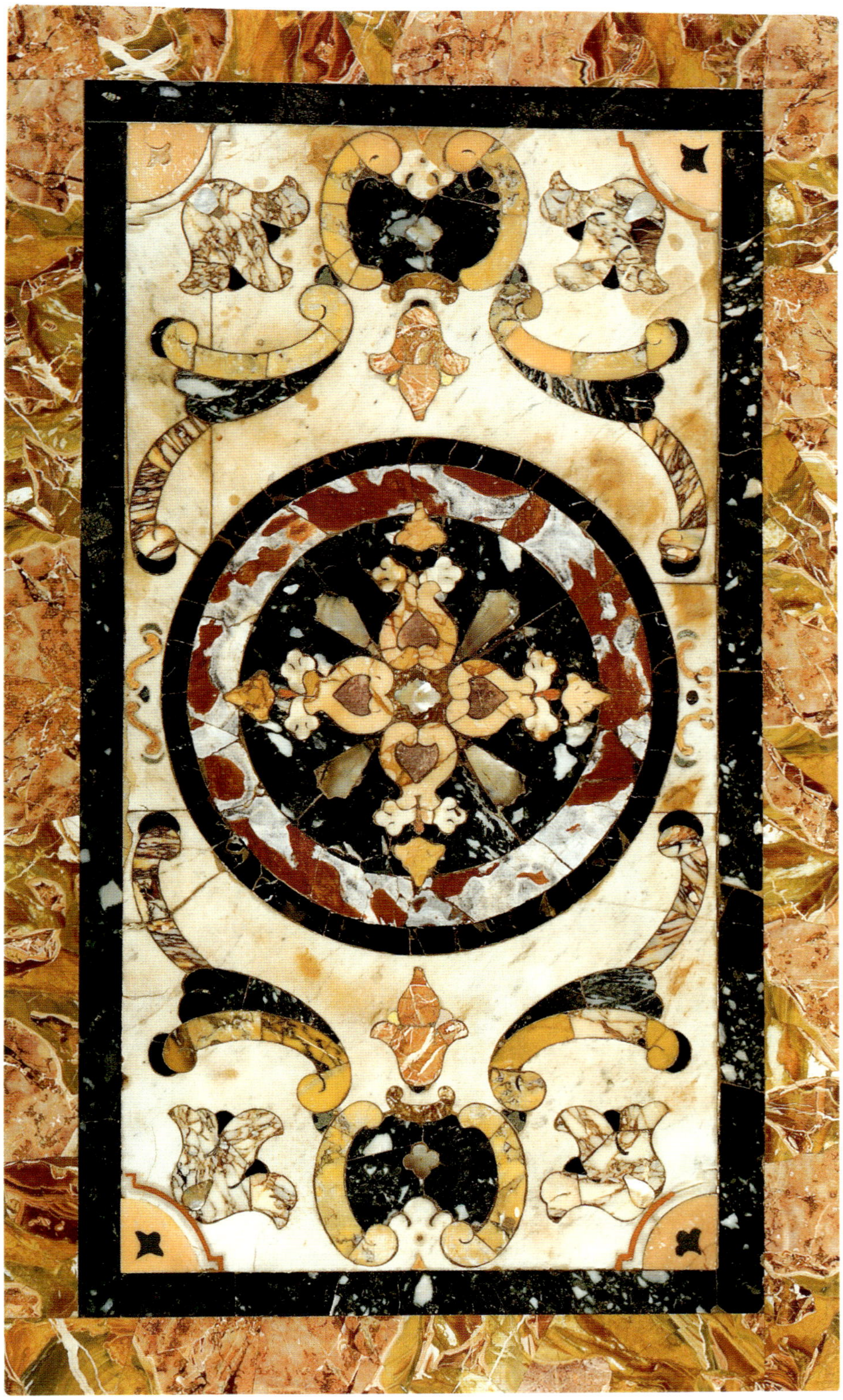

PROVENANCE: Giuseppe Constantini, Rome, 1971.

DESCRIPTION: Rectangular panel of coloured and variegated marbles, with a large central roundel, and scrolls and palmettes at the corners, executed and inlaid with breccia and coloured marble with smaller roundels of mother-of-pearl.

COMMENTARY: This inlaid panel was probably designed for the front of an altar and is characteristic of the output of Neapolitan marble workshops in the second half of the seventeenth century. Both the quality of the marble and the design, with its large, central roundel and surrounding volutes, suggest comparisons with the inlaid floor of the Certosa di San Martino in Naples.[1]

NOTE

1 Rossi, 1967, pl. 15.

41. FOUR PANELS

Central Italy, seventeenth century
Coloured marble, panels (combined): 144.8 × 92.1 × 5.0 cm (57 × 36¼ × 2½ in)
(MM63)

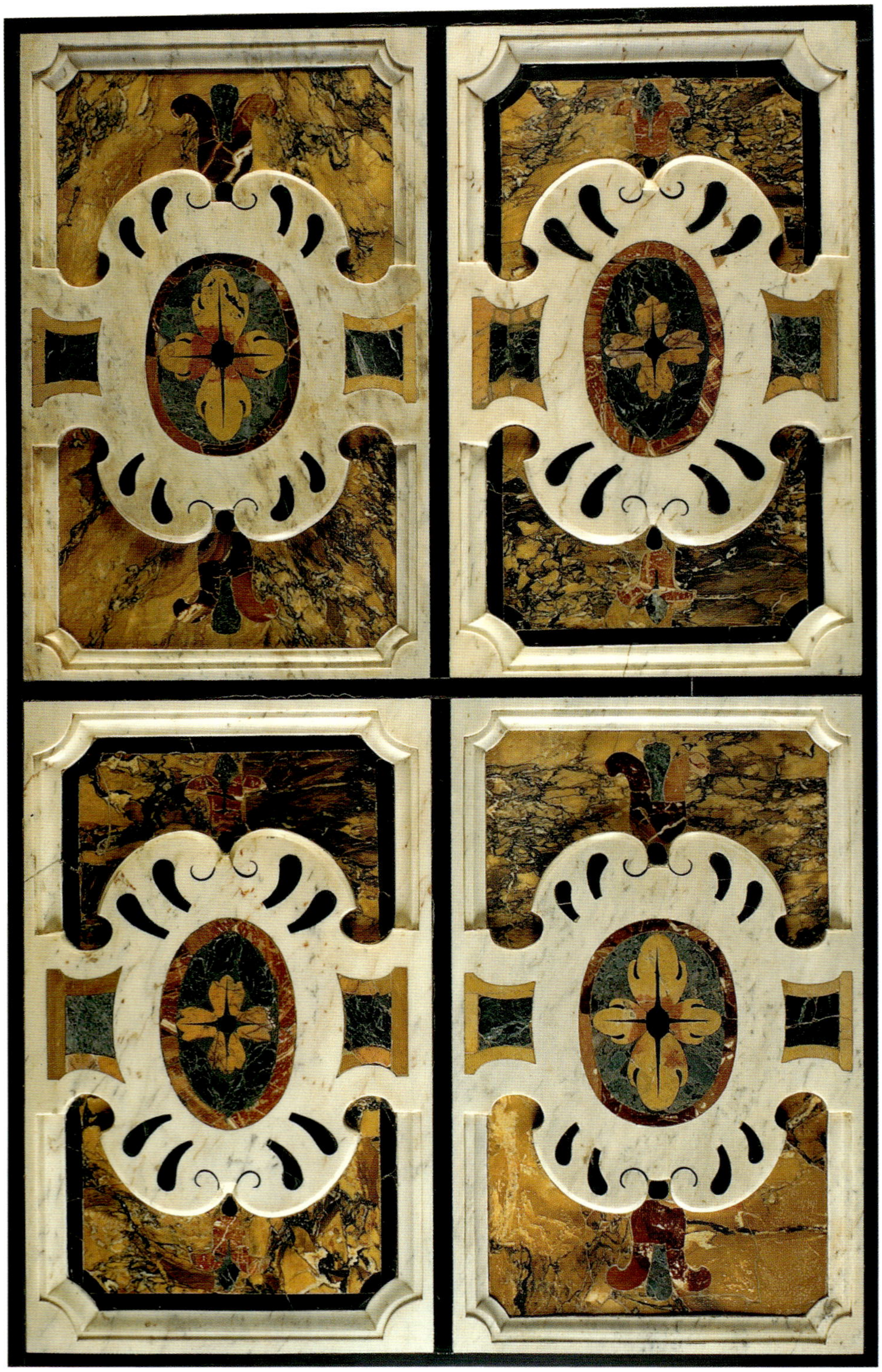

PROVENANCE: Dino Levi, Florence, 1969.

DESCRIPTION: Four rectangular panels of yellow marble with borders and cartouches of white marble relief. At both ends of the cartouches are palmettes; in the centre is a rosette.

COMMENTARY: It is not known where these panels originated, but they were probably designed to ornament the upper steps of an altar. Decoration of this type has frequently been recorded in churches in Tuscany, at the high altar in the Duomo in Prato, for example. The style of the inlay and the combination of intarsia with relief features could also connect these panels with seventeenth-century Roman inlay work for altars and walls, such as the Caetani chapel in Santa Pudenza in Rome.[1] However, the combination of flat and relief mosaic and the technique of the central rosettes and of the palmettes bordering the cartouches may indicate that these belong to a less opulent Neapolitan tradition and derive from the fashion set by Cosimo Fanzago (1591–1678).

NOTE

1 Di Castro, Peccolo, and Gazzaniga, 1994, figs. 33, 40, 51.

42. TABERNACLE DOOR

Rome or Naples, early eighteenth century
Chalcedony, jasper, gilt bronze, silver, 53.3 × 32.7 × 7 cm (21 × 12⅞ × 2 in)
(TU92)

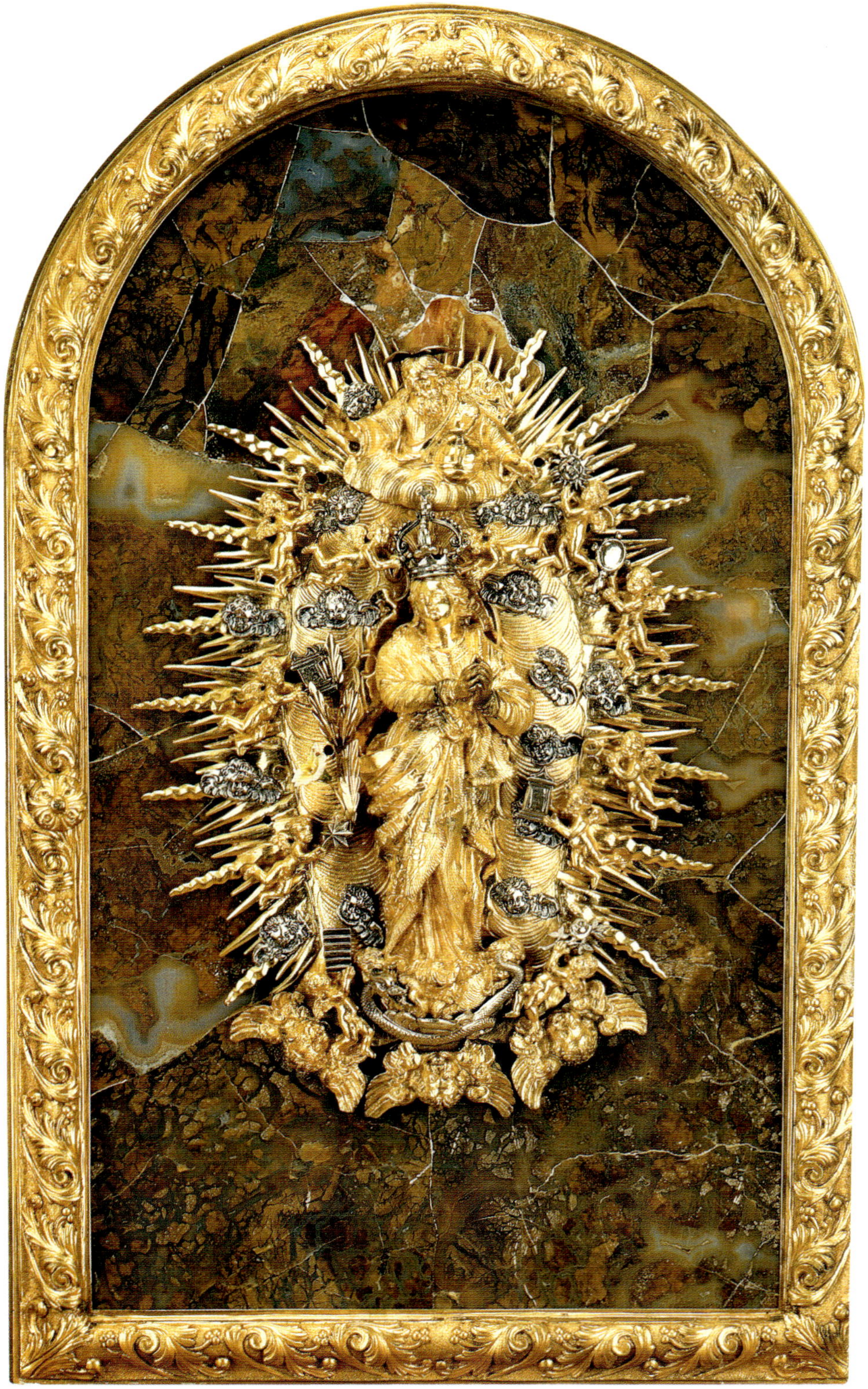

PROVENANCE: Alberto di Castro, Rome, 1976.

DESCRIPTION: A round-headed door with central panel veneered in mosaic of chalcedony and jasper. The centre is applied with a relief plaque in gilt bronze and silver depicting the Virgin of the Immaculate Conception trampling the monster, surrounded by cherubim. The gilt-bronze frame is decorated with a border of acanthus leaves.

43. TABERNACLE DOORS

Southern Italy, possibly Naples, early eighteenth century
A: Lapis lazuli, gilt bronze, 61.6 × 31.1 × 8.6 cm (24¼ × 12½ × 3⅜ in) (TU90)
B: Jasper, gilt bronze, 62.5 × 31.1 × 8.9 cm (24⅝ × 12¼ × 3½ in) (TU91)

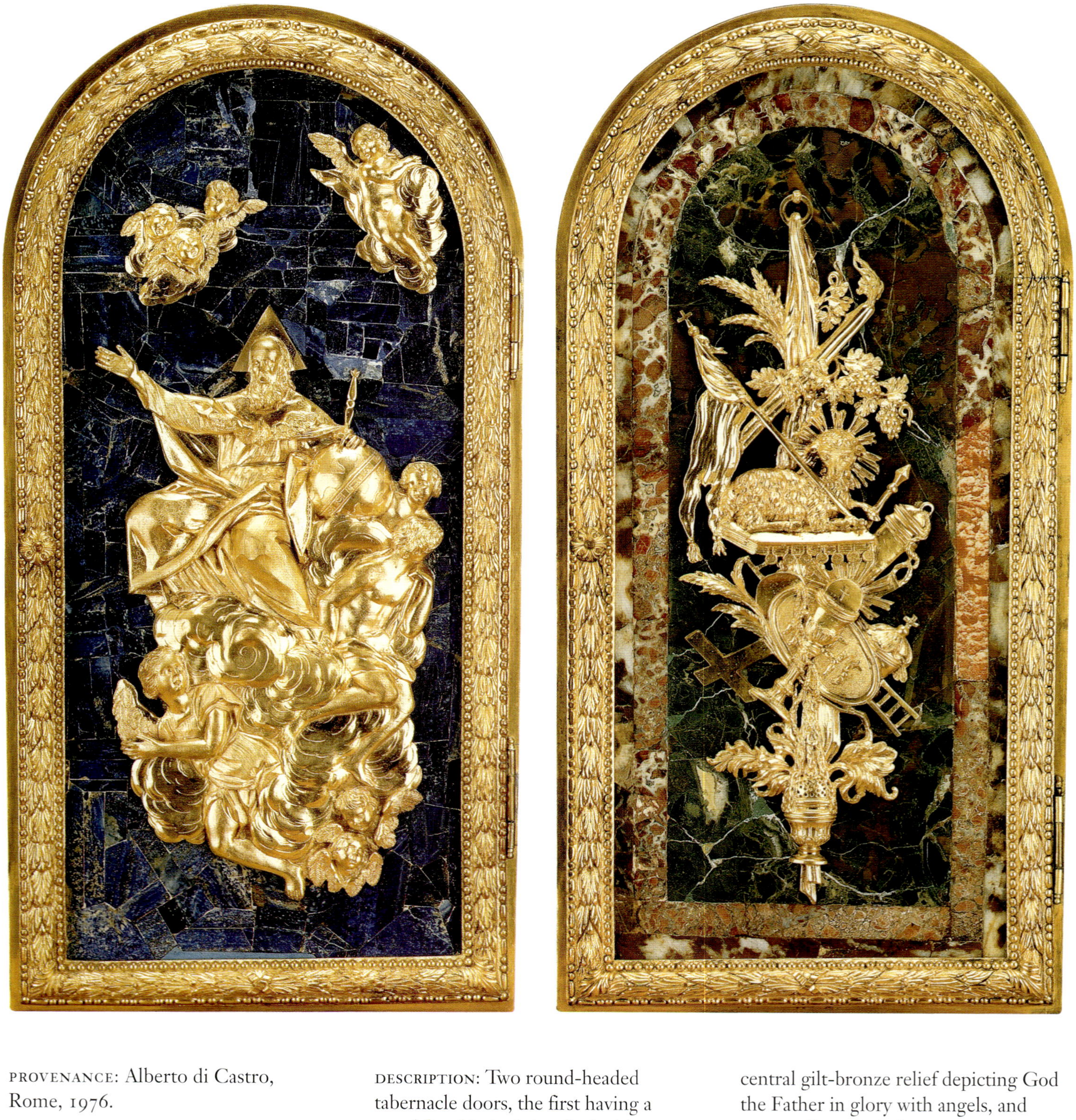

PROVENANCE: Alberto di Castro, Rome, 1976.

DESCRIPTION: Two round-headed tabernacle doors, the first having a panel faced in lapis lazuli, the blue stone acting as a background to a central gilt-bronze relief depicting God the Father in glory with angels, and two smaller reliefs depicting angels in flight. The frame is of gilt bronze chased with a garland of laurel leaves. The door still has its original handles and hinges. The second door has a panel inlaid with mosaic of jasper of various hues. In the middle is a bas-relief of gilt bronze depicting an allegory of the Eucharist with symbols of the Passion: the chalice, the host, the Agnus Dei seated on the Gospels, the thurible, grapes and wheat. The gilt-bronze border is identical to that of the first door.

COMMENTARY: The dimensions of these three doors and the design of their borders indicate that they came from the same opulent marble tabernacle. They share features with others produced in Neapolitan workshops in the first quarter of the eighteenth century. Similar designs and techniques are to be found in the door on the marble altar in the church of Santa Maria Donnaregina Nuovo in Naples, executed between 1701 and 1702.[1]

It is possible to find examples of bronze reliefs with a stone background in Roman ecclesiastical decorations. The most important work of this kind is the altar in the Coronaro Chapel (Rome, Santa Maria della Vittoria) by Gian Lorenzo Bernini (1598–1680). Depicting the Last Supper, this work is in gilt bronze on a lapis-lazuli background.[2]

NOTES

1 *Civiltà del 600 a Napoli* 1984, p 334, no. 5.29.
2 Di Castro, Peccolo and Gazzaniga 1994, fig. 152.

44. RELIQUARY

Naples, first half eighteenth century
Silver, silver gilt, green Corsican jasper, chalcedony, paper, wood, 61.6 × 21 × 16.8 cm (24¼ × 8¼ × 6⅝ in)
1999.57 (TU88)

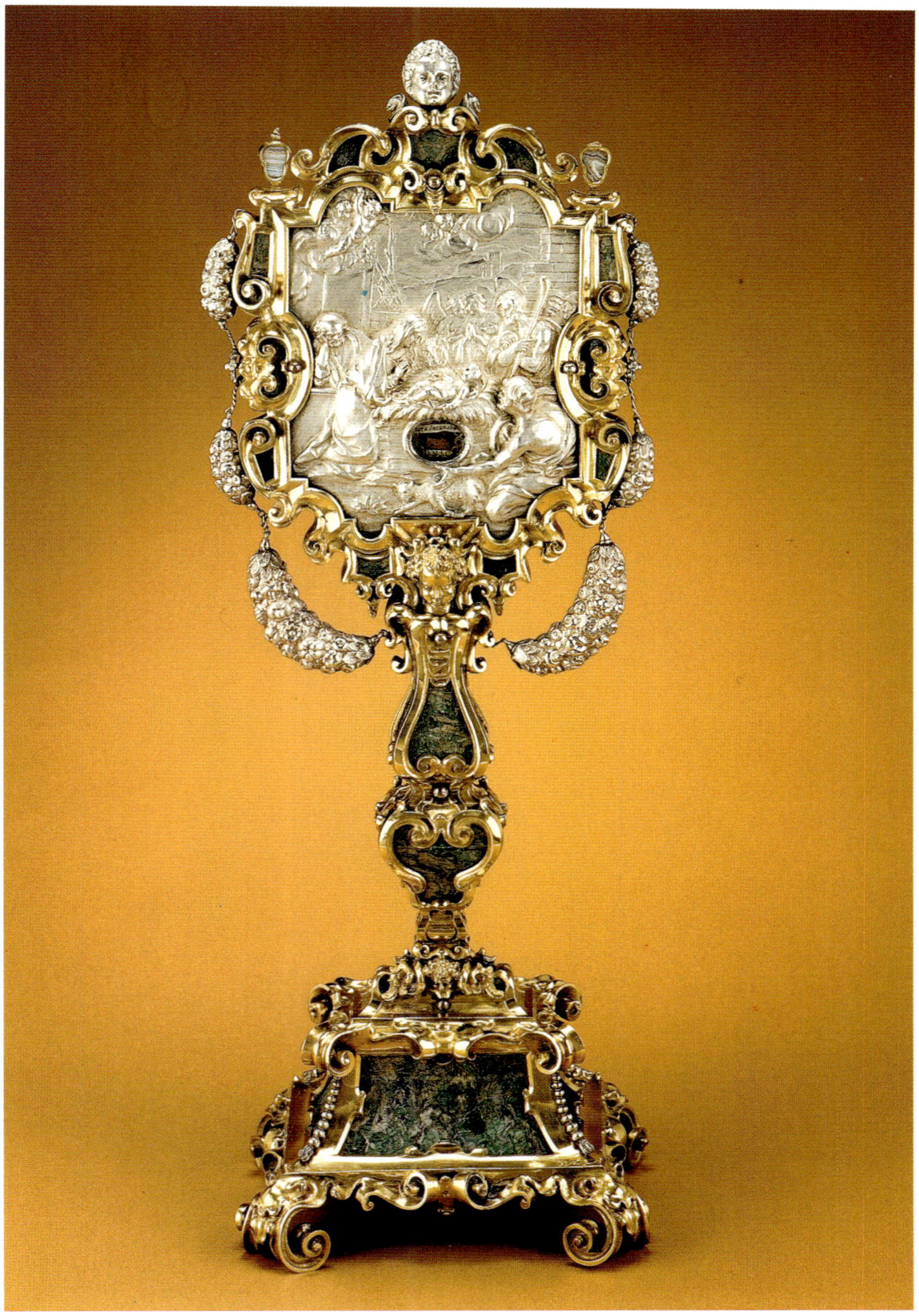

PROVENANCE: Alberto di Castro, Rome, 1976.

DESCRIPTION: Reliquary with a case decorated with a silver bas-relief depicting the Nativity, with a multilinear frame and an opening that allows a glimpse of the relic of the holy crib inside. The outer edge is of gilt bronze with volutes and framed panels of Corsican green jasper. At the top is a cherub's head; on the sides are festoons of embossed fruit and flowers attached by small chains. Another cherub's head marks the joint between the reliquary panel and the support, the latter a baluster of Corsican jasper with voluted edges of gilt bronze. The Corsican jasper base is also bordered with volutes and cartouches of gilt bronze. Around the sacred wood fragment is an inscription on paper that reads SACRA INCUNABULA D. N. J. C. (sacred birthplace of our Lord Jesus Christ).

COMMENTARY: This reliquary's elegant combination of *pietre dure*, silver, and silver gilt link it with the Neapolitan taste in church ornamentation at the end of the seventeenth century and first half of the eighteenth century. It also has a direct connection with the designs of Orazio Scoppa (fl. c. 1642–43), the Neapolitan goldsmith who was responsible for a series of 18 etchings between 1642 and 1643 that show designs for sacred and secular furnishings.[1] These designs are highly ornate, with volutes, cartouches, cherub's heads, and garlands. For many years they constituted the chief source book in the workshops of Neapolitan silversmiths; marks on the borders indicate that they were reprinted several times. The Gilbert Collection reliquary is a simplified synthesis of features from Scoppa's repertoire and is similar in design to the etching of a monstrance, which has an octagonal reliquary panel edged with a multilinear voluted cornice, from which dangle cherubs' heads and festoons of fruit.[2]

NOTES

1 G.N.S., inv. F.C. 13136-53; Catello 1981, p. 145; *Civiltà del 600 a Napoli* 1984, pp. 310-13.

2 *Civiltà del 600 a Napoli* 1984, p. 313.

45. TWO ARCHITECTURAL PANELS

Italy, early eighteenth century
Marble, each: 235.3 × 67.7 cm (92 5/8 × 25 7/8 in)
1996.222; 1996.223 (MM62AB)

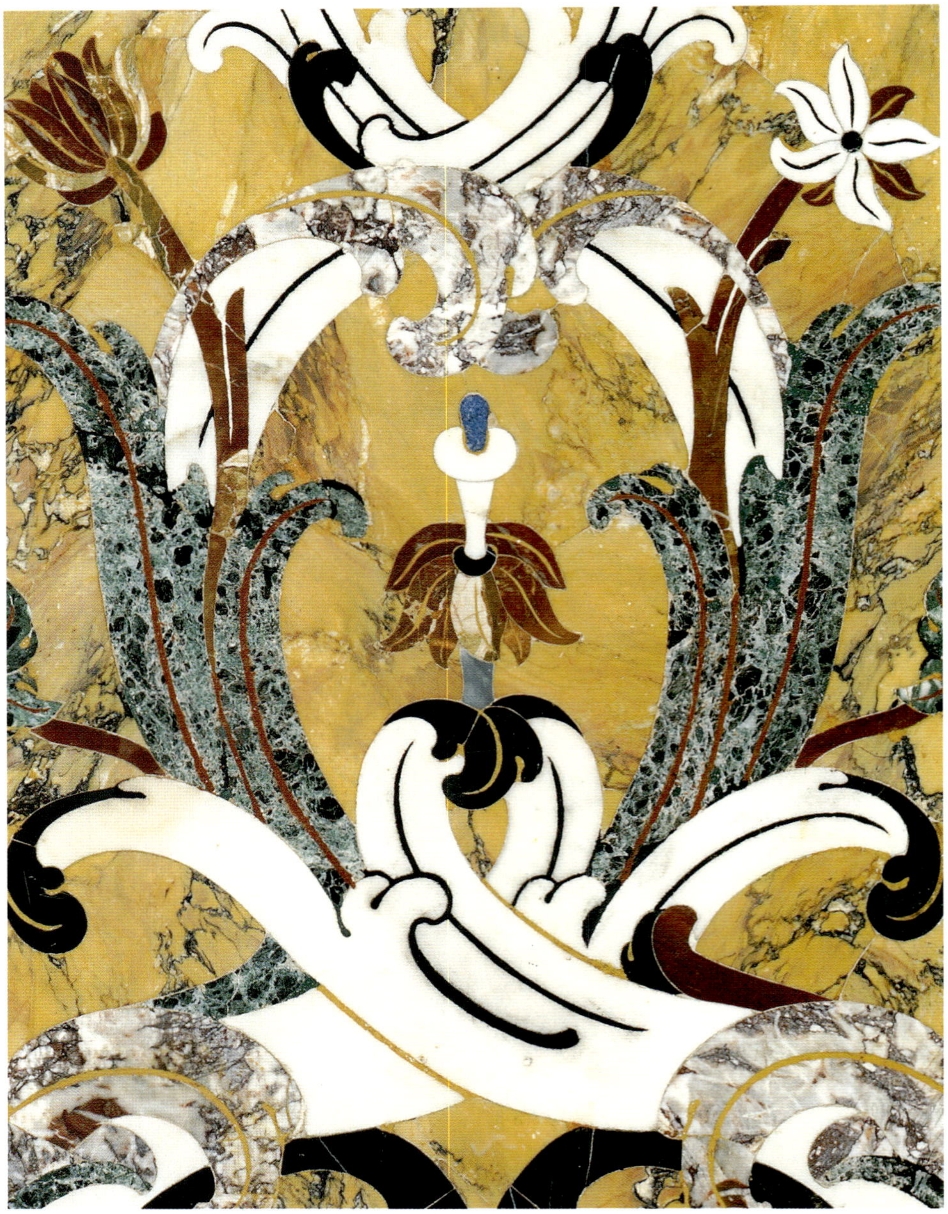

PROVENANCE: Arturo Ferrante, Rome, 1969; Los Angeles County Museum of Art.

LITERATURE: González-Palacios 1977a, no. 13; González-Palacios and Röttgen 1982, no. 13.

EXHIBITIONS: Los Angeles, 1975, 1977.

DESCRIPTION: Pair of panels made of fragments of antique yellow marble with black marble borders and a band of white marble around the edges. The short sides are inlaid with plant motifs in marble of diverse colours: yellow, green, black, white, antique red, and gray breccia. The inlay is similar in the two panels, but not identical.

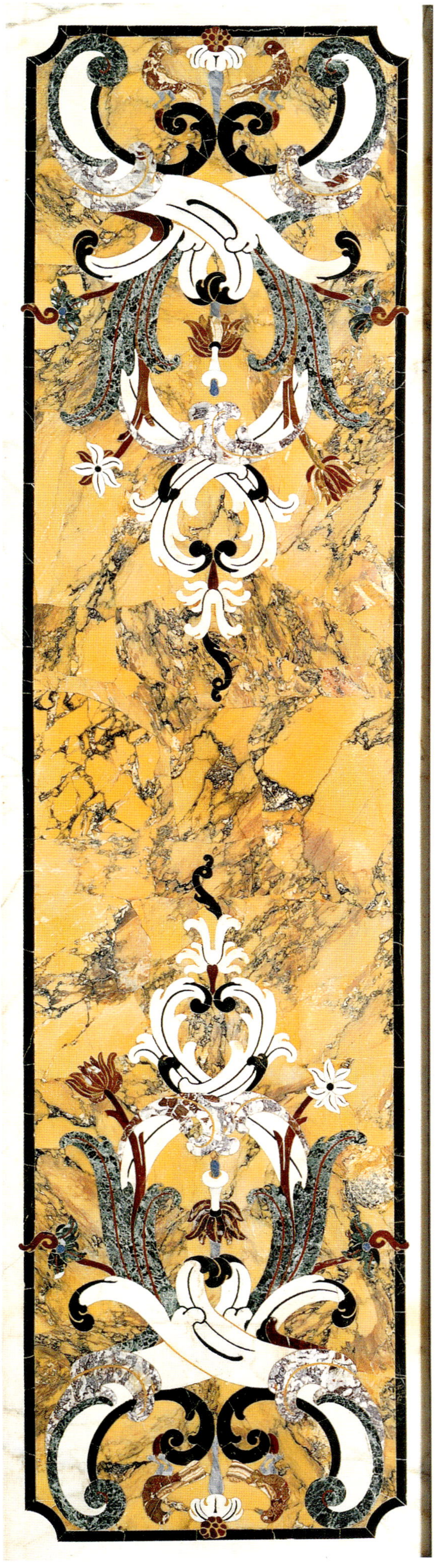
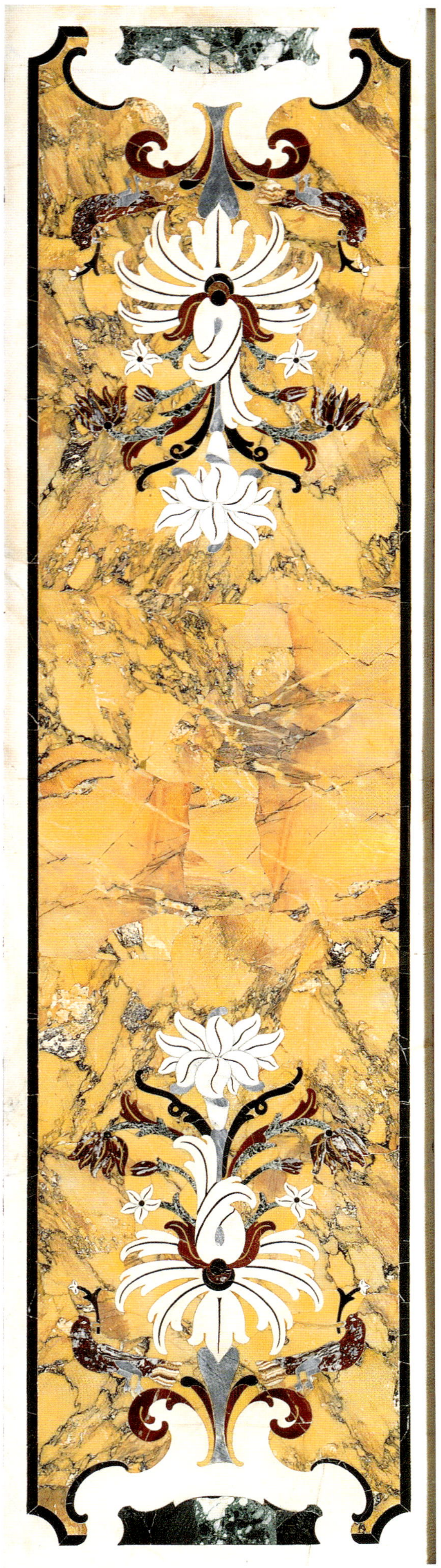

COMMENTARY: These panels can be dated to the first half of the eighteenth century and were probably made in the workshop in Naples that developed in the wake of the activity of Cosimo Fanzago, who was responsible for the spread of the art of stone intarsia throughout Naples and the Campania.[1] Panels of this type occur frequently in churches in the Campania from the second half of the seventeenth century and early eighteenth century, where they were used to cover walls and pilasters. The closest equivalent to the Gilbert Collection panels is provided by those of inlaid stone on the pilaster in the Duomo in Amalfi. Fanzago developed a new local style of ornamentation in Naples that would survive until the rococo period. He succeeded in abandoning the dense floral schemes in use by Neapolitan marble workers, which were often derived from fabric designs. Having absorbed the Roman taste for marble wall facing, Fanzago devised a style of inlay for the architectural mouldings consisting of opulent plant patterns, with extended and somewhat simplified tendrils and rosettes that were particularly suitable for reproduction in series if need be.

NOTE

1 Cantone 1984.

46-47. TWO PAIRS OF ALTAR BALUSTRADES

A: Naples, first half eighteenth century
White and coloured marbles, two sections each: 74.9 × 189.2 × 20.3 cm
(29½ × 74½ × 8 in)
1996.364 (TU44)
B: Naples, first half eighteenth century
White and coloured marbles, two sections each: 81.3 × 228.6 × 23.5 cm
(32 × 90 × 9¼ in)
1996.365 (TU47)

PROVENANCE: Dino Levi Florence, 1972; Los Angeles County Museum of Art, Los Angeles.

EXHIBITIONS: Florence, 1971; Los Angeles, 1975; Los Angeles, 1977.

DESCRIPTION: Two pairs of altar balustrades made of white marble with red and yellow marble inlay on the sides and on the altar rails. The first pair are pierced with vertical rectilinear cartouche shapes between the balusters; the second has lyre-shaped sections between the pilasters.

COMMENTARY: These works depart from the traditional Italian balustrade design, which usually consisted of a sequence of three-dimensional balusters of various shapes, invariably with vase-shaped bases. The work done in Naples in the late seventeenth century changed this standard pattern somewhat. In the staircase designed by Cosimo Fanzago inside the monastery of San Martino in Naples, balusters carved in the round alternate with two-dimensional, fretted balusters with double scrolls at the top and flared bases. In the high altar of the chapel of Santa Maria delle Anime del Purgatorio in Naples, also by Fanzago, three-dimensional balusters have been replaced by sheets of white marble cut in elaborate patterns like lace; the white marble surrounds panels of different-coloured marble.

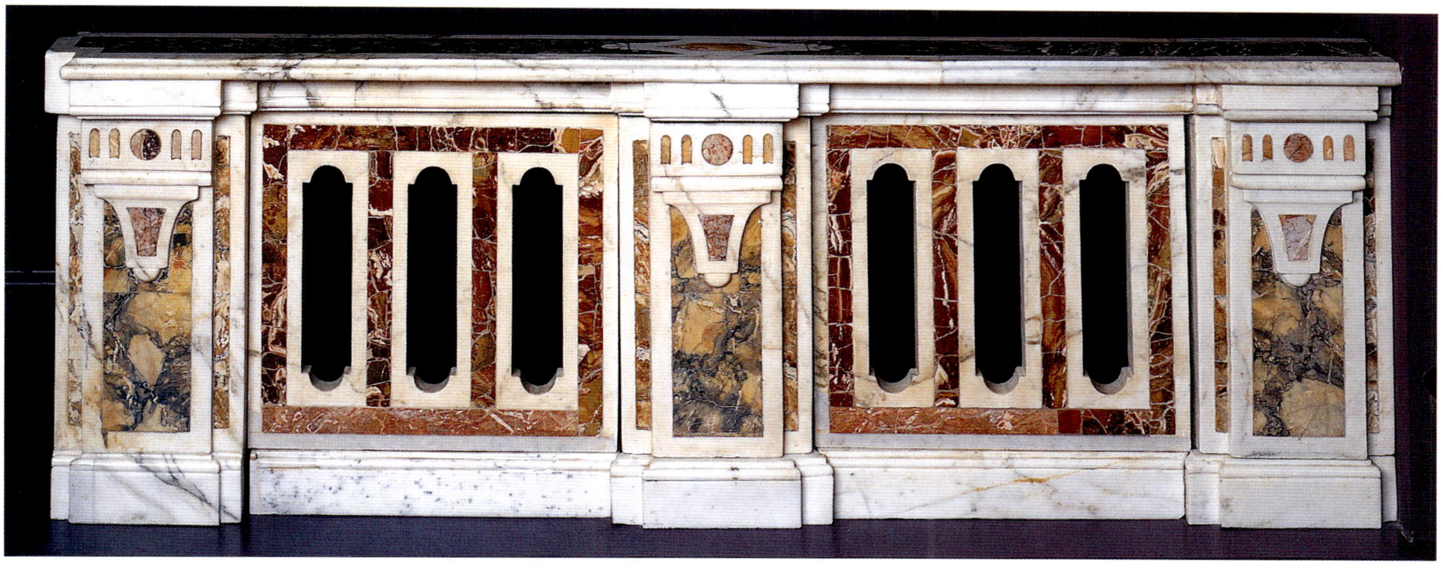

48. HOUSE ALTAR

Rome, c. 1750
Alabaster, amethyst, marble, silver gilt, wood, tortoiseshell
58.4 × 38.1 × 25.4 cm (23 × 15 × 10 in)
1996.845 (TU89)

PROVENANCE: Alberto di Castro, Rome, 1976.

LITERATURE: González-Palacios 1977a, no. 15; González-Palacios and Röttgen 1982, no. 15.

EXHIBITION: Los Angeles, 1977.

DESCRIPTION: House altar consisting of a white marble base on a plinth with three steps, curved at the front, and an architectural upper part. The base has four brackets with volutes, one on each side and two in the front, with silver-gilt mounts comprising acanthus leaves and cherubs' heads. In the centre is an alabaster door with a crown and a monogram of entwined initials. Inside, the floor of the recess is lined with tortoiseshell inlaid with plant motifs in silver gilt. On the upper part, six amethyst columns and two fluted alabaster pilasters on the corners have Corinthian capitals and bases of silver gilt. These support an entablature of carved marble decorated with silver-gilt festoons and stars. On top of this is a half dome with a decoration of coffers outlined in silver and containing silver stars. Two silver-gilt angels kneel on the entablature, and a pair of putti, also of silver, on the dome. Their position, along with two holes bored in the edge of the dome to hold either screws or fastenings, suggests that they must originally have supported a coat-of-arms or a cartouche.

COMMENTARY: González-Palacios' entry in the 1982 catalogue of the Gilbert Collection of mosaics reads as follows:

> The purpose for which this precious object was created is still a mystery. It was probably a royal present made without a designated recipient. It appears to have been made in Rome, where such rich materials were used throughout the eighteenth century. The angels on top recall Gian Lorenzo Bernini's angels on the altar of the Cappella del SS. Sacramento in the Vatican. The crown surmounting the initials on the door panel appears to be French since it has the Bourbon fleurs-de-lys around it. The initials are difficult to decipher: they seem to be *MJL* which could stand for Marie Josephe [1731–67], the wife of Louis XV's son, the Dauphin Louis (1729–65), who died in 1765. The monogram may also be interpreted as two *Ls* facing each other, the initial of the Dauphin himself.

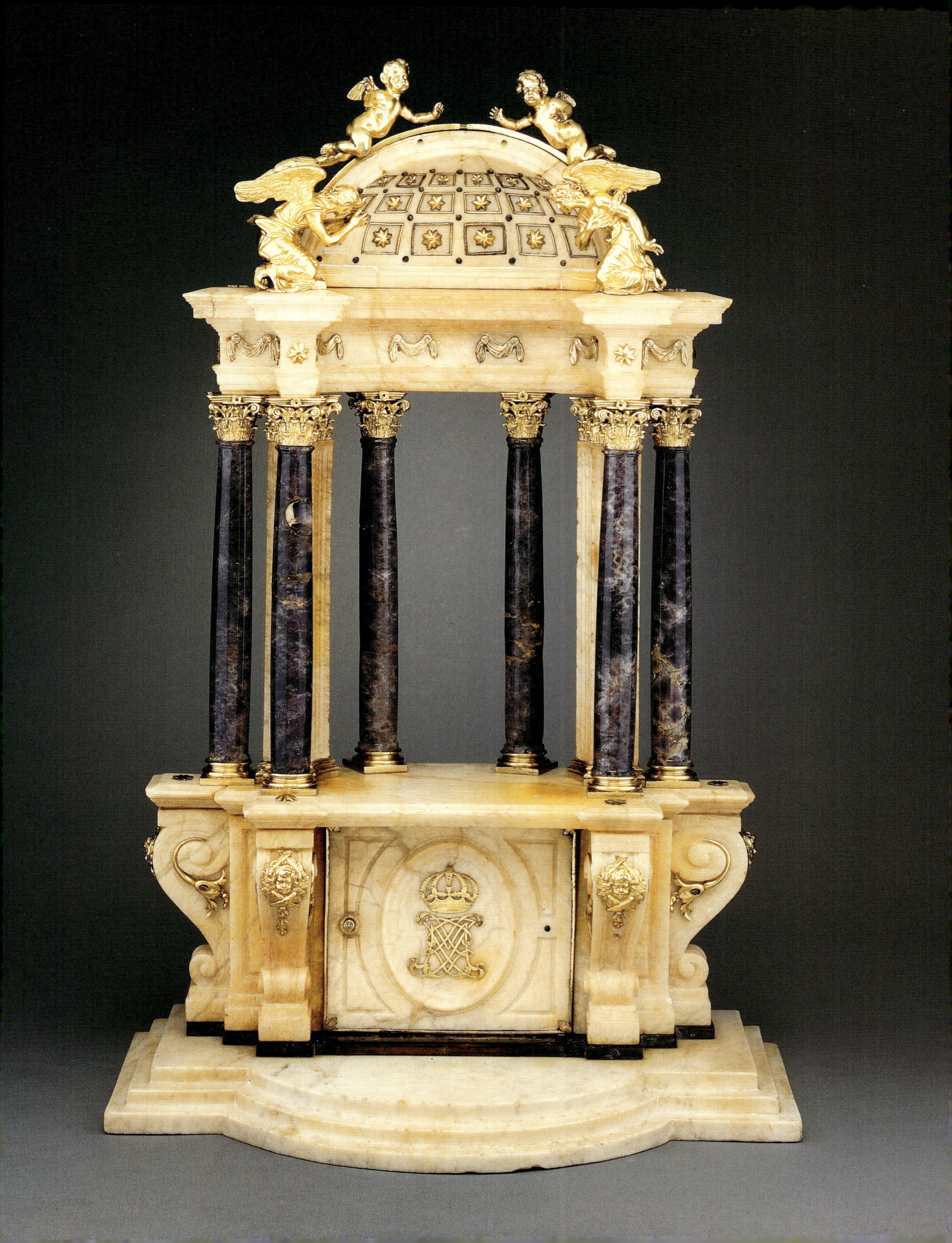

Snuffboxes

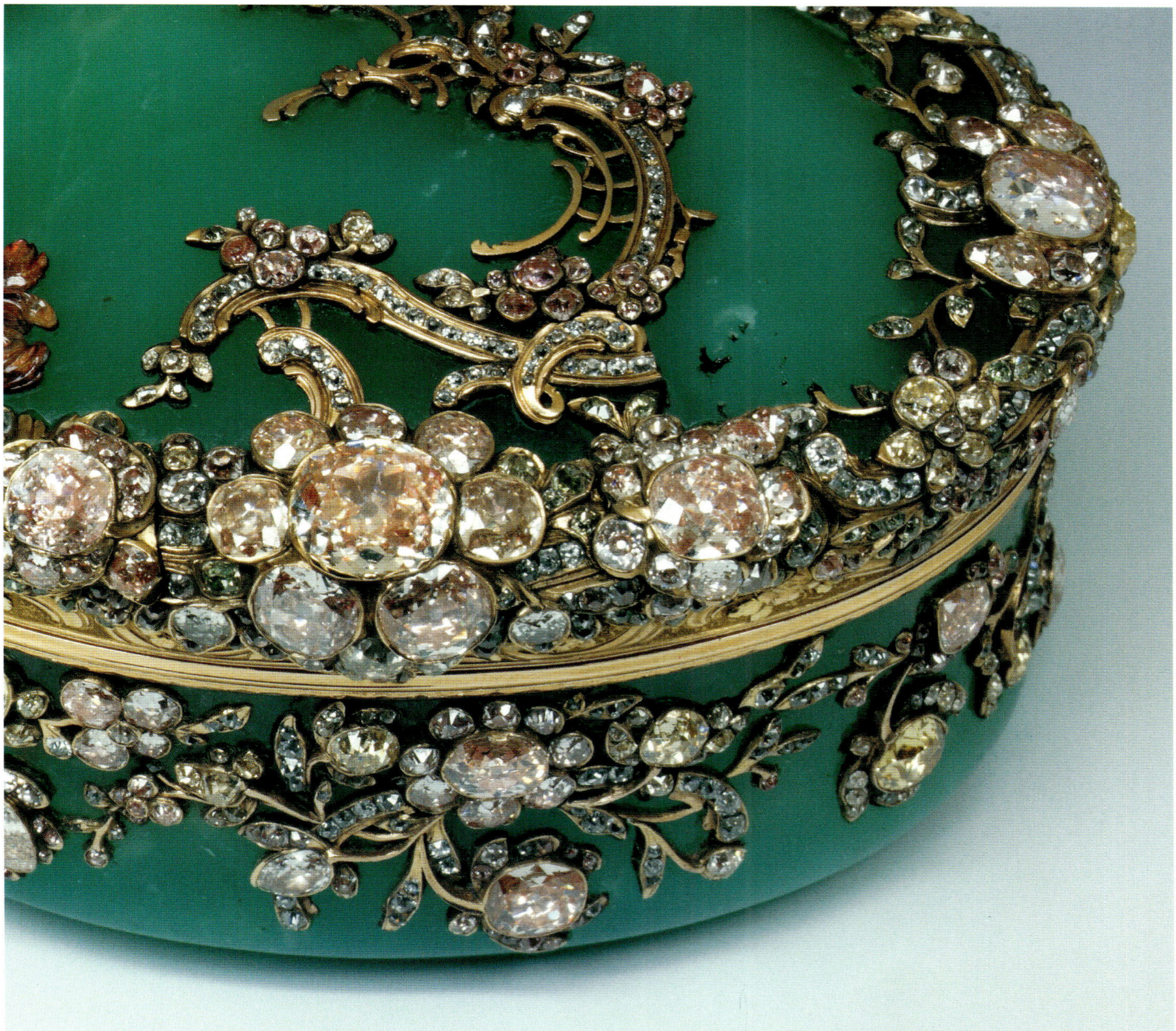

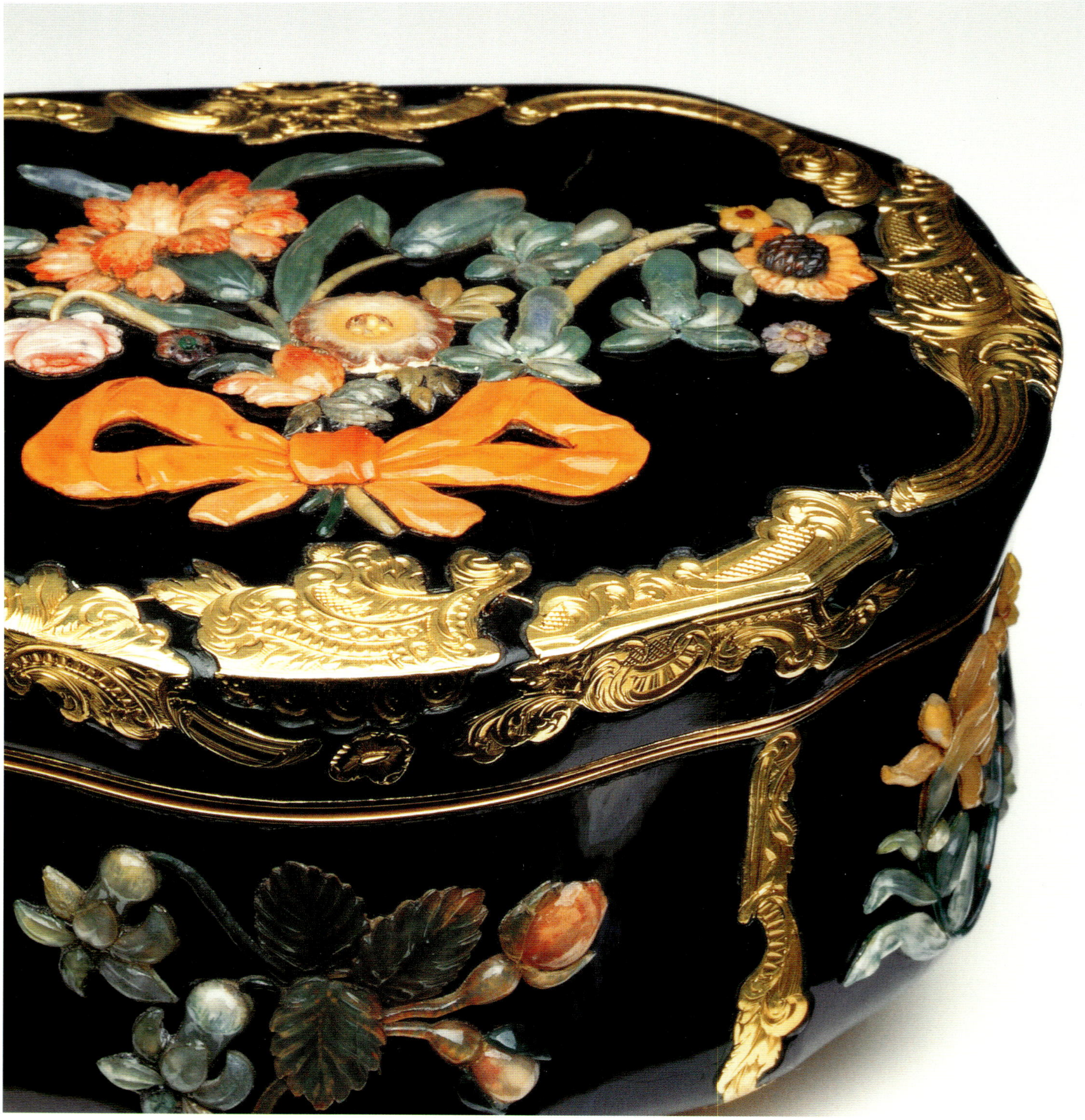

SNUFFBOXES

The earliest snuff canisters were made of inexpensive materials such as horn and wood. Change came during the eighteenth century, when their manufacture became the prerogative of goldsmiths all over Europe. They used their talents to create lavish objects with intricate panels of enamel and precious stones. Even the Grand Ducal workshops became involved. With the renewed interest in the carving of semiprecious stones in late seventeenth-century Florence, the making of snuffboxes expanded.[1]

The earliest contemporary information about the manufacture of snuffboxes comes from Giuseppe Antonio Torricelli (1662–1719), who noted in 1718: 'I have also made vases, drinking vessels, cups, and snuffboxes with screw tops, and I was the inventor of these screw tops in *pietra dure*, they had not been used before.'[2] Spiral grooves cut around the edge of the lid and base allowed the top to screw on, eliminating the need for a separate mount with metal hinges. However, there were problems when materials of differing density were used: the tiny dimensions and thin walls posed the danger of breakage during the carving stage. So the attempts made by Torricelli to perfect screw tops may have been a short-lived experimental phase.

During the Lorraine period, the production of snuffboxes was given new stimulus by Louis Siries, who had previously worked as a goldsmith in Paris and was already experienced in the craft.[3] An agate snuffbox, signed by the artist, was made to the same circular design as Torricelli's snuffboxes.[4] Instead of a screw top with chiselled grooves however, this has a border in chased gold. Boxes of this type were catalogued in the Grand Ducal Collection at the end of the eighteenth century.

Although information relating to *pietre dure* snuffboxes is relatively scarce, occasional examples show that other workshops were also making snuffboxes in semiprecious stones. In Naples, c. 1800, there was an interesting variation at the Real Laboratori, where boxes were carved out of petrified wood. Examples were also produced by the Buen Retiro workshop in Madrid and that of Johann Christian Neuber (1736–1808) in Dresden.

During the early years of Siries' activity, the revival of the snuffbox saw experimentation with form and an attempt to produce Florentine boxes to wider European tastes. Boxes were made in a variety of forms, some in the cartouche shape beloved of the age of rococo, others simply circular, oval, or rectangular. All were carved from two blocks of stone, one for the lid, another for the base. A number of documents dating to the last three decades of the eighteenth century describe snuffboxes of various types, the most common consisting of a gold framework with ten panels of *pietre dure*.

NOTES

1 For the production and spread of snuffboxes in Europe, see Nocq and Dreyfus 1930; Snowman 1966; Truman 1991.

2 Quoted in Zobi 1853, p. 272, CFR Appendix B.

3 Pinto 1977, vol. 2, pp. 614–15.

4 Giusti 1992, p.113, fig. 32.

Previous page
Enlarged detail of cat. no. 52

Opposite
Enlarged detail of cat. no. 56

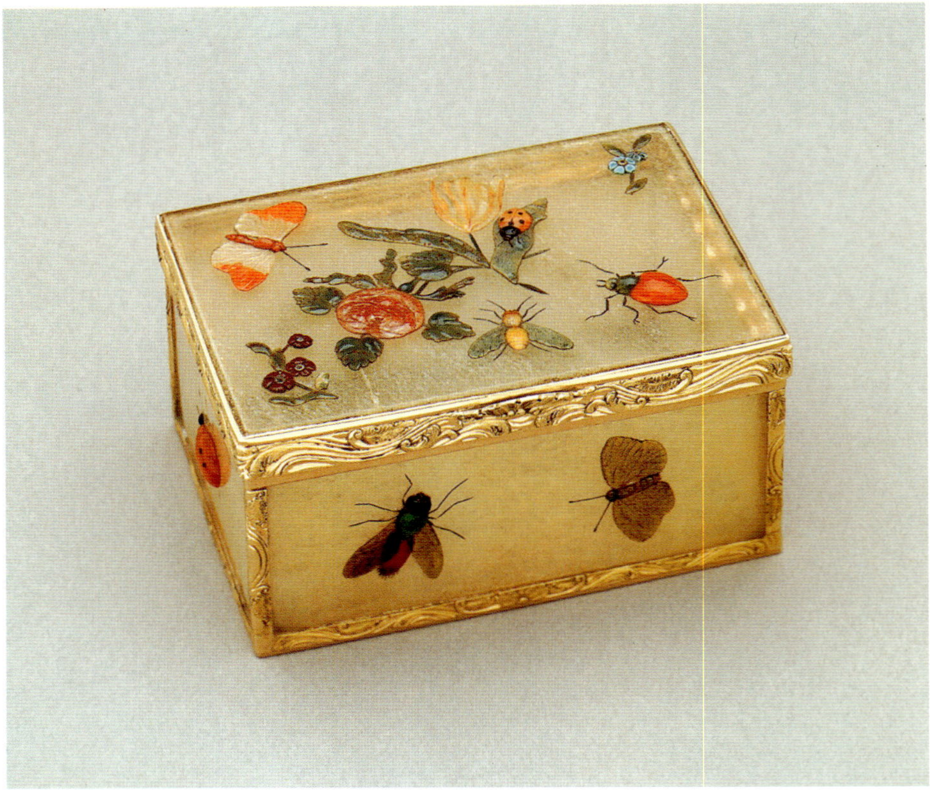

49. SNUFFBOX

Berlin or Dresden, signed F. L. Hoffman, c. 1750
Alabaster, hardstone, gold, 7.3 × 5.3 × 3.9 cm (2 7/8 × 2 1/16 × 1 9/16 in)
1996.470 (GB122)

PROVENANCE: S. J. Phillips, London, 1987.

LITERATURE: Snowman 1966, pls. 539–40; Snowman 1990, pls. 615–16; Moncrieff 1991, p. 73; Truman 1991, no. 66.

EXHIBITIONS: London, 1990; Los Angeles, 1991.

DESCRIPTION: A rectangular snuffbox composed of six panels of pale gold alabaster set with gold mounts chased with scrolls and flowers. The cover and sides are applied with naturalistic insects and flowers of carved coloured hardstones, those on the top in relief. The base is signed F. L. HOFFMAN.

COMMENTARY: Snuffboxes of this type can be found in the Danish Royal Collection and in the Victoria and Albert Museum in London.[1] There is some mystery surrounding the identity of the craftsman, Hoffman. Boxes signed or attributed to Hoffman are discussed by both Kenneth Snowman and Charles Truman, who indicate that there may have been a dynasty of goldsmiths by that name. There is also uncertainty as to whether the technique of raised stonework on this box should be associated with the workshops of Frederick the Great in Berlin or the Saxon court at Dresden. Truman favours the first of these choices.

NOTE

1 Snowman 1966, nos. 575, 598.

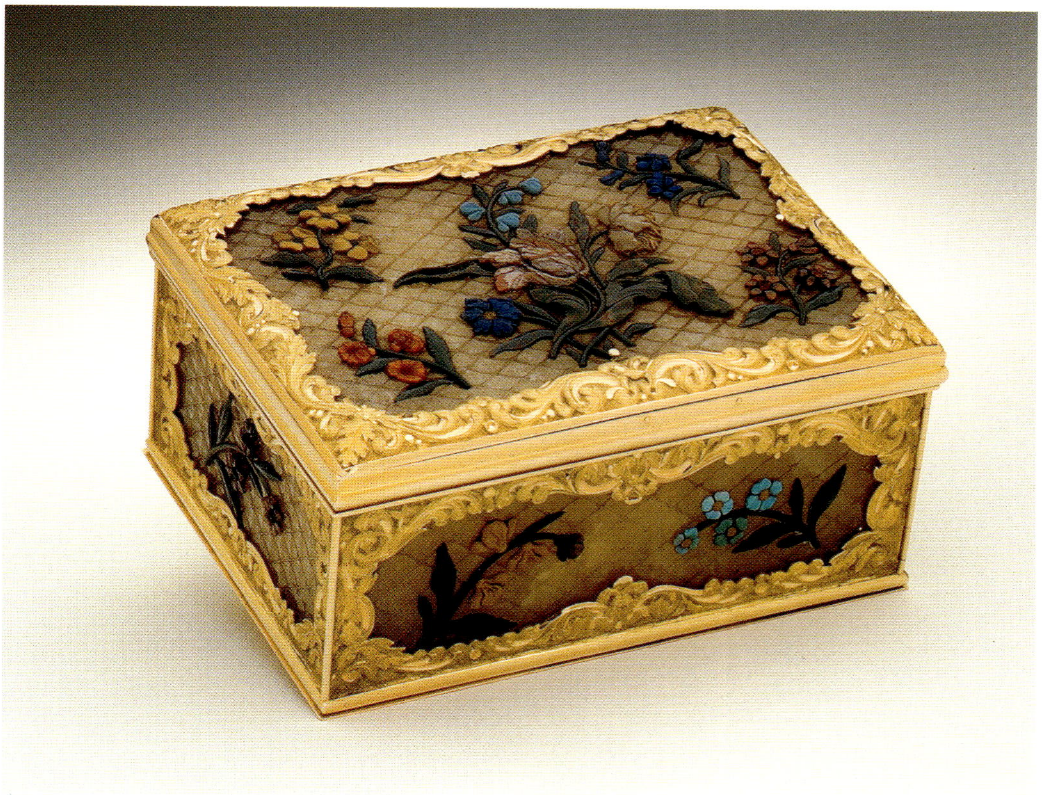

50. SNUFFBOX

Paris, 1817–19, L. B. Benard (fl. c. 1817)
Agate, bloodstone, chalcedony, jasper, lapis lazuli, turquoise, gold, 8.4 × 6.3 × 4.2 cm (3⅝ × 2½ × 1½ in)
1996.524 (GB175)

PROVENANCE: Christie's, London, 10 November 1993, lot 97; S. J. Phillips, London, 1993.

EXHIBITION: Memphis, 1994.

DESCRIPTION: A rectangular snuffbox consisting of six panels of chalcedony cut in a pattern of diamond-shaped lozenges, mounted *à cage* in gold chased with volutes and foliage, and with reeded borders. The cover and sides are encrusted with naturalistic floral hardstone-relief decoration of chalcedony, bloodstone, agate, jasper, turquoise and lapis lazuli.

COMMENTARY: Charles Truman and other authorities agree that, based on its marks, this box is most likely to be a product of a French workshop in the early nineteenth century. Its cagework mounts are very much in the English taste of the 1750s and 1760s (less frequently adopted by the French), while the hardstone elements such as blond panels, relief-hardstone carving and sprigs of flowers appear to be derived from Berlin stonework such as that on a Gilbert Collection box by Hoffman (cat. no. 49). Mid-eighteenth-century hardstones of this type, however, would have been stylised, not naturalistic as in this box. An additional argument for the early nineteenth-century date is the diamond-cut ground characteristic of glass cutting at that time.

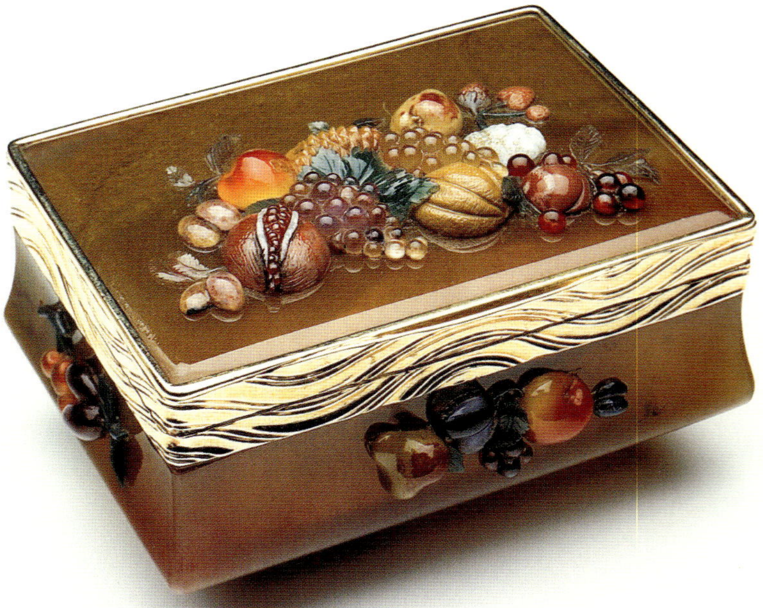

51. SNUFFBOX

Germany, probably Berlin, mid-eighteenth century
Agate, *pietre dure*, gold, 7.8 × 5.8 × 3.3 cm (3 1/16 × 2 5/16 × 1 5/16 in)
1996.380 (GB12)

PROVENANCE: Wartski, London, 1979.

LITERATURE: Habsburg-Lothringen 1983, no. 37; Snowman 1990, pl. 624; Moncrieff 1991, p. 73; Truman 1991, no. 70.

EXHIBITIONS: London, 1990; Los Angeles / Memphis, 1991–92; San Francisco, 1996.

DESCRIPTION: An oblong snuffbox carved from gold-coloured agate, the lid and sides applied with carved hardstone relief depicting clustered fruit and foliage. The gold mounts are chased with a wave pattern.

COMMENTARY: Charles Truman suggests[1] that this box originated in a Berlin workshop, based on comparison with Gilbert Collection hardstone boxes with similarly applied ornament (cat. nos. 55, 56) and other boxes from the collection of Frederick the Great of Prussia, as well as with an example at the Musée du Louvre, which has comparable clusters of fruit.[2] He cautions, however, that the simplicity of the mounts may possibly suggest that the box could have been made in the early nineteenth century.

NOTES

1 Truman 1991, p. 203.
2 Baer 1980, pp. 100–105; Solodkoff and Habsburg-Lothringen 1983, pp. 36–41; Grandjean 1981, no. 420, fig. 30.

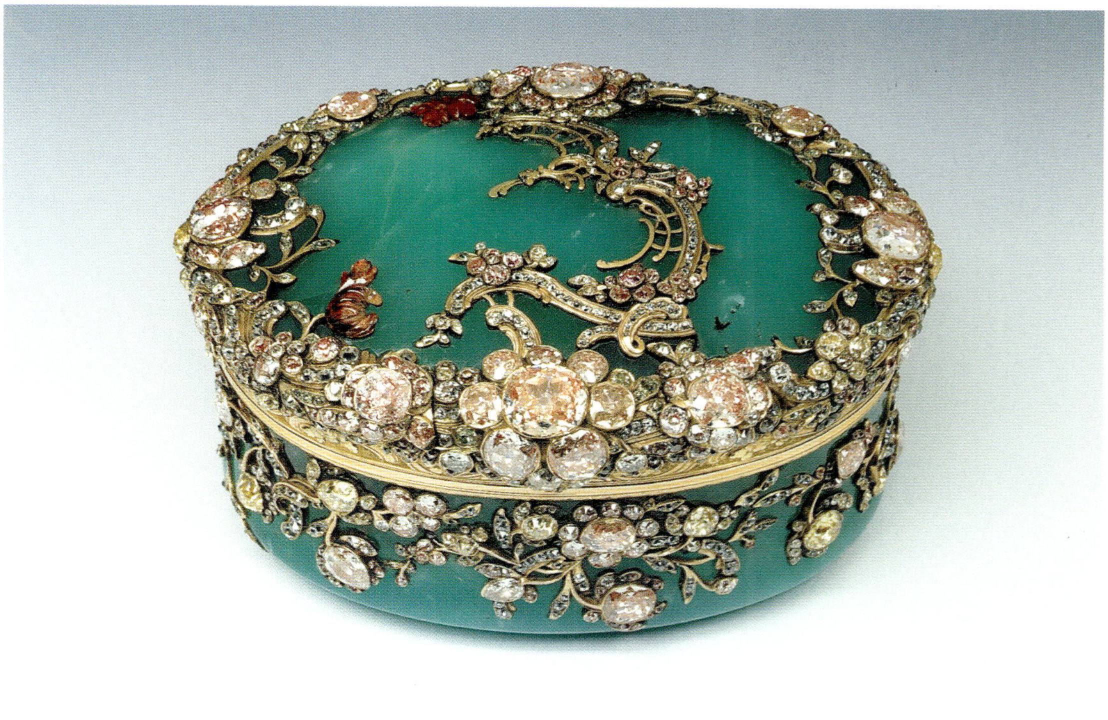

52. SNUFFBOX

Berlin, c. 1755
Chrysoprase, diamonds, hardstones, foil, gold, 10 × 7.8 × 4.9 cm ($3^{15}/_{16}$ × $3^{1}/_{16}$ × $1^{15}/_{16}$ in)
1996.469 (GB120)

PROVENANCE: Frederick II of Prussia; presented by Frederick to his brother Augustus Wilhelm; King Frederick William II of Prussia; Prince Frederick of Prussia, thence by descent; Christie's, sale, Geneva, 11 November 1986, lot 444; S. J. Phillips, London, 1986.

LITERATURE: Seidel 1901, no. 15; *Christie's Review* 1987, p. 323; Spector 1991, pp. 94–95, no. 2; Truman 1991, no. 71, no. 121; Potsdam 1993, no. 36.

EXHIBITIONS: Los Angeles / Memphis, 1991–92; Munich, 1992; Potsdam, 1993.

DESCRIPTION: An oval, gold-mounted hardstone snuffbox, the chrysoprase box and cover carved from single pieces of chrysoprase set with diamond, gold and hardstone scrolls, vines and flowers, the diamonds over pink, green and yellow foil. The sides of the base are similarly applied with relief hardstones and gems. Two small, red hardstone flowers are on the cover, and one appears to be missing from the lower-right quadrant.

COMMENTARY: Eight chrysoprase snuffboxes belonging to Frederick the Great are recorded by Paul Seidel. Five of these have been accounted for: one is found in the Thyssen-Bornemisza Collection, Lugano, three are in Schloss Charlottenburg, Berlin, and the Gilbert Collection example is in London. In a more recent exhibition catalogue documenting the snuffboxes known to have belonged to Frederick the Great, Winfried Baer dates all the chysoprase boxes to around 1765.[1] With regard to the Gilbert Collection snuffbox, however, this date would conflict with the provenance of the box, which, according to Charles Truman, came from Frederick's brother, Augustus Wilhelm (d. 1758), to whom the King is supposed to have presented it. Baer proposes an alternative provenance (and later date): from the Empress Augusta Victoria (1858–1921), wife of Emperor Wilhelm II (1854–1941), then to Prince Oscar of Prussia (1888–1958).

An earlier dating of this box, to about 1755, as proposed by Truman, could be made based on its shape, which is a very regular oval. Many of the snuffboxes owned by Frederick are more modern and relaxed in design. Not only is the style of this box markedly rococo, the shape of the cartouche on the cover is the same as in many of the royal snuffboxes and in the drawings of Jean Guillaume George Krüger (b. 1728). This London-trained designer, who moved to Berlin in 1753, designed a series of snuffboxes in the Prussian royal collection (see cat. no. 59).

NOTE
1 Potsdam 1993, p. 54.

53. SNUFFBOX

Berlin, c. 1765
Agate, diamonds, *pietre dure*, gold, foil, 10.5 × 8 × 5.2 cm (4 1/8 × 3 1/8 × 2 1/16 in)
1996.479 (GB131)

PROVENANCE: Frederick III of Prussia; King Frederick William III of Prussia; Prince Albrecht of Prussia; M. Solover, Paris; King Farouk of Egypt; The Palace Collections of Egypt, sale, Sotheby's, Cairo, Koubbeh Palace, 13 March 1954, lot 726; Robert Lehman Collection, New York to 1977; Harry Winston, New York, 1988.

LITERATURE: Seidel 1901, pls. 16A, 16b; Klar 1929, pl. 18; Snowman 1966, pls. 546–47; Baer 1980, p. 104; Solodkoff and Habsburg-Lothringen 1983, pp. 38, 40, figs. 8–9; Snowman 1990, 444–45, pls. 736–37; Moncrieff 1991, p. 73; *Connoisseur* March 1954, 'The Egyptian Royal Collections', pp. 43–44; Truman 1991, no. 72; no. 122; Baer 1993, no. 37.

EXHIBITIONS: Berlin, 1929; London, 1990, no. 59; Los Angeles / Memphis, 1991–92; Potsdam, 1992–3; Munich, 1992.

DESCRIPTION: A cartouche-shaped snuffbox with lid and base carved from two blocks of brown agate. The body consists of seven panels of the same agate; the cover, made of two pieces of stone, and the sides of the body, are applied with floral motifs of inlaid gold set with diamonds. The base and walls are bordered with a gold frieze chased with leaves and flowers and set with brilliants. On the gold bezel is the inscription: FRIEDRICH DER GROSSE BESASS MICH. FRIEDRICH WILHELM III UEBERGAB MICH / SEINEM SOHNE ALBRECHT ZUM FIDEIKOMMIS IN SEINER FAMILIE, (translated by Charles Truman as: Frederick the Great had me, Frederick Wilhelm II gave me to his son Albrecht as the inalienable property of his family). On the base is a hardstone-relief panel of a dog stalking a duck.

COMMENTARY: As Truman has observed, the inscription on this snuffbox 'provides a firm link with Frederick the Great, which is lacking in the majority of boxes associated with his commissions'. He further states that this box is not attributable to any of the goldsmiths who supplied the Prussian court, but is from the same outside atelier that provided several other Gilbert Collection boxes (cat. nos. 53–58).

The scene on the base of the box is taken from *Cigne et Barbet*, a painting by Jean-Baptiste Oudry (1686–1755), Superintendent of the Gobelins manufactory, although here, a mallard replaces the swan.[1] Truman relates that the scene appears in two snuff-boxes of *vernis*, a European version of oriental lacquer: one in the Thyssen-Bornemisza Collection, Lugano,[2] the other in the Felix Doisteau Collection.[3]

NOTES
1 For a history of Oudry's painting and its use in decorative arts, see Truman 1991, p. 215.
2 Somers-Cocks and Truman 1984, no. 59.
3 Sale, Paris, 16–17 June 1928, lot 153.

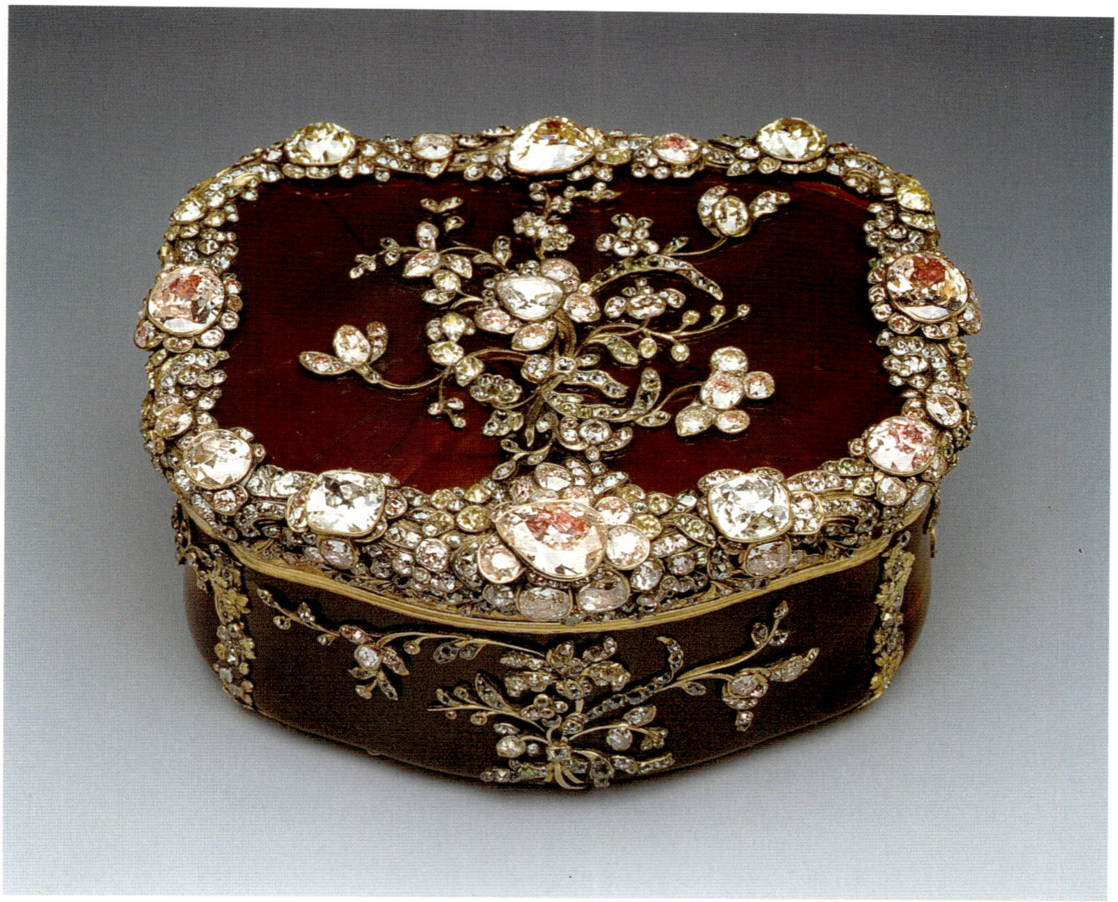

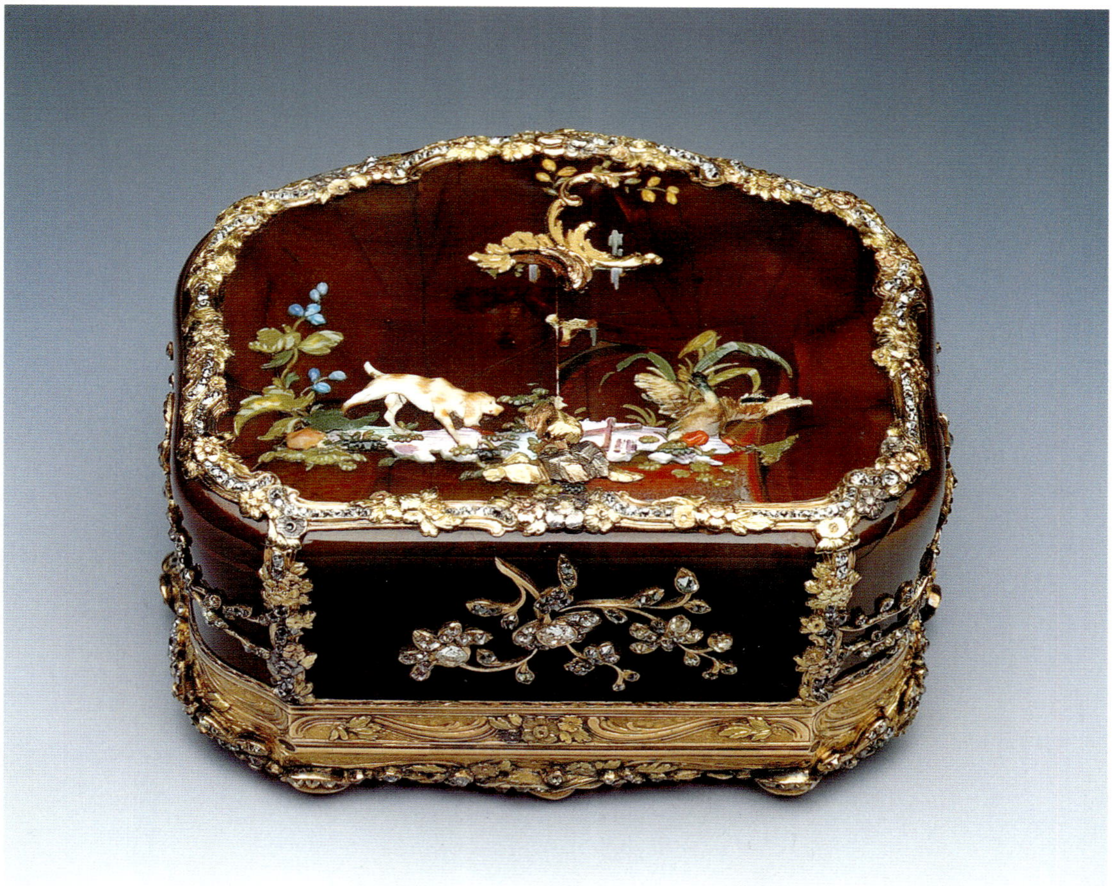

54. SNUFFBOX

Berlin, c. 1765
Mother-of-pearl, gold, diamonds, rubies, hardstones, foil, 10 × 8 × 5.2 cm (3 15/16 × 3 3/16 × 2 1/16 in)
1996.405 (GB45)

PROVENANCE: Frederick II of Prussia; Duke of Mecklenburg-Schwerin, 1914; Dukes of Anhalt-Dessau, 1929; Christie's, Geneva, 11 May 1982, lot 176 (property of a German Royal House); S. J. Phillips, London, 1982.

LITERATURE: Biermann 1914, pl. 630; Klar 1929, fig. 4; Habsburg-Lothringen 1983, no. 38; Solodkof & Habsburg 1983, 36, 38, figs. 5–6; *Apollo*, vol. CXX, no. 274, April 1986, p. 283, pl. VI; Prince Michael of Greece, *Crown Jewels* 1983, ill., p. 52. Snowman 1990 pl. 738; *Connaissance* 1987, ill. p. 11; Richardson 1983, p. 112; Truman 1991, no. 73; Spector 1991, no. 3; Munich 1992–93, no. 43; Potsdam 1993, no. 128; Hapsburg 1997, fig. 269.

EXHIBITIONS: Darmstadt 1914, no. 24; Los Angeles / New York / Virginia Museum of Fine Arts, 1986–87, no. 31; Los Angeles / Memphis, 1991–92; Munich, 1992–93; Potsdam, 1993; San Francisco, 1996.

DESCRIPTION: A cartouche-shaped snuffbox composed of panels of mother-of-pearl with three-colour gold *à cage* mounts chased with flowers and scrolls, set with diamonds, and applied with flowers and foliage of amethyst, citrine and coloured or foiled quartz. The edge of the lid is studded with diamonds, six of which are larger than the others – five cushion-shaped and one pear-shaped. Also around the edge of the cover are eight flowers with petals made of rubies. The central portion of the cover bears a dense pattern in the rococo style consisting of intertwined volutes from which emerge relief tulips, peonies and roses of various coloured quartzes. The same design can be found on the sides and the base.

COMMENTARY: Charles Truman comments that this box was apparently unknown to experts in the field of Frederick the Great snuffboxes in 1901.[1] He also observes what is

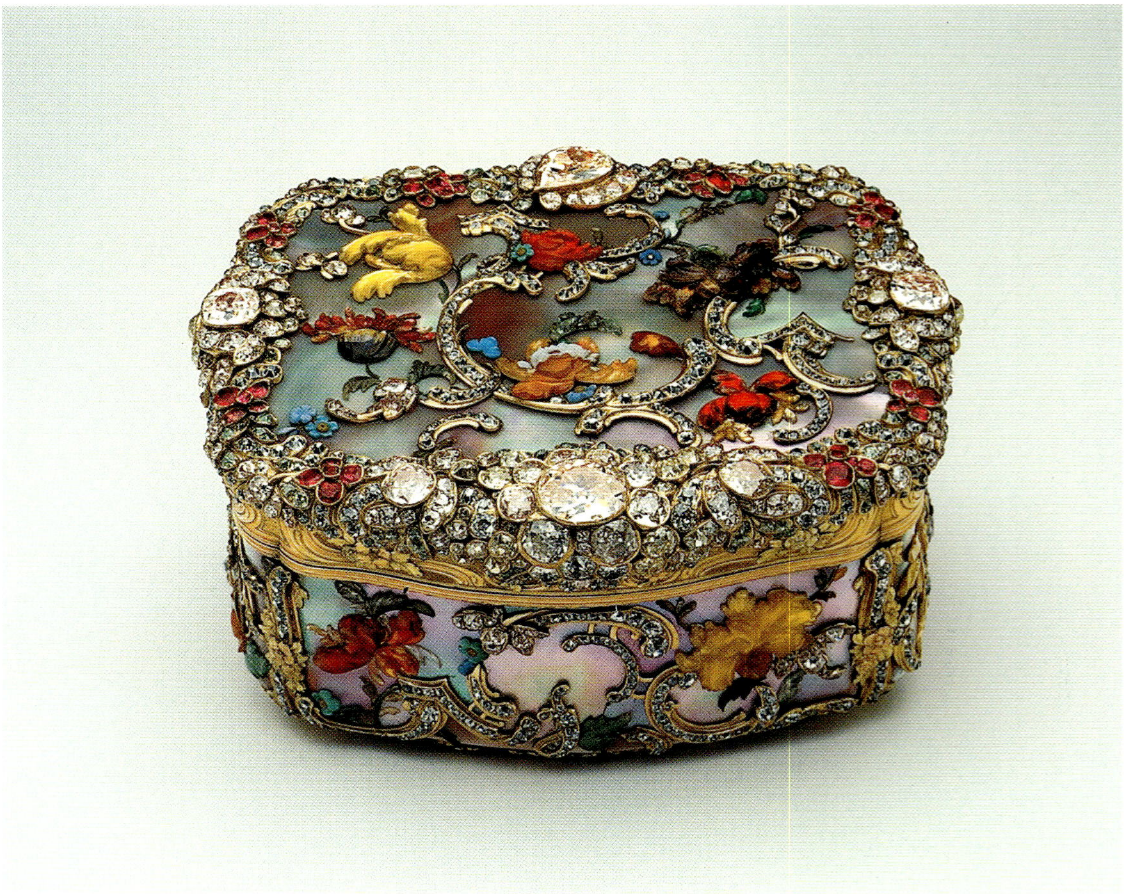

manifestly evident, that the box is one of the most extraordinary and resplendent of its type, and the only one known to employ reflective and iridescent mother-of-pearl for its body. He cites several examples using similarly raised hardstone flowers such as those in the Musée du Louvre (Grandjean 1981, no. 420), the collection of Robert Lehman (Metropolitan Museum of Art, New York),[2] and two other Gilbert Collection boxes (cat. nos. 53, 58). He also suggests a possible attribution to Baudesson, who made another Frederick the Great snuffbox, now in the Gilbert Collection, with similar mounts (cat. no. 54).

NOTES

1 Truman 1991, p. 219, referring to Paul Seidel.
2 Illustrated in Snowman 1966, pls. 548–49.

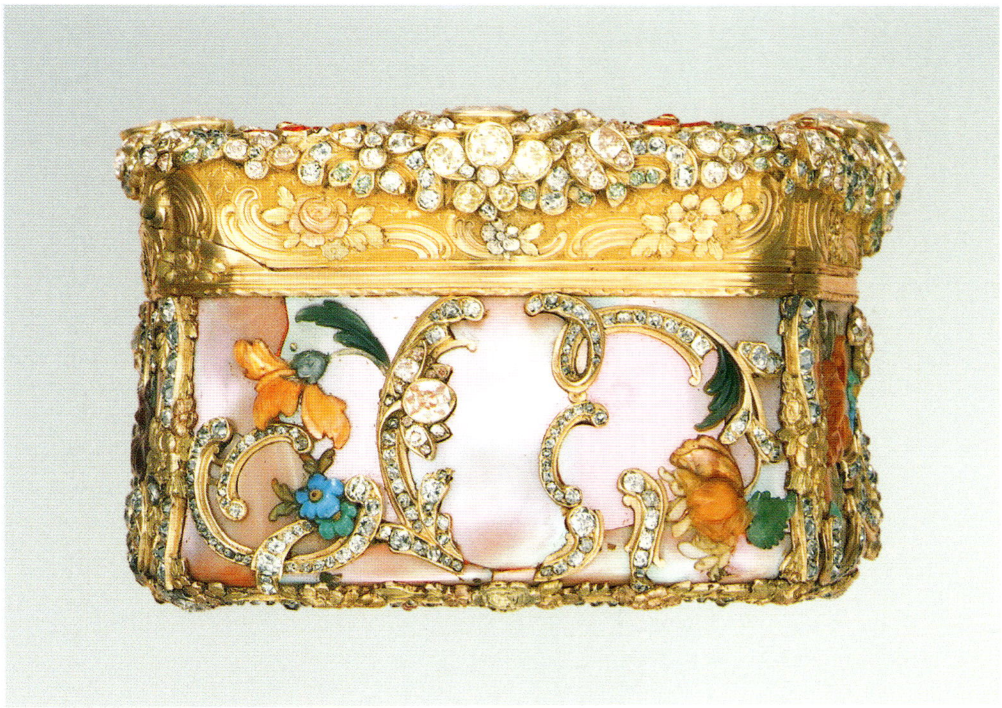

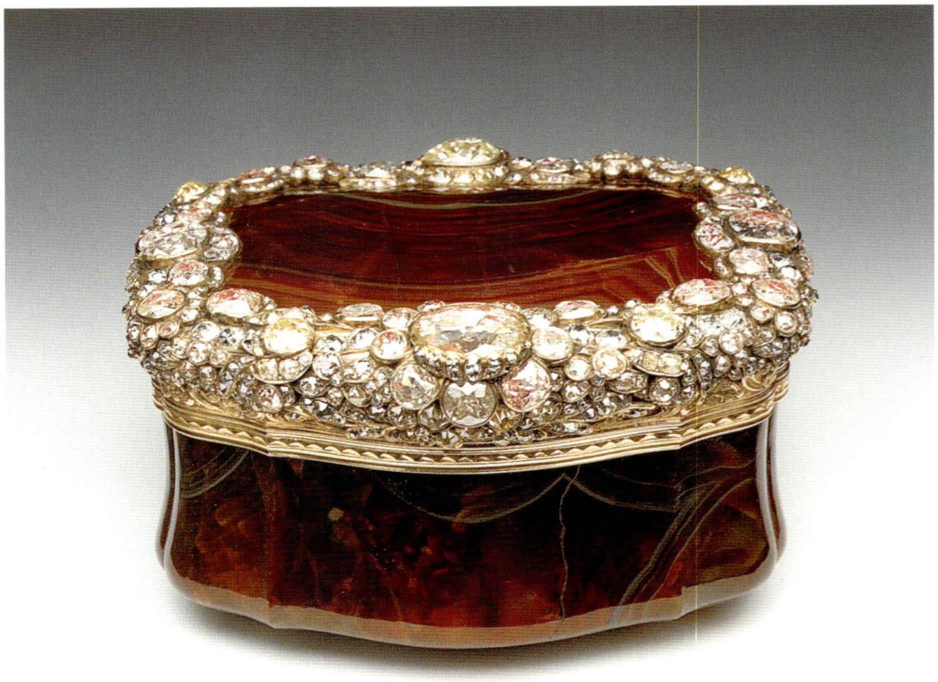

55. SNUFFBOX

Berlin c. 1765
Agate, gold, diamonds, foil, 9.3 × 7.9 × 4.6 cm ($3^{11}/_{16}$ × $3^{1}/_{8}$ × $1^{15}/_{16}$ in)
1996.440 (GB90)

PROVENANCE: Charles Engelhard, sale, Christie's, 28 June 1972, lot 41; A. Neuhaus, Würzburg; S. J. Phillips, London, 1984.

LITERATURE: Christie's, London, 28 June 1972, lot 41; Christie's *Review of the Season* 1972, p. 213; Figueiredo 1992, ill. p. 11; Truman 1991, no. 74; Sullivan 1991, p. 17; *Friedrich der Grösse* 1992, no. 124; Baer 1993, no. 39.

EXHIBITIONS: Bath, 1973, no. 244; Los Angeles / New York / Richmond, 1986–87, no. 32; Los Angeles / Memphis, 1991–92; Munich, 1992–93, no. 124; Potsdam, 1993, no. 39.

DESCRIPTION: A cartouche-shaped snuffbox carved from a block of brown agate with a cover carved of the same stone. The varicoloured gold mounts are chased with flowers and scrolls, while the border of the cover is lavishly set with four large, cushion-shaped diamonds and a myriad of smaller stones, some over yellow and pink foil. The inside of the lid has a gold border chased with flowers and scrolls.

COMMENTARY: Charles Truman believes that this extraordinary box is another made for Frederick the Great by the hand or workshop of Daniel Baudesson. He bases this attribution on the coloured-gold chasing, particularly that of flowers, comparable to that on another gold box in the Gilbert Collection signed by Baudesson (cat. no. 54).

The snuffboxes that belonged to Frederick the Great are generally decorated with gold mounts and set with jewels on the side and base. In this example, however, the agate body is unadorned, and the diamonds are concentrated around the border of the lid. Two other boxes that belonged to the King are decorated in the same way (Hermitage, St. Petersburg; Schloss Charlottenburg, Berlin).[1] Both of these examples are carved from agate and have lids with diamond-studded borders. Like the Gilbert Collection snuffbox, neither of them is marked, but all three seem to have been made by the same craftsman.

NOTE
1 Potsdam 1993, nos. 40–41.

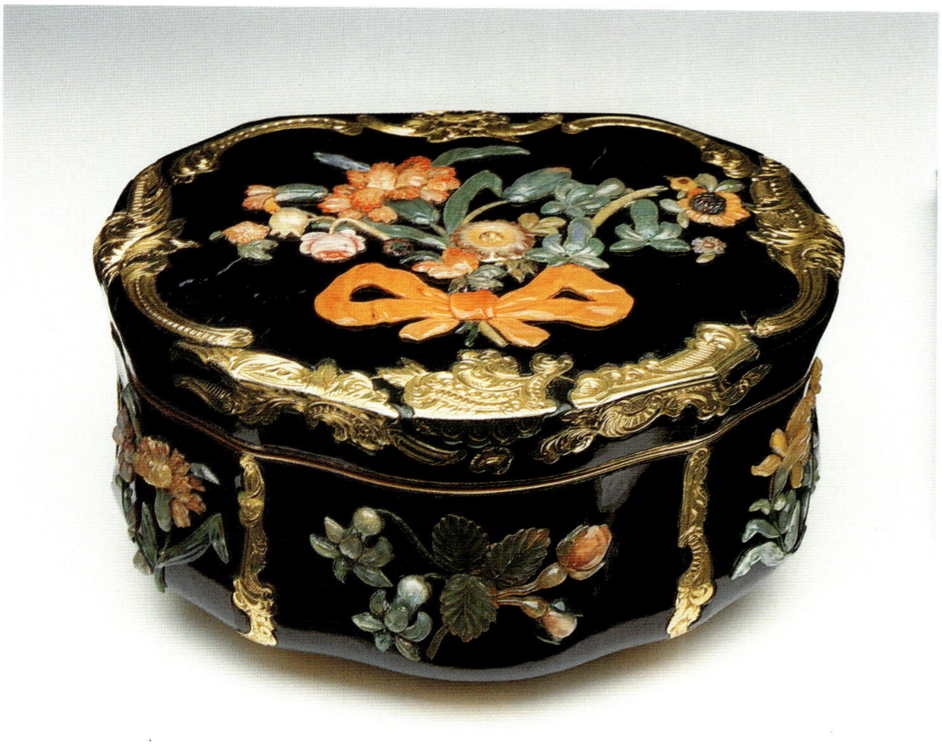

56. SNUFFBOX

Berlin, c. 1865
Black marble, *pietre dure*, *pietre tenere*, gold, $3\frac{7}{8} \times 3\frac{1}{16} \times 1\frac{15}{16}$ in ($9.8 \times 7.7 \times 4.9$ cm)
1996.488 (GB140)

PROVENANCE: Christie's Geneva, 11 May 1982, lot 194; Kugel, 1989.

LITERATURE: Truman 1991, no. 75; Potsdam 1993, no. 50.

EXHIBITIONS: Los Angeles / Memphis, 1991–92; Potsdam, 1993; Munich, 1993.

DESCRIPTION: A cartouche-shaped snuffbox, the base fashioned from several pieces of marble; the lid, from a single piece. The sides are encrusted with naturalistic designs inlaid in *pietre dure* and *pietre tenere*, bordered by gold finely chased with scrolls, shell, and foliage.

COMMENTARY: Charles Truman has stated that 'both the treatment of the hardstone and of the gold mounts place it with the group of boxes associated with Frederick the Great'.[1] Especially conspicuous are its structural and decorative links with the exquisite snuffbox from the Thurn und Taxis collection, made to a design by Jean Guillaume George Krüger (cat. no. 59). Similarities include the cartouche shape, the style of workmanship, and the use of dark stone as a background to brilliantly coloured floral designs. The encrustation in very low relief with finely inlaid leaves and flowers, as well as the actual arrangement of the floral designs, especially on the side panels, are very similar on both snuffboxes.

The creator of this elegant piece remains a mystery, although Truman has linked the mark VB, visible on the gold mount, with the widow of the Parisian jeweller Louis Buyrette, who called herself the 'Veuve Buyrette' (Widow Buyrette). The Buyrette workshop was last heard of in 1743–45, when the name of the Veuve Buyrette occurs along with that of Daniel Baudesson in connection with an important commission for the court of Schwerin.[2] In fact, the snuffbox exhibited here seems stylistically in advance of the last years of documented activity of the Buyrette workshop, and it is therefore difficult to connect the piece with that particular studio.

NOTES
1 Truman 1991, p. 223.
2 Baer 1993, p. 71.

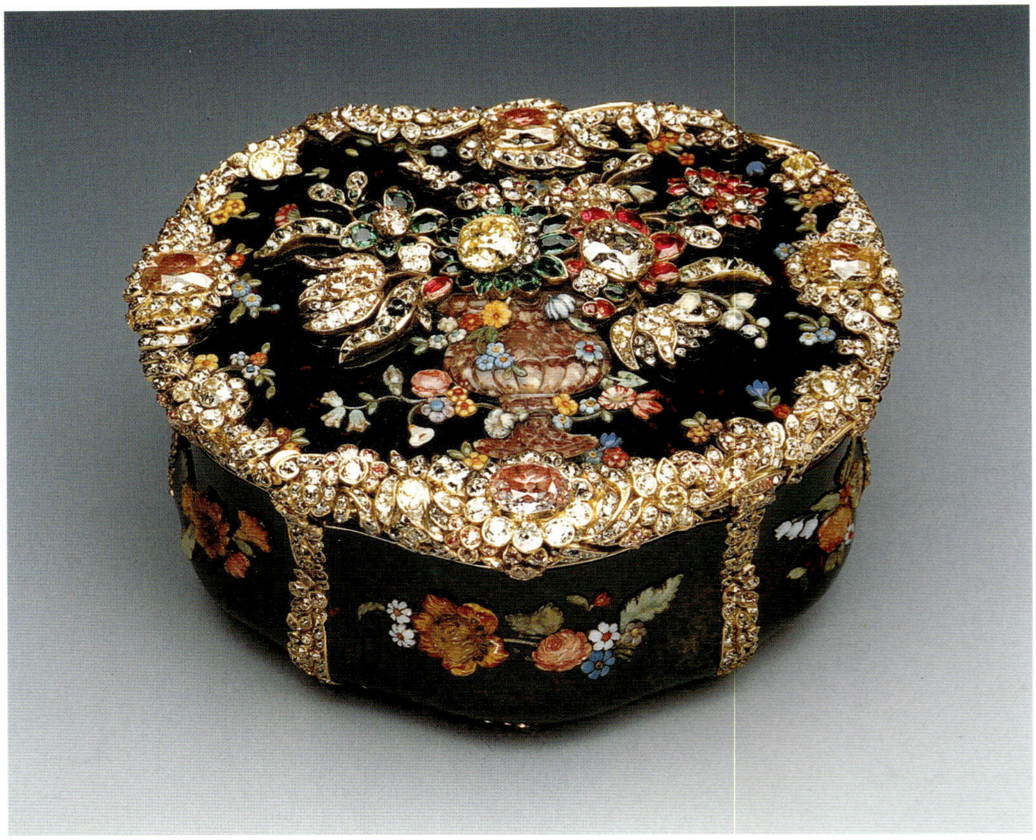

57. SNUFFBOX

Berlin c. 1775, after a design by Jean Guillaume George Krüger
Bloodstone, gold, hardstones, diamonds, emeralds, foil, 10 × 8.4 × 5 cm (4 × 3 3/8 × 1 15/16 in)
1996.516 (GB167)

PROVENANCE: Frederick II of Prussia; Traditionally Fürstin Therese, born Duchess of Mecklenburg-Strelitz and wife of Fürst Carl Alexander; the Thurn und Taxis Collection; Sotheby's, sale, Geneva, 17 November 1992, lot 144; S. J. Phillips, London, 1992.

LITERATURE: Dragadze 1988, p. 87; Truman 1991, p. 207; Sotheby's *Art at Auction* 1992–3, pp. 11, 233; Potsdam 1993, no. 46, pp. 74–75.

EXHIBITIONS: Munich, 1992–93; Potsdam, 1993.

DESCRIPTION: A cartouche-shaped snuffbox mounted *à cage* with gold, the body composed of seventeen separate panels of bloodstone, the cover set with a lavish display of yellow, clear, and foil-tinted diamonds. On the cover is a central depiction of a glass vase simulating porphyry, overflowing with stylised flowers and foliage of hardstones and diverse gems within a similarly decorated floral border. Among the flowers represented are tulips, carnations, lilies-of-the-valley, convolvulus, roses and forget-me-nots. The six side panels are separated by vertical gold and diamond columns and applied with hardstone and glass sprays of flowers, the base similarly applied with a floral bouquet. The border is of clear diamond scrolls and flowers.

COMMENTARY: Charles Truman has recently taken into consideration Dr Winfried Baer's view that snuffboxes with elaborate diamond and hardstone decoration such as this date from late in the reign of Frederick the Great (Munich 1992–93; Potsdam 1993). But he points out that the design for this box is clearly taken from one of the 20 surviving designs of Krüger. Krüger went from Paris to the *Fabrique Royale de Berlin* in 1753, and returned to Paris by 1774, later returning to Berlin where he died.[1] The 20 designs date from before 1774, and are in a high rococo style that would have been out of fashion in the 1770s. Truman notes that apart from the Gilbert Collection box, there are only three other known snuffboxes after Krüger's designs, and these are dated by Baer respectively 1770, 1765–70, and 1772.[2]

NOTES

1 Truman 1991, cat. no. 21.

2 Potsdam, nos. 45, 46, 54.

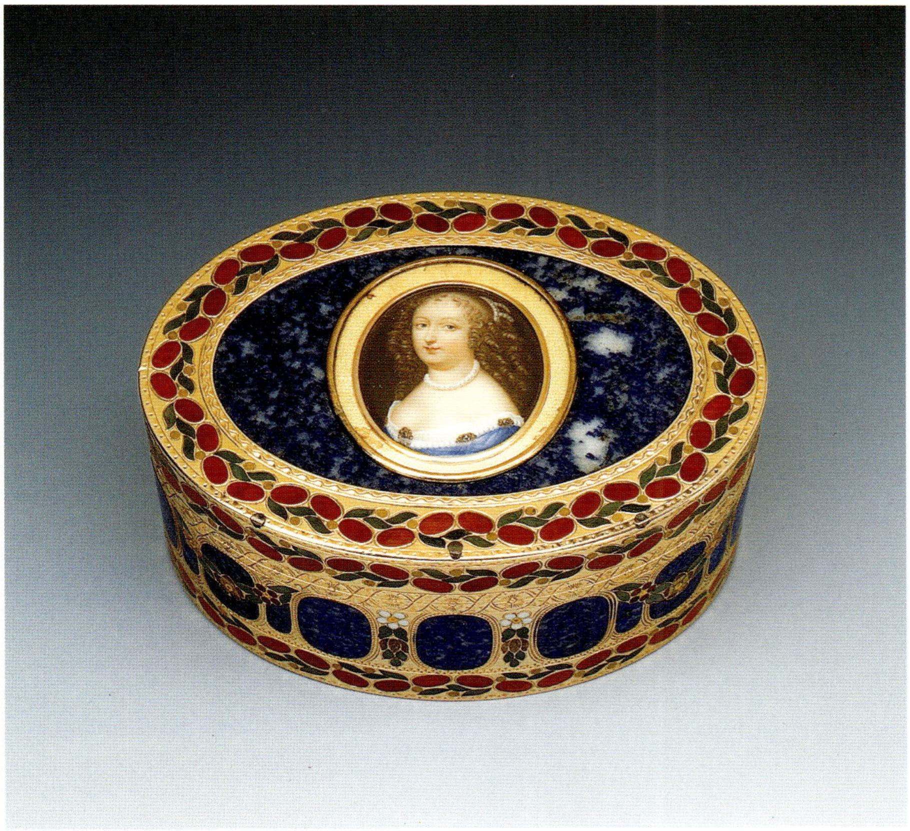

58. SNUFFBOX

Box: Dresden, c. 1780, Johann Christian Neuber (1736–1808); Miniature: French School
Gold, lapis lazuli, hardstones, marble, glazed-enamel miniature, 8.7 × 7.6 × 3.7 cm (3 7/16 × 2 5/8 × 1 7/16 in)
1996.433 (GB81/MM233)

PROVENANCE: Viscount Bearstead; S. J. Phillips, London, 1976.

LITERATURE: Norton & Norton 1938, pl. 40; González-Palacios 1977, no. 22; González-Palacios and Röttgen 1982, no. 22; Habsburg-Lothringen 1983, no. 39; Truman 1991, no. 78.

EXHIBITIONS: Los Angeles / Atlanta / San Antonio / Richmond / Seattle, 1977–79; New York / Richmond, 1986–87; San Francisco, 1996.

DESCRIPTION: An oval, gold-mounted hardstone snuffbox, the cover and base of lapis lazuli with a border of gold inlaid with a wavy string of oval, red carnelian beads interspersed with green jasper laurel leaves, the cover with a central oval miniature of a lady in a chased gold, glazed setting. The sides of the box have vertical ovoid reserves of lapis lazuli interspersed or hung with swags of hardstone and marble flowers and fruit below a band of chased gold and with upper and lower borders like that of the cover and base.

COMMENTARY: This box is one of the few signed works by the important Dresden goldsmith, Johann Christian Neuber. His work uses the technique known as *zellenmosaik* – the setting of small hardstones in frames or cells. Both Neuber and the Saxon goldsmith C. G. Stiehl (1708–92) utilised this method, which had been developed by Neuber's father-in-law, Heinrich Taddel (fl. 1739–d. 1769?), Director of the Green Vaults in Dresden from 1739. While González-Palacios (1982) attributed the box to Stiehl, Charles Truman later attributed it to Neuber, based on the more geometric quality of Neuber's work.[1]

The sitter of the miniature has been variously identified as Henrietta Maria (1609–69), consort of Charles I, and Charlotte Aglae, granddaughter of Louis XIV, although neither seems entirely convincing.

NOTE

1 Truman 1991, no. 78; Snowman 1966, p. 101.

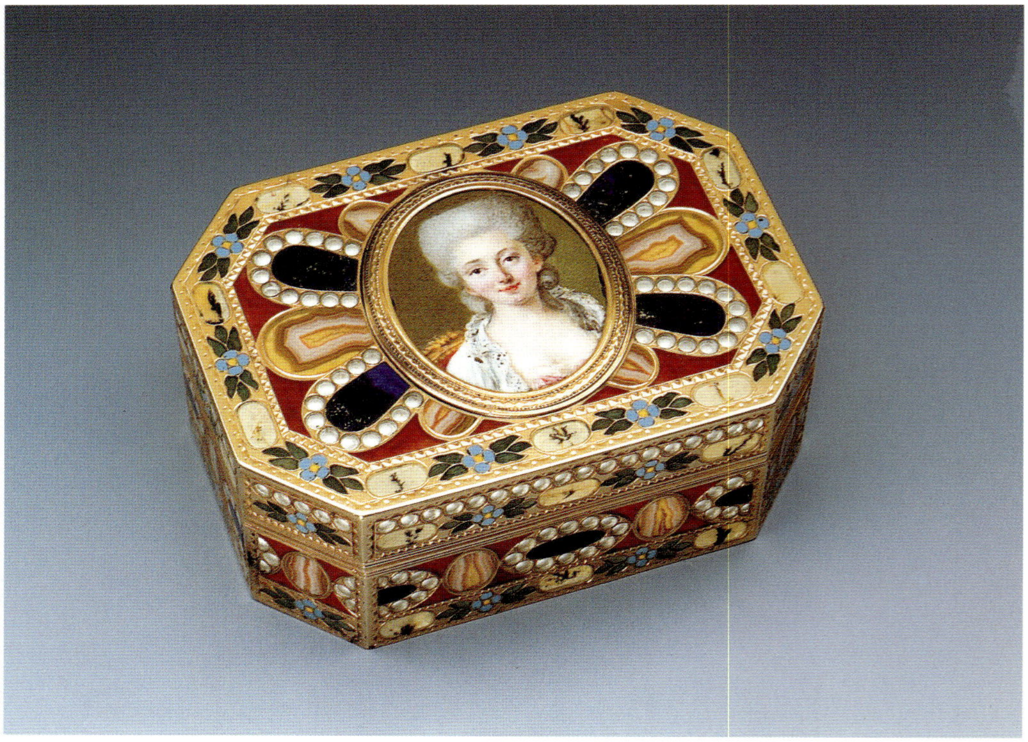

59. SNUFFBOX

Box: Dresden, c. 1780, attributed to Johann Christian Neuber; Miniature: German or French School, enamel, c. 1780
Gold, agate, bloodstone, carnelian, jade, lapis lazuli, quartz, turquoise, enamel over foil, enamel miniature,
8.2 × 6.9 × 3 cm (3 1/4 × 2 11/16 × 1 3/16 in)
1996.483 (GB135)

PROVENANCE: Garrard and Co., London 1987.

LITERATURE: Holzhausen 1935, fig. 20; Truman 1991, no. 79.

EXHIBITIONS: Los Angeles / Memphis, 1991–92.

DESCRIPTION: A rectangular snuffbox with canted corners, set with *zellen-mosaik* of agate, bloodstone, carnelian, jade, lapis lazuli, quartz, turquoise and simulated pearls of enamel over foil. The faux-pear bordered lapis and the yellow agate are arranged on a pattern of radiating ovoid petal shapes on a carnelian ground around the portrait miniature in the centre of the box's cover. The outer border of the cover is a band of inlaid foliage and flowers. The sides of the box have an upper band of faux-pearls and a central section of oval agate and lapis on carnelian between borders matching that on the cover.

COMMENTARY: Charles Truman (1991, no. 79) compares this box with one in the Victoria and Albert Museum. He has previously pointed out that the use of enamel over foil to create the effect of pearls was a characteristic of the Neuber workshop.

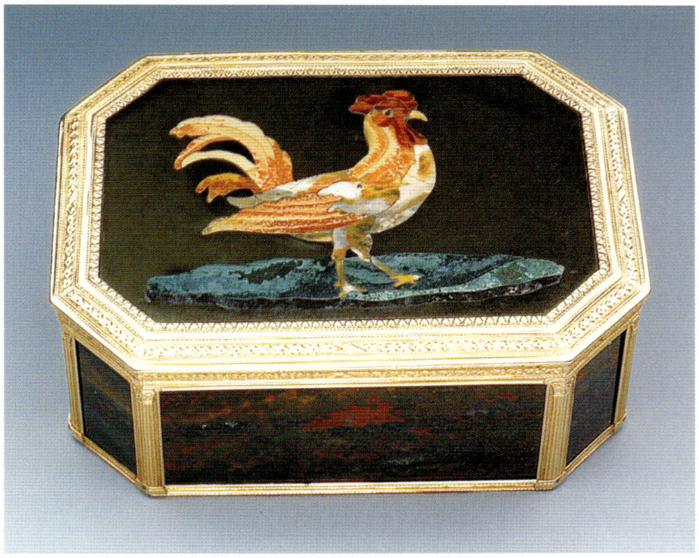

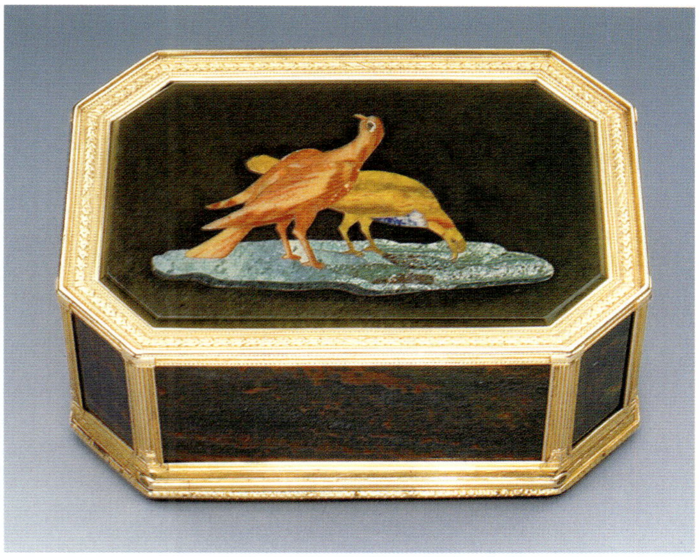

60. SNUFFBOX

Hardstones: Florence, Grand Ducal workshops, c. 1785; Mounts: Paris, Adrien-Jean Maximilien Vachette, c. 1786–7
Pietre dure, jade, bloodstone, gold, 8.4 × 6 × 3.3 cm (3 5/16 × 2 3/8 × 1 5/16 in)
1996.496 (GB148)

PROVENANCE: Commander Clare Vyner, removed from Studley Royal, Yorkshire, sale, Christie's 21 June 1966, lot 88; S. J. Phillips, London, 1989.

LITERATURE: Truman 1991, no. 34.

EXHIBITIONS: Los Angeles / Memphis, 1991–2.

DESCRIPTION: An octagonal box consisting of ten panels of stone with gold *à cage* mounts chased with stylised foliage and pilasters. The jade base and lid are decorated with hardstone inlay depicting a cockerel (on the lid) and two hens (on the base). The walls are of bloodstone, and the inside is lined with gold panels.

COMMENTARY: The mosaics on this snuffbox are associated with Florentine production at the end of the eighteenth and beginning of the nineteenth centuries. The drawings for these inlaid hardstone panels still survive in the Archivio dell'Opificio delle Pietre Dure in Florence (fig. 11). Scenes of barnyard fowl were popular in decorative arts and often taken from paintings by northern artists such as Paul Potter (1625–54) and Melchior de Hondecoeter (1636–96). Their works exerted a tremendous influence on subsequent generations of artists, providing an abundance of sources that were copied in many media. Numerous examples are in the Gilbert Collection of micromosaics. The subject matter of cockerels was especially popular in France, where it was a national symbol.

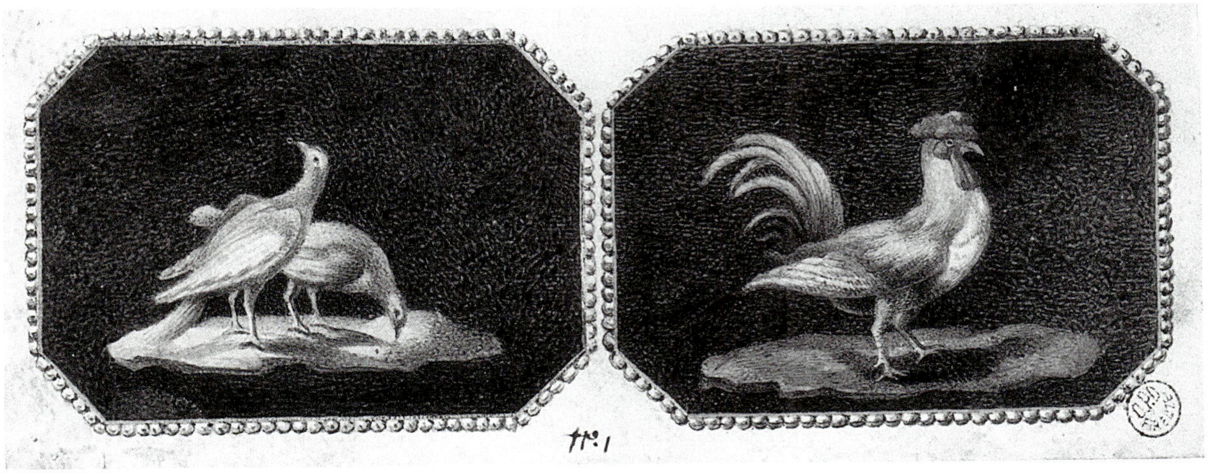

FIG. 11 Watercolour designs for *pietre dure* plaques.

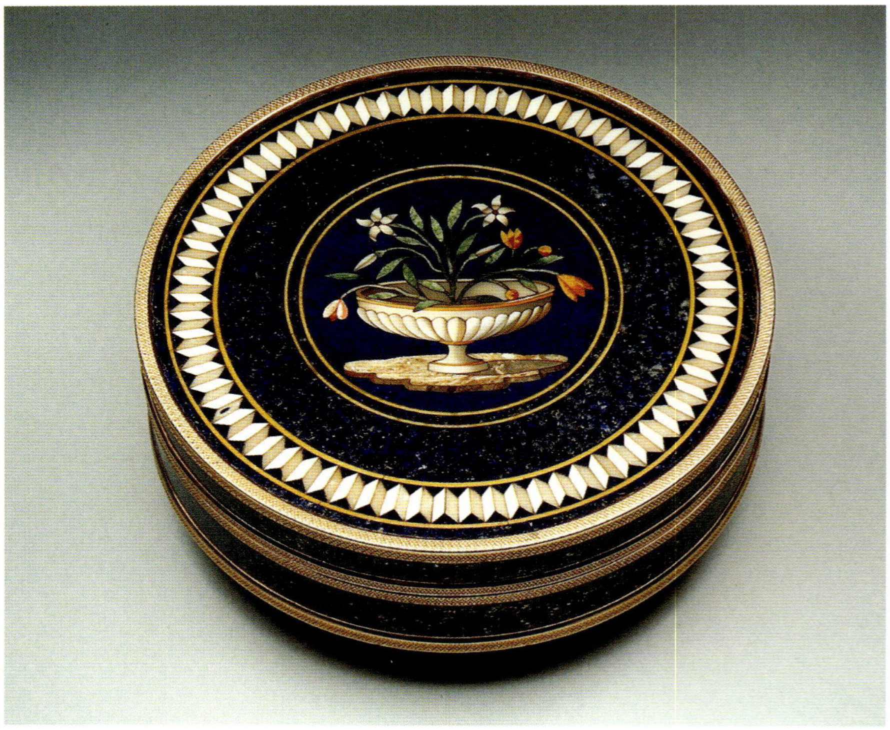

61. BONBONNIÈRE

Florence, Grand Ducal workshops, c. 1800
Lapis lazuli, chalcedony, agate, *pietre dure*, gold, 8 × 2.2 cm (3 1/8 × 7/8 in)
1996.570 (MM251)

PROVENANCE: A La Vieille Russie, New York, 1976.

LITERATURE: Truman 1991, no. 142; Figueiredo 1992, ill. p. 17.

EXHIBITIONS: Los Angeles / Memphis, 1991–2.

DESCRIPTION: A round *bonbonnière*, lined with gold and mounted with matted-gold bands. The lid and base are made from two circular pieces of lapis. On the lid is a vase of chalcedony holding *pietre dure* flowers within concentric rings of lapis and other hardstone. The outermost band is a white zigzag pattern. On the base, within a similar surround, is an agate bouquet of flowers tied with a ribbon.

COMMENTARY: Depictions of flowers in *pietre dure* were produced at the Grand Ducal workshops in Florence from the seventeenth century. One large example can be found on the Gilbert Collection cabinet with a vase on the central door (cat. no. 3). Round, oval and octagonal shaped *pietre dure* plaques depicting vases of flowers were made expressly for snuffboxes, and were produced in great quantity at the Grand Ducal workshops in Florence at the end of the eighteenth and early nineteenth centuries.[1] The preparatory sketch of the lid and base of this snuffbox are in the Archivio dell'Opificio delle Pietre Dure in Florence [2] (figs 12 and 13). The vase of flowers on the cover of the Gilbert Collection box resembles the composition on the top of an early nineteenth-century octagonal snuffbox whose design is attributed to Carlo Carlieri (Victoria and Albert Museum).[3]

NOTES
1 González-Palacios 1986, vol. 1, pp. 118–20.
2 Thanks to Anna Maria Giusti for making a photograph of this sketch available.
3 *Splendori di Pietre Dure* 1988, p. 212.

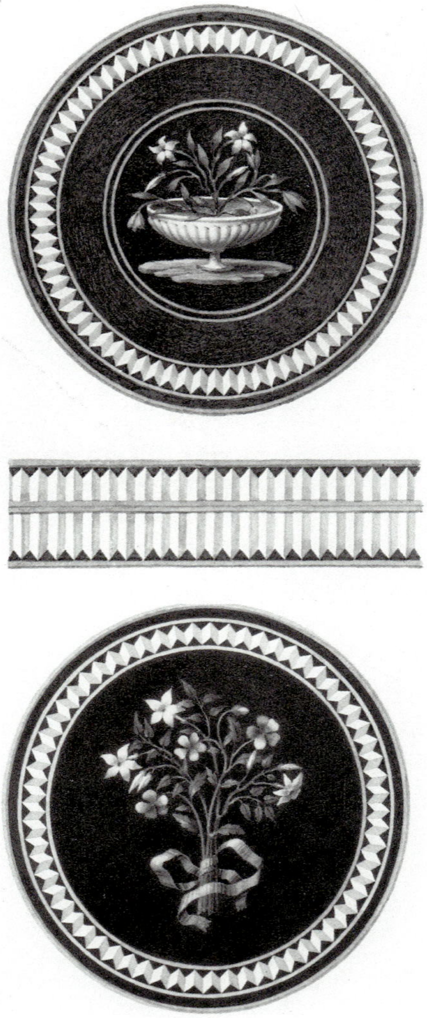

FIGS 12 & 13. Watercolour designs for *pietre dure* panels.

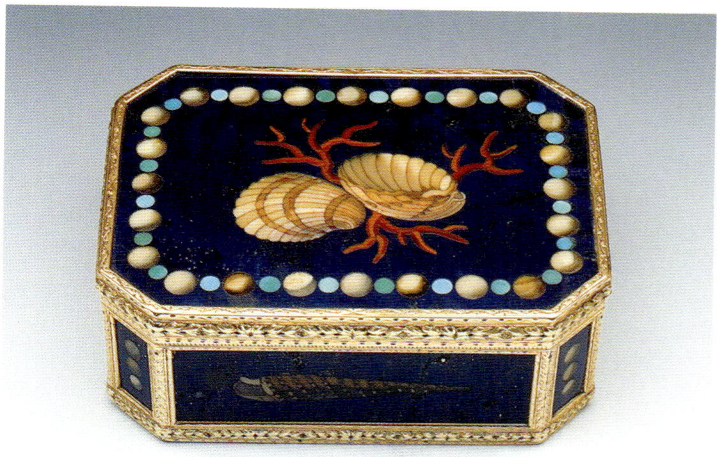

62. SNUFFBOX

Florence, Grand Ducal workshops, c. 1800
Lapis lazuli, chalcedony, turquoise, *pietre dure*, *pietre tenere*, gold, 6.8 × 5 × 2.7 cm (2 11/16 × 1 15/16 × 1 1/16 in)
1996.475 (GB127)

PROVENANCE: S. J. Phillips, London, 1987.

LITERATURE: Truman 1991, no. 141.

EXHIBITIONS: Los Angeles / Memphis, 1991–92.

DESCRIPTION: A rectangular snuffbox with canted corners composed of ten panels of lapis lazuli in *à cage* gold mounts engraved and chased with stylised foliage. The cover depicts two scallop shells and branches of coral, with a border of agate and turquoise pellets, while the base displays two conical shells with coral and the same border. The sides of the box have similar shells and each of the canted corners has three pellets.

COMMENTARY: Snuffboxes of this type frequently appear in documents relating to the Grand Ducal workshops in the last two decades of the eighteenth century. An invoice dated 3 February 1792 establishes the price of a snuffbox, apparently very similar to the one in the Gilbert Collection. Made of Persian lapis lazuli, it was octagonal and bore inlaid shell patterns with branches of coral and pearls. The valuation put on it by the secretary to the crown was 2,543 *lire*.[1] There are a number of drawings of snuffboxes conforming to the same type in the Archivio dell'Opificio dell Pietre Dure in Florence (fig. 14).[2]

NOTES
1 González-Palacios 1986, vol. 1, pp. 118–20, no. 86.
2 Thanks to Anna Maria Giusti for making these designs available.

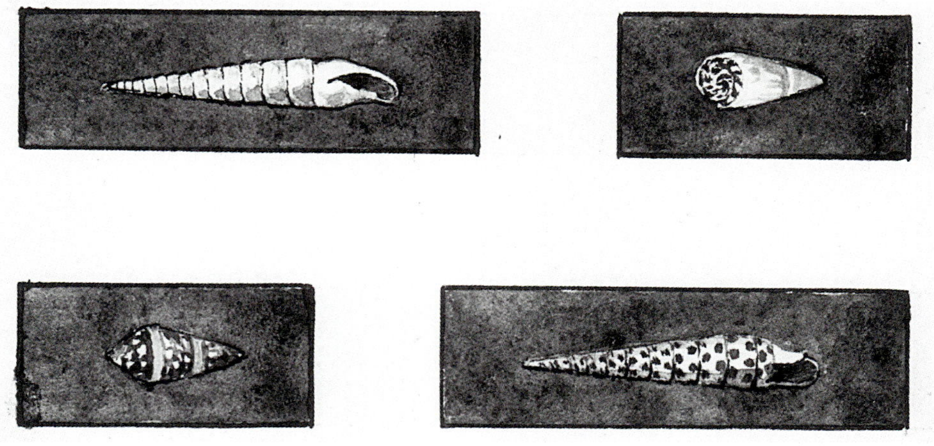

FIG. 14. Watercolour designs for *pietre dure* side panels.

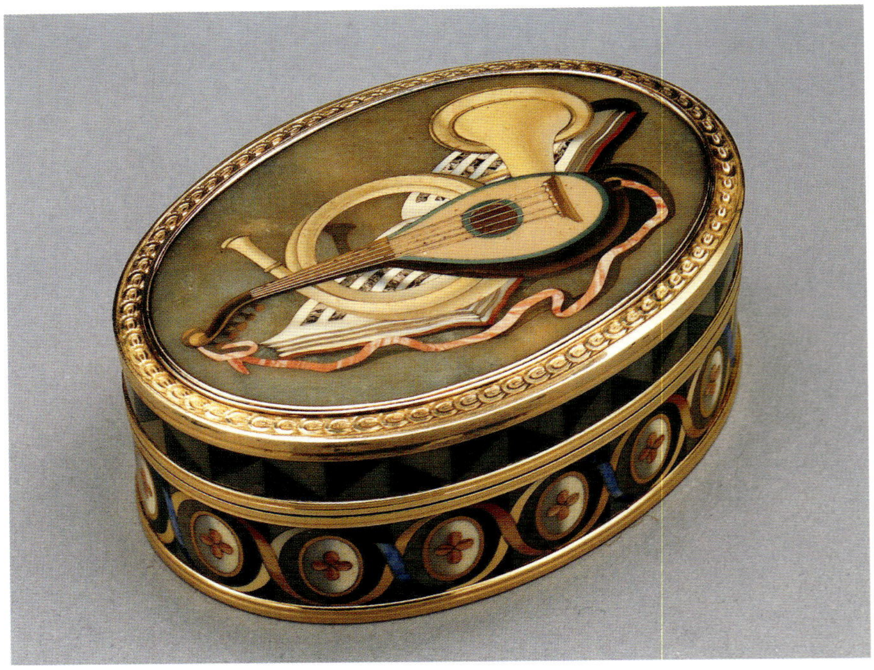

63. SNUFFBOX

Florence, Grand Ducal workshops, late eighteenth/early nineteenth century
Jade, *pietre dure*, *pietre tenere*, gold, 8.9 × 6.4 × 3.5 cm (3½ × 2½ × 1⅜ in)
1996.525 (GB176)

PROVENANCE: Jack and Belle Linsky Collection, sale; Sotheby's, New York, 6 and 8 December 1993, lot 219.

LITERATURE: Snowman 1966, p. 448, pls. 891–92; Snowman 1990, p. 448, pls. 891–92.

DESCRIPTION: An oval snuffbox with chased-gold mounts. The cover consists of a panel of jade with a still life of a musical score and instruments, a mandolin and horn in *pietre dure* and *pietre tenere*. The base is made of another piece of jade and depicts a violin, bow, and musical score of stone mosaic. The gold sides of the box are decorated with two borders of stone mosaic with a geometrical pattern of triangular parquetry and a frieze of entwined ribbons enclosing rosettes.

COMMENTARY: The two compositions of musical instruments are very similar to those inlaid in the corners of the frame for a picture on the theme of Music, made in the Grand Ducal workshops to a design by the Florentine painter, Giuseppe Zocchi (1711–67).[1] Zocchi was employed for the decoration of the palaces of Florence and was a painter of history, genre and landscapes. Snowman observes that Zocchi's composition of instruments is in the tradition of Italian musical still-life painting from Fra Damiano da Bergamo (d. 1549) and Evaristo Baschenis (1617–77) to Gino Severini (1883–1966).[2] Between 1776–1780, Zocchi had made *modelli* for this and for three other pictures depicting the themes Painting, Sculpture and Architecture (Museo dell'Opificio delle Pietre Dure).[3]

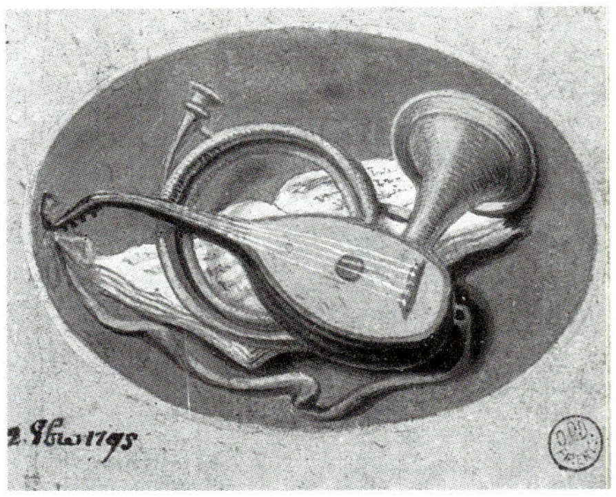

FIG. 15. Design for panel.

Documents published by González-Palacios relating to the production of snuffboxes during the last two decades of the eighteenth century mention oval snuffboxes defined as being 'for men', with *à cage* covers made by the Florentine goldsmith, Clemente Capecchi, who frequently contributed the gold details to the boxes produced in the *pietre dure* workshops. Although the use of jade was not particularly common in the Florentine workshop, there are various documents of the period that refer to jade boxes.[4] The drawing for this snuffbox, dated 22 October 1795, is in the Museo dell'Opificio delle Pietre Dure in Florence (fig. 15).

NOTES
1 Giusti 1995, fig. 29.
2 Snowman 1990, p. 448.
3 González-Palacios 1986, vol. 1, pp. 84–85, 97, 99.
4 González-Palacios, 1986, vol. 1, pp. 120–28, nos. 72, 82, 102, 107.

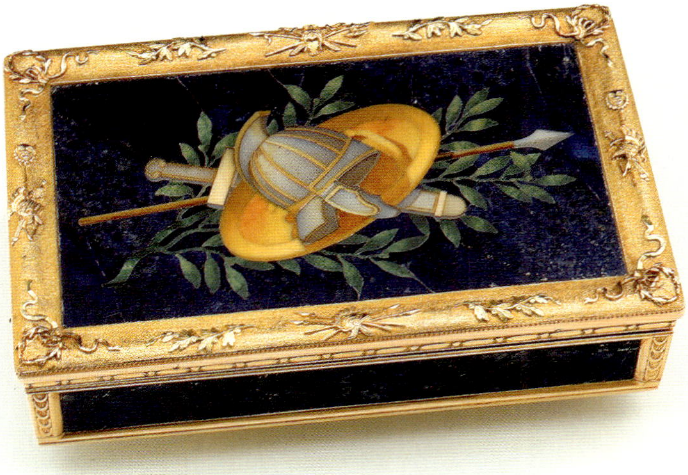

64. SNUFFBOX

Florence, Grand Ducal workshops, probably made to a design by Giovan Battista Giorgi, 1822
Lapis lazuli, *pietre dure*, *pietre tenere*, gold, 8.5 × 5.2 × 2.2 cm (3 3/8 × 2 1/16 × 7/8 in)
1996.531 (GB183)

PROVENANCE: Kugel, Paris, 1994.

LITERATURE: Snowman 1990, pls. 891–92; Giusti 1992, p. 120, pl. 66 and p. 260, n. 133.

DESCRIPTION: A rectangular snuffbox mounted *à cage* in chased gold, consisting of six panels of lapis lazuli, the cover depicting a military trophy composed of *pietre dure* and *pietre tenere*.

COMMENTARY: A document at the Opificio delle Pietre Dure in Florence dated 11 September 1822, describes a snuffbox very similar to the one in the Gilbert Collection: 'On this day 11 September (1822) – a snuff box of lapis lazuli with *pietre dure* work on the lid representing a military device consisting of a helmet placed on an upturned shield – delivered on the said date to His Excellency the Prince, the Chief Majordomo. The costs are as follows; labour *lire* 866.13.4 / stone *lire* 140 / various expenses *lire* 60'.[1] There are various pen and ink designs for snuffboxes depicting military trophies in the Archivio del Museo dell'Opificio in Florence. The snuffbox in the Gilbert Collection bears distinct similarities to two watercolour designs for lapis lazuli boxes (inv. nos. 123–124; figs. 16 and 17).

A huge collection of designs for military trophies was to be found in the catalogue of furnishings and decorations published by the architects Charles Percier (1764–1838) and Pierre-François-Leonard Fontaine (1762–1853) in a number of editions between 1802 and 1812 (see cat. no. 111). In the Grand Ducal workshops a martial design was used by Carlo Carlieri for a lavish sweetmeat dish made of lapis lazuli, begun in the workshop in 1807 at the request of Marie-Louise de Bourbon, Queen of Etruria. Snuffboxes with military trophies on the lid seem to derive from the same collection of designs.[2]

NOTES
1 Archivio dell'Opificio delle Pietre Dure, misc. 1, fasc. 5. The document transcribed above was first quoted by Anna Maria Giusti.
2 Galleria d'Arte Moderna, Florence; González-Palacios 1986, vol. 1, pp. 47–52.

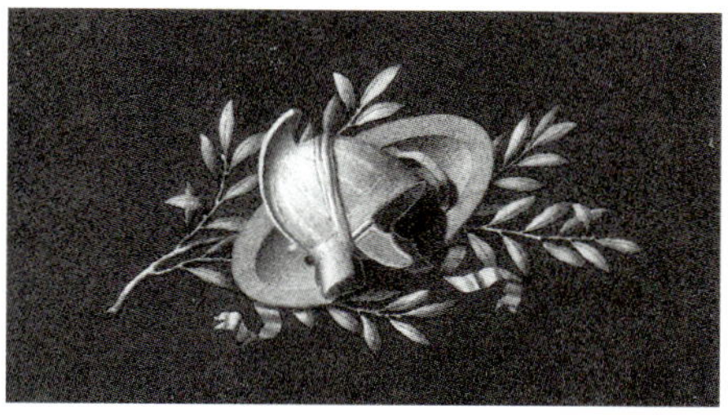

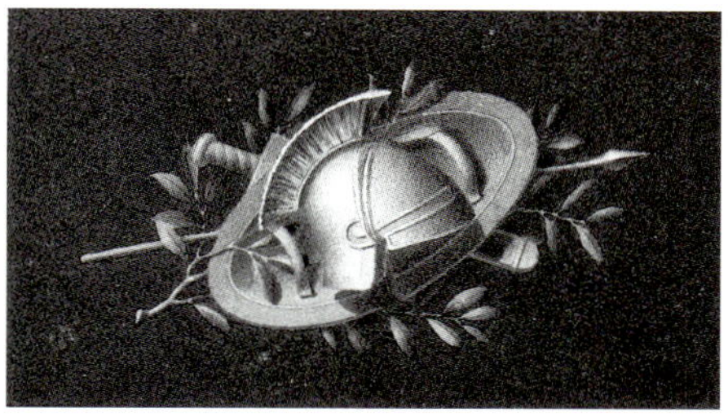

FIGS 16 & 17. Watercolour designs for *pietre dure* panels.

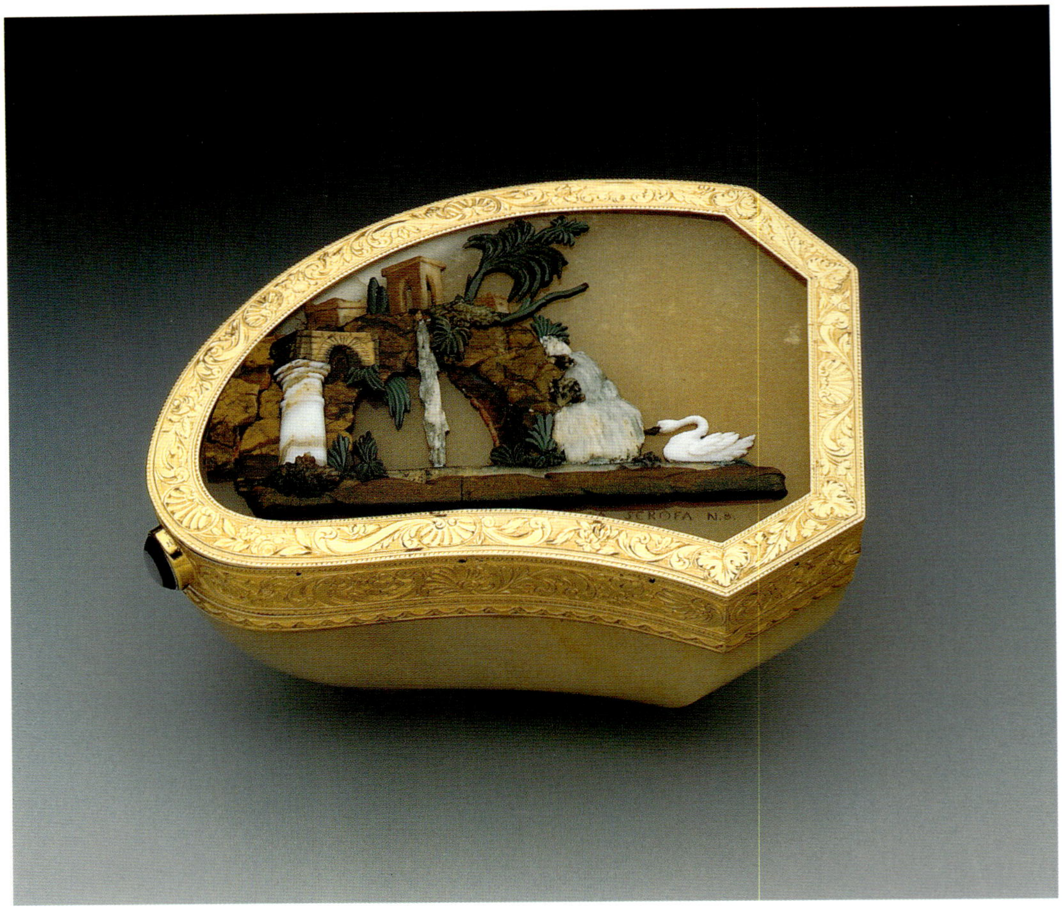

65. SNUFFBOX

Box: Gabriel-Raoul Morel, Paris, 1819/38; cover: signed by G. Morelli, Rome c. 1810
Chalcedony, agate, hardstones, gold, 9.5 × 7.6 × 4.7 cm ($3\frac{3}{4}$ × 3 × $1\frac{7}{8}$ in)
1996.431 (GB79/MM219)

PROVENANCE: S. J. Phillips, London, 1975.

LITERATURE: Habsburg-Lothringen 1983, no. 60; González-Palacios 1977, no. 50; González-Palacios and Röttgen 1982, no.54; Truman 1991, no. 44.

EXHIBITIONS: London, 1973; Los Angeles / Atlanta / San Antonio / Richmond / Seattle, 1977–79; Los Angeles / New York / Richmond, 1986–87; Los Angeles / Memphis, 1991–92.

DESCRIPTION: A kidney-shaped, hardstone box, the body composed of chalcedony, the cover applied with a hardstone cappricio featuring a mountain town, possibly Tivoli, a waterfall, and a swan in the right foreground. At the lower right base is an inscribed signature, G. (?) MORELLI F, IN ROMA VIA DELLA SCROFIA N. 8, covered up to the lower half of 'della' by the gold mounts. These are chased with scrolls, foliage, and shells and the thumbpiece is composed of agate.

COMMENTARY: The identity of the 'Morelli' who signed the hardstone cover of this snuffbox has been disputed over the years. The signature is probably that of Giovanni Morelli, a noted nineteenth-century Piedmontese mosaicist, sculptor and intaglio artist. He has also been desribed as a stone carver who worked on inlaid furniture, candelabra, frames, figurines, birds and floral sculpture. Several sources state that he collaborated with the famous mosaicist and hardstone artist, Giacomo Raffaelli, in Milan around 1804, and that he also operated in London and St. Petersburg.[1] Morelli also worked on the tabletop, *Achilles Heel* for the Vatican Mosaic workshop and has been mistakenly identified as Giuseppe Morelli.[2] He may also be the artist responsible for the Gilbert Collection micromosaic picture of Tivoli dated 1820 (Hanisee-Gabriel 2000, cat. no. 45).

NOTES

1 *Dizionario Enciclopedico Bolaffi dei Pittori e degli Incisori Italiani*, VIII, p. 12; *Corna, Dizionario dell' Storia dell'Arte in Italia* 1915, p. 373; Thieme Becker, XXV, p. 135-6; Nagler 1840, vol. 10, p. 532. Petochi 1981, p. 62.

2 Ledoux-Lebard, 1977, pp. 212, 216.

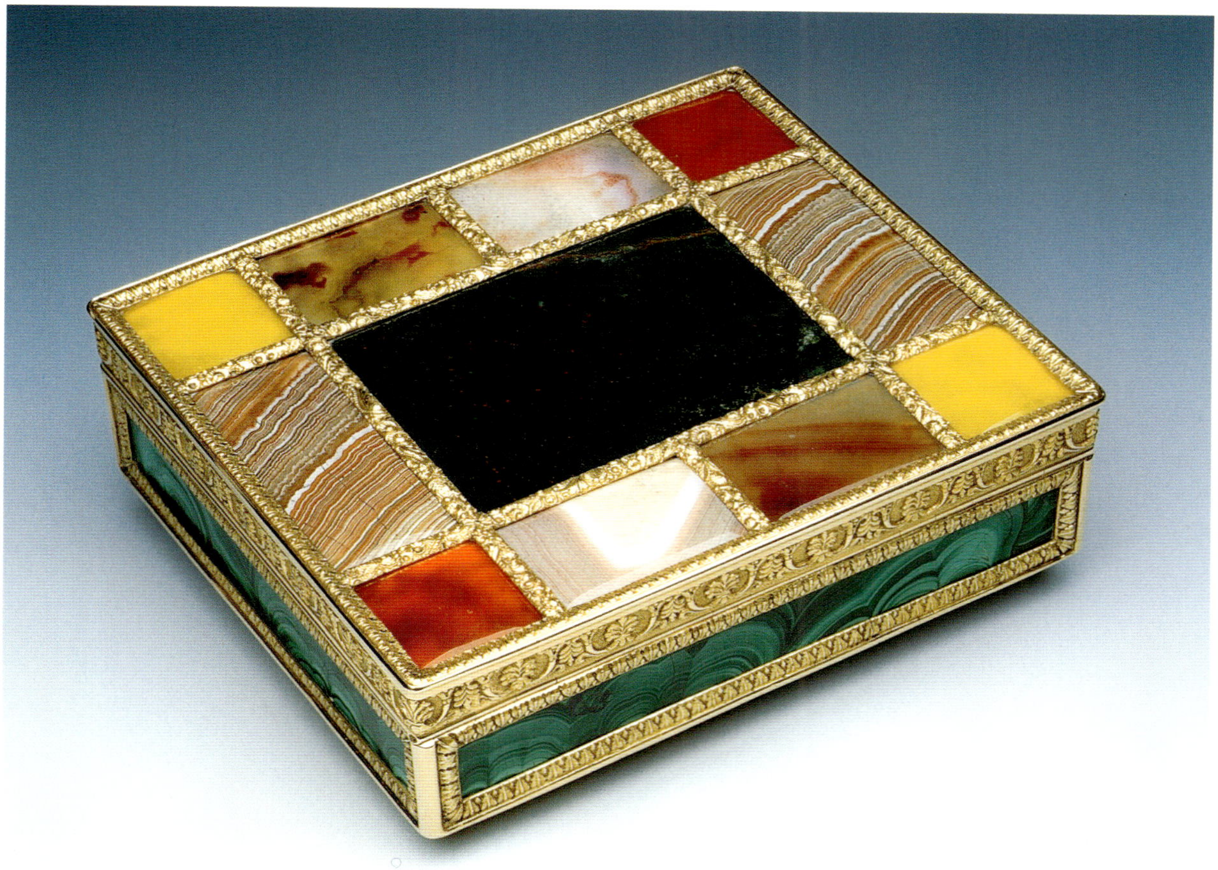

66. SNUFFBOX

Rome, c. 1828, Giovanni Andrea Mascelli (1796–1870)
Bloodstone, agate, malachite, lapis lazuli, chalcedony, quartz, foil, glazed-ivory miniature,
11.4 × 9.5 × 3.2 cm (4½ × 3¾ × 1¼ in)
1996.392 (GB28)

PROVENANCE: S. J. Phillips, London 1980.

LITERATURE: Habsburg-Lothringen 1983, no. 6; Truman 1991, no. 147; Figueiredo 1992, pp. 18–19.

EXHIBITIONS: Los Angeles / New York / Richmond, 1986–87; Los Angeles / Memphis, 1991–92.

DESCRIPTION: A rectangular, gold-mounted box, the cover composed of 11 rectangular panels of coloured specimen hardstones (bloodstone, agate, malachite, lapis lazuli, and chalcedony) framed in gold chased with anthemions and foliage. The base consists of panels of lapis lazuli and adventurine quartz, the sides of the box set with malachite. Inside the cover, in a similarly chased gold frame, is a rectangular, half-length portrait miniature on ivory of a man wearing a dark coat, holding the front of a red-lined cloak with his right hand, and wearing on his left lapel the Neapolitan Order of Saint Januarius and the Turkish Order of the Crescent (identified by Charles Truman). The inside of the base is lined with gold.

COMMENTARY: The brothers Giovanni Andrea (1796–1870) and Giovacchino Mascelli were partners in Rome with a goldsmith's shop at 90/91 Piazza di Spagna. The box is engraved inside in script: FRATELLI MASCELLI A ROMA AND RIGHT HONOURABLE SIR WILLIAM DRUMMOND 1828. Drummond (1770–1828) attended Christ Church, Oxford, and became an MP for St. Mawes, Cornwall in 1795. In 1801 he was sworn to the Privy Council and appointed envoy extraordinary to the court of Naples, and in 1803 became Ambassador to Constantinople. He retired in 1809, and died in Rome in 1828.[1]

NOTE

1 Thanks to Charles Truman for the biographical information.

Hardstone Pictures

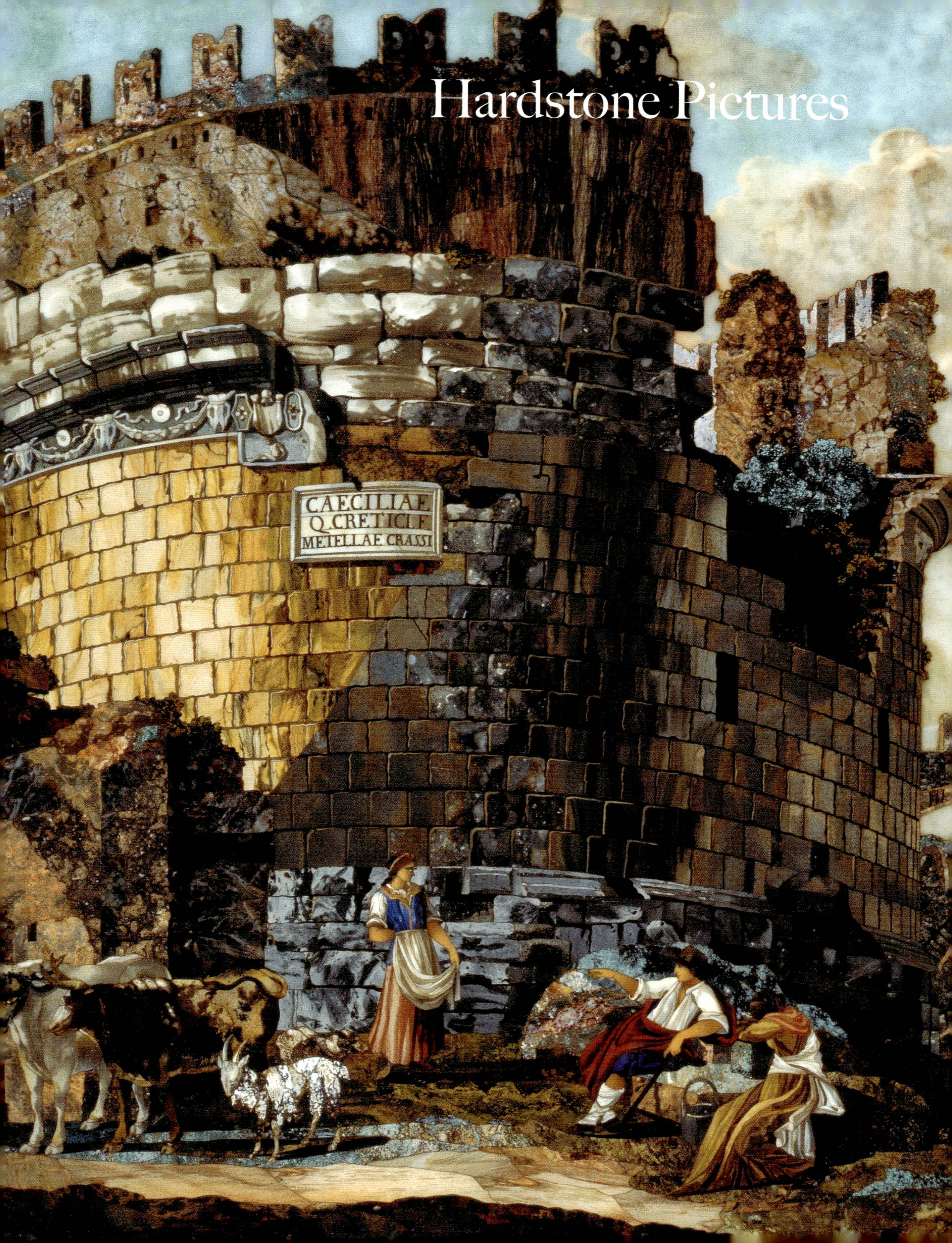

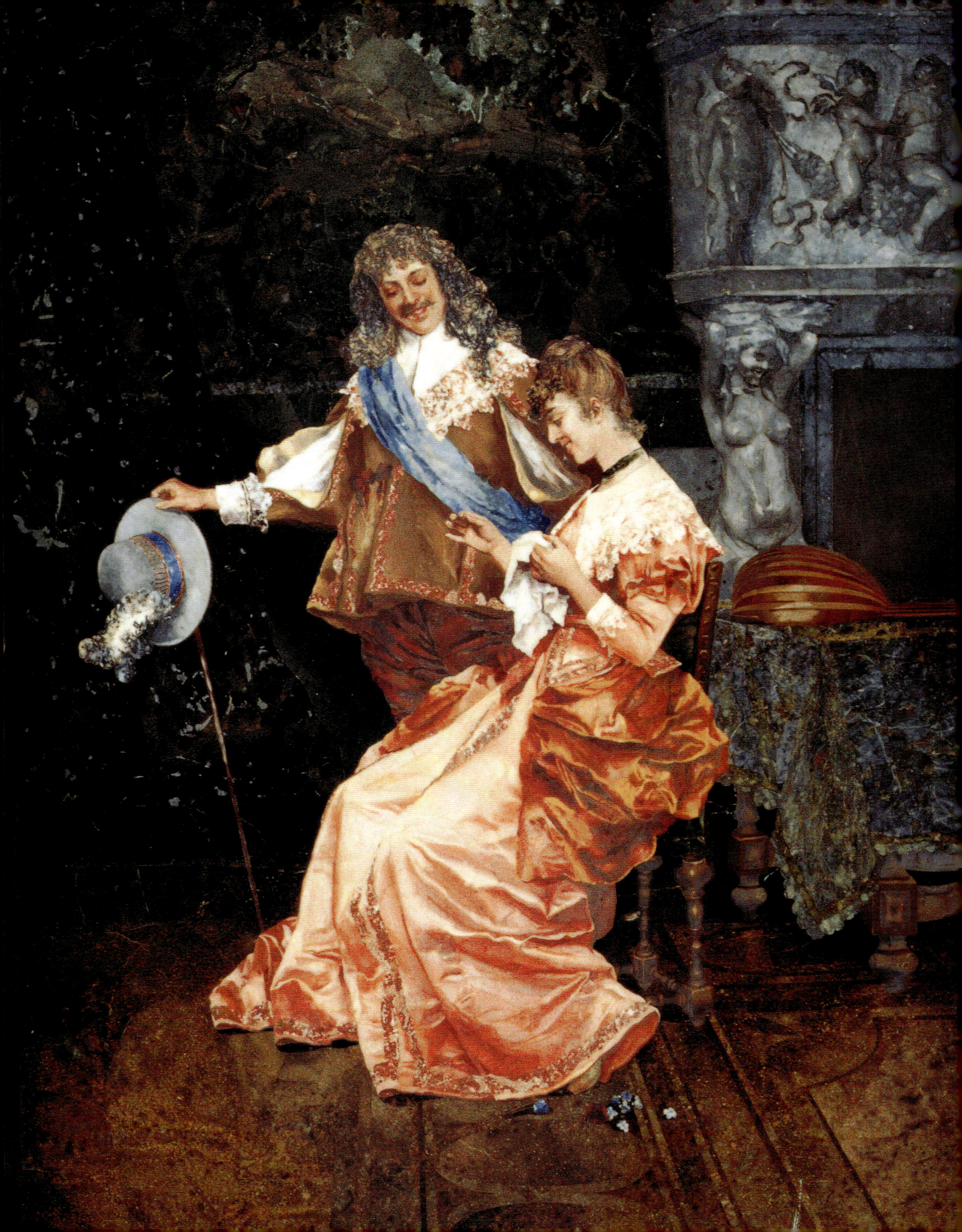

HARDSTONE PICTURES

In sixteenth-century Europe, the pictorial potential of stones in their natural colours aroused the enthusiasm of collectors, painters and stone carvers alike. At a time when contemporary culture was widely focused on scientific inquiry and the development of technical knowledge, sensitivity to products of the natural world led to the search for an 'everlasting' type of picture. Amateur scientists took a great interest in unusual stones, seeing images of different kinds in their natural markings. In the wake of this popular hobby, artists began to imitate nature, improving on the colours and veining of marble, alabaster, lapis lazuli, jasper, agate, and other stones by enhancing the inherent designs with traditional oil painting techniques. This art form fell somewhere between mineralogy and traditional painting and was highly successful in the second half of the sixteenth century and throughout the seventeenth century.

Giorgio Vasari discusses the art of painting on stone in his *Life of Sebastiano del Piombo* (c. 1485–1547), commenting that the Venetian artist had tried out this technique and that:

> it pleased everyone a lot because in this way paintings were made eternal and could not be assailed by fire nor by woodworm. So he began making many paintings on stone, and surrounding them with ornamental borders of mixed stones which looked very beautiful when polished. It is true to say, however, that when the works of art were completed they could only be lifted or moved with the greatest difficulty because they were so heavy. Nevertheless many people were attracted by the novelty of the new method and by the beautiful results, and they gave him money to work for them.[1]

Stones of different kinds, of different colours, and with different markings were used to give a variety of effects. Filippo Lauri (1623–94), in his *Baptism of Christ*, for example (cat. no. 99), used a panel of amethyst, mounting it in a frame decorated with *pietre dure*.

In Florence, craftsmen of the Grand Ducal workshops began trying to perfect their mosaic technique, aiming to make their work look as much like brush painting as possible. According to Antonio Zobi,[2] 'the time at which real painting began to be imitated in Florence with natural coloured stones inlaid in mosaic to portray objects as if they had been painted with a paint brush' was chronicled by a document dated 1597 relating to a portrait of Cosimo I by the painter Domenico Cresti (called Il Passignano; c. 1560–1636). The portrait was given to the stoneworker Francesco Ferrucci (1497–1585) to be transformed into a mosaic picture (Museo dell'Opificio delle Pietre Dure, Florence). Ferdinand I wrote in a letter to Count G. Bardi di Vernio in 1601: 'We have now invented a new way of constructing marble mosaics using different shaped pieces and great ingenuity and skill; we can

Previous page
Detail of cat. no. 70

Opposite
Detail of cat. no. 74

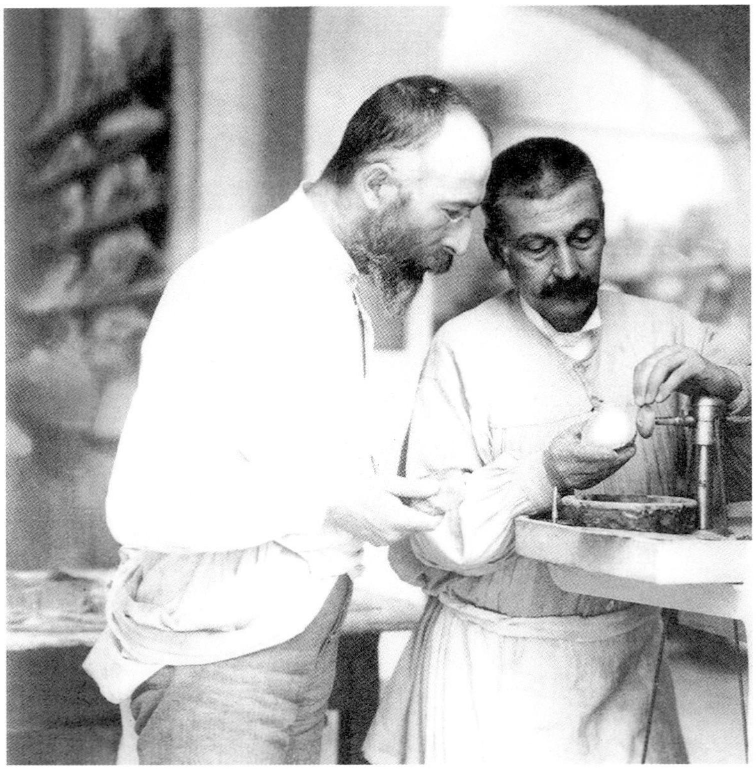

FIG. 18 Giovanni Montelatici (left) in his workshop, c. 1900.
Photo courtesy of Arte del Mosaico, Florence.

make likenesses of people using natural colours for the whole face. We have just had a portrait done like this of His Holiness [Pope Clement VIII]'. The face was 'portrayed in such a life-like manner, just as a portrait painted with a brush might be'. The Grand Duke went on to recommend that the portrait be viewed in the correct light, hung high up and from a distance, so that its qualities might be appreciated to the full. His strictures were probably engendered by his awareness that the technique was still in its infancy and that the pieces of mosaic might not be laid with absolute precision. Nevertheless, taken at a glance, the result was very convincing. This portrait was recently acquired by the J. Paul Getty Museum, Los Angeles.[3]

By the early seventeenth century, such experiments with mosaic were developing in different directions, imitating various styles of painting, from landscape to figure painting to scientific illustration. Once the interest in portraiture described above had waned, the technique was applied to mosaic work on household and ecclesiastical furnishings. *Pietre dure* pictures conceived as separate objects came back into fashion after the middle of the eighteenth century. During the Lorraine period, when Louis Siries was in charge of the court workshop, 'all effort was directed towards representing people, landscapes and architecture, and other subjects proper to the art of painting'. Great skill was needed to 'match the pieces exactly, searching out markings and natural shading in the stones in order best to imitate the necessary tones and half tones, and to give weight to the objects being depicted'.[4]

The mid-nineteenth century saw the art of stone painting enter a period of stagnation. It returned to life in the 1880s with two panels designed by Edoardo Marchionni (1873–1923), decorated with a landscape, a small girl gathering flowers, and the goddess Flora. The panels were used in 1883 to decorate a drawing room jardinière.[5] In private workshops as well, there was a revival of interest in the form.

At this time, when Florentine mosaic work was experiencing its most devastating crisis, unable to develop in any creative way, it took a skilful mosaicist, Giovanni Montelatici, to realise that a revival of painting in *pietre dure* would restore dignity to the art of hardstone mosaic, which, at a technical level, had reached its peak. At the end of the nineteenth century he set up a partnership with Galileo Chini, the artistic director of his workshop, and soon their work began to gain popularity. In 1897, a *pietre dure* picture by Montelatici entitled *A Difficult Letter* (present location unknown) was one of the most prominent exhibits by a Florentine artist during a charity exhibition in the city. Its price was estimated at 6,000 *lire*, among paintings costing between 40 and 1,000 *lire*.[6] International renown, however, was won by a work born of the union between Montelatici and Chini, the latter being responsible for the design. This was described as an 'imposing table' with a picture of the Annunciation (present location unknown); it was sent to the Exposition Universelle in Paris in 1900, where it won the gold medal and was immediately sold to a 'very rich foreign collector'.[7] Following this success, Montelatici became the founding member and director of the workshop called La Musiva, which is still functioning today.

The first decades of the twentieth century saw a period of intense activity at La Musiva, with Montelatici's works selling successfully to foreign buyers. His products, and those of his sons Mario (1894–1974) and Alfonso (active late nineteeth and early twentieth century), embraced the whole repertory of Florentine Macchiaioli and post-Macchiaioli painting and captured the effects of light in stone mosaic with stunning virtuosity. The Montelatici's production covered just about every subject, with heavy emphasis on sentimental domestic scenes with glimpses of rural life. A favourite theme is child poverty, sentimentally viewed, as in *The Stocking* and *Two Little Tykes*, by Mario Montelatici, both in the Gilbert Collection (cat. nos. 76, 77). These are directly derived from paintings of the Tuscan Macchiaiolo school and from Southern Italian painters who were themselves inspired by Victorian sentimental art. Also popular are scenes of gallantry derived from French literature, made popular in Italy by Francesco Vinea (1845–1902); Alfonso's large picture depicting a cavalier and his lady in a wine cellar is also typical (cat. no. 76). Any subject inspired by nostalgia for vanished worlds could be turned into a mosaic: a painting by the Florentine artist Raffaello Sorbi (1844–1931) for example, is the model for another picture by Mario Montelatici in the Gilbert Collection (cat. no. 74).

NOTES

1 Vasari 1568, vol. 5, p. 679.
2 Zobi 1853, p. 184.
3 Fusco and Hess 1994.
4 Zobi 1853, pp. 296–97.
5 Museo dell'Opificio delle Pietre Dure, Florence; Giusti, Mazzoni, and Pampaloni Martelli 1978, figs. 374–75.
6 *Catalogo della Esposizione* 1897, p. 6, no. 195.
7 *Arte del mosaico* 1928.

67. THE TOMB OF CECILIA METELLA

Florence, Grand Ducal workshops, after a cartoon by Ferdinando Partini, 1795
Pietre dure, marble, alabaster, pigment, gilt bronze, 54.3 × 76.4 cm (21 3/8 × 30 1/16 in)
1996.242 (MM92)

PROVENANCE: Ferdinand III of Lorraine; Palazzo Pitti; Opificio delle Pietre Dure, Florence; Pope Pius IX; Giorgio Rovelli, Rome, 1971; Los Angeles County Museum of Art.

LITERATURE: Zobi 1853, p. 299; Avery and Emperatori 1975, no. 22; González-Palacios 1977a, no. 18; Giusti, Mazzoni and Pampaloni Martelli 1978, p. 329; González-Palacios and Röttgen 1982, no. 18.

EXHIBITIONS: Los Angeles, 1975; London, 1975; Los Angeles, 1977; Jerusalem, 1995.

DESCRIPTION: A mosaic picture in *pietre dure* with view of the Tomb of Cecilia Metella, antique ruins, peasants, two cows, and a goat. The alabaster background of sky has been painted from behind to give the effect of clouds.

COMMENTARY: Taking as his inspiration the mosaic pictures in the Kaiserhaus, Vienna, Louis Siries proposed to Ferdinand of Lorraine the execution of a cycle of pictures for a particular part of the Palazzo Pitti. As the subject, he suggested 'ancient buildings', remarking that 'architecture is the subject that can be represented most perfectly'. Having received the Grand Duke's consent, he asked the painter Ferdinando Partini to prepare the *modelli*. The paintings, dating from 1794 to 1797, are still to be seen in the Museo dell'Opificio delle Pietre Dure in Florence.[1]

The first picture in the series was a view of the Pantheon in Rome. This seems not to have satisfied Siries, since for the subsequent drawings, he advised Partini to get the two volumes of *Vedute di Roma*, engraved by Gian Battista Piranesi (1720–78) between 1748 and 1778. The next pictures were closely based on Piranesi's work: the mosaic version of *The Tomb of Cecilia Metella* was completed in 1795, and views of the Temple of Peace, the Temple of Janus, the Ponte Molle, and the Foro di Nerva were all completed in 1796 (with the assistance of the painter Giovan Battista Dell'Era; 1765–1798). The series, completed in 1798, was immediately dispersed. The French invaded the following year, and among the works of art selected by the Commissaire Joly to take back to Paris were the views of the Pantheon and *The Tomb of Cecilia Metella*.[2] Both were returned in 1815.

The Tomb of Cecilia Metella, certainly the most successful picture in the series, was then presented to Pope Pius IX by Leopoldo II in 1857. A replica ordered by Leopold was to be sent to the International Exhibition in London in 1862 (Museo dell'Opificio delle Pietre Dure, Florence), but according to Demetrio Carlo Finocchietti,[3] it was not ready in time and was sent to the Paris Exhibition in 1867 instead (the archive of the Museo dell'Opificio contains a drawing possibly used for the execution of the replica). The version in the Gilbert Collection, as has been noted by González-Palacios, is the original one.

This picture shows one of the most celebrated Roman archaeological sites, (the tomb is also known by the name *Capo di Bove*, because of the frieze of *bucrania* – stylised ox skulls, usually a decoration on a temple or altar – running beneath the battlements). Dating from the first century BC, the tomb is one of the most impressive sights along the Appian Way. Cecilia Metella, a loved Roman heroine, was the fourth wife of Lucius Cornelius Sylla, dictator of Rome (r. 82–79 BC), and daughter of Quintus Caecilius Metellus. The circular tower, built 79 years before Christ, is about 70 ft in diameter. It was converted into a fortress for the Gaetani family by their relative, Pope Boniface VIII.

The tomb was a famous resting place for tourists, artists, and learned men. The interior was at one time supposed to have contained treasures and works of art, but it is now bare. The white marble sarcophagus, believed to belong to Cecilia Metella, was removed to the court of the Farnese Palace by Pope Paul III.

NOTES
1 Giusti, Mazzoni, and Pampaloni Martelli 1978, p. 328, no. 549.
2 Zobi 1853, p. 298.
3 Finochietti 1863.

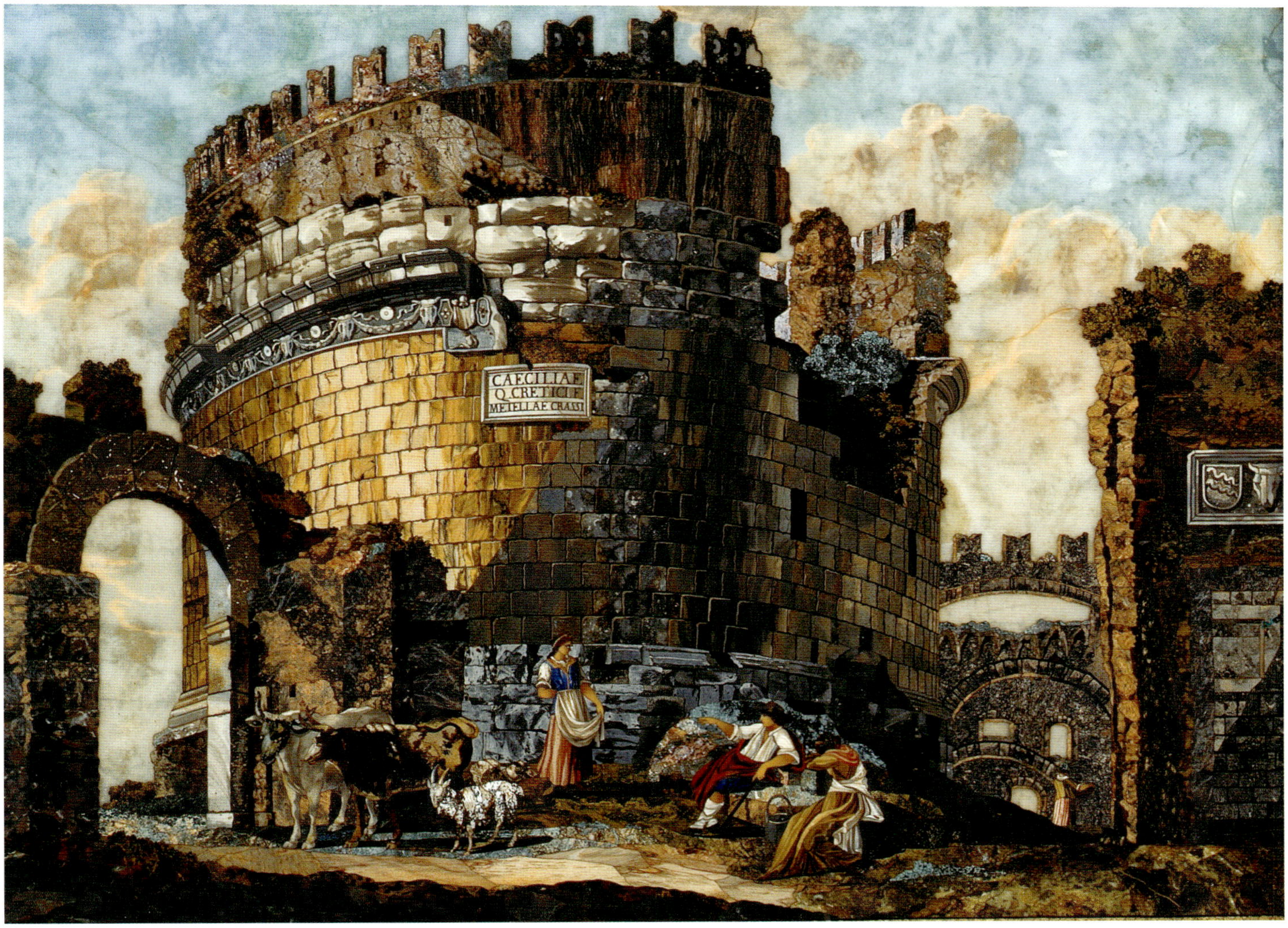
CAECILIAE
Q. CRETICI F
METELLAE CRASSI

68. PAIR OF STILL LIFES WITH FLOWERS

Florence, late nineteenth century
Pietre dure, *pietre tenere*, marble
A: 26.4 × 18.7 cm (10 3/8 × 7 3/8 in); 1996.581 (MM43A)
B: 26.7 × 18.7 cm (10 1/2 × 7 3/8 in); 1996.582 (MM43B)

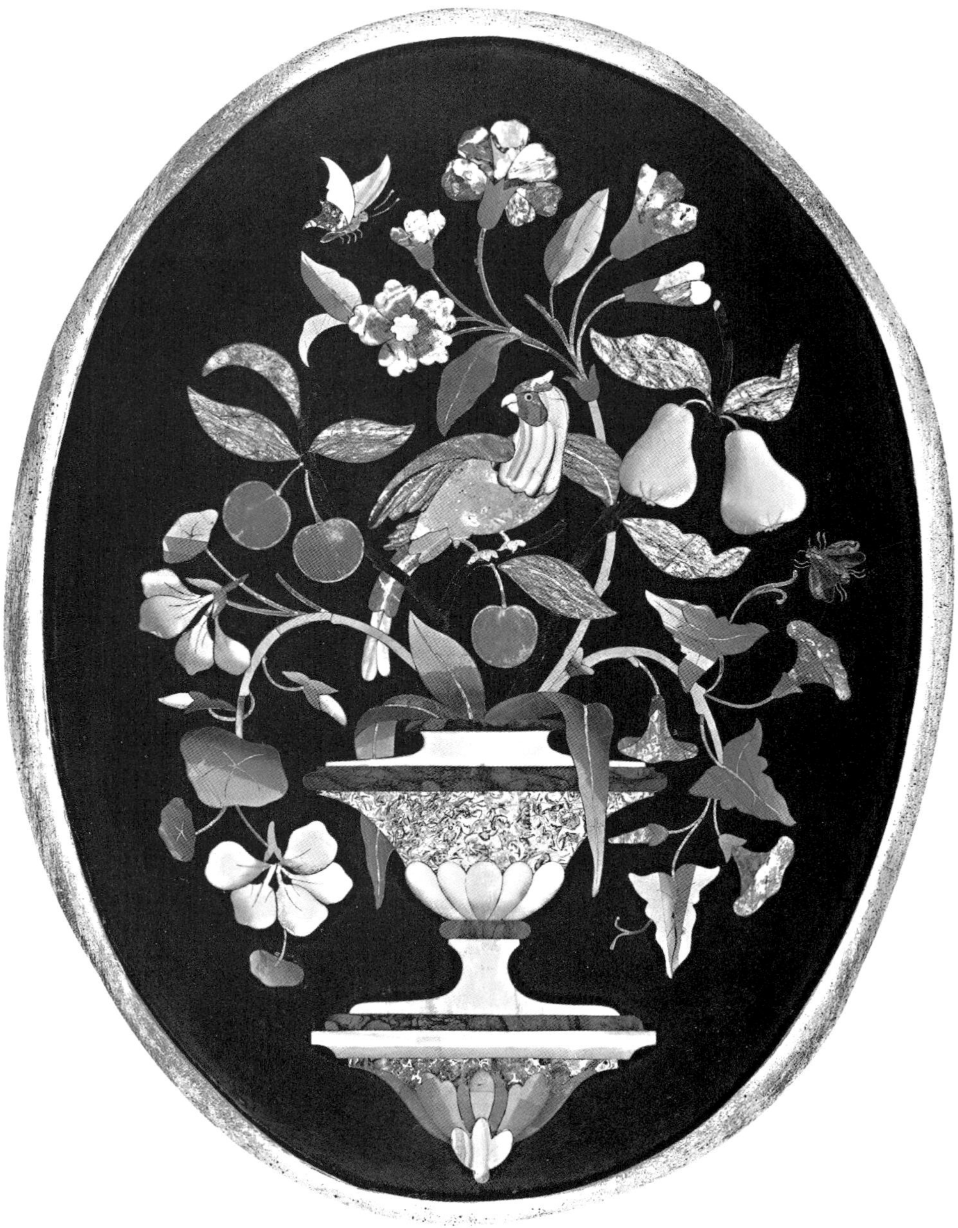

PROVENANCE: Grace Elliot, Los Angeles, 1966.

DESCRIPTION: Two oval medallions made of *pietre dure* and *pietre tenere* on a background of black marble. The mosaic designs are of two vases, each with a slightly different arrangement of flowers, fruit, birds, butterflies, and bees.

COMMENTARY: These late nineteenth-century panels were probably made to decorate the doors of a pair of cabinets (see cat. no. 16). They are typical examples of the work made by private workshops in Florence in the style of the Grand Ducal baroque mosaics produced during the seventeenth century.

69. DRINKING CAVALIER

Florence, c. 1880
Pietre dure, *pietre tenere*, 31.1 × 21 cm (12¼ × 8¼ in)
1996.217 (MM52)

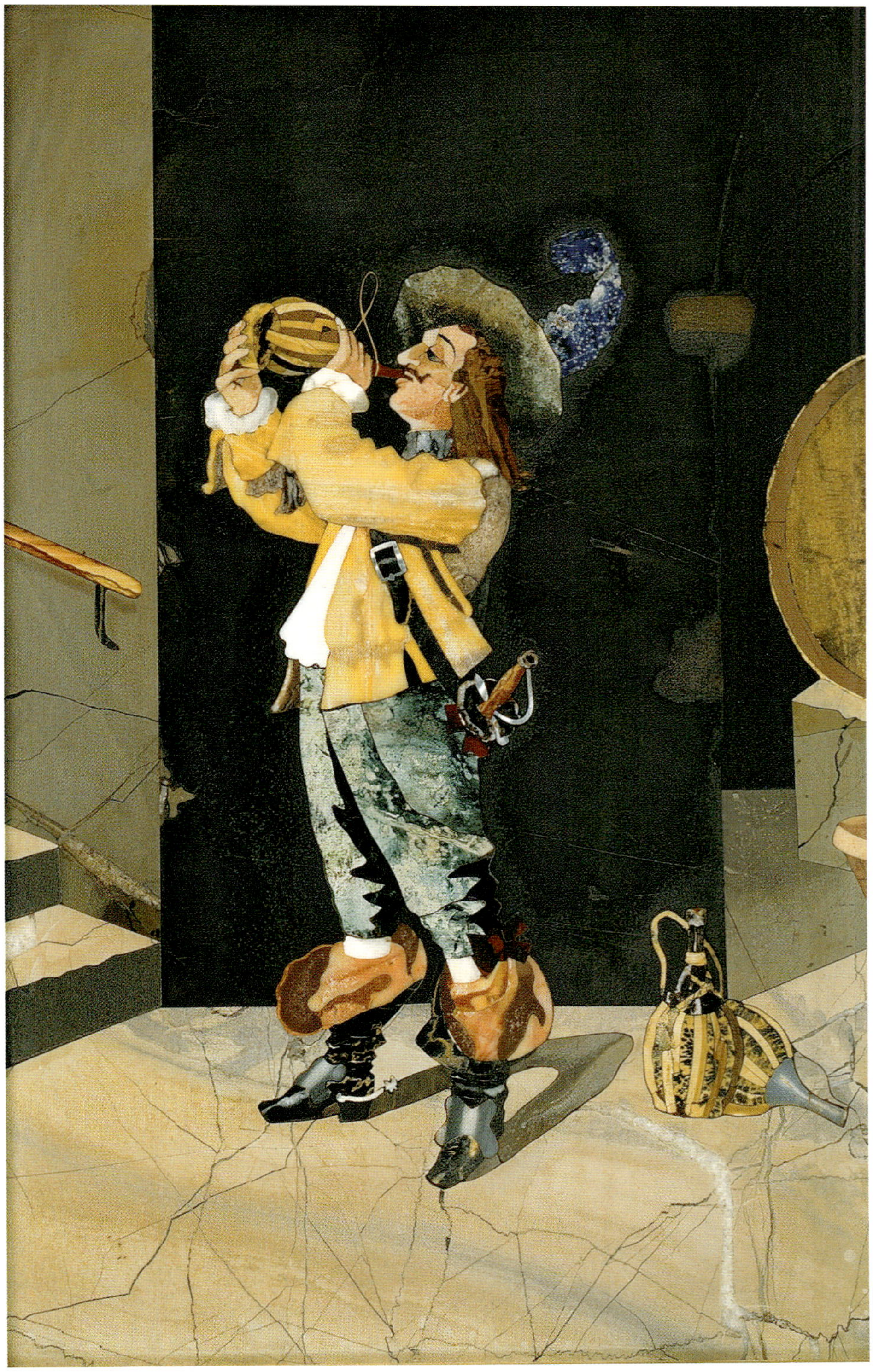

PROVENANCE: J. and P. van Brink, New York, 1969.

DESCRIPTION: Rectangular mosaic picture showing a cavalier in seventeenth-century costume drinking from a wine bottle in a cellar.

COMMENTARY: An identical *pietre dure* picture of a cavalier signed E. PAOLUCCI/FIRENZE, from c. 1880 was sold at auction.[1] Another larger one (87 × 72 cm) from the workshop of Peter Bazzanti and Son has also emerged on the market.[2] Both were probably copied from a painting in the style of Francesco Vinea. Other works to the same design include one in micromosaics (See Hanisee-Gabriel 2000, cat. no. 93).

NOTES

1 Sotheby's, London, on 25–28 July 1983.

2 Christie's (20 February 1992, lot 135).

70. FOX AND CHICKENS

Florence, private workshop, late nineteenth century
Pietre dure, coloured marble, 34.3 × 27.3 cm (13½ × 10¾ in)
1996.207 (MM34)

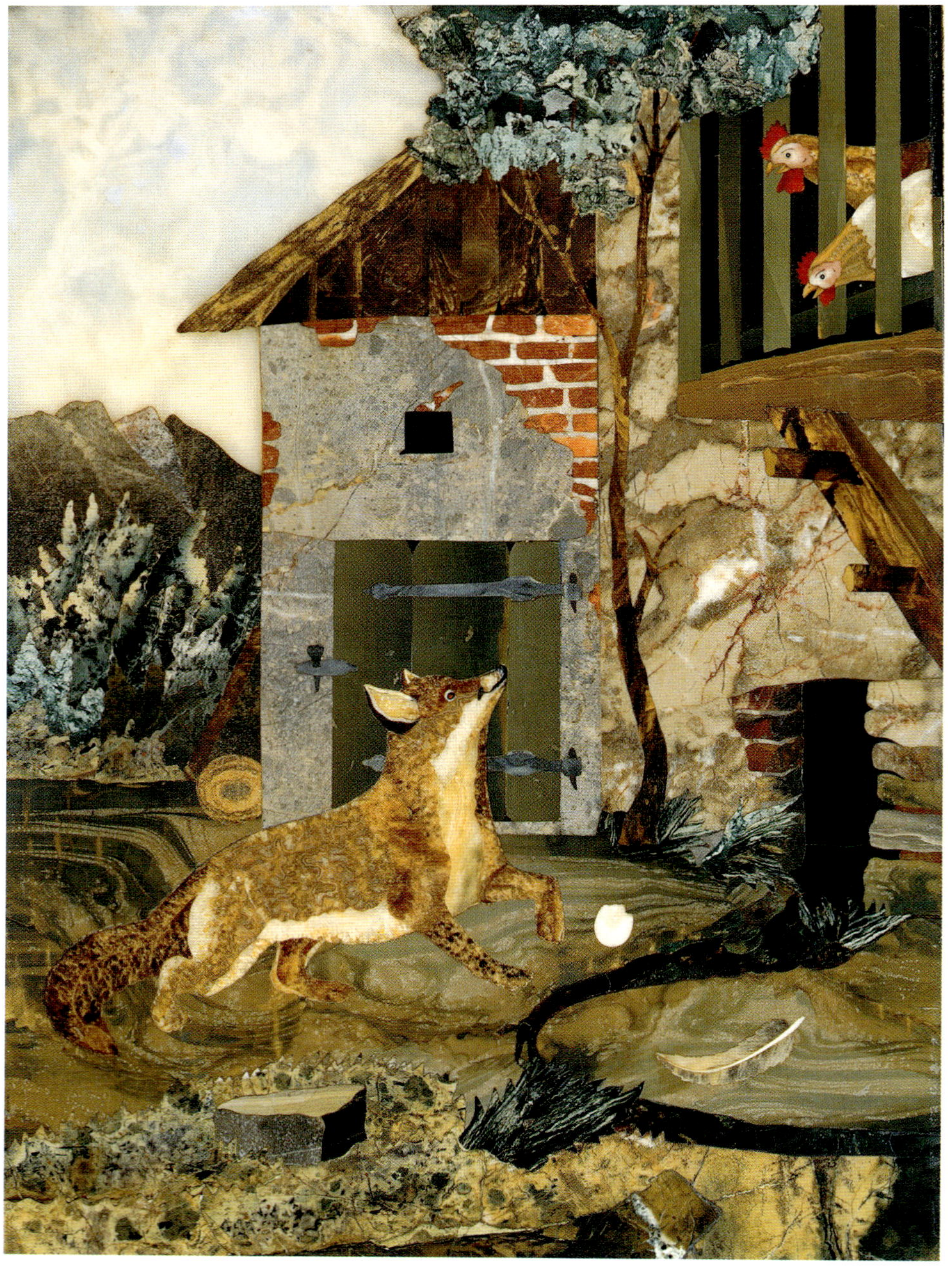

PROVENANCE: Amadeo de Castro, Rome, 1969.

LITERATURE: Avery and Emperatori 1975, no. 13.

EXHIBITIONS: Los Angeles, 1975; London, 1975; Los Angeles, 1977.

DESCRIPTION: A rectangular *pietre dure* and coloured marble panel showing a farm scene with a fox (who has just eaten an egg) stalking a pair of chickens in a henhouse.

71. FLIRTATION

Florence, A. Sandrini, late nineteenth century
Marble, chalcedony, alabaster, lapis lazuli, gilt wood, 147 × 79.5 × 8.8 cm (57⅞ × 31½ × 3½ in)
1996.356 (MM298)

PROVENANCE: Christie's, sale, London, 2 June 1995, lot 169.

EXHIBITION: Los Angeles 1996.

DESCRIPTION: A firescreen with a circular spreading base and gilt-wood rectangular frame decorated with foliage and scrolls. The frame is surmounted by a crown within an escutcheon with a Florentine lily. The mosaic panel depicts a chivalric scene showing a cavalier and lady in seventeenth-century dress in a room decorated in the baroque taste, with a chimneypiece and a draped table. An inscription incised on the reverse reads: DIPINTO DAL PROF. F. VINEA/FLIRTATION/ESEGUITO IN MOSAICO A FIRENZE VIA DEI FOSSI NO. 4 NEL LABORATORIO DI A. SANDRINI DIRETTO DA GINO PANERAI.

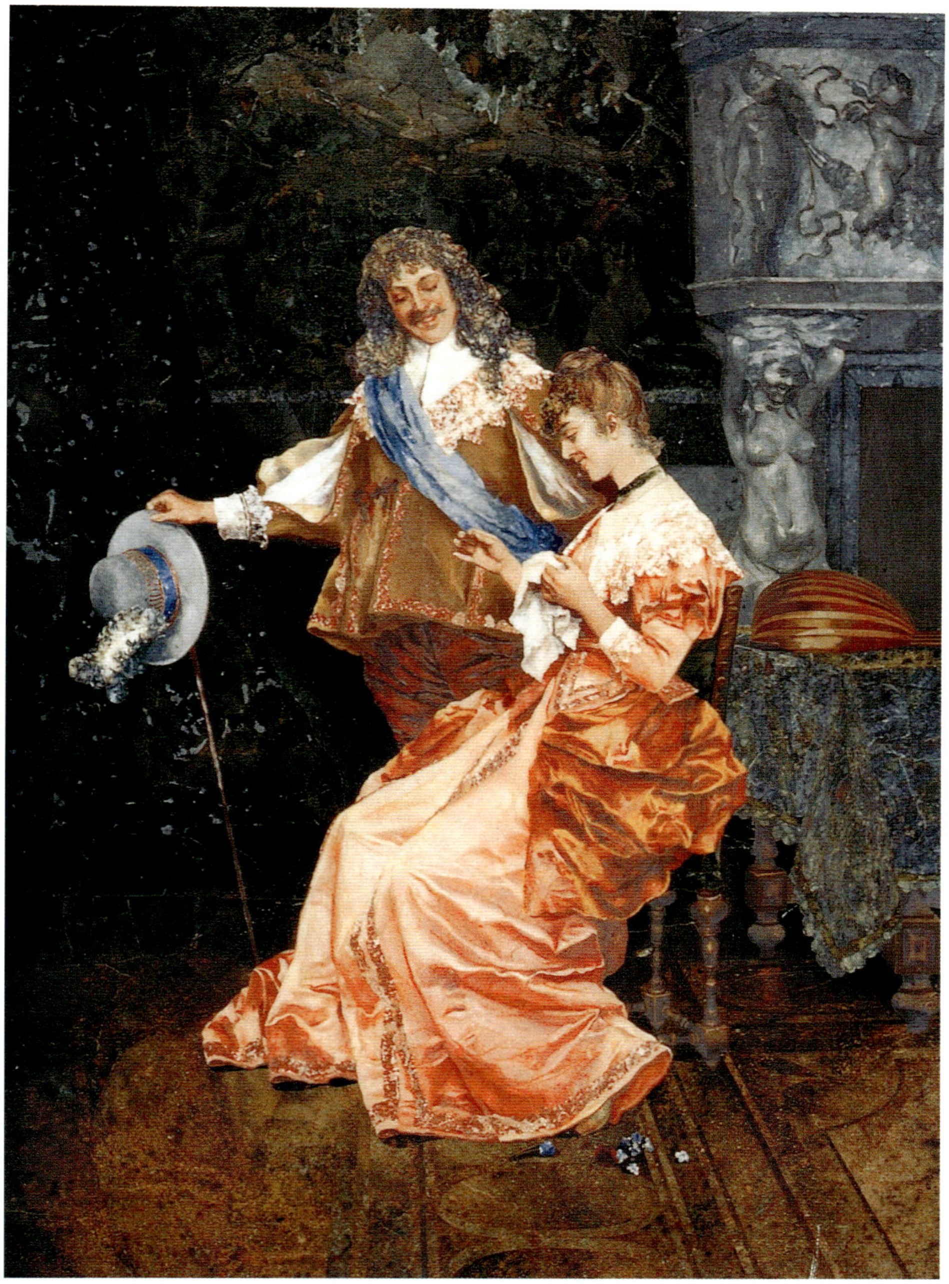

COMMENTARY: The inscription documents the origin of the subject matter as a painting by Francesco Vinea entitled *Flirtation*. Vinea created several versions of this subject, one of which was the model for a large hardstone picture by Alfonso Montelatici in the Gilbert Collection (cat. no. 76). The inscription also indicates that the mosaic was made in the Florentine workshop of A. Sandrini, directed by Gino Panerai. No information about this workshop is known.

The choice of the subject, together with the richly carved gilt-wood frame, suggests a late nineteenth-century date. The hardstone picture is very similar to a number of works sent to the Bruxelles Exposition in 1897 by the renowned Florentine manufactory Ugolini, as seen in a contemporary photograph of its display (see fig. 2, p. 14).

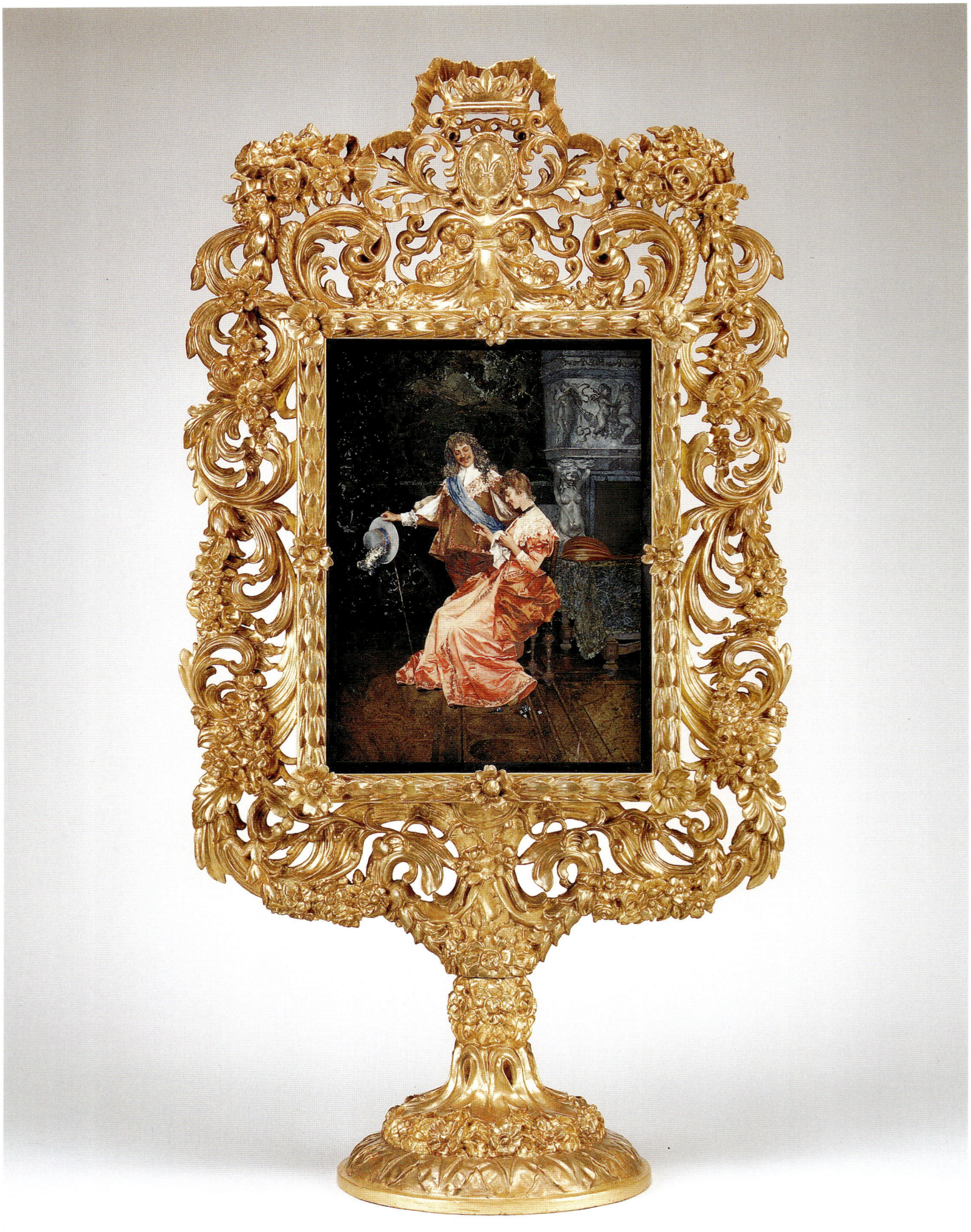

72. PIAZZA DELLA SIGNORIA, FLORENCE

Florence, attributed to Alfonso Montelatici (active late nineteenth/early twentieth centuries), late nineteenth century
Pietre dure, marble, Albarese limestone, alabaster, clock movement, 109.2 × 85.1 cm (43 × 33½ in)
1996.324 (MM231)

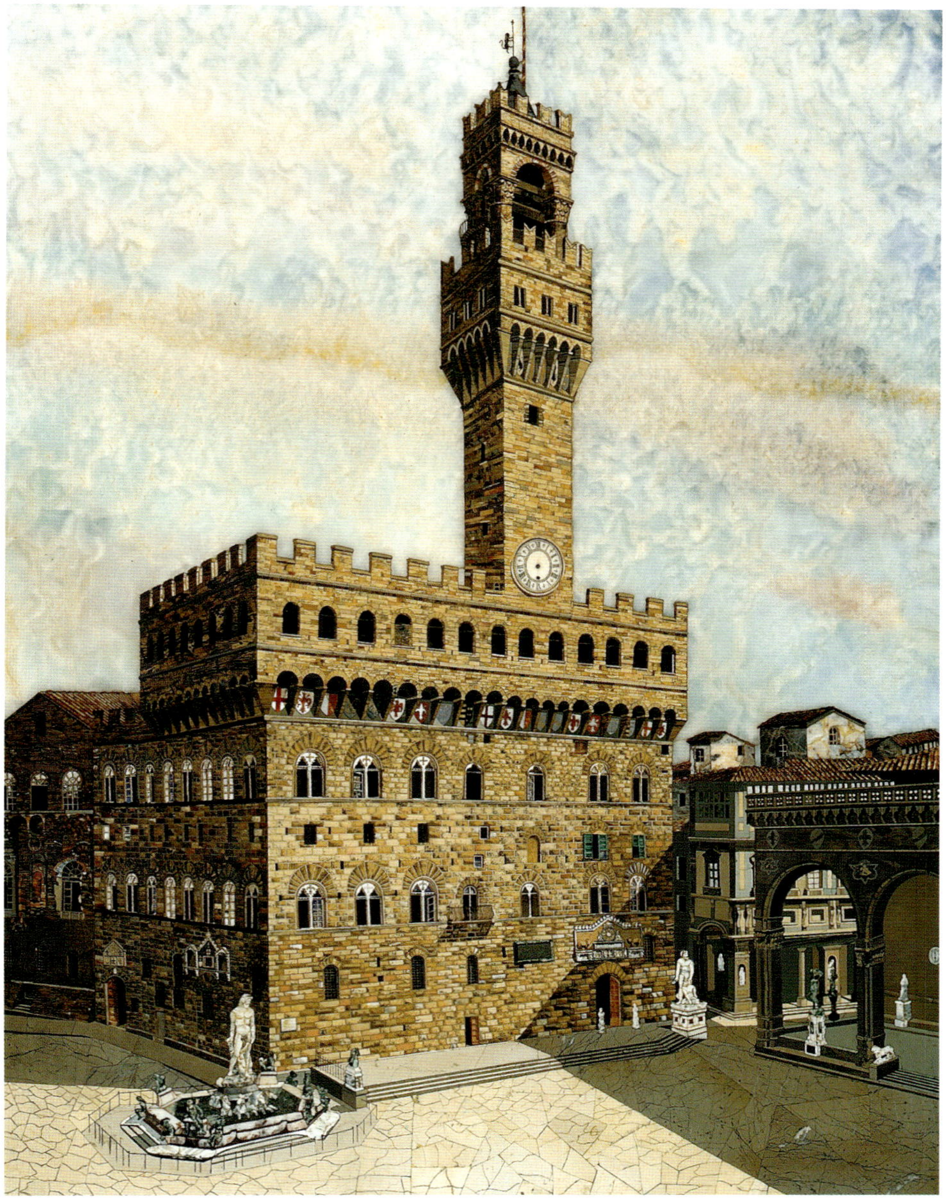

PROVENANCE: Nestle, Inc, New York, 1975; Los Angeles County Museum of Art.

LITERATURE: González-Palacios and Röttgen 1982, no. 115.

EXHIBITION: Los Angeles, 1977.

DESCRIPTION: A large view of the Piazza della Signoria in Florence, made of *pietre dure*, marble, Albarese limestone, and alabaster. On the bell tower of the palace is a clock mechanism.

COMMENTARY: Although this picture is not signed, it can probably be attributed to Alfonso Montelatici, who, of all the turn-of-the-century mosaicists in Florence, was the most attracted to large formats and big, coloured backgrounds. The view is most likely to have been taken from a photograph. The absence of Michelangelo's *David*, which originally stood in front of the Palazzo della Signoria, indicates that it dates from after 1873, the year in which the statue was removed to the Museo dell'Accademia.

73. FLIRTATION

Florence, Alfonso Montelatici (active late nineteeth/early twentieth centuries), early twentieth century
Pietre dure, 114.3 × 88.9 cm (45 × 35 in)
1996.186 (MM4)

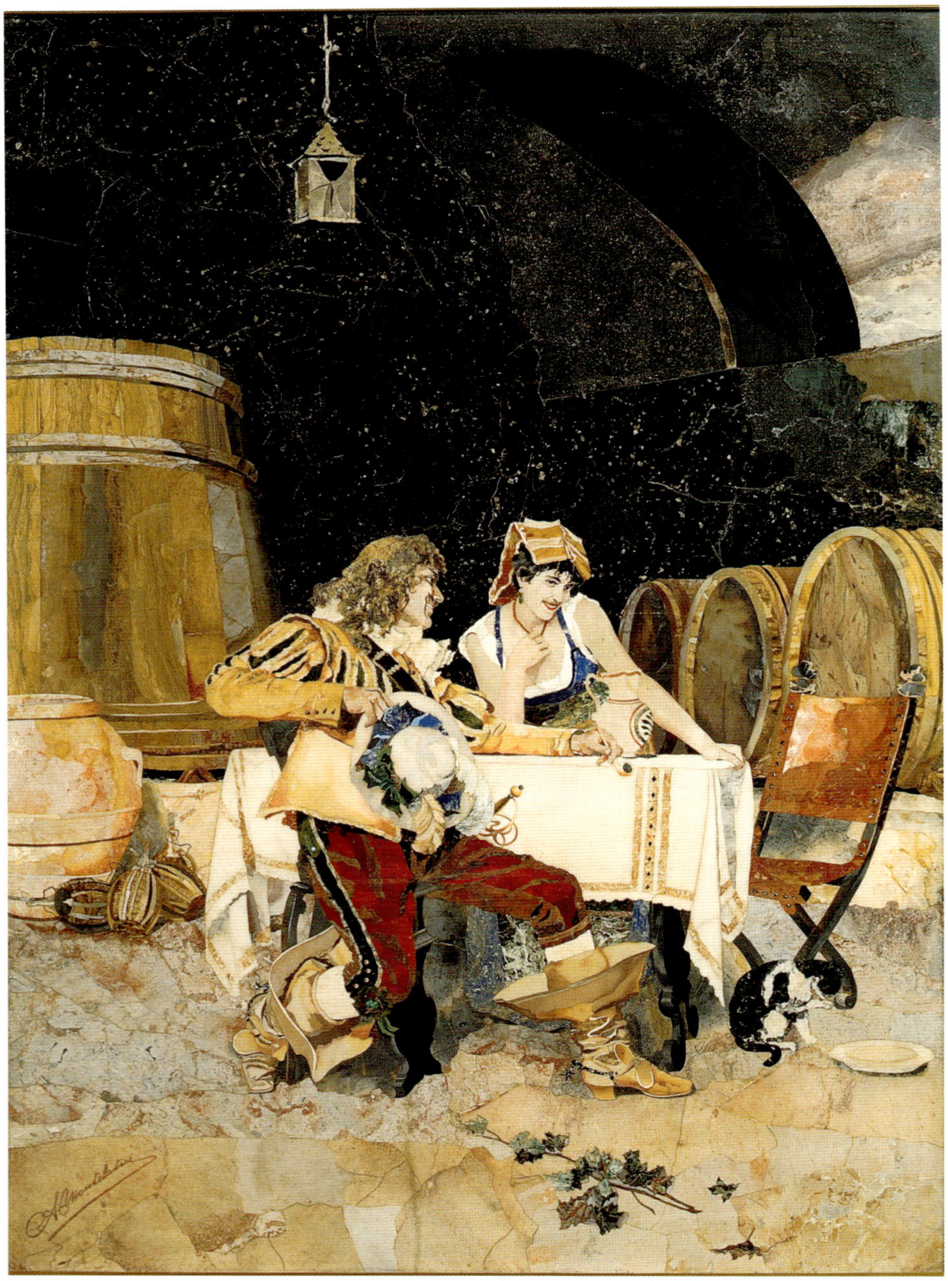

PROVENANCE: Sotheby's, London, sale, 24 July 1969, lot 75; Los Angeles County Museum of Art.

EXHIBITION: Los Angeles, 1977.

DESCRIPTION: A mosaic picture in *pietre dure* and *pietre tenere*, signed *A. Montelatici*. It shows a cavalier in seventeenth-century costume with a woman in a wine cellar.

COMMENTARY: This picture shows Montelatici's extraordinary technical skill in imitating painting in stone. It is based on *Flirtation* by Francesco Vinea.[1] Compared with the other members of the Montelatici family, Alfonso preferred large-scale works and themes of gallantry. His works show a marked preference for broad patches of colour and assertive backgrounds.

NOTE

1 Signed and dated 1870; Sotheby's, New York, 24 February 1983, lot 83.

74. ROMAN IDYLL

Florence, Mario Montelatici (1894–1974), 1923
Pietre dure and *pietre tenere*, 39.4 × 58.4 cm (15½ × 23 in)
1996.349 (MM284)

PROVENANCE: Butterfield and Butterfield, 8–11 November 1988, lot 3827.

DESCRIPTION: A hardstone picture, signed by Mario Montelatici and dated 1923, showing a young man and woman holding hands in a garden. They are wearing classical robes and sandals and are seated together on a stone bench. A brown-and-white dog watches attentively, while sunlight filters through the branches of trees that appear in the background against a blue sky.

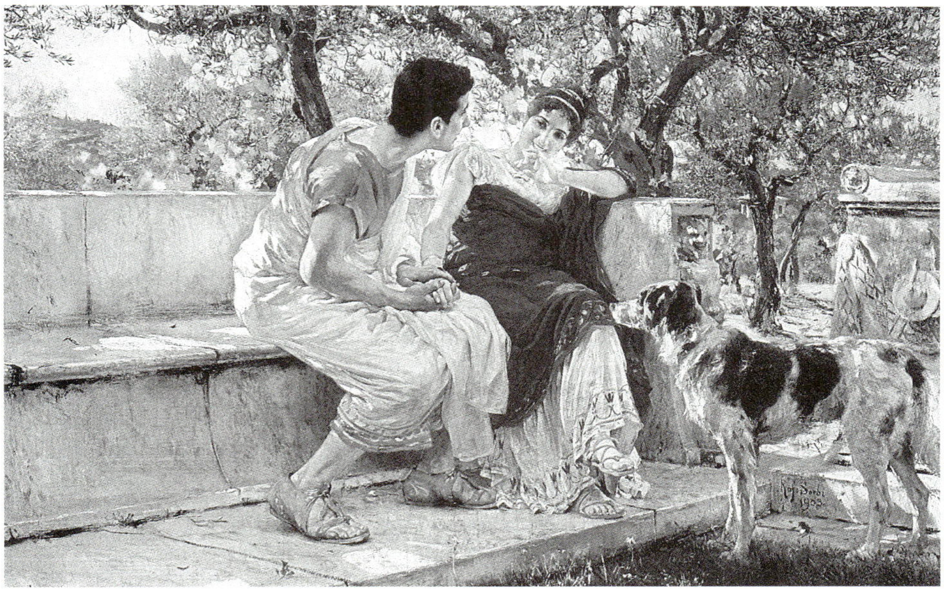

FIG. 19 Rafaello Sorbi, *Roman Idyll.*

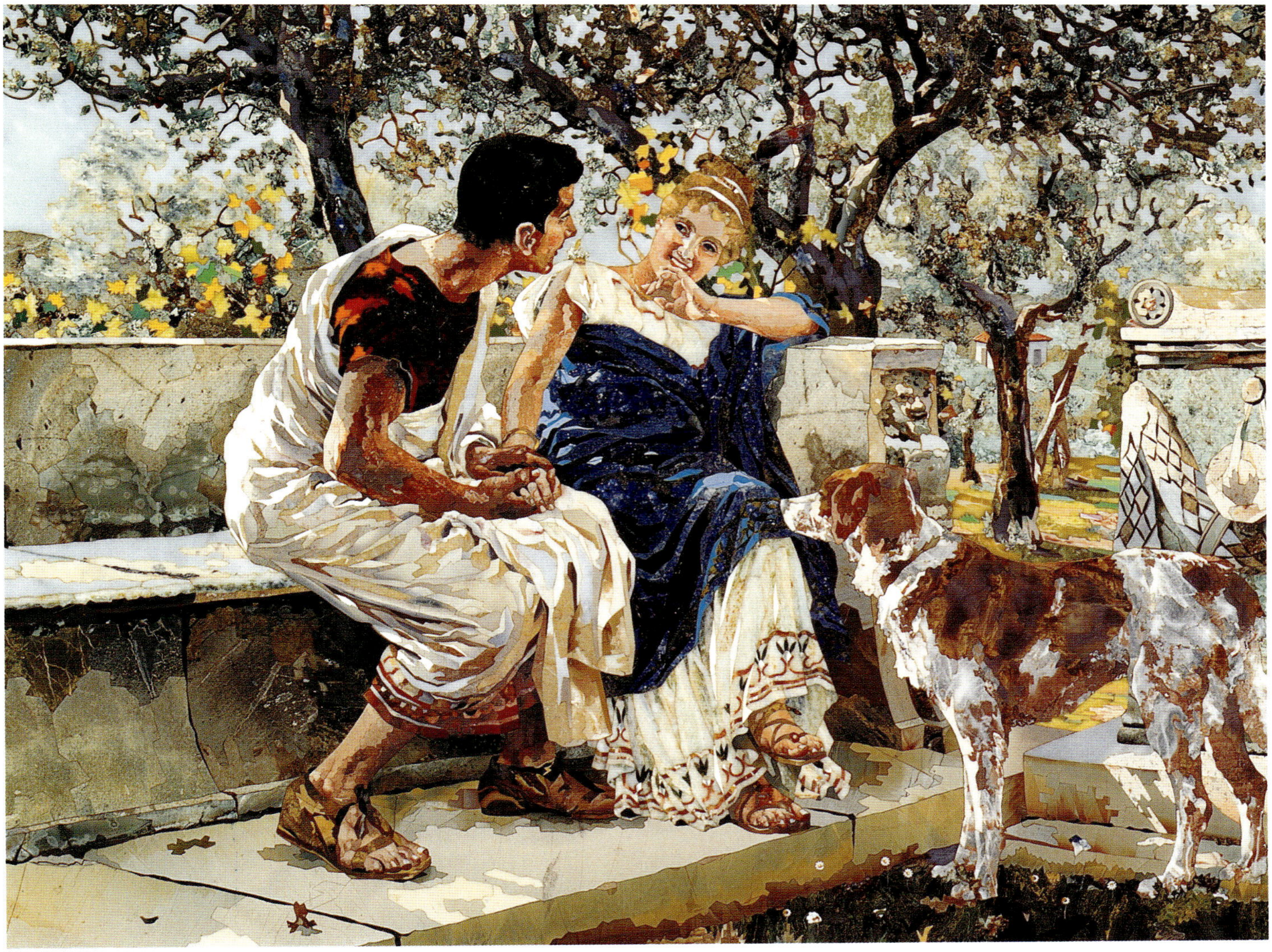

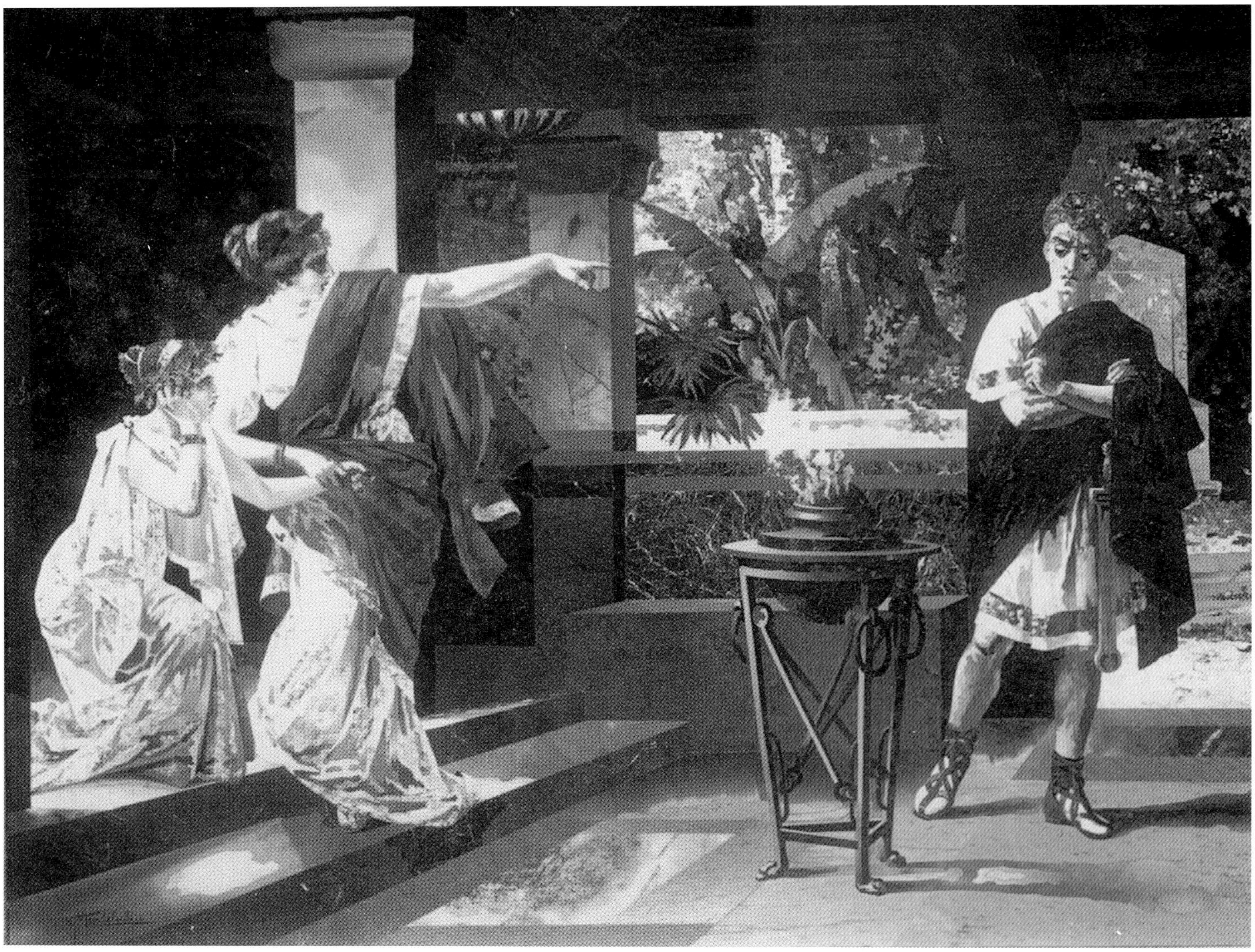

FIG. 20 Archival photograph of mosaic picture by Montelatici.
Photo courtesy of Metello Montelatici

COMMENTARY: This picture is a reduced version of the painting *Roman Idyll* (fig. 19) by the Florentine artist Raffaello Sorbi.[1] Montelatici's rendering of the painting is very faithful, particularly in the effects of light and shade achieved by the use of a great variety of *pietre dure* and *pietre tenere*, cut into small, irregular tessellations. These are laid in such a way as to imitate the chiaroscuro effects achieved with a brush. A related picture (fig. 20) by Mario Montelatici on a classical theme is known from an old photograph owned by, his son, Metello Montelatici.

NOTE

1 Parronchi 1988, p. 86, fig. 26.

75. RETURN FROM THE MARKET

Florence, Mario Montelatici (1894–1974), 1928
Pietre dure, white and *bardiglio* marble, onyx, gabbro, albarese limestone, 66 × 92.5 cm (26 × 36½ in)
1996.355 (MM296)

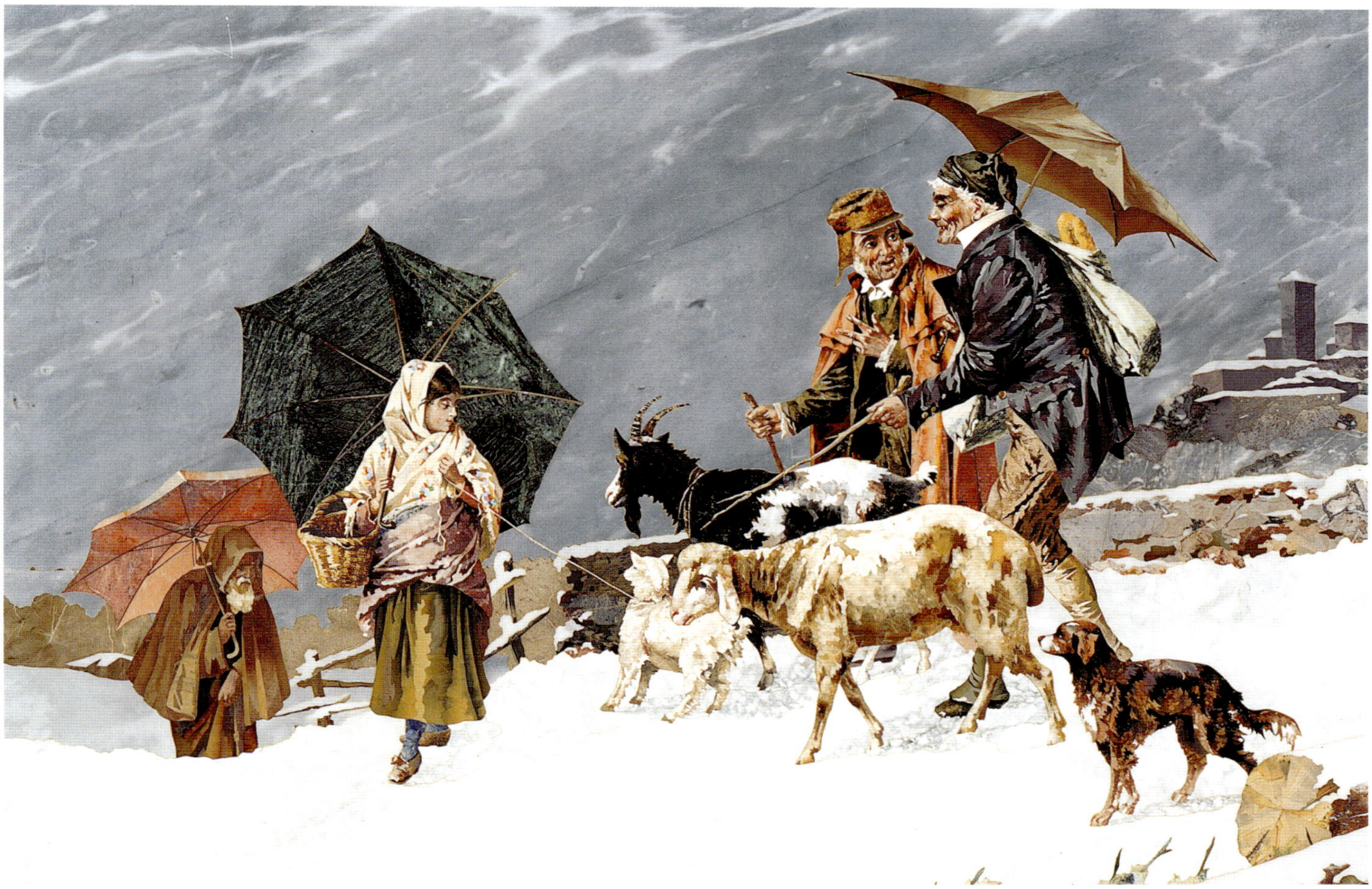

PROVENANCE: Arte del Mosaico, Florence, 1928; Marjorie Merriweather Post; Donald J. Trump; Christie's, sale, New York, 30 March 1995, lot 199.

DESCRIPTION: A hardstone plaque depicting a genre scene of a monk, two elderly men, a young woman, and various animals returning home from the market in a snowstorm. An inscription on the back reads: 1928 ESEGUITO DA/MANO MONTELATICI/DI GIOVANNI ARTE MUSIVA/FIRENZE.

COMMENTARY: As the inscription indicates, this work was made by Mario Montelatici, Giovanni's son, at the Arte Musiva in Florence. The subject is derived from a painting by Stefano Bruzzi (1835–1911) that received a prize in the Parma Exhibition of 1888 (now in the Bruzzi Family Collection, Piacenza).

This hardstone plaque is one of the most spectacular pictures made by Mario Montelatici, who exploited the mimetic potential of Tuscan marbles and hardstones. The grey slab of *bardiglio* marble with white veins realistically imitates the stormy sky, while the fine, white Carrara marble gives a wonderful effect of snow on the street. The other Tuscan stones – onyx, gabbro, and albarese limestone – are finely cut and fitted together to form a hardstone micromosaic, typical of this artist, giving the details of the figures and landscape as well as his characteristic light and shadow effects.

The work was part of a commission submitted to the Florentine workshop, Arte del Mosaico, by the American heiress and art patron Marjorie Merriweather Post in 1927 for Mar a Lago, her estate at Palm Beach, Florida. Other objects commissioned were a round centre table[1] and a large table (12.3 × 1.7 m) inlaid in marbles and hardstones for the villa's dining room. Before these were sent to Florida, these works were exhibited and photographed in the Montelatici workshop.

NOTE

1 Christie's, New York, 30 March 1995, lot 38.

76. THE STOCKING

Florence, Mario Montelatici (1894–1974), 1938
Pietre dure, pietre tenere, 47 × 35.9 cm (18½ × 14⅛ in)
1996.250 (MM101)

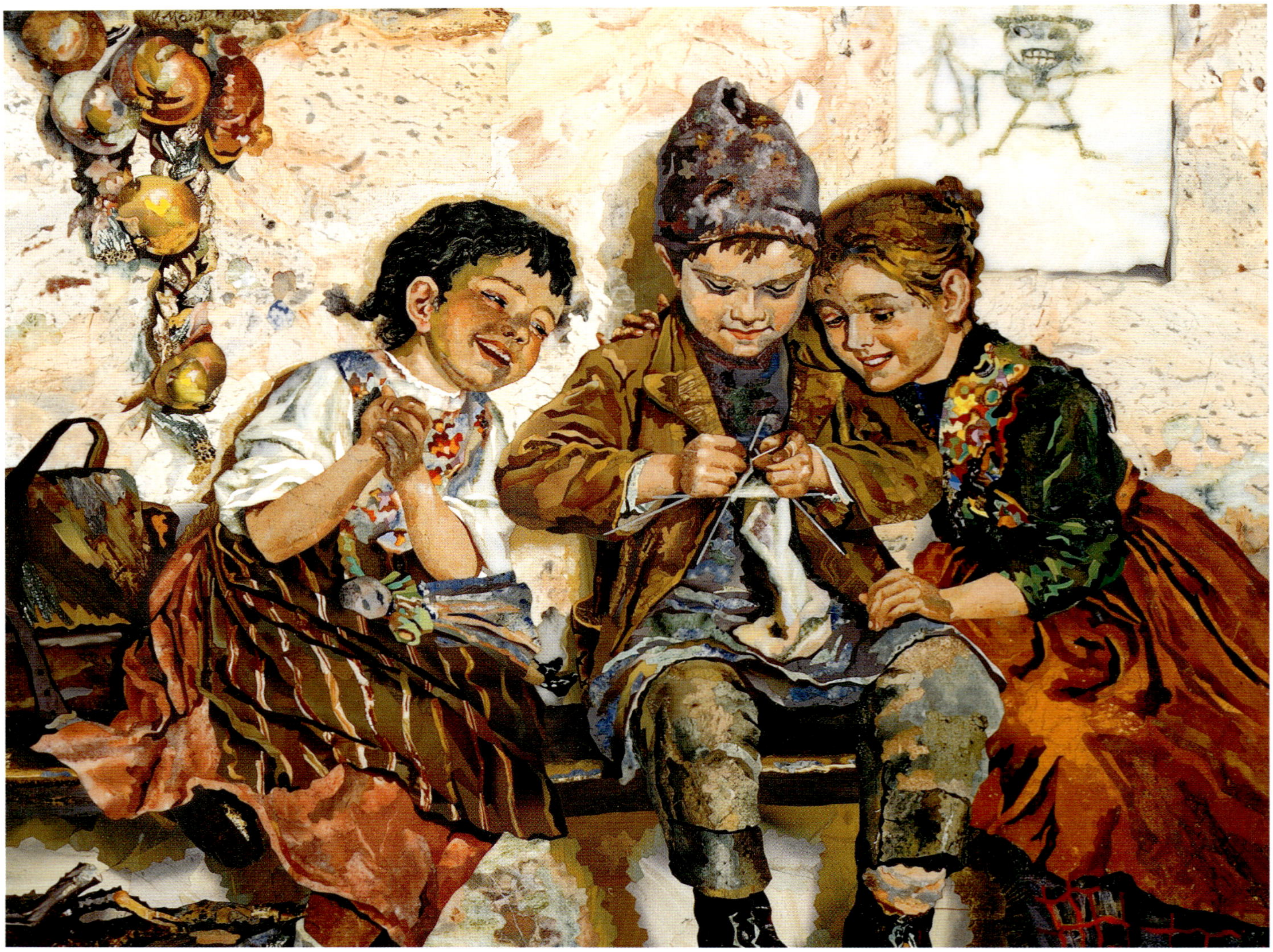

PROVENANCE: Arte del Mosaico, Florence, 1972.

DESCRIPTION: A mosaic picture in *pietre dure* and *pietre tenere*, signed by Mario Montelatici. It depicts two girls teaching a boy how to knit.

COMMENTARY: The subject of this picture is taken from a painting by Edmond Adler (Austria, 1871–1975), entitled *His First Knitting Lesson* (illustrated in Hook and Poltimore, *Popular 19th Century Painting. A Dictionary of Genre Painters*, 1986, p.176). Mario Montelatici particularly liked the subject of childhood (see also cat. no. 77).

77. TWO LITTLE TYKES

Florence, Mario Montelatici (1894–1974), second quarter twentieth century
Pietre dure, 47.9 × 34.9 cm (18⅞ × 13¾ in)
1996.219 (MM59)

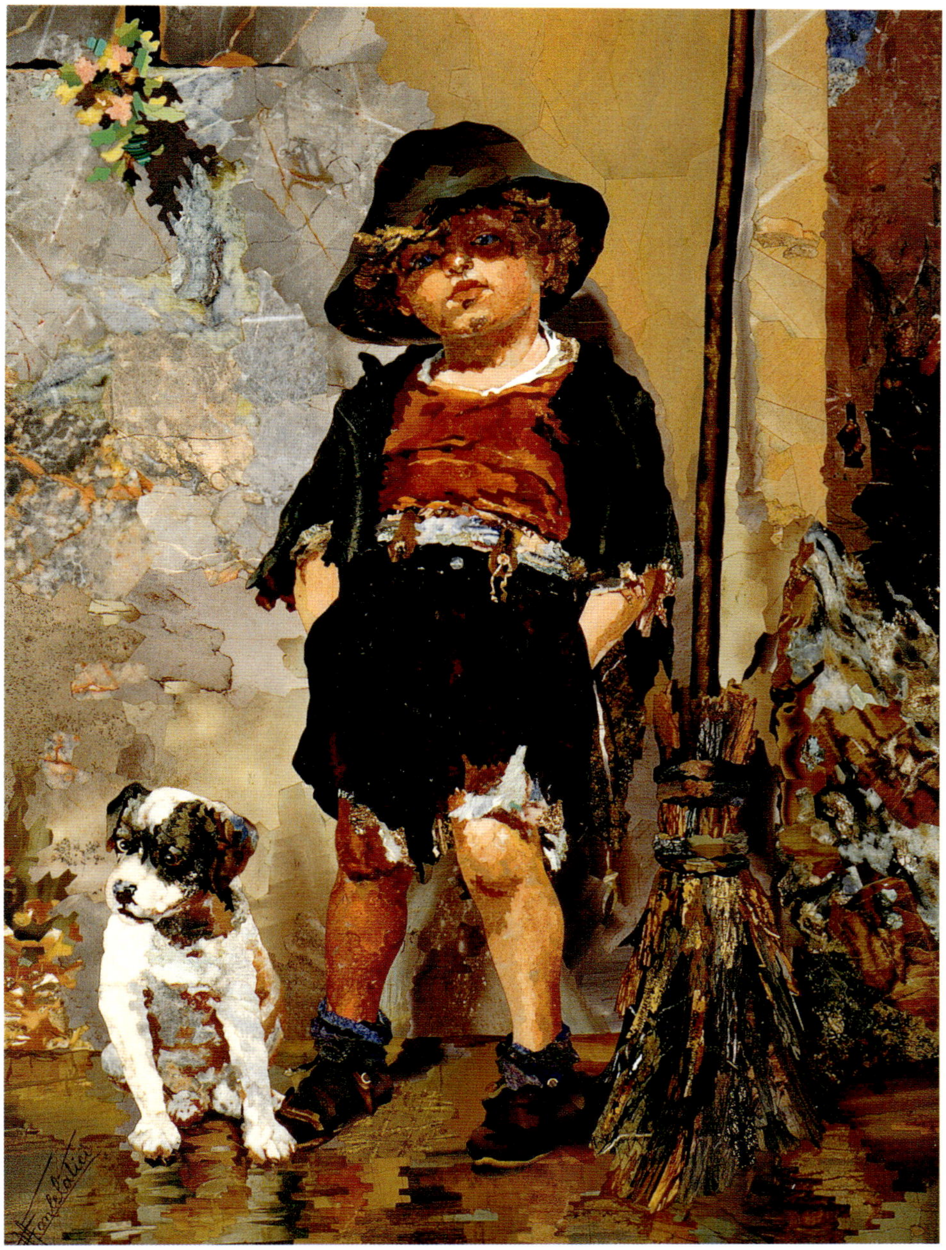

PROVENANCE: Arte del Mosaico, Florence, 1962.

LITERATURE: Avery and Emperatori 1975, no. 19; González-Palacios 1977a, no. 99; Casey 1978, p. 31; González-Palacios and Röttgen 1982, no. 116.

EXHIBITIONS: Los Angeles, 1975; London, 1975; Los Angeles, 1977.

DESCRIPTION: A hardstone picture signed *M. Montelatici*, lower left. The work depicts a child with a dog.

COMMENTARY: This realistic work is an example of the technical skill of Mario Montelatici at its most spectacular. It is also typical of his favourite theme – child poverty – a popular subject taken from contemporary post-Macchiaioli artists.

78. THE CATCH

Florence, Fernando Chisio (b. 1908), mid-twentieth century
Pietre dure, 71.4 × 47.9 cm (28 1/8 × 18 7/8 in)
1996.208 (MM37)

PROVENANCE: Arte del Mosaico, Florence, 1975.

LITERATURE: González-Palacios and Röttgen 1982, no. 117.

DESCRIPTION: A hardstone mosaic, signed *Fernando Chisio*, lower left. Two boys are depicted in a hilly landscape, the older boy showing the younger a glass jar with a frog he has caught in the stream beneath the bridge.

COMMENTARY: Fernando Chisio was a notable pupil of Giovanni Montelatici. He retired in 1975 and presently lives in Florence. He is famous for his pictures of Tuscan country views.

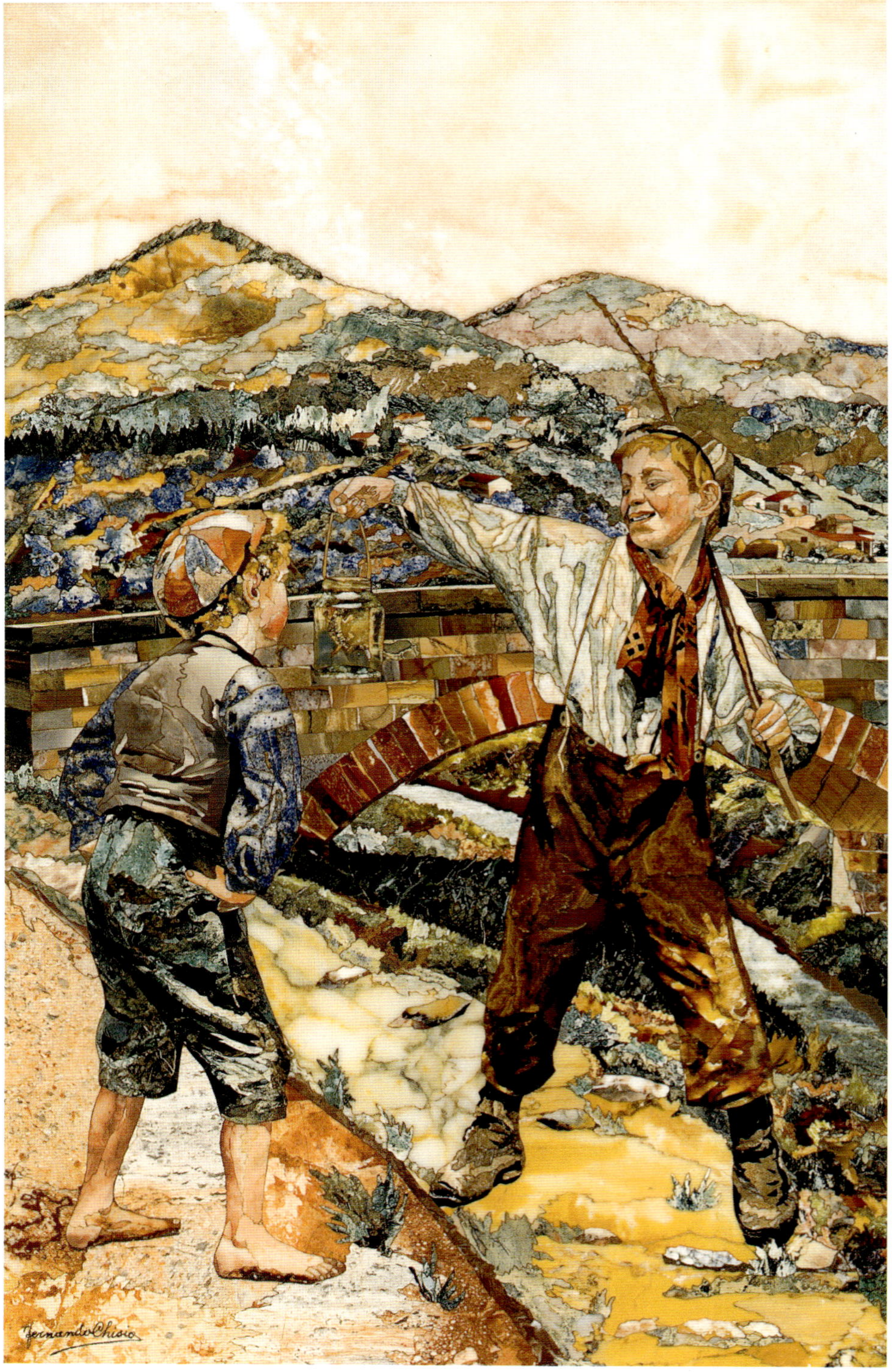

79. STREET SCENE

Florence, Fernando Chisio (b. 1908), mid-twentieth century
Pietre dure, black marble, mother-of-pearl, 33 × 24.8 cm (13 × 9¾ in)
1996.209 (MM38)

PROVENANCE: Arte del Mosaico, Florence, 1975.

DESCRIPTION: A picture in hardstone mosaic, signed by Fernando Chisio, showing a view of a hillside road that passes between two buildings.

COMMENTARY: This mosaic was inspired by the twisting roads in the small towns and villages around Florence. The theme is one of the most popular with the mosaic workshops still in operation in Florence.

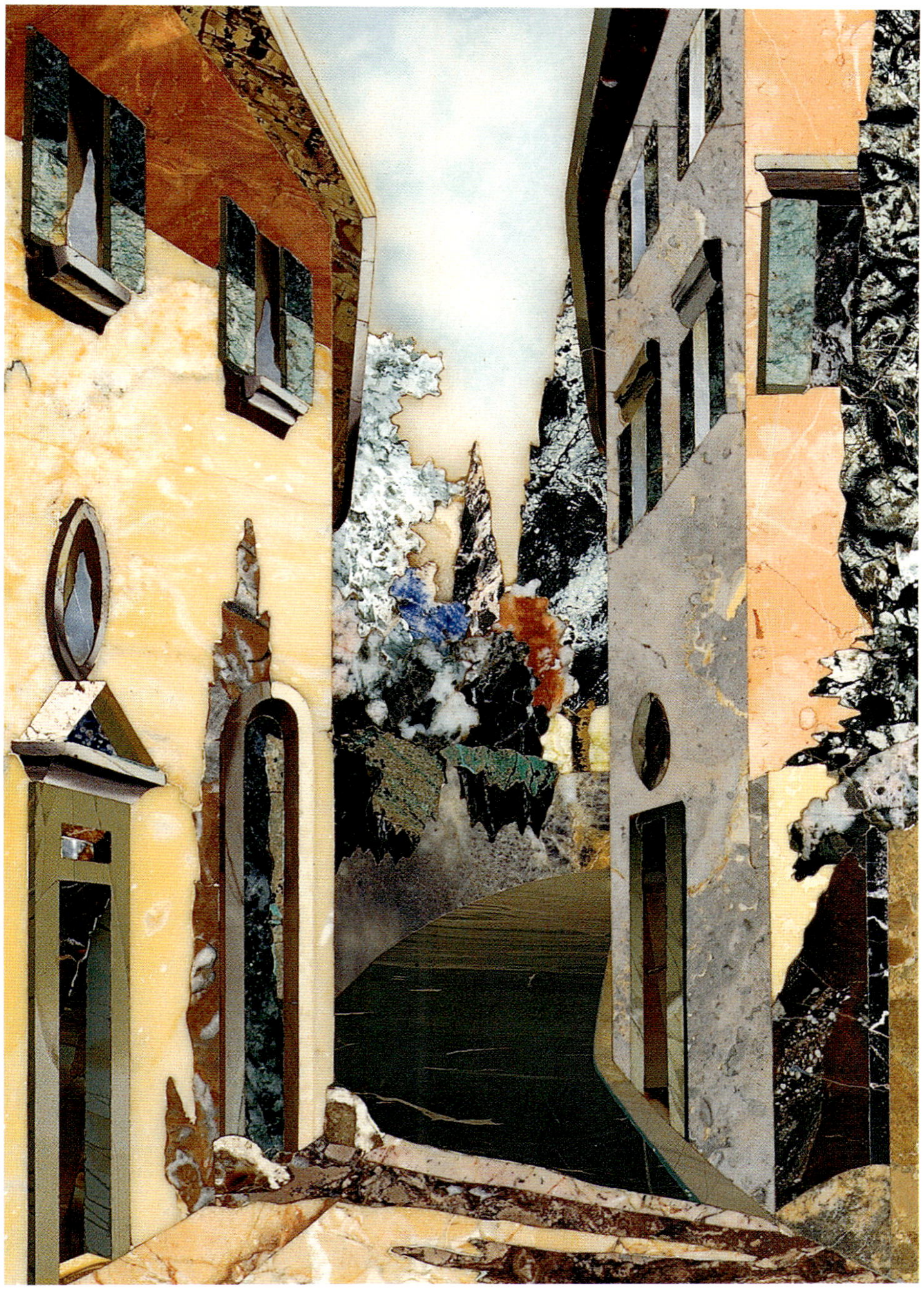

Miscellaneous Objects

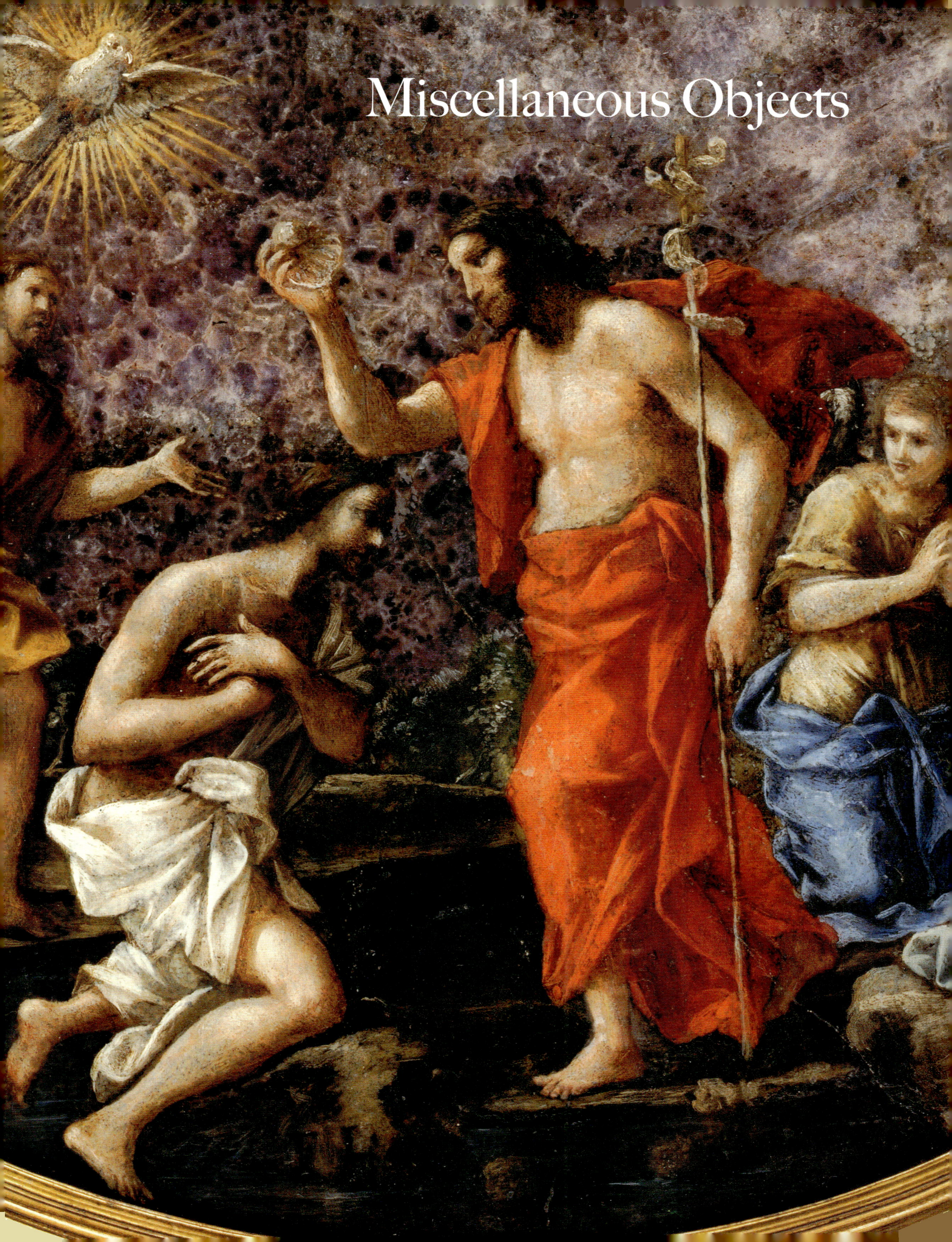

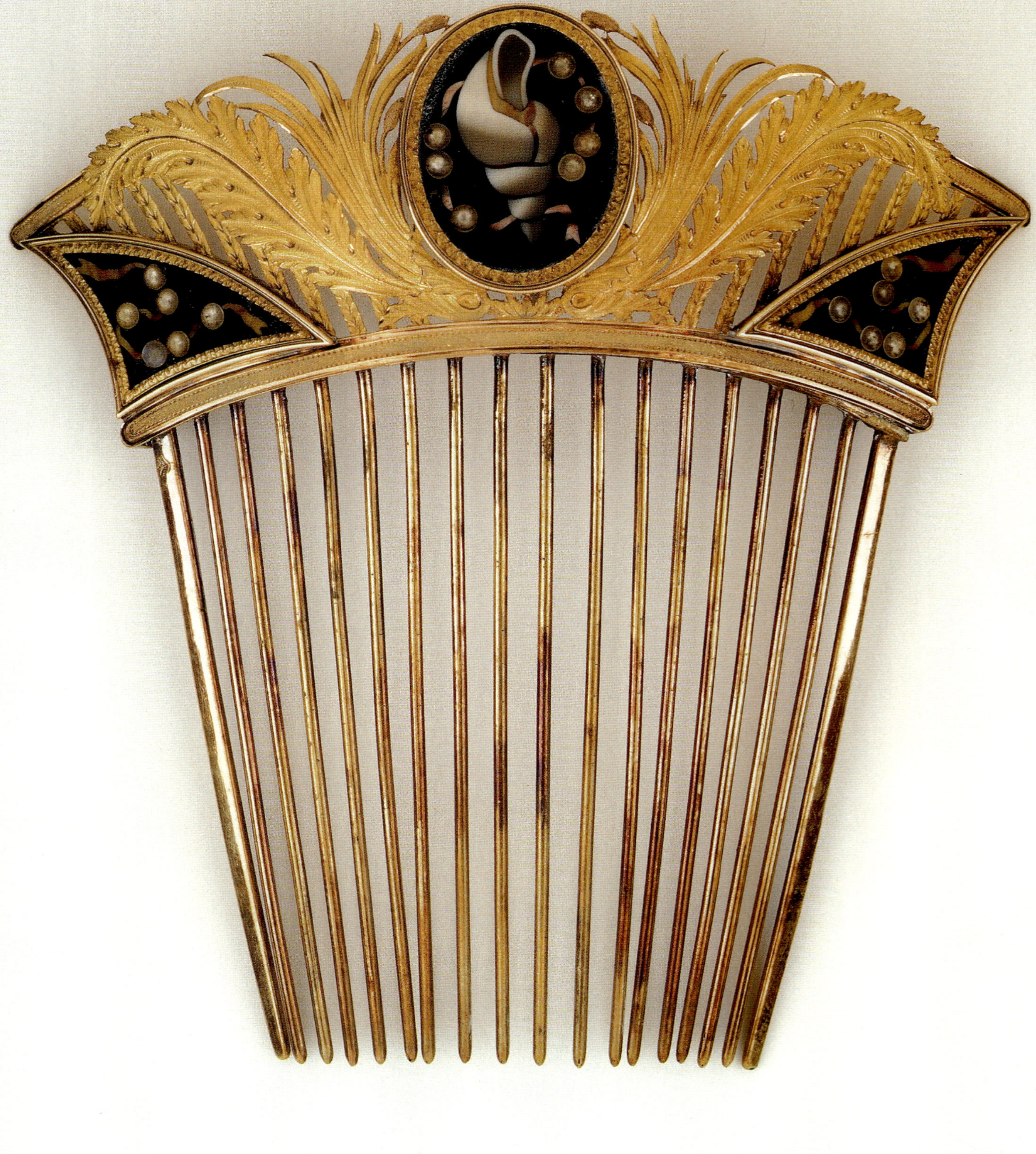

MISCELLANEOUS OBJECTS

In sixteenth-century Europe, the pictorial potential of stones in their natural colours aroused the enthusiasm of collectors, painters and stone engravers alike. At a time when contemporary culture was widely focused on scientific enquiry, the development of technical knowledge and sensitivity to products of the natural world, scientific collectors took a great interest in unusual stones, seeing images of different kinds in their natural markings. These were known as *pietre figurate* or figured stones. In the wake of this popular hobby, artists began to imitate nature, improving on the colours and veining of polychrome marble, alabaster, lapis lazuli, jasper, agate and other stones, and skilfully enhancing their inherent designs using traditional oil painting techniques to create precious objects. They developed a form that lay somewhere between mineral curiosity and work of art, which proved highly successful in the second half of the sixteenth and throughout the seventeenth centuries.

Behind all this experimental activity was the idea of the 'everlasting picture', the result of a combination of the Renaissance interets in curiosities of the natural world and attempts to add value to painting by making it eternal.[1] This found its most perfect expression in the stone mosaics made by Florentine craftsmen. They came closer than anyone else to absolute mastery of the techniques of *pietre dure* mosaic work. In the early seventeenth century they were able to render both figures and landscapes with extraordinary naturalism, considerably advancing the art of 'painting in stone'.

Figured stones, in which irregularities within the material suggest the outlines of an indentifiable animal or landscape view, had already been described with great interest in classical literature; collectors of objets d'art and curiosities kept examples of *pietre figurate* in their cabinets.[2] The brilliant, varied colours of stones are a vivid manifestation of the decorative potential hidden in a natural product, and this fascinated scholars, who regarded the pictures that emerged from the spots and striations as truly miraculous. This idea of a work of art enclosed in matter until released by man comes close to some of the concepts of Platonism.

In the list of gems and precious stones in the thirty-seventh book of his *Naturalis Historia*, Pliny mentions a natural phenomenon observed in a unique stone belonging to Phyrrhus, the famous King of Epirus. In it could be seen a picture of Apollo and the Muses, not obtained by the 'skill of any person', but by a miracle of nature.[3] Other authors and collectors described similar wonders. The revival of stone collecting in the sixteenth century drew on the whole reservoir of classical learning. Whenever a particular stone is described in classical literature, miracles and prodigies are invoked. These were the ideal attributes of the treasures and curiosities being sought in the latter half of the sixteenth century to stock the *Wunderkammern* and private museums in Europe.

Amongst these treasures, certain unusual stones mentioned in documents relating to the collections of the Grand Dukes of Florence stand out: an oval

Previous page
Detail of cat. no. 80

Opposite
Comb (enlarged) from the parure in cat. no. 87

panel of agate in which, 'by a prodigy of nature', the coat-of-arms of the House of Medici can be discerned (Museo di Mineralogia, Florence); a small chalcedony salt cellar, also from the Medici Collections, which bears a blemish that, thanks to a little judicious retouching, resembles a swan (Museo di Mineralogia, Florence).[4]

The illustrious Bolognese doctor and naturalist, Ulisse Aldrovandi (1522–1607), boasted a hoard of such curiosities, as did the private museum of Settala (1664) in Milan, and the Cospi Collection in Bologna (1677), both of the latter possessing stones bearing the outline of a cross on a bearded face.[5]

Aldrovandi, compiled a large encyclopaedia of the natural sciences, including a comprehensive list of these unusual stones bearing a variety of pictures and designs, accompanied by a sheaf of illustrations.[6] The theoretical side of this phenomenon was dealt with exhaustively in other books about natural history, which heralded the birth of modern mineralogy.

The writings of Athanasius Kircher (1602–1680) complement those of Aldrovandi. In Volume VIII of his book on mineralogy (1664),[7] Kircher systematically investigates the origins and causes of figured stones, classifying them by subject: celestial and terrestrial elements, living creatures and religious pictures. The explanation he gives for their formation is fourfold: chance, natural predisposition, magnetism between similar forms and divine intervention.

Kircher also provides a chemical formula for achieving the same effects by artificial means, prompting the suspicion that some of the mineralogical curiosities mentioned or illustrated in the various collections are in reality the result of skilful experiments in the chemistry laboratory.

The trend for painting on stone was evidently well underway in the middle of the sixteenth century, when Vasari dedicated one of his chapters to 'oil painting on stone'.[8] The chapter entitled *Del dipingere in pietra olio, e che pietre siano buone* ('Of painting in oils on stone, and which stones are suitable') provides some interesting technical information. He discusses experiments with painting on slate, and on finer varieties of stone such as the marble blends, serpentine and porphyry. He returns to the same question in his biography of Sebastiano del Piombo. The passage quoted on p.111 continues

> He [executed] a Christ Crucified and a picture of Our Lady in stone for Don Ferrante Gonzaga, sending them to Spain; these were considered very successful and Sebastiano was paid five hundred *scudi* by Messer Niccolò da Cortona, the Cardinal of Mantua's agent in Rome.[9]

Painters like Titian had also succumbed to the idea of their paintings being rendered 'eternal': his *Mater dolorosa* (1554) in the Prado, for instance, is painted on a slab of marble. For his *Annunciation* (before 1641) in the Pinacoteca, Naples, Annibale Carraci used an alabaster background. The genius of artists specialising in busy crowd scenes, filled with people and descriptive details, gave renewed vigour to the art of painting on stone in the early years of the seventeenth century.

Background materials varied considerably, according to the desired effect. In Tuscany, limestone from the valley of the Arno is characterised by striations that suggest rocky landscapes, and this led to a successful blending of natural 'painting with stone' and artificial 'painting on stone'. These so-called *paesine* (landscape stones) or *lineato dell' Arno* were amongst the most sought-after stones in the early sixteenth century because they gave such a convincing landscape background to sacred and mythological scenes, as well as to Arcadian and maritime compositions. The colouring of the *paesina* oscillates between greyish-yellow and various shades of red-brown produced by iron hydroxide, and is used to depict landscape with dramatic geological faults, fantastic ruins, crumbling towers and pyramids, or the outline of city walls in a disquieting, lunar landscape. The presence of scraps of vegetable material in the stone gives the effect of scattered bushes and trees. Sometimes, the stone bears horizontal folds, which can convey the idea of undulations in the landscape, a sea shore or a strip of sky. Both kinds of marking are often to be found in the same piece of stone, making the representation of landscape even more vivid and realistic.

The spectacular views created from sheets of *terra di paese dell'Arno* made the stone greatly sought after. In 1777, the naturalist Georg Wolfgang Knorr described the different varieties of the Tuscan limestone, remarking on its exceptional ornamental qualities. So decorative was it, that sometimes collectors would simply frame untouched pieces of the stone.[10]

The natural landscapes in the Tuscan limestone fired painters' imaginations with dreams of dramatic, primordial landscapes where time hangs suspended. Rocky, arid mountain ranges with a few dry shrubs, a glimpse of a ruined wall, an obelisk, a pyramid, all suggesting the aftermath of a natural disaster, a recent earthquake or conflagration. Against such backgrounds, the artist inserted tiny figures to make scenes from epic poems, or from Dante's *Commedia* (*Divine Comedy*, finished 1321), the Old Testament or the lives of the Saints. The small panels by the painter Filippo Napoletano (?Rome 1630), a favourite of Grand Duke Cosimo II and his circle, depict the lives of the hermits.

A series of seven pictures is documented in the Medici archives, of which only two have so far been identified – the *Temptation of St. Anthony* and *Mary Magdalene in the Desert* (Museo dell'Opificio delle Pietre Dure, Florence). In some cases, the formation of the stone provides backgrounds exactly suited to stories from the Old Testament, like Lot and his daughters (Museo di Mineralogia, Florence), or the destruction of Sodom and Gomorrah (private collection, Rome), both of which bear stylistic similarities to the work of Filippo Napoletano.

Sometimes, when the pieces of limestone are cut and polished, the craftsmen are reminded of episodes from Ariosto's *Orlando Furioso* (1532); from the atmosphere of dread emerge the figures of Ruggero and Angelica (Museo dell'Opificio delle Pietre Dure), or the turbulent, crowded scene of the capture of Jerusalem as recounted by Tasso, depicted by Antonio Tempesta (1555–1630) (Galleria Borghese, Rome).

Elsewhere, in an unrivalled symbiosis of subject and material, we are shown scenes from the realms of the damned, as in the small picture of Dante and Virgil in Hell (Museo dell'Opificio delle Pietre Dure, Florence), attributed to Francesco Ligozzi. This may originally have been a pendant to another paesina depicting an episode from Dante's *Purgatorio*.[11]

When the veins on the stone are disposed in such a way as to recall calm seas, boats and galleons are appropriate additions, or they may form the background for Old Testament stories like Jonah and the whale, as is the case with several of these works also attributed to the circle of Filippo Napoletano (Opificio delle Pietre Dure, Florence). Antonio Tempesta exploited the markings of a particular piece of stone, divided by wavy parallel veins, as the background for the *Crossing of the Red Sea* (Galleria Borghese, Rome).

At the beginning of the seventeenth century, the main centre for artists specialising in this type of work was Rome. Filippo Napoletano worked there before being summoned to the court of Florence by Grand Duke Cosimo II between 1618 and 1621. Also in Rome was Cornelis van Poelenburgh (Utrecht 1586–1667), whose painting *Latona Transforming the Lycian Shepherds into Frogs*, inspired by an episode from Ovid's *Metamorphoses*,[12] is executed in oils on lapis lazuli. When lapis bears no markings to suggest a background it is occasionally used to evoke the sea in marine paintings like Antonio Tempesta's *Pearl Fishing* (Louvre, Paris), presented to the Grand Duke Cosimo by Pietro Strozzi. Until the second half of the eighteenth century, this was one of the valuable objects displayed in the Tribuna degli Uffizi.[13]

Stones of different kinds and colours and with different markings were used to give a variety of effects. Jacques Stella (1596–1657) used a mottled marble for the background of a small picture of the deluge. Domenico Cresti, called Il Passignano (Passignano 1558/60–1638) painted a Descent from the Cross on alabaster. Filippo Lauri, in his *Baptism of Christ* in the Gilbert Collection, used a panel of amethyst. The use of slate, remarked on by Vasari, was particularly in favour in the early seventeenth century following a period of experiment with light and shade, and strongly contrasted nocturnal scenes in imitation of Caravaggio. There are examples of this in the work of Filippo Napoletano: his *Burning of Troy* and *Persephone Abducted to Hades* (both in the Palazzo di Montecitorio, Rome), in Giovanni Bilivert's (1576– 1644) *Mystic Marriage of St. Catherine* (1642, Florence: SS Annunziata) and in Agostino Tassi's (1580–1644) *Paesaggio Notturno* (Landscape Nocturne), probably before 1610).

The climax of painted-stone collecting within Medici court circles came during the reign of Grand Duke Cosimo II (r. 1609–21), encouraged by his passionate interest in the arts and sciences. He took delight in beautiful artefacts obtained from a synthesis of the two. Works of a similar nature also figure in the inventory of property belonging to Don Lorenzo de' Medici in 1649; mention is made of 'two Albarese limestone paintings with ships, framed in black stones separated by arabasques of gold thread'.[14] These may be two of the series of three marine paintings with galleons now in the Museo dell'Opificio delle Pietre Dure. This type of painting is part of the larger phenomenon of the collection of gemstone paintings by the Medici family, including miniatures painted on copper, silver, parchment and *pietre dure* of various kinds. Even Cardinal Carlo, the brother of Cosimo II, was a passionate collector. He had in his possession, for example, stones painted by Antonio Tempesta, which he had acquired in Rome.[15] Paintings on stone also figure in the inventories of Vittoria della Rovere.[16]

In Rome, these precious paintings were often incorporated into a tabernacle for private worship. In Palazzo Pallavicini the tabernacle contains an amethyst on which is painted an Adoration of the Magi.[17] In Oberlin, Ohio, there is a small altar with a painting of Abraham and Isaac painted on amethyst by Jacopo Ligozzi; another, in the Victoria and Albert Museum, London, bears a picture of the Flight into Egypt.[18]

At the beginning of the seventeenth century, painted stone decoration became very fashionable in Augsburg, where it was used in the making of cabinets sold by the dealer Philipp Hainhofer. These pieces were elaborately constructed and were enriched with sumptuous inlaid ornamentation, like the Kunstschranken made for Philip II of Pomerania (1617, formerly in the castle in Berlin, but destroyed during World War II), and for Gustavus Adolfus of Sweden (1632); another was acquired by Archduke Leopold V of Tirol and presented by him to Grand Duke Ferdinand II, who removed it to Florence in 1628 (Museo degli Argenti, Florence). These cabinets were made by craftsmen in Augsburg, though Hainhofer followed the production of each one personally and selected the materials to be used. In his correspondence with his brother (who was in Florence in 1611) there is frequent mention of 'Florentine stone with trees and landscapes';[19] in fact, he purchased stones in Florence and had them painted by German artists before setting them into the complicated inlay work of the cabinets. Johann Koenig (1586–1635) painted the *Day of Judgment* and the *Crossing of the Red Sea* on two pieces of agate. There is also a marble plaque bearing a picture of a naval battle (after Callot) painted by an unknown artist. They were used to decorate the Kunstschrank of Gustavus Adolfus of Sweden (Universites Konstsamling, Upsala). The so-called 'German cabinet', which has remained in the Florentine collection to this day, is richly decorated with stones – jasper and landscape stone painted with stories from the Old and New Testaments.[20] The cabinets described above are the most famous of those produced in Augsburg, but others appear on the market from time to time. An example, now in the Paul Getty Museum, Malibu, has a series of different stones painted with allegorical figures and portraits of illustrious women.

NOTES

1 On this subject cf. M. Chiarini, 'Pittural su pietra', in *Anitichità Viva*, 2, 1970, pp. 6 et seq.; *La pittura su pietra*, catalogue of the exhibition, Florence, 1970; P. Della Pergola, Galleria Borghese, *Opere in mosaico, intarsi e pietra paesina*, Rome 1970; A. Ottani Cavina, 'I dipinti su lavagna', in *Bolaffi Arte*, 1971, no. 6, pp 22–24; Guisti, Mazzoni, *Pampaloni Martelli*, 1979, pp. 344–346; M. Hirst, *Sebastiano del Piombo*, Oxford, 1981; P. Boccard (ed.), *Del dipingere e scolpire in pietra*, catalogue of the exhibition, Genoa 1985.

2 This subject has been dealt with exhaustively in J. Baltrusaitis, *Aberrations. Quatre essais fur les légendes des formes*, Paris, 1957.

3 Gaius Plinius Secondus, *Storia Naturale*, Books 33–37, Turin 1988, vol. v. p. 749.

4 Massinelli, 1990, pp. 111–34, fig. 19; 1992, pp. 211–225.

5 Baltrusaitis 1957.

6 U. Aldrovandi, B. Ambrosino, Museum Metallicum, Bologna, 1648.

7 A. Kircher, *Mundus Subterraneus*, 1664.

8 Vasari, 1568, vol. I, pp. 189–90.

9 G. Vasari, op. cit., vol. v, p. 679.

10 G. W. Knorr, *Receuil des monuments des catastrophes que le globe de terre a essuyées, dessinées, gravées et enluminées d'après les originaux, avec leur description*, 1777, quoted in R. Caillois 'D'étranges délires de marbre', in: *Connaissance des Arts*, no. 139, September 1963, pp. 36–43.

11 Both recorded in the Villa del Poggio Imperiale in 1624 (ASF. GM479. c. 13).

12 Book vi, verses 313–381.

13 A. Cecchi, 'La pêche des perles aux Indes, une peinture d'Antonio Tempesta', in *Revue du Louvre et des Musées de France*, 1, 1986, pp. 45–57.

14 *La quadreria di Don Lorenzo de' Medici*, catalogue edited by E. Borea, Florence 1977, p. 103.

15 Chiarini 1970, op. cit., p. 7.

16 ASF. Misc. Med. 12.

17 *Splendori di pietre dure* 1988, p. 145.

18 González-Palacios 1980 II, p. 18, fig. 2; p. 33.

19 Baltrusaitis 1957, p. 52.

20 Alfter, 1986.

80. BAPTISM OF CHRIST

Rome, Filippo Lauri (1623–94), second half seventeenth century
Oil on amethyst, chalcedony, lapis lazuli, *pietre dure*, ebony, rosewood, pewter, silver, gilt bronze, 44.1 × 52.1 cm (17 3/8 × 20 1/2 in)
1996.284 (MM139)

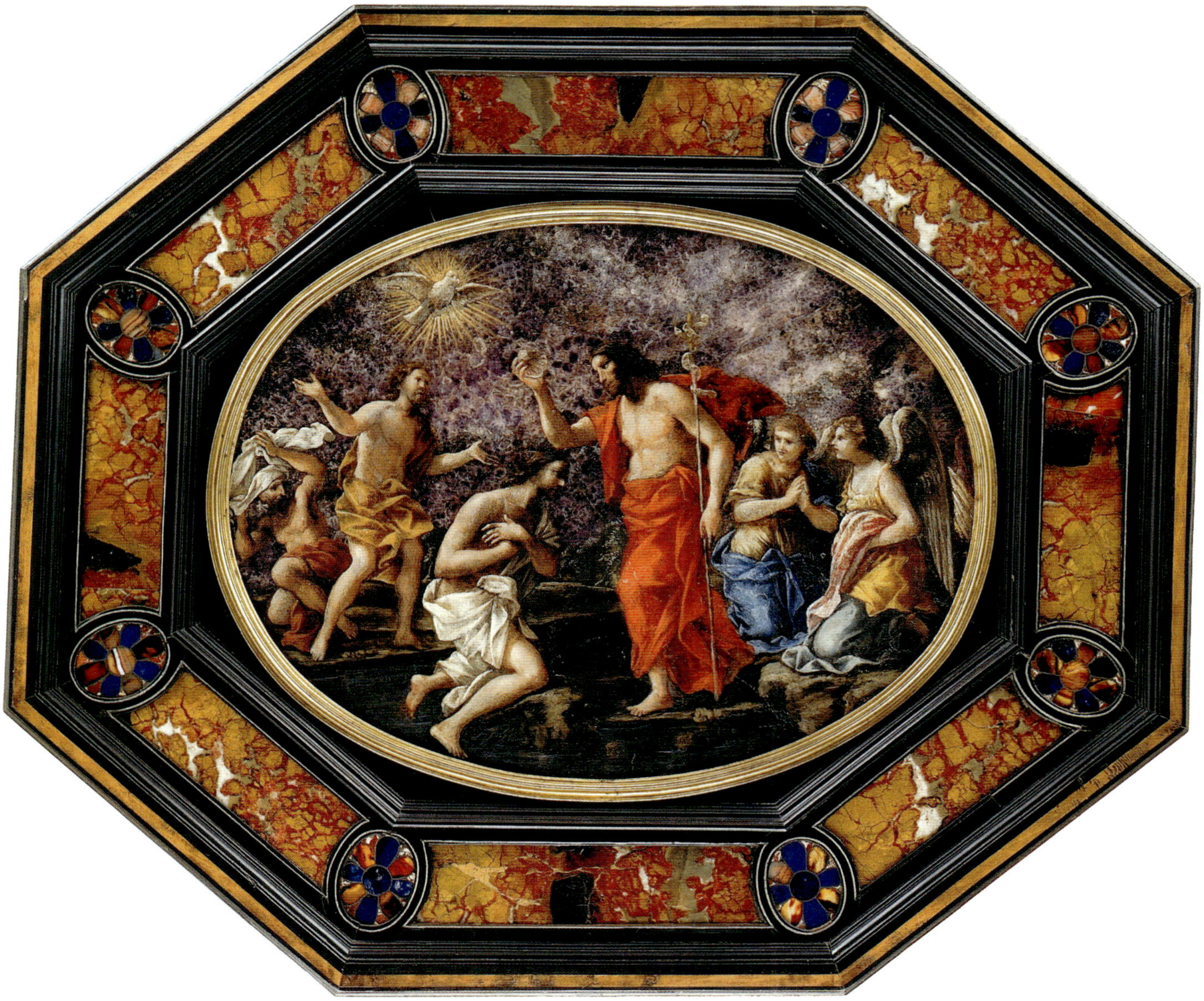

PROVENANCE: Alberto di Castro, Rome, 1972.

LITERATURE: Lizanni 1970, fig. XXVI–VII; Avery and Emperatori 1975, no. 30; González-Palacios 1977, figs. 1, 3, 4; González-Palacios 1977a, no. 2; Hagans 1977, ill. p. 31; González-Palacios and Röttgen 1982, no. 2; González-Palacios 1984, vol. 2, p. 65, fig. 109.

EXHIBITIONS: Los Angeles, 1975; London, 1975; Los Angeles / Atlanta / San Antonio / Richmond / Seattle, 1977–79.

DESCRIPTION: An oval panel of amethyst painted with a scene of the Baptism of Christ. The panel, edged with gilt bronze, is inserted into an octagonal ebony frame inlaid with jasper. In the corners of the frame are four inlaid rosettes of chalcedony and lapis lazuli edged in pewter. The scene depicts Jesus kneeling on a rock in the River Jordan. In front of him stands Saint John the Baptist, who is holding a staff in his left hand and a shell in his right, from which he is baptising Jesus. Above left is the Holy Spirit in the form of a dove, radiating light on the scene below. On the viewer's left of Jesus are two men awaiting baptism; on the right are two kneeling angels. In the centre of the rock upon which Jesus kneels are the artist's signed initials: FL.

COMMENTARY: Filippo Lauri was the son of Baldassar Lauwers of Antwerp (c. 1570/76–1645), a talented landscape painter who was a student and follower of Paul Brill. Lauri was best known for the small paintings of religious and mythological figures that retained the flavour of his Flemish heritage. His cabinet pictures were in great demand by Italian collectors and foreigners, but most of the private patrons of small works were from outside Italy.

During his adult career, Lauri lived in the area of the Piazza di Spagna in Rome, an artist's enclave populated by painters from throughout Europe. He was particularly close to Nicolas Poussin (1600–82), Claude Lorraine (1594–1665) and Gaspard Dughet (1615–75), all of whom influenced his work. His career was long and financially successful. One of his most important commissions was a fresco cycle (1656–57) for the Gallery of Pope Alexander VII (r. 1655–67?) in the Quirinale Palace, a project utilising the talents of several artists under the supervision of Pietre Cortona (1596–1669).[1] A medal cast in his honour by the French Royal Academy depicts him painting nature with the Latin motto *Aemulat et superat* (He emulates and he surpasses).[2]

The provenance of the painting in the Gilbert Collection is not documented. However, such paintings were made for both ecclesiastical and lay clients. This particular subject could have been commissioned for a variety of reasons: for a church or baptistery named after Saint John the Baptist, or for a private devotional chapel, particularly for a person named Giovanni, or Giovanni Battista (John, or John the Baptist). Other examples of this type of painting on stone can be found on the cabinet of Sixtus V at Stourhead, Wiltshire, and on a reliquary at the Victoria and Albert Museum.[3]

NOTES

1 For information on artists working on Quirinale Palace fresco, see Wittkower 1985, note 34, pp. 330, 448.

2 For further biographical information on this artist, see Riccio, 1959. Thanks to Jeremy Parzen of Los Angeles for his help in translating this article.

3 González-Palacios and Röttgen 1982, no. 2.

81. BUST OF FAUSTINA MINOR

Rome, seventeenth century
Porphyry, breccia, 50 × 33 × 22 cm
(19⅝ × 13 × 8⅝ in)
(TU84)

PROVENANCE: Orsini collection, Rome; Mallett and Son (Antiques) Ltd, London, 1974.

DESCRIPTION: A head-and-shoulders, female portrait bust, the head and pedestal carved of red porphyry, the drapery of breccia with irregular fragments of white and red inserted in a dark gray mastic. The hair is in close, stylised waves, the facial features stylised and frontal in pose.

COMMENTARY: This portrait is connected with a series of busts of the Antonine period (AD 161–80). The facial features are recognisable as those of Faustina Minor (c. AD 125– c. 175/6), the wife of Emperor Marcus Aurelius (r. AD 161–180). There are other similar examples of this genre, including one in the Louvre and two – one genuinely antique and the other pseudo-antique – in the Uffizi Gallery.[1] If the Gilbert bust is compared with the other known portraits of Faustina, it would appear to derive from a head in the Capitoline Museum in Rome, which has a white marble face, hair of black marble dressed close to the head, and shoulders of 'flowered' alabaster.[2] The Gilbert portrait echoes all the descriptive details of face and hair, but the pose is completely frontal, whereas the Capitoline bust is slightly turned to the left. The use of hard material such as porphyry makes the copy look somewhat stiffer than the original. The drapery, less voluminous in the Capitoline bust, follows the same pattern of folds.

Porphyry came from Asia Minor and was frequently used in Imperial Rome.[3] Because it is so hard, and therefore difficult to carve, porphyry has always been a rare stone for

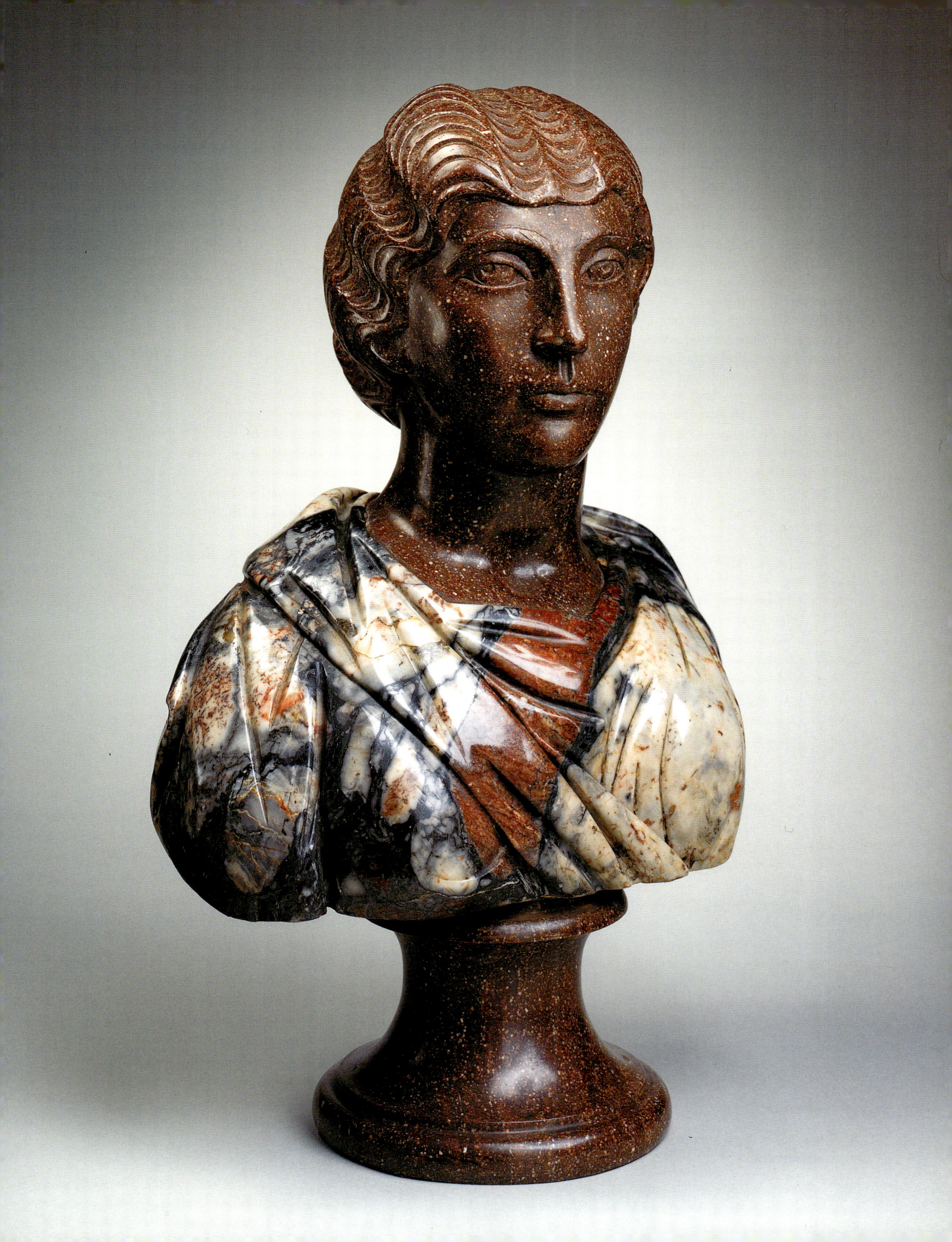

sculpture and, since classical times, has been particularly prized for symbolic as well as commercial reasons. In Rome, the stone was reserved for the emperor. It came back into use in Florence in the mid-sixteenth century when the sculptor Francesco Ferrucci del Tadda (1497–1585) from Fiesole revived the techniques of porphyry cutting thanks to the use of various abrasives. According to Giorgio Vasari (1511–74), the new technique was invented by Cosimo I (r. 1569–74) and handed down to Ferrucci del Tadda.[4] A nineteenth-century label glued to the back of this bust bears the coat-of-arms of the Orsini family and the caption, PRINCIPE ORSINI ASSISTENTE AL SOLIO PONTIFICIO, which indicates (as in the case of cat. no. 101) that it came from the scattered collection of this Roman family. It has not yet been possible to document this collection fully.

NOTES

1 Bernoulli 1891, vol. 2, p. 194, pl. 52; Mansuelli 1960, vol. 2, p. 188, no. 124.
2 Fittschen and Zancher 1983, vol.2, p. 83, pls. 142–43.
3 Gnoli 1987, pp. 174–77.
4 Di Castro Moscati 1987, pp. 242–48.

82. PORTRAIT OF A WOMAN WITH A DIADEM

Rome, seventeenth century
Porphyry and oriental alabaster, 60 × 33 × 16 cm (23 ¼ × 13 × 6¼ in)
(TU83)

PROVENANCE: Orsini collection, Rome; Mallett and Son (Antiques) Ltd, 1974.

DESCRIPTION: A portrait bust composed of carved porphyry depicting a woman with hair tied at the nape of her neck, wearing a diadem carved in relief with a central vase between radiating stalks of wheat. The shoulders are draped in oriental alabaster; the pedestal is of porphyry.

COMMENTARY: This is a faithful seventeenth-century copy of an ancient Roman bust made of white marble with alabaster shoulders now in the Capitoline Museum in Rome.[1] The work is identified as a portrait of Livia as Ceres. Livia Drusilla (AD 56 BC?–29), was the wife of Tiberius Claudius Nero, and by him the mother of Tiberius (r. AD 14–37), second Emperor of Rome, and Drusus Senior (39–9 BC). She later divorced her husband to marry Augustus (r. AD 27 BC–14), thus becoming the first Empress of Rome.

Other examples of this type of bust include genuine archaeological pieces and pseudo-antiques. A later copy by the Roman sculptor and restorer Bartolomeo Cavaceppi (1716–99) can be seen in the castle of Worlitz in Germany.[2] Like the bust of Faustina Minor (cat. no. 81), it bears a label on the back with the words, PRINCIPE ORSISNI ASSISTENTE AL SOLIO PONTIFICIO, which indicates that it came from the scattered collection of the celebrated Roman family. The piece is unidentifiable from the Orsini inventories published to date, although it would fit very well into a group of busts on antique themes made in porphyry and coloured marble and cited as belonging to the family collection.[3] Copies from the antique in costly marbles, alabaster and porphyry were very common in Rome, and portrait heads and sculpture of this type were frequently found among the furnishings of the major residences of the city in the seventeenth and eighteenth centuries.

NOTES

1 Fittschen and Zancher 1983, vol. 2, pp. 3–4, pl. 3.
2 Bernoulli 1891, vol. 2, pp. 3–4.
3 Rubsamen 1980.

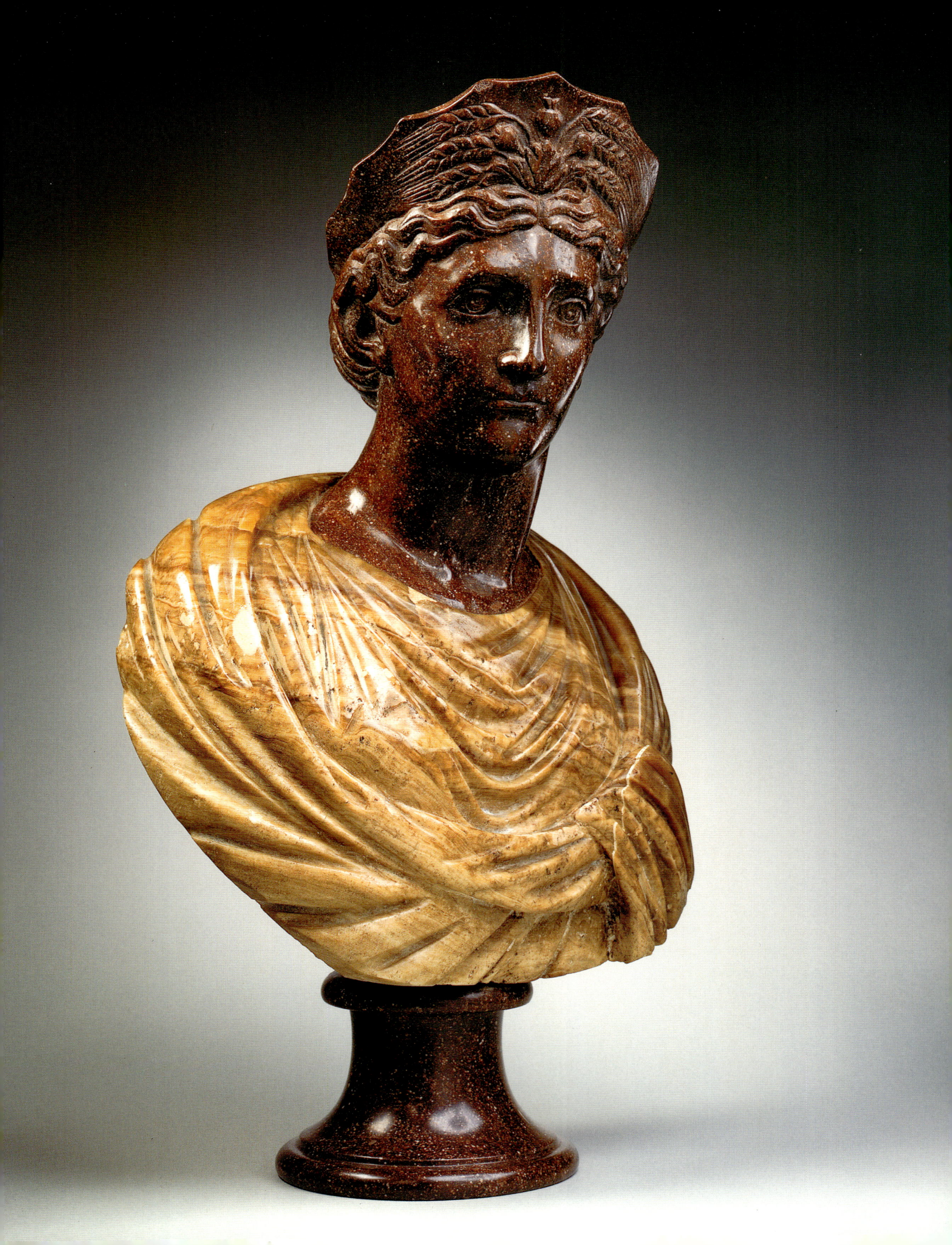

83. PAIR OF PUTTI

Naples, late seventeenth to early eighteenth century
White marble, *bardiglio* marble, coloured breccia, and gilt bronze, A: 68.6 × 40.6 × 40.6 cm (27 × 16 × 16 in);
B: 68.6 × 45.7 × 40.6 cm (27 × 18 × 16 in)
(TU39AB)

PROVENANCE: Alberto di Castro, Rome, 1972.

DESCRIPTION: Two putti of white marble carved in the round. One, with short-cropped hair, holds a garland of flowers in its left hand; drapery covers his groin and flows behind his back. The other, with longer curly hair and wearing drapery like a mantle over his head, raises his right arm. The figures are seated on cushions of *bardiglio* marble edged with cord and tassels of gilt bronze. The bases are faced with coloured breccia edged in white marble. The front mouldings bear a cartouche and carved acanthus leaves at the sides.

COMMENTARY: The combination of polychrome materials and certain other characteristics exhibited by these sculptures link them to Naples in the late-seventeenth and early eighteenth centuries. Putti constituted a recurrent subject in the prolific output of the marble masons of Naples in the second half of the seventeenth century. Plump cherubs in whimsical poses are frequently found in the opulent, elaborate decoration of baroque churches in the region.

The iconography of these sculptures is uncertain, but the wreath and drapery might indicate that the putti are allegories of Spring and Winter – the works may have belonged to a series of four representing the seasons. The two putti, designed as a pair and belonging to the same decorative scheme, were almost certainly executed in the same workshop, but must have been completed by craftsmen with dissimilar training. The surface treatment of the statues points to two different hands: Spring is delicately shaded and has a gauzy transparency; Winter has a heavily accentuated contrast of light and shadow, particularly in the folds of the drapery, the rendering of the hair, and the anatomical features. Spring's sheer drapery flutters at the back of the statue; Winter's fabric falls heavily and is furrowed by deep folds.

According to contemporary sources, prototypes of the work of the Flemish artist François Duquesnoy (1594–1643) were used frequently in sculptors' studios as models. Giovanni Battista Passeri, for instance, recorded a 'number of putti made by him in high relief, not very large, for various occasions; they are a great help and support to teachers of art'.[1] Filippo Baldinucci reported, 'From time to time the Flemish artist made different models of charming putti, which, when they were finished, would be sent to teachers' studios'.[2] In fact, the wide diffusion of the graceful cherubs can be estimated by the huge incidince of putti in late baroque sculpture.[3] Spring belongs to this tradition, reiterating a standard type already much in use in artists' studios. The relationship between this and a small terracotta sketch in the Musée des Arts, Lille, is worthy of note, the terracotta being ascribed to Duquesnoy.[4]

The works of artists such as Lorenzo Vaccaro (1655–1706) and Pietro and Bartolomec Ghetti, documented in Naples from 1645 to 1689, were an important factor in the spread of this type of ornamental sculpture, in combination with showy wall decorations in marble mosaic. Analogies with Winter can be found, for instance, in the pair of cherubs on the altar of the Milano family in the church of San Lorenzo Maggiore in Naples, executed by the Ghetti brothers between 1698 and 1710.[5]

NOTES
1 Passeri 1772, p. 106.
2 Baldinucci 1846, vol. 2, p. 318.
3 Fabianski 1985.
4 Photograph in the Istituto Tedesco, Florence, no. 227247.
5 Fittipaldi 1980, figs. 25–26, 39–40; Rizzo 1984, figs. 6–7.

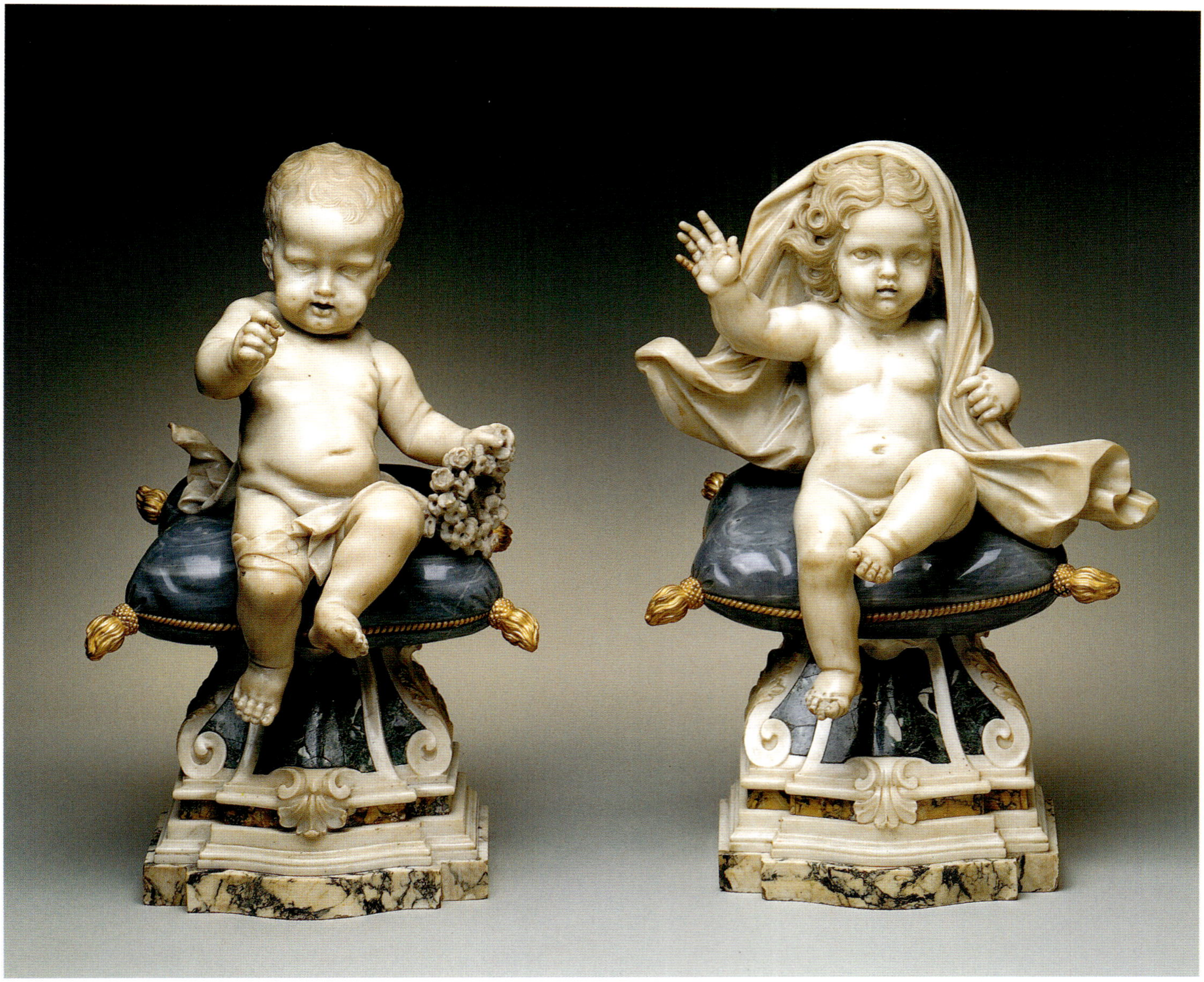

84. PAIR OF EWERS

England, Matthew Boulton (1728–1809) and John Fothergill (d. 1782), 1772
Derbyshire spar, fluorite, and gilt bronze, 49.2 × 21.6 × 12.7 cm ($19\frac{1}{2} \times 8\frac{1}{2} \times 5$ in)
(TU96AB)

PROVENANCE: First Earl of Sefton, then by descent to Hugh William Osbert Molyneux, seventh Earl of Sefton, Croxteth Hall, Liverpool; Christie's, London, sale, 17 September 1973, lot 115; Alberto di Castro, Rome, 1976.

LITERATURE: Christie's *Review of the Season* 1974, p. 444; *Italian Art & Antiques* November 1996, pp. 2, 46–47; *Connaissance des Arts* October 1996. pp. 82, 128.

DESCRIPTION: A pair of amphorae, each carved from two blocks of fluorite. The neck and handle of each are of cast gilt bronze with acanthus leaves around the lip and on the handle, and three satyrs: one on the handle, one on the base of the handle, and one on the front. The stone body of each ewer is attached to its base by a wreath of lanceolate leaves. Each bronze pedestal is fluted, with a garland around the foot, and stands on a smooth, square base.

COMMENTARY: The scheme for these ewers appears in a catalogue of designs by Matthew Boulton and John Fothergill. The only way in which the design differs from the actual vessels is that it includes a horizontal band of bronze beneath the satyrs' heads on the base of the handle and front of the ewer. This band would have served both as further ornament and as a cover for the joint between the blocks of fluorite. These ewers were supplied by Boulton and Fothergill to the First Earl of Sefton in 1772; their delivery is recorded in a letter from Boulton and Fothergill to Lord Sefton dated 19 May 1772. The price was 14 guineas. Other examples of ewers made from this design include one in private hands and a pair in the Birmingham Museum and Art Gallery, which also lacks the band.[1]

Boulton's factory in Soho, Birmingham, specialised in the production of vases, candelabra, and perfume burners with gilt-bronze mounts. He made extensive use of stones such as marble, fluorite, and quartz.

NOTE
1 Goodison 1974, pp. 131, 199, no. 248, pl. 49.

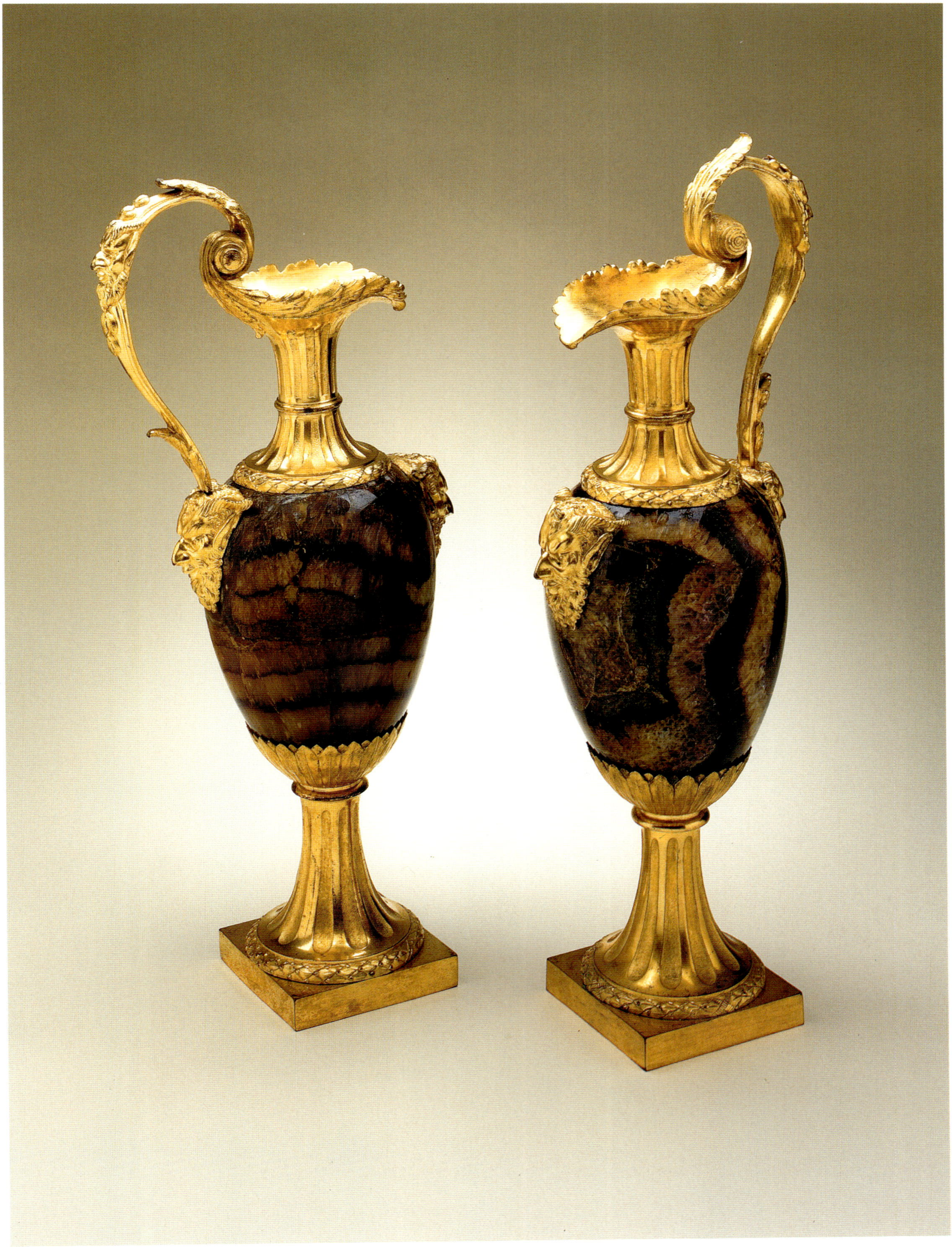

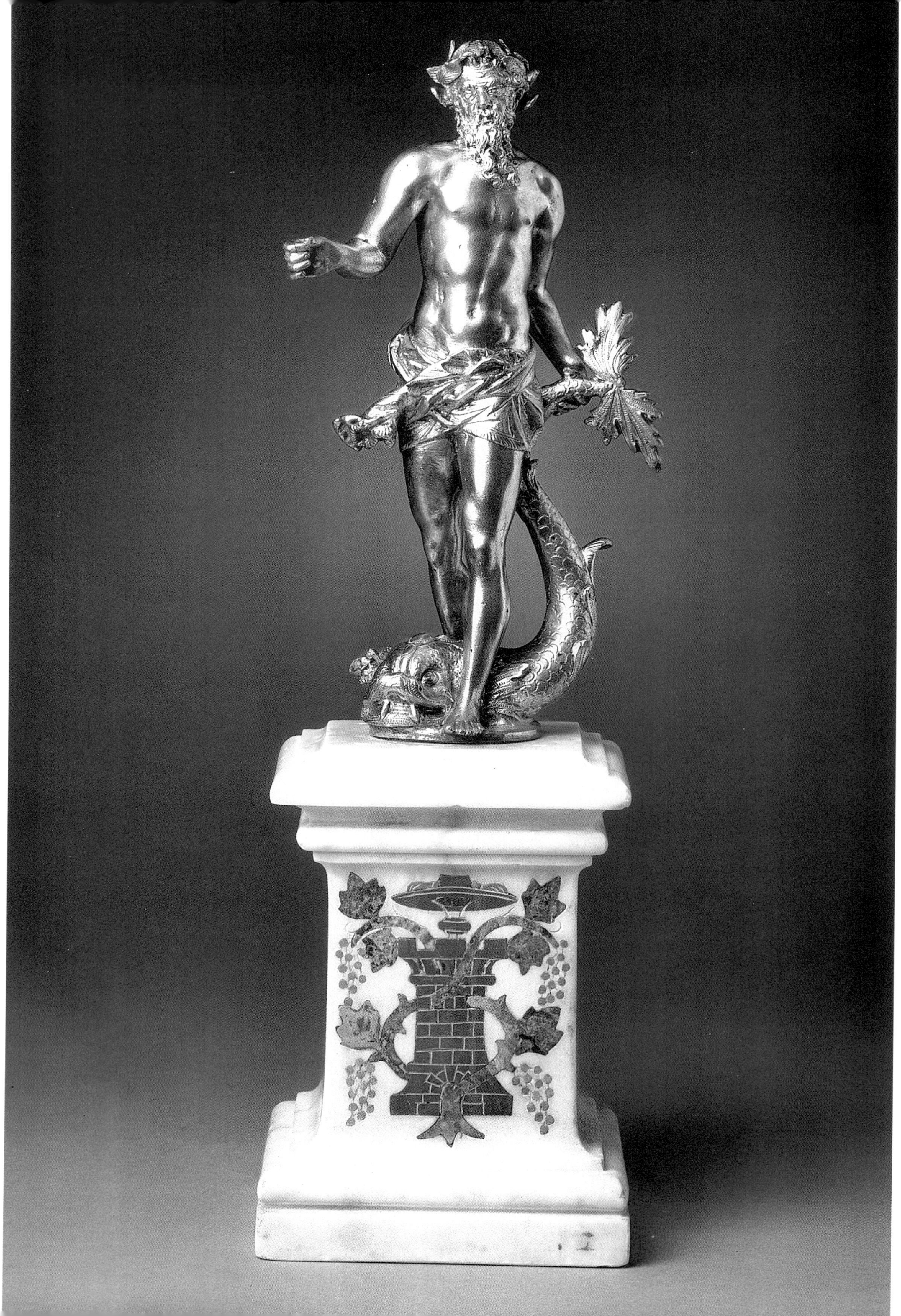

85. NEPTUNE

Italy, probably Venice, after Gerolamo Campagna (1549–c. 1625), sixteenth century
Gilt bronze, marble
Figure: 5 × 14 × 8.5 cm (29⅞ × 5½ × 3⅜ in); base: 17.4 × 12.5 × 12.5 cm (6⅞ × 5 × 5 in)
(TU149)

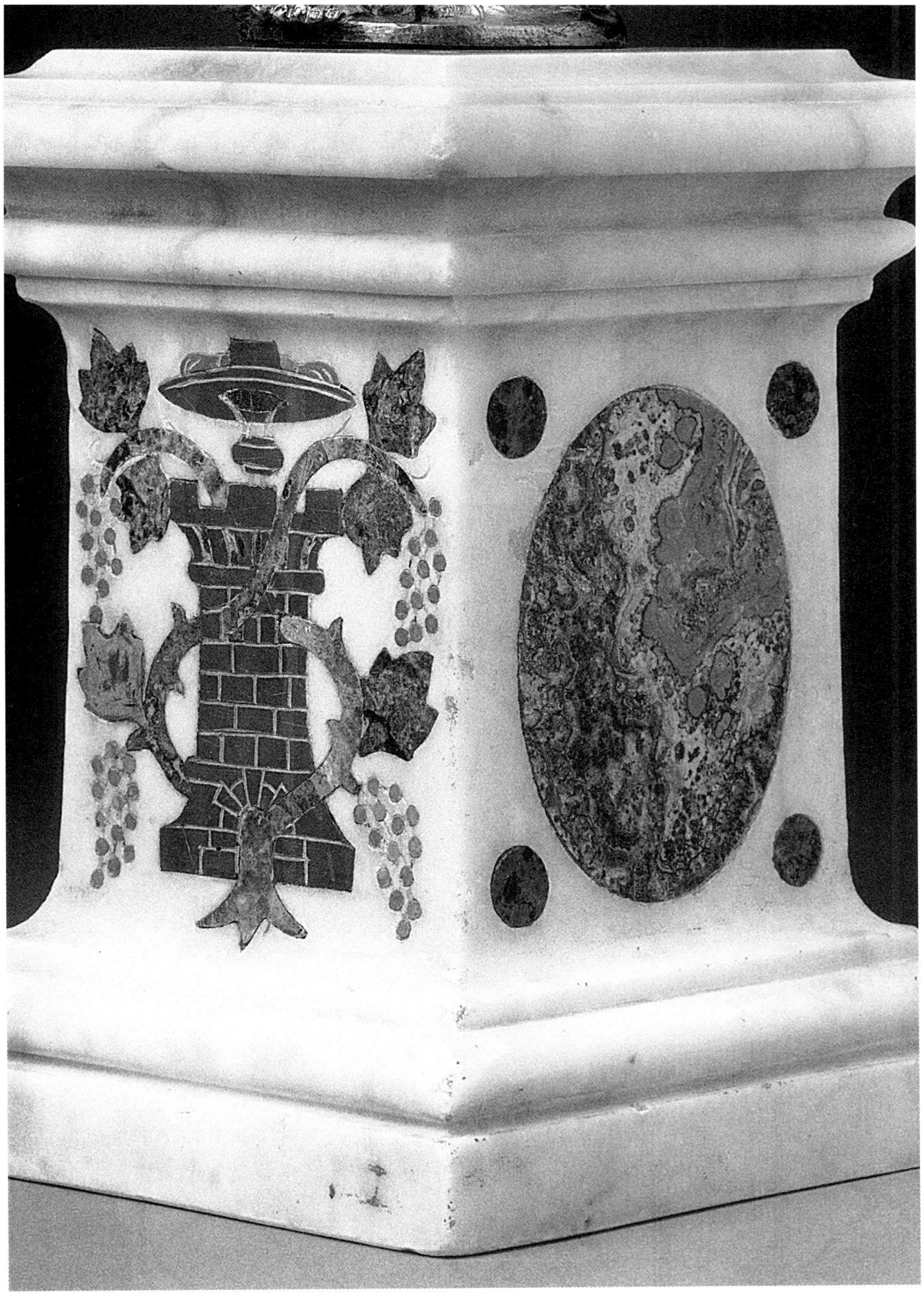

PROVENANCE: Christie's, London, 8 December 1987, lot 159.

DESCRIPTION: A gilt-bronze statuette of Neptune astride a dolphin, his left hand grasping the upraised dolphin's tail, his right hand extended, indicating that he once held a trident, now missing. The statuette stands on a marble base, which has an unidentified coat-of-arms on one side and inlaid ovals of marble bordered by smaller discs of marble on the opposite side. The coat-of-arms includes a red-brick tower surmounted by a bishop's crown, and is entwined with vines, leaves, and four clusters of grapes.

COMMENTARY: This statuette is in the style of Gerolamo Campagna, one of the most prominent and influential Venetian sculptors of the sixteenth century, who specialised in dynamic and expressive biblical figures. In addition, he contributed subjects from classical mythology such as two marble statuettes of Hercules and Mercury (c. 1582) for the chimneypiece of the Doge's Palace in Venice, and allegorical figures of War, Peace, and Minerva (c. 1585, Doge's Palace). His first bronzes were monumental figures of St. Mark, St. Francis, and the Crucifixion (1589–90; Il Redentore, Venice). In the last of these, the crucified Christ typifies the 'sensuous treatment of the nude male figure', which can be seen echoed in the Gilbert bronze Neptune.[1] Among his smaller works are a pair of bronze statuettes of angels holding candlesticks of about the same date (Santa Maria del Carmelo). After numerous major large scale commissions, he produced several more bronze statuettes around 1606.[2]

NOTES
1 *The Dictionary of Art*, vol. 5, p. 532. Entry by Bruce Boucher.
2 *The Dictionary of Art*, vol. 5, pp. 531–34.

86. NOTEBOOK

Dresden, attributed to Johann Christian Neuber (1736–1808), c. 1800
Pietre dure, miniature on ivory, gold, silk, 11.7 × 8.3 × 1.3 cm (4⅝ × 3¼ × ½ in)
1996.319 (MM218)

PROVENANCE: King Farouk of Egypt, sale, Sotheby's, Cairo, The Palace Collections of Egypt, Koubbeh Palace, 18 March 1954, lot 703; Baron de Redé, sale, France; Sotheby's, sale, Monaco, 25–26 May 1975, lot 41.

LITERATURE: *Princely Taste*, Israel Museum, 1995, p. 75.

EXHIBITIONS: Los Angeles / Atlanta / San Antonio / Richmond / Seattle, 1977–79; Jerusalem, 1995.

DESCRIPTION: A notebook composed of gold and lined with red watered silk. The cover is inlaid with multi-coloured hardstone lozenges set in cells in the manner of *Zellenmosaik*. The centre of each cover is set with an oval, gold-framed miniature: Louis XVI on the front and Marie Antoinette on the back. A gold pencil serves to lock the notebook by being inserted through loops on the right-hand side.

COMMENTARY: The attribution to Neuber by González-Palacios seems well founded, based on the exquisite workmanship of the *Zellenmosaik* – Neuber's trademark. (For further information on Neuber, see cat. nos. 58, 59). The miniatures, while originally attributed to Sicardi by Christie's, have not been firmly identified with that artist.

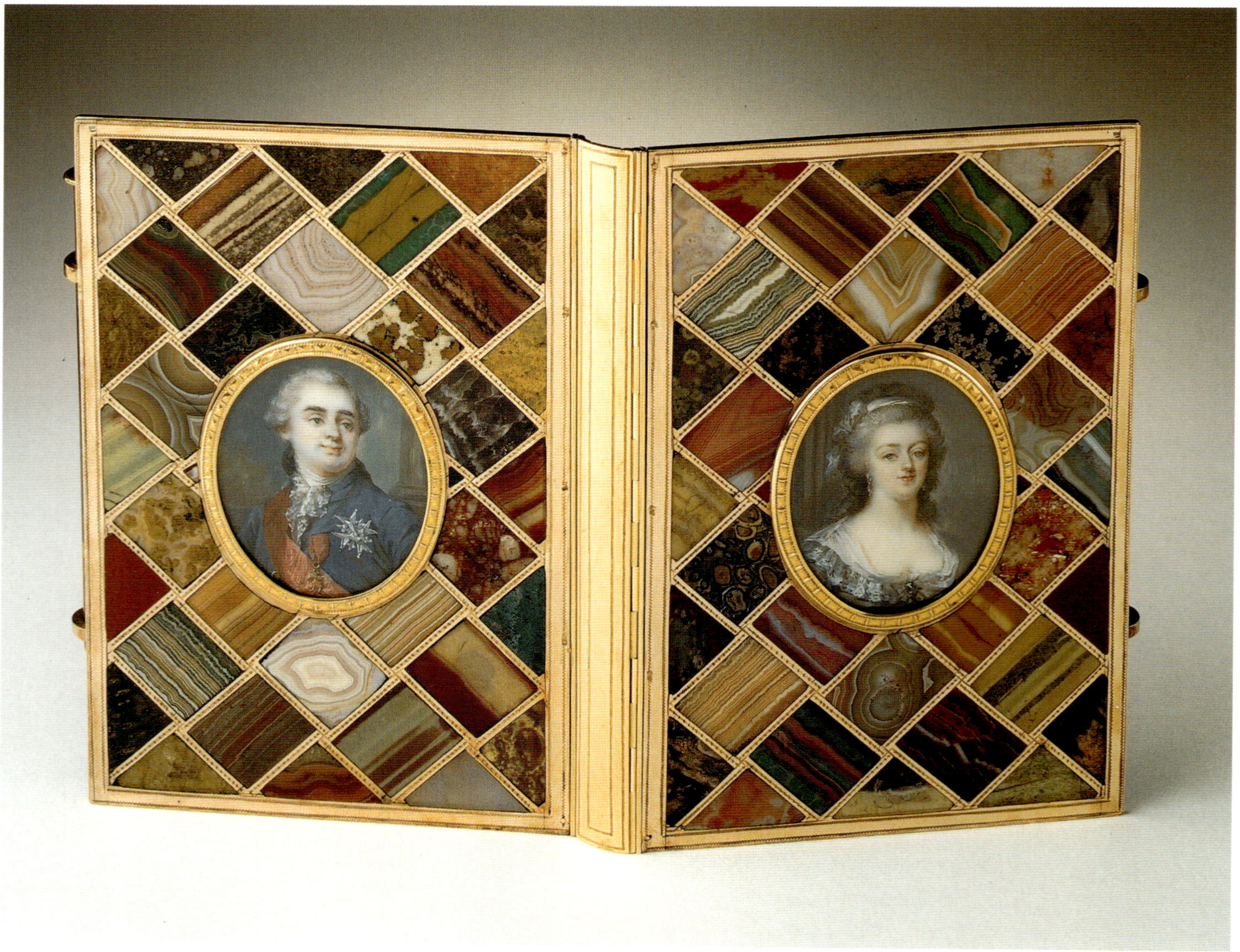

87. PARURE

Naples, Real Laboratorio, c. 1808
Pietre dure, lapis lazuli, chalcedony, gold, comb: 11.7cm (4 5/8 in); tiara: 14.6 cm (5 3/4 in); necklace: 44.8 cm (17 5/8 in); earrings: 5.4 cm (2 1/8 in)
1996.305 (MM186)

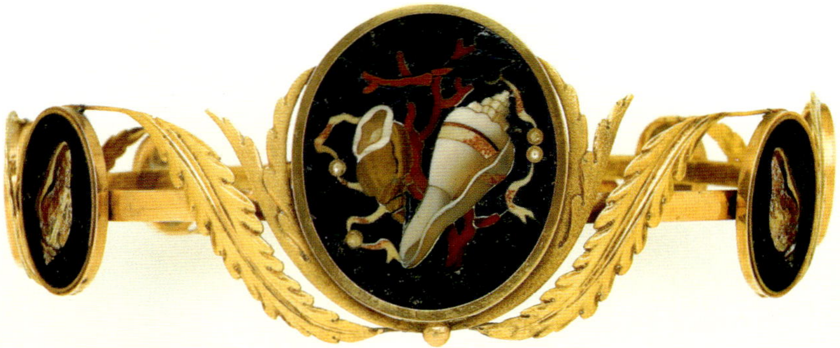

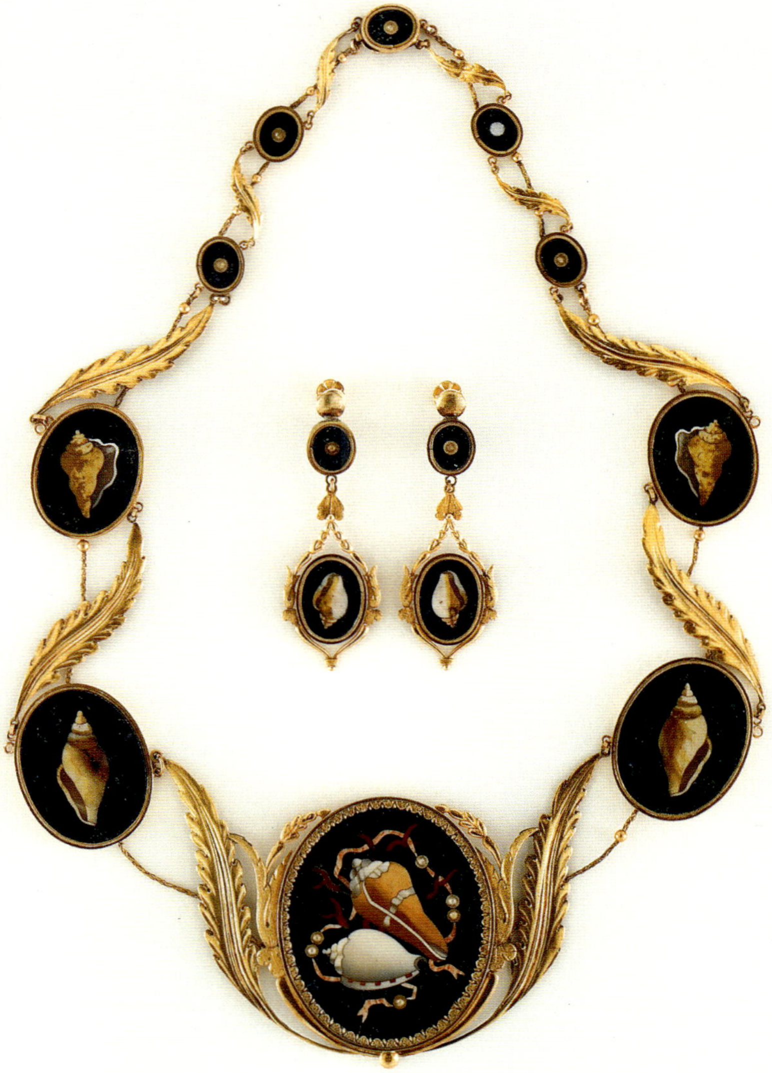

PROVENANCE: Caroline Murat, Queen of Naples; Delessert family; Marthe Bocher; Jacques Kugel, Paris, 1975.

LITERATURE: González-Palacios 1977a, no. 30; Wilson 1980, p. 100; González-Palacios 1982b, pp. 69–70; González-Palacios and Röttgen 1982, no. 32; *Designers West* 1987, p. 120; Giusti 1992, pp. 235, 246, pl. 122; *Princely Taste* 1995, p. 77.

EXHIBITIONS: Los Angeles / Atlanta / San Antonio / Richmond / Seattle, 1977–79; Jerusalem, 1995.

DESCRIPTION: A matched set of gold jewellery consisting of a comb, tiara, necklace and a pair of earrings. The individual plaques are made of lapis lazuli inset with shells and pearls in *pietre dure* mosaic. There are 24 mosaic plaques in all. The comb has a French import mark (a swan in an oval) of the type stamped after 1893 on objects coming from countries without customs. The clasp and earrings have an unidentified mark with the initials ET in a rectangle.

COMMENTARY: The origin of this elegant parure is unclear, having been ascribed to the workshops of both Naples and Florence. Originally González-Palacios thought it was made in the Grand Ducal workshops in Florence, but on the basis of documents found by him in the archives of Naples, he suggested that the Gilbert Collection parure was made there, a hypothesis endorsed by the fact that their original owner was Caroline Murat.[1] In 1982, Alvar González-Palacios linked a drawing in the archives of the Opificio delle Pietre Dure in Florence with the Gilbert Collection jewellery. The unsigned drawing is dated 22 October 1798 and is probably by Leopold Cioci who, in 1792, became a designer and selector of stones in the Opificio.

Various examples of lapis lazuli jewellery of this type were produced in the Grand Ducal workshops in Florence at this time. A necklace commissioned by 'Milord Mongommery', for example, was finished in 1799.[2] Numerous other unpublished designs are in the archives of the Opificio delle Pietre Dure. The jewellery designs and patterns created in Florence in the final decade of the eighteenth century were still fashionable during the following decade, and it seems likely that the royal workshop in Naples, which made *pietre dure* jewellery, would have repeated the same sort of styles. Documents located by González-Palacios do, in fact, relate to lapis lazuli jewellery made in the Real Laboratorio in Naples, referring particularly to the production of two combs, two necklaces, and two pairs of earrings – evidently matching sets similar to the Gilbert parure.[3] The documents date from 1809, and it is quite plausible that the jewellery described was made expressly for the queen, who had so recently come to live in the city. It is appropriate to relate them to the set in the Gilbert Collection.

This parure still has its original Moroccan red leather case, decorated with an embossed gold border of sphinxes and amphorae. In the centre is an initial C and a royal crown. The tradition that this set of jewellery belonged to Caroline Murat, Queen of Naples, is substantiated by the presence of her monogram on the box and by a document dated 30 May 1894, accompanying it. The document is an extract of the will of Madame Gabriel Delessert, who left the set to Marthe Bocher and mentioned its provenance.

NOTES

1 González–Palacios 1977a, no. 30; González-Palacios and Röttgen 1982, no. 32; González-Palacios 1982b, p. 122.

2 González-Palacios 1986, vol. 1, p. 123, no. 117.

3 González-Palacios 1982b, p. 70; A. S. N. M. I. sec. inv. 5074.

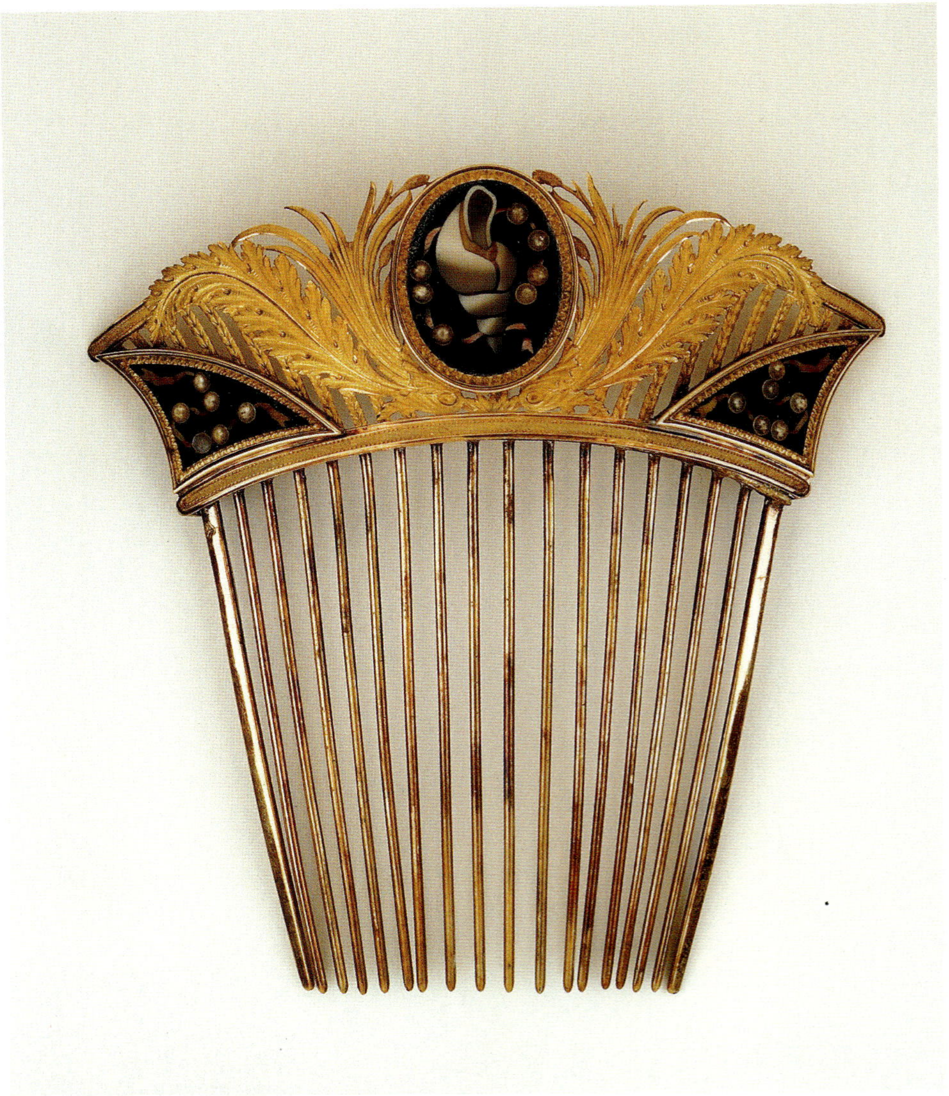

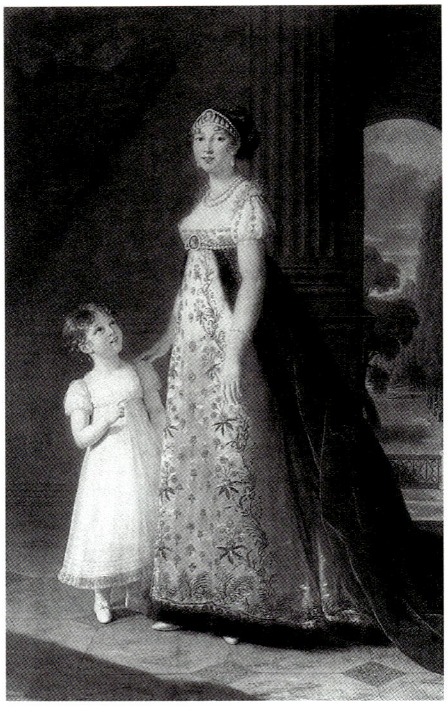

FIG. 21. Portrait of Caroline Murat, Queen of Naples, c. 1806, by Marie Vigée Lebrun, Chateau de Versailles.

88. CENTREPIECE

Possibly Austria, mid-nineteenth century
Malachite, bronze, gilt bronze, 60.8 × 39.2 × 34.3 cm (24 × 15½ × 13½ in)
(TU119)

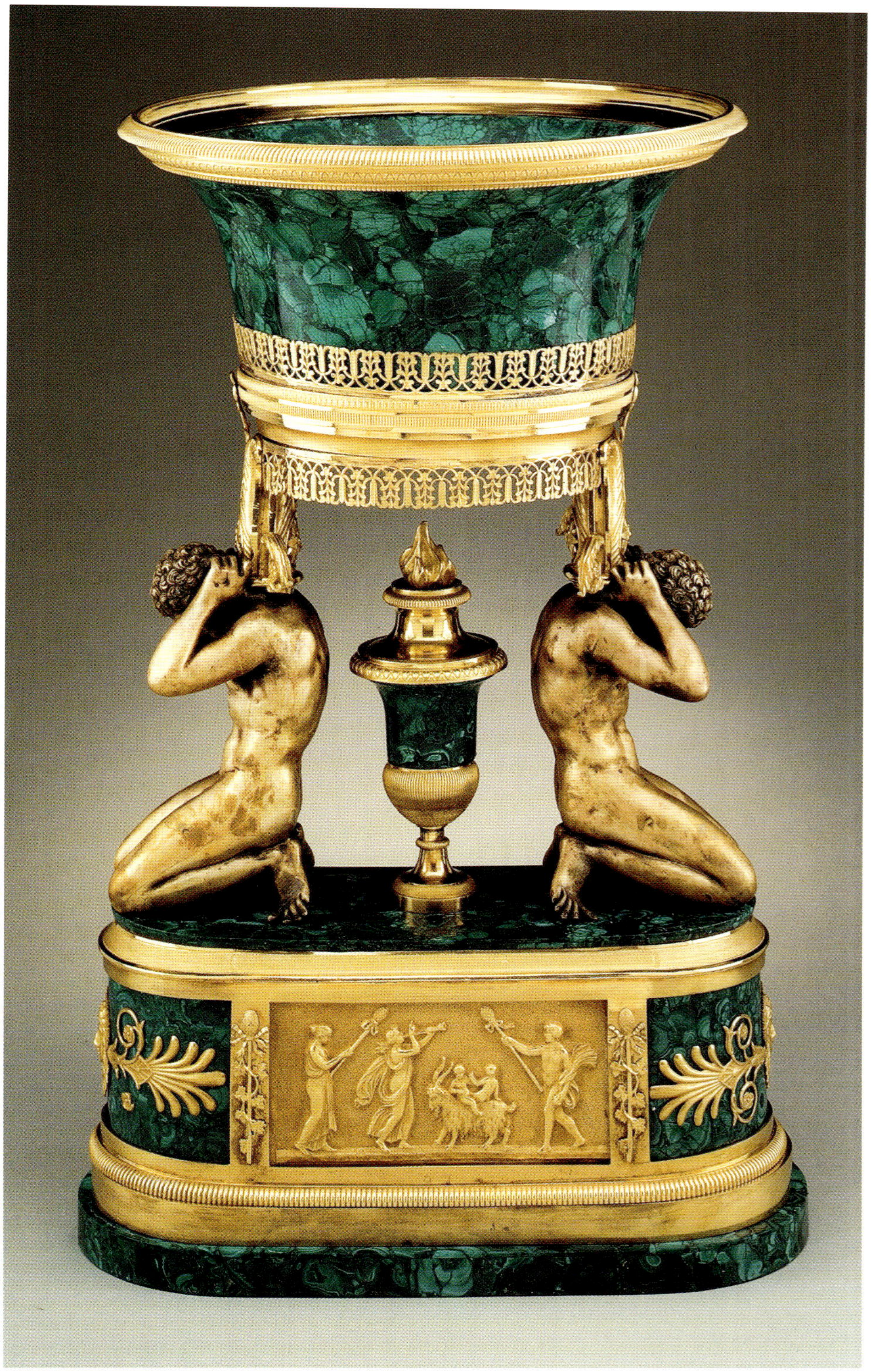

PROVENANCE: Louise Bouvier Drexel Morrell, Philadelphia; Rare Art, New York, 1978.

DESCRIPTION: A vase with a malachite bowl, edged at the lip and base with gilt bronze and supported by two figures of kneeling Moors of bronze with a dark-brown patina; these are on an oval base of malachite mosaic with gilt-bronze borders. On top of the base is a smaller vase with a torch. Two rectangular gilt-bronze plaques on the front and back of the base are chased with scenes of bacchanals; the ends of the base have gilt-bronze mounts of two palmettes with a mask in the centre.

COMMENTARY: The bronzes on the base of this centrepiece are almost identical to the decorations on a Viennese clock of 1810.[1] The shape of the oval base and the style of the bronze pedestal connect this object with Viennese workshops in which malachite was sometimes used.

NOTE
1 Ottomeyer and Proeschel 1986, vol. 2, p. 408, no. 50.20.2.

89. TWO-HANDLED VASE

St. Petersburg, mid-nineteenth century
Malachite and gilt bronze, 59.2 × 50.5 × 32 cm (23 3/8 × 20 1/4 × 12 5/8 in)
(TU25)

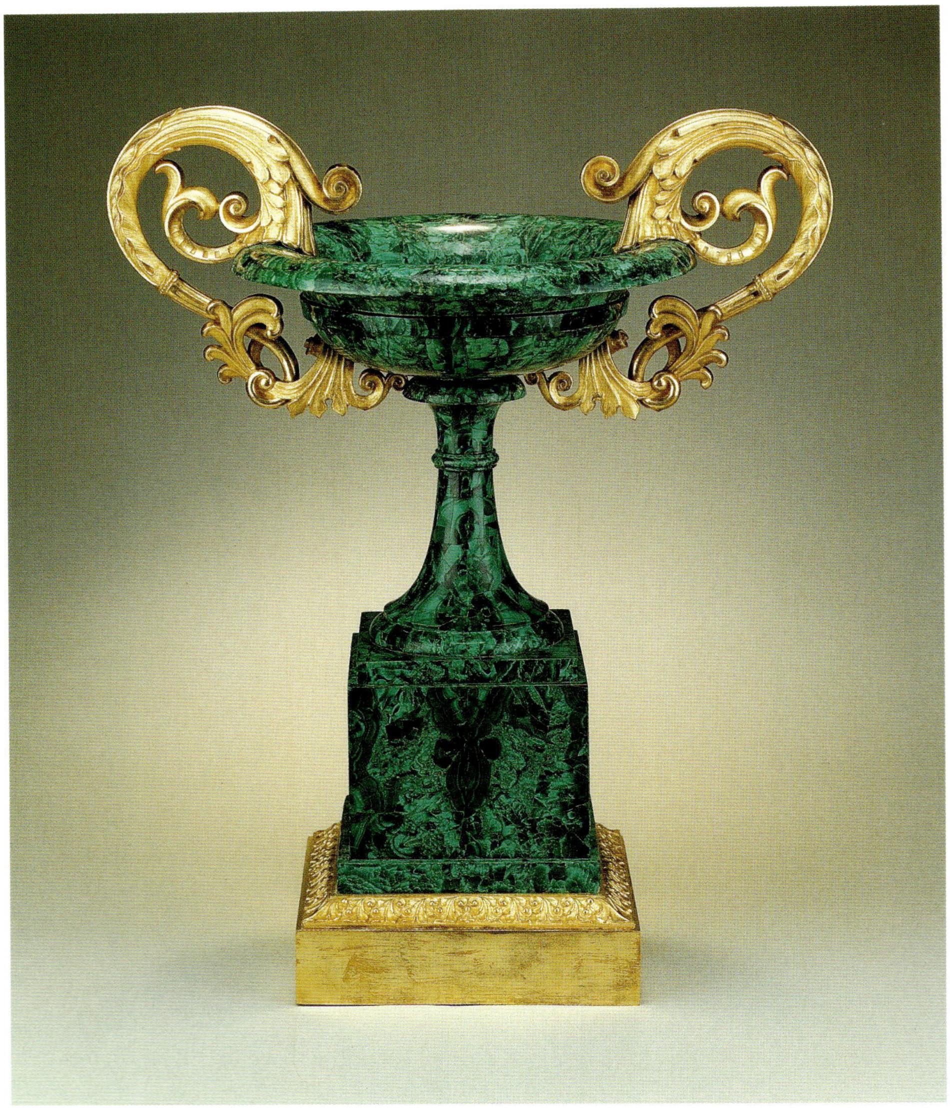

PROVENANCE: Charles J. Winston, New York, 1968.

DESCRIPTION: A malachite vase with a circular bowl and supporting foot on a stepped, square malachite pedestal. The plinth and raised volute handles are of gilt bronze.

COMMENTARY: As indicated by the inscription on the base: G. G. MULLER, ST PETERSBURG, this vase comes from one of the many private workshops in the Russian city. Malachite objects produced by the Russian workshops were very much admired at the Great Exhibition in London in 1851 for their technical virtuosity. Large vases similar to this can be found in the Hermitage in St. Petersburg.[1]

NOTE

1 (inv. no. KM–326a.b).

90. MODEL OF MUMTAZ MAHAL'S CENOTAPH

India, Uttar Pradesh, Agra, first half nineteenth century
Pietre dure, white marble, 19.2 × 54.2 × 21.6 cm (7½ × 21⅜ × 5½ in)
1996.354 (MM291)

PROVENANCE: Michael and Henrietta Spink, London, 1993.

EXHIBITION: Los Angeles, 1993.

DESCRIPTION: A model fashioned from a single block of white marble enriched with elegant *pietre dure* inlay.

COMMENTARY: This model of the cenotaph of the Mughal Empress, Mumtaz Mahal (1598–1631), is a virtually exact copy of the original in the Taj Mahal, in Agra, India. It was made in the nineteenth century when numerous finely crafted models of Indian monuments were created for English patrons who wanted a memento of their service in, or trip to, India. The marble was quarried in the Maicrana mines near Jaipur, Rajasthan, and the hardstones used for the inlay were obtained from various imported and indigenous sources.

The *pietre dure* technique used for the model was originally taught to Indian artists in the seventeenth century by Florentine craftsmen lured to the Mughal court by accounts of its fabled riches by returning travellers. A number of Italian artists are known to have worked in India during the period and there are surviving records of trade, royal gifts, and missionary and diplomatic exchanges between the Mughal court and the Medici family of Florence.[1]

Mumtaz Mahal (Exalted One of the Palace) was the second wife and true love of the Mughal Emperor, Shah Jahan (r. 1628–58). She married Shah Jahan at the age of 14 in May 1612 and died on 17 June 1631, after giving birth to their fourteenth son. The Taj Mahal (Crown of the Palace, derived from her imperial sobriquet) was built in her honour as a memorial mausoleum between 1632 and 1643. For security reasons, her body is interred in a cenotaph within a secluded crypt beneath a false cenotaph on the main floor that is enclosed within an elaborate *pietre dure* marble screen. Her husband was later entombed by her side in an analogous pair of cenotaphs. While all of the cenotaphs are similar in overall form, each is embellished with different inscriptions and decorative designs. Both of Mumtaz Mahal's

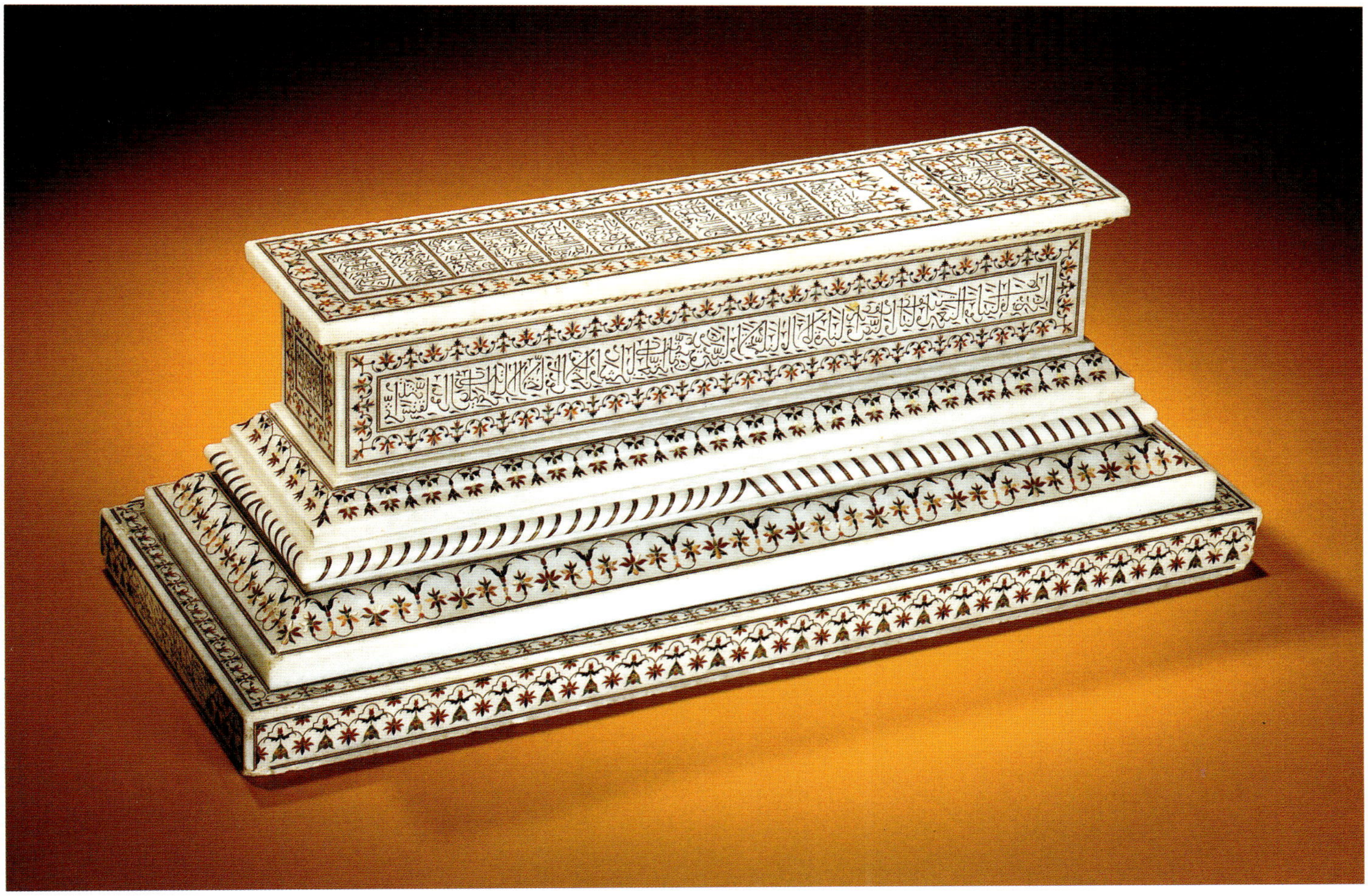

cenotaphs are graced with verses from the *Qur' an*, the holy book of Islam, and the lower cenotaph is also inscribed with the 99 names of god. Each of the Empress' cenotaphs has an identical historical epitaph on the lower moulding of the southern end (viewer's right in the photograph): 'The illumined grave of Aijumand Banu Begam, entitled Mumtaz Mahal, who died in the year 1040 [1631]'. The model in the Gilbert Collections replicates the upper cenotaph.[2]

NOTES

1 Jones 1987.

2 *Qur 'anic* inscription on the upper cenotaph and model:

Top of cenotaph, northern end (viewer's left)

[SURA 41: *HA HIM*, OR *AL-FUSSILAT*, 'THE EXPLANATION']

In the Name of God, the Merciful, the Compassionate.
O Living, O Eternal I beseech Thy Mercy! Said the Blessed
and Great God

30. *Verily those who say, 'Our Lord is God!' and further*
stand straight and steadfast; unto them the Angels
shall descend, saying: 'Fear ye not! Neither be ye
grieved! But rejoice ye in the Paradise which ye have
been promised!'

[SURA 40: *AL-MU' MIN*, 'THE BELIEVER']
7. 'O Lord! Who Reaches over All Things, in Mercy and
Knowledge. Forgive, then, those who turn in
Repentance, and follow Thy Path; and preserve them from
the Penalty of the Blazing Fire!'
8. 'And allow them, O Lord! To enter the Gardens of Eden
which Thou hast promised unto them and unto the
righteous among their fathers, their wives, and their
posterity – for Thou art surely the All-mighty, the
All wise!'

Eastern side (not shown in photograph)

[SURA 83: *AL-TATFIF*, 'THE SHORT MEASURE']
Said the Almighty –
22. Truly the righteous shall be in Bliss,
23. Upon raised couches, gazing –
24. Thou shalt observe in their faces the radiancy of Bliss!
25. They shall be given to drink of a pure wine, sealed:
26. The seal whereof shall be musk – and for this, let those
Aspire who have aspirations! –
27. An[d?] mingled therewith shall be the waters of Tasnim:
28. A Fountain whereat do [to?] drink ...

Southern end (viewer's right in photograph)

[28. Contd.] ... Those Nearest unto God!

[SURA 41: *HA HIM*, OR *AL-FUSSIAT*, 'THE EXPLANATION']

30. Verily those who say, 'our Lord is God!'...

Western side (viewer's front in photograph):

[30. Contd.]... And further, stand straight and steadfast:
unto them the Angels shall descend, saying: 'Fear ye
not! Neither be ye grieved! But rejoice ye in the
Paradise which ye have been promised!'

[SURA 2: *AL BAQARAH*, 'THE COW']

286. 'O Lord! Place not upon us a burden greater than we
Have strength to bear! Blot out our sins, and grant us
Forgiveness! Have Mercy upon us! Thou art our...
Protector: help us therefore against ...

Northern end (not shown in photograph):

[286. contd.]... the people of the unbelievers!'

[SURA 59: *AL HASHR*, 'THE ASSEMBLY']

22. He is God! Beside Whom there is no God! He is the
Knower of the unseen and the seen! He is the All-
merciful, the All-compassionate![2]

Tranlations from W. E. Begley and Z. A. Desai, pp. 235–39.

Entry by Stephen Markel, Curator of Indian and Southeast Asian Art, Los Angeles County Museum of Art.

91. PENDANT CROSS

Florence, c. 1850
Pietre dure, marble, gold, 10 × 5.7 cm ($3\frac{15}{16} \times 2\frac{1}{4}$ in)
1996.629 (MM259)

PROVENANCE: Hancocks and Co., London, 1977.

DESCRIPTION: A small, black marble cross inlaid with *pietre dure* depicting sprays of white campanula and green leaves, the top pierced and holding a gold loop.

COMMENTARY: This product is characteristic of the private workshops of Florence in the late nineteenth century. They produced a constant supply of jewellery, such as brooches, earrings, and pendants decorated with simple inlaid hardstones. Jewellery of this type was also produced by the Opificio delle Pietre Dure, where examples can still be seen.

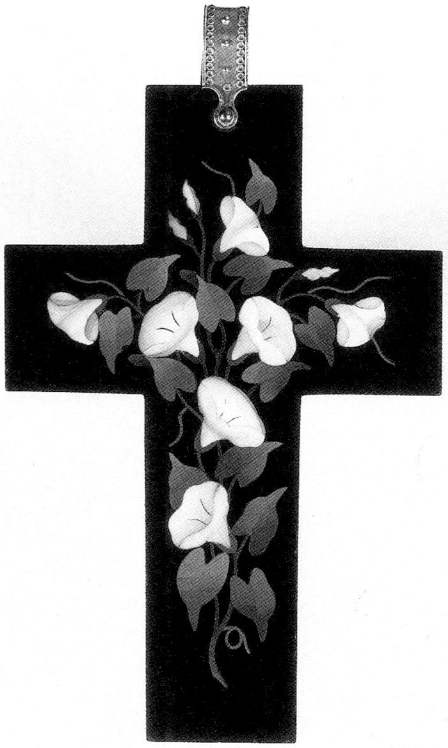

92. PLAQUE WITH COAT-OF-ARMS

Nineteenth century
Coloured marbles, 20.3 × 17.1 cm (8 × 6¾ in)
1996.578 (MM26)

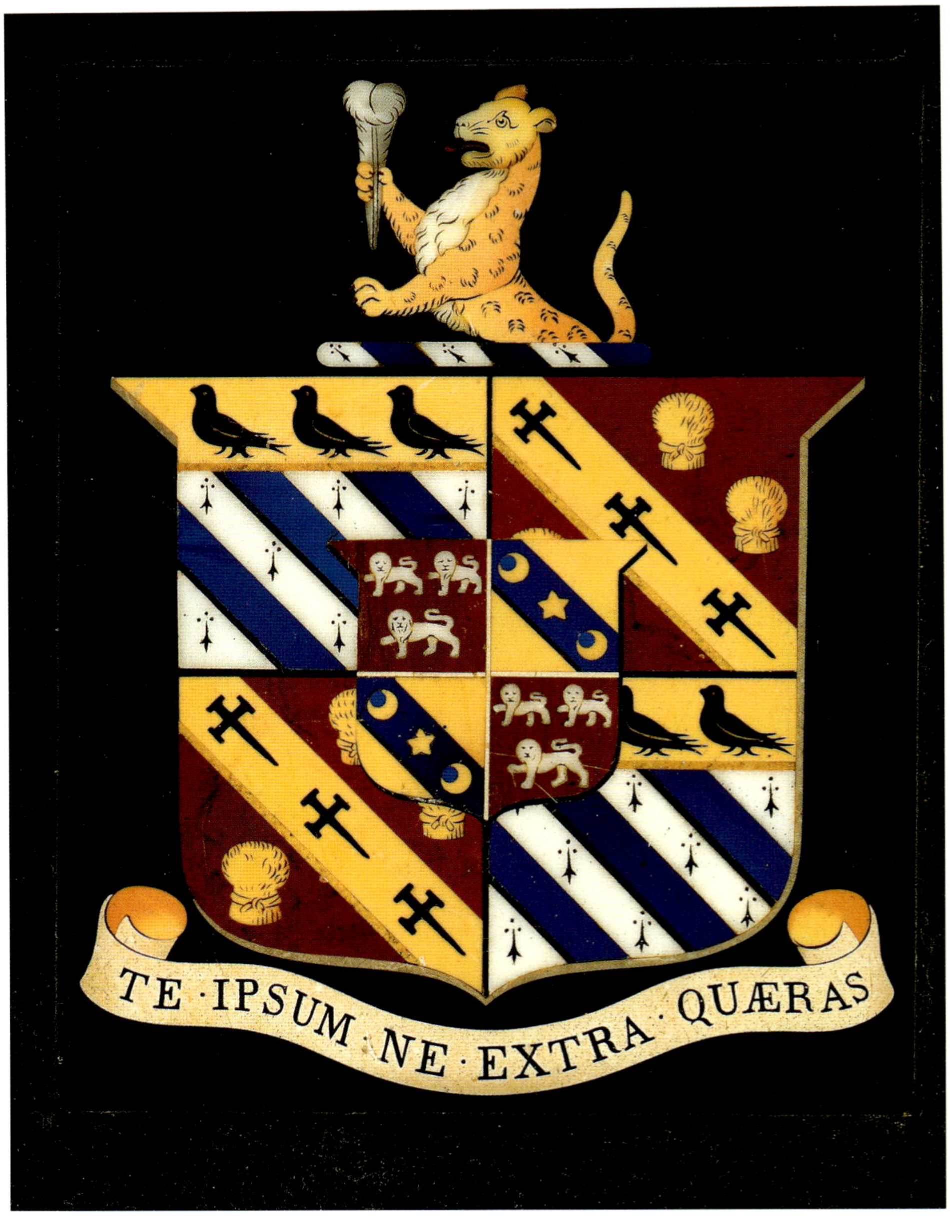

PROVENANCE: A. Cook, London, 1969.

EXHIBITION: Los Angeles, 1977.

DESCRIPTION: A rectangular piece of black marble inlaid with a cartouche-shaped coat-of-arms of coloured marbles with a white scroll below, which displays the motto TE IPSUM NE EXTRA QUERAS.

COMMENTARY: The arms are those of Pocklington of Nottinghamshire and Cumberland, quartering Rowe and with others in pretence.

93. RUNNING STAG

Dayton, Ohio, Herman Sachs, (1889–1940), c. 1920
Scagliola, 24.2 × 37.8 cm (9⁵⁄₈ × 14⁷⁄₈ in)
1996.583 (MM44)

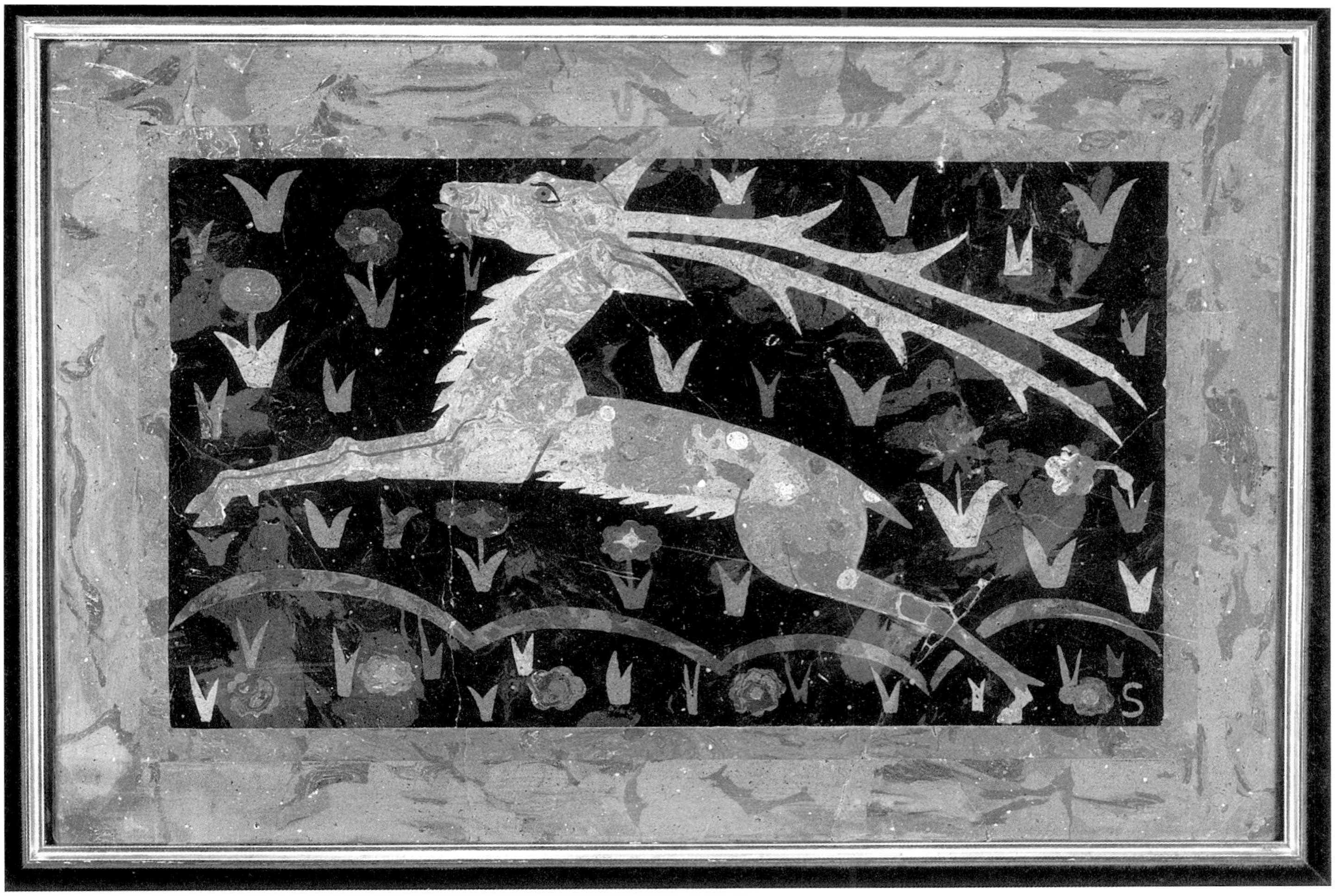

PROVENANCE: Antique Mart, Los Angeles, 1966.

LITERATURE: *Dayton Journal*, 9 October 1921, p. 3.

EXHIBITIONS: Dayton, 1921; Los Angeles, 1977.

DESCRIPTION: A rectangular *scagliola* picture depicting a stylised deer running in a landscape. The work is initialled S at the bottom right.

COMMENTARY: Herman Sachs was both an artist and an art educator. A Romanian by birth, he was held as a civilian prisoner in Germany during the early part of World War I, declining to be Director of the German Industrial Art Schools. He was able to emigrate instead to the United States where he became a naturalised citizen. He later returned to Europe for 12 years to study art in France, Austria, Switzerland, and Germany, where he ran an art school in Munich for a while. Eventually he returned to Chicago to head Hull House, an arts and crafts centre, and was also in charge of the Chicago Industrial Art School. Subsequently, he served as director of the Dayton Art Museum and School of Industrial and Fine Arts. Along with his books on the techniques of painting and batik, Sachs was also co-author (with S. Mollier) of a text on anatomy for artists.

This *scagliola* picture of a deer suggests the influence of Franz Marc (1880–1916), a member of the German Expressionist movement, who specialised in painting animals, and was killed in action near Verdun. The picture is made with a type of paste obtained from artificially coloured marble powder. Its use in this work exemplifies Sach's broad range and experimental approach. *Running Stag* was illustrated in the *Dayton Journal* in 1921 in a review of an exhibition of the artist's works, which included intarsia items, a cartoon for a tapestry with a flower design, and objects in batik, ceramics, and other media.

APPENDIX A

Modern Commesso Mosaics

The works presented in this section are the result of an experiment conducted by the Florentine workshops in the 1950s and 1960s with respect to the techniques used in traditional works. Through the initiative of Lando Bartoli, the director of the Opificio delle Pietre Dure, painters and artisans were invited between 1952 and 1954 to present sketches to be carried out in *commesso* mosaic. Creators of cartoons were Mauro Bini, Alvaro Monnini, Renato Bittoni, Ugo Blasi, Gianni Spadolini, and Bartoli himself. Those carrying out the work, besides the ones doing the sketches, were Renato Bresci, Renzo Ciampi, and Renzo Biondi. The initiative was supported by the Florentine artisan shops of Fiaschi, Menegatti, Nenci, Bencini, Calderoni, Fracassini, and La Musiva, also by the work of Richard Blow, a painter and American scholar passionately fond of these works. In these years, the workshop also instituted courses for young artisans by the painter Mauro Bini and the old master Angiolo del Sarto.

The *commessi* here collected are made with delicate materials and therefore are of easier and more fluent workmanship. They often employ Tuscan stones, like limestone from the Arno, igneous rocks from Impruneta (in the region of Florence), and marbles from the Apuan Alps, to which are joined some of the best-known Italian and foreign limestones. 'Poor' materials also occur, sometimes side by side with lapis lazuli and malachite. While they cannot be compared to the preciousness of *pietre dure*, they are endowed with exceptional chromatic richness.

During the 1950s Richard Blow served as an agent through whom mosaic work was exported to the United States. In order to sell these works, he obtained an import licence and a registered trademark in New York in 1951, helping to spread the taste for stone mosaic work in America and guaranteeing the continued existence of the few workshops still functioning in Florence.

A collection of modern hardstone pictures is in the Museo dell' Opificio delle Pietre Dure in Florence (Baldini, Giusti, and Pampaloni Martelli 1979, pp. 361–63).

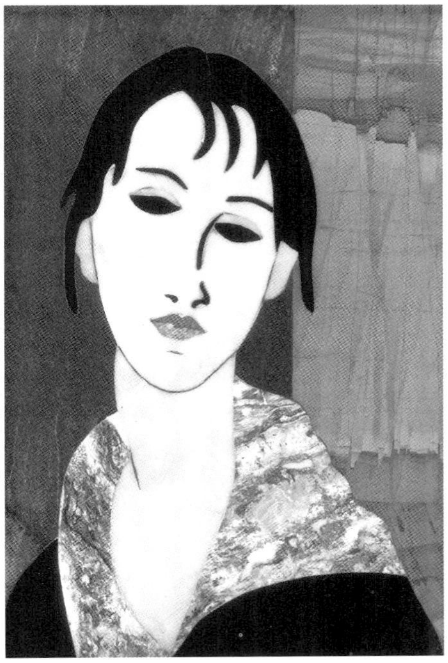

94. WOMAN (AFTER MODIGLIANI)

Florence, third quarter 20th century
Pietre dure, 17.8 × 12.1 cm (7 × 4$^{3}/_{4}$ in)
1996.585

PROVENANCE: Arte del Mosaico, Florence, 1966.

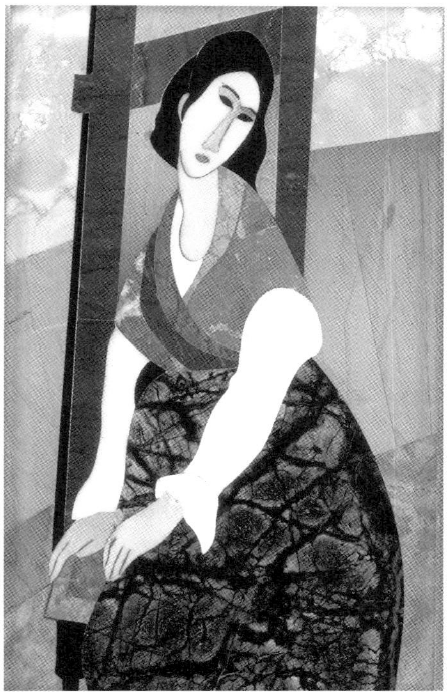

95. SEATED WOMAN (AFTER MODIGLIANI)

Florence, mid 20th century
Pietre dure, 22.9 × 14.6 cm (9 × 5$^{3}/_{4}$ in)
1996.588

PROVENANCE: Arte del Mosaico, Florence, 1966.

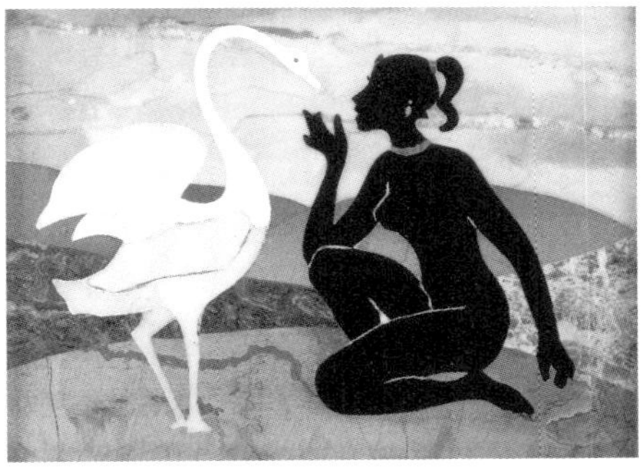

96. SWAN AND KNEELING WOMAN

Florence, third quarter 20th century
Pietre dure, 14 × 19.1 cm (5$^{1}/_{2}$ × 7$^{1}/_{2}$ in)
1996.984

PROVENANCE: Arte del Mosaico, Florence, 1966.

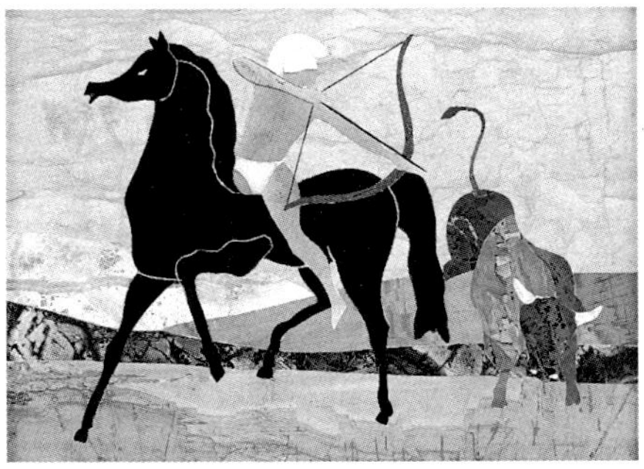

97. HUNTER ON HORSEBACK

Florence, third quarter 20th century
Pietre dure, 16.5 × 22.9 cm (6½ × 9 in)
1996.591

PROVENANCE: Arte del Mosaico, Florence, 1966.

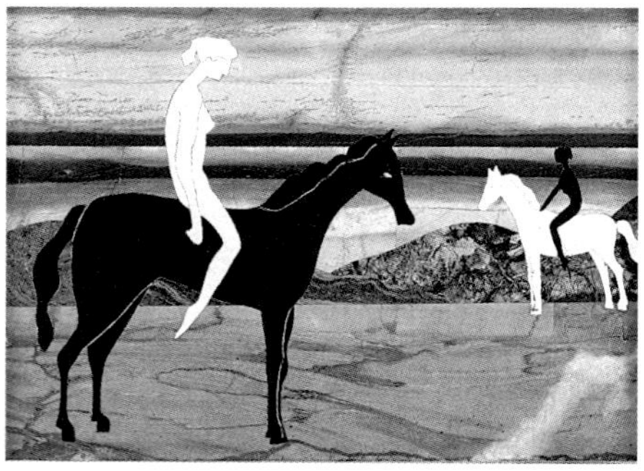

98. WOMEN ON HORSEBACK

Florence, third quarter 20th century
Pietre dure, 15.2 × 20.3 cm (6 × 8 in)
1996.589

PROVENANCE: Arte del Mosaico, Florence, 1966.

LITERATURE: Hillier 1975, p. 271, fig. 8.

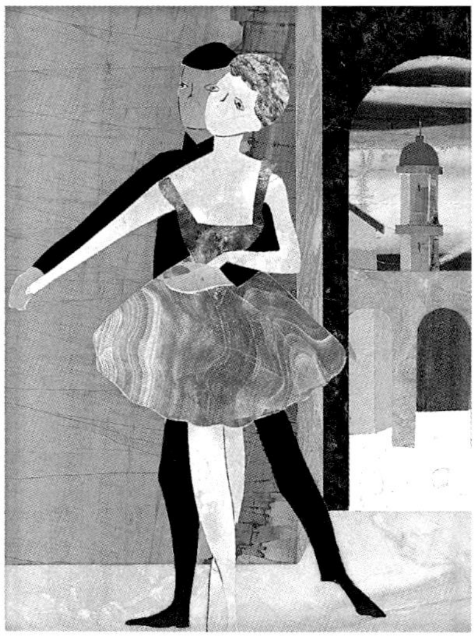

99. BALLET DANCERS

Florence, third quarter 20th century
Pietre dure, 21 × 15.9 cm (8¼ × 6¼ in)
1996.586

PROVENANCE: Arte del Mosaico, Florence, 1966.

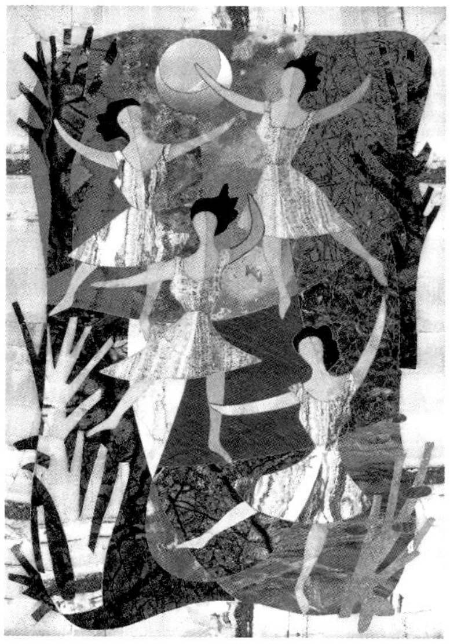

100. DANCERS

Florence, third quarter 20th century
Pietre dure, marble, 24.1 × 34.3 cm (9½ × 13½ in) (MM48)

PROVENANCE: Arte del Mosaico, Florence, 1966.

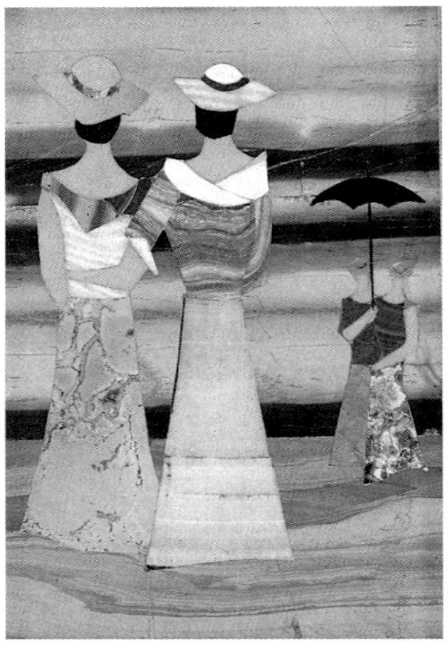

101. FOUR WOMEN

Florence, third quarter 20th century
Pietre dure, 22.9 × 17.1 cm (9 × 6¾ in)
1996.218

PROVENANCE: Arte del Mosaico, Florence, 1966.

EXHIBITIONS: Los Angeles, 1975; London, 1975.

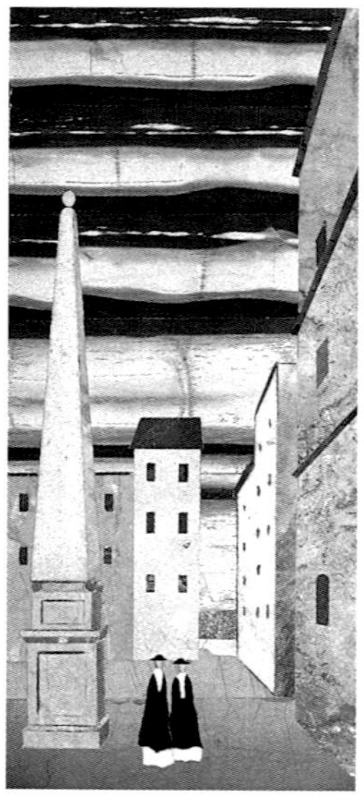

102. TWO PRELATES

Florence, third quarter 20th century
Pietre dure, 40.6 x 31.8 cm (16 × 12½ in) (MM49)

PROVENANCE: Setay, Beverly Hills, 1965.

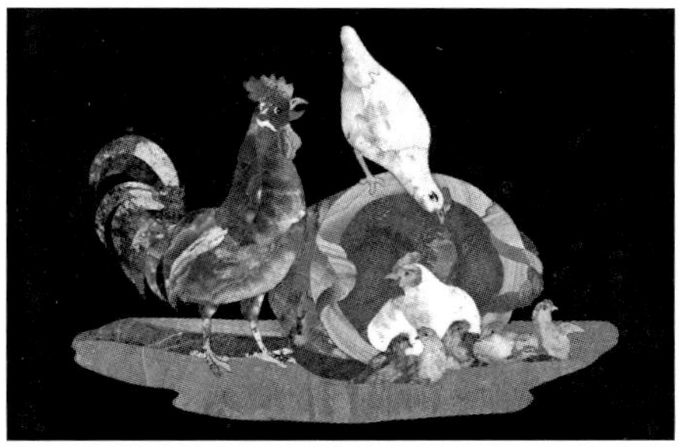

103. ROOSTER, HENS AND CHICKS

Florence, third quarter 20th century
Pietre dure, 20.3 × 12.7 cm (8 × 5 in)
1996.584

PROVENANCE: Old World Imports, Los Angeles, 1965.

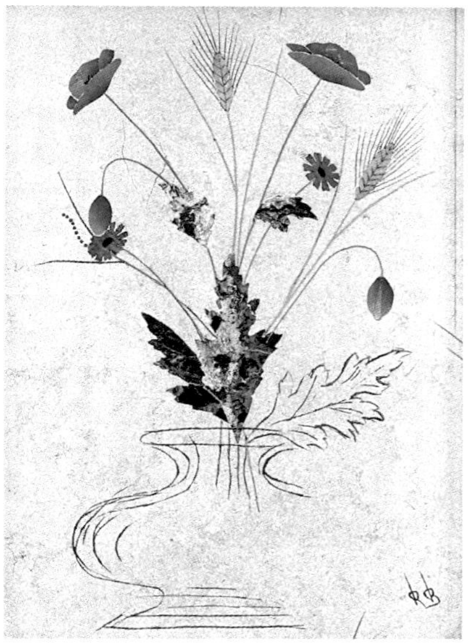

105. FLOWERS AND WHEAT

Florence, third quarter 20th century
Pietre dure, 36.8 × 27.3 cm (14½ × 10¾ in) 1996.592

PROVENANCE: Gina Contini, Florence, 1969.

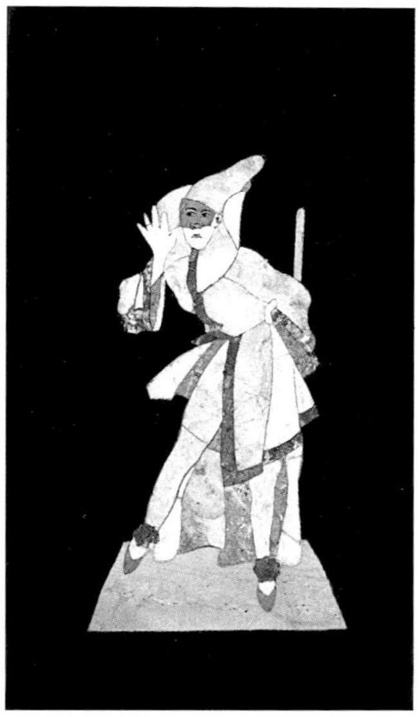

107. CARNIVAL FIGURE

Florence, third quarter 20th century
Pietre dure, 30.5 × 35.6 cm (12 × 14 in)
1996.593

PROVENANCE: Arte del Mosaico, Florence, 1966.

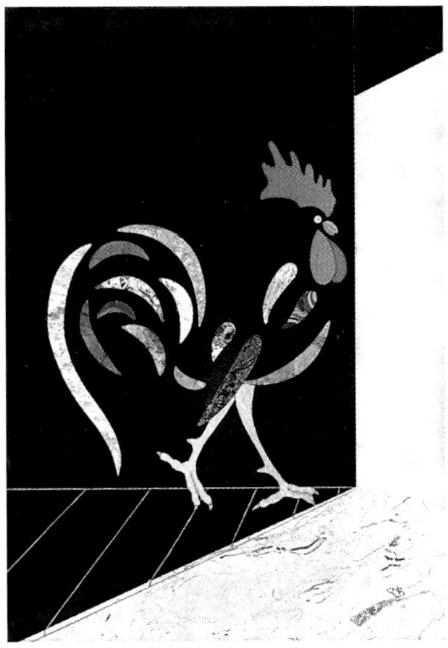

104. ROOSTER

Florence, third quarter 20th century
Pietre dure, 37.1 × 27.9 cm (14⅝ × 11 in)

PROVENANCE: Gina Contini, Florence, 1966.

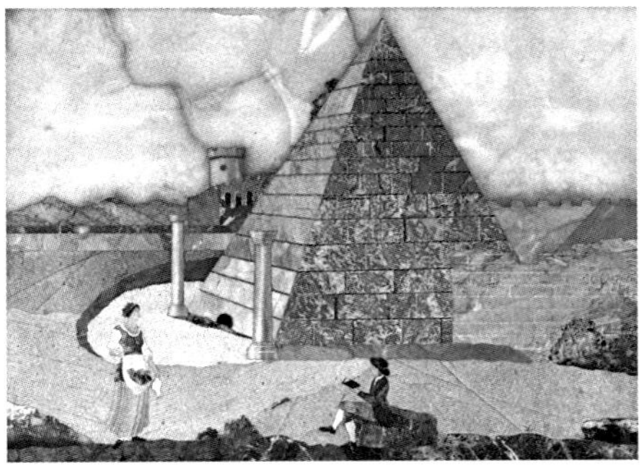

106. PYRAMID OF CAIUS CESTIUS

Florence, third quarter 20th century
Pietre dure, 16.5 × 25.4 cm (6½ × 10 in)
1996.590

PROVENANCE: Arte del Mosaico, Florence, 1966.

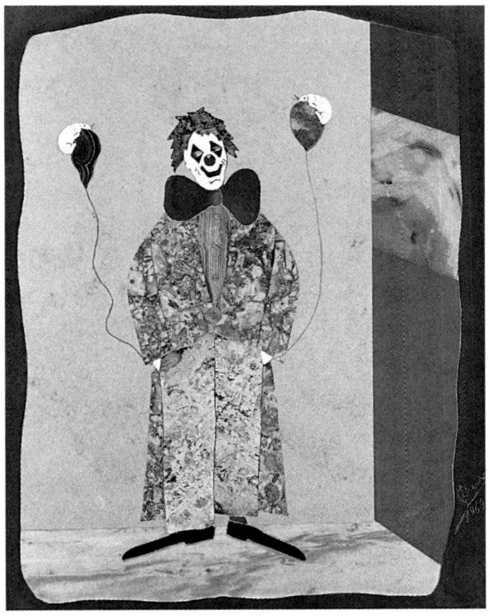

108. CLOWN

Florence, 1969
Pietre dure, 40.6 × 34.9 cm (16 × 13¾ in) (MM170)

PROVENANCE: Gina Contini, Rome, 1969.

APPENDIX B

Materials

The types of stones most widely used for decorative work such as mosaics, glyptics, and sculpture can be divided into two categories: *pietre tenere* and *pietre dure* (softstones and hardstones). Particular stones were chosen for their markings, variety of colour, and hardness.

The degree of hardness is based on a scale drawn up in 1816 by the German physicist Friedrich Mohs; this identifies ten levels of hardness, each exemplified by a mineral that is widely to be found in nature, the name of which thus becomes a term of comparison for all other minerals possessing a similar structure. The criterion for the classification of minerals is the degree to which one mineral can be scratched compared with another.

The sequence of minerals on the Mohs scale is as follows:

I. TALC

II. GYPSUM

Particularly friable minerals are located between 1 and 1.5 on the scale; these include the various types of ALABASTER, the chalky one from the countryside around Volterra (hardness 1 – 1.5), or the ORIENTAL QUINCE or MARINE varieties with attractive veining and coloured markings of harder stone (between 2.5 and 3), widely used both in Imperial Rome and in sixteenth-century mosaics.

III. CALCITE

Rocks fall between 3 and 3.5 on the scale. They present various types of structure and a huge range of colours. Amongst the CALCAREOUS ROCKS the variety found in Tuscany and known as ALBARESE was particularly appreciated for the landscape effects created by the grey-brown streaks in the stone. According to the arrangement of the streaks, the stone is generally defined as PAESINA (landscape) if it gives the impression of an environment with rocks or mountains, or LINEAR if it contains undulations reminiscent of seascapes. METAMORPHIC rocks with crystalline structure, generally known as MARBLE, were very widely used in antiquity. Many varieties were to be found in different parts of the Roman Empire, and these were often reused in mosaic work after the middle of the sixteenth century. In art history, the term 'antique marble' was applied to a huge range of materials with varied and often very striking colours, whose structure is in fact different from that of marble: these are the varieties of BRECCIA, sedimentary clastic rocks made of large, rough fragments bound together by a calcareous cement. Volcanic rocks with granular structure such as ORIENTAL GRANITE were also used by the ancient Egyptians and Romans. Further detailed illustrations of these rocks, their origins and their uses, can be found in Gnoli, Borghini. A typical sample of so-called antique marbles can be found in the Roman table in the Gilbert Collection (cat. no. 19).

The compact black marble known as PARAGON comes from Flanders and was generally used as a background in the typical Florentine hardstone mosaics of the baroque period. The compact red marble from VERONA also had a variety of uses. Gray BARDIGLIO is a less highly prized marble from the Apuan Alps in Tuscany; it had a variety of uses, from architectural finishes to Florentine hardstone mosaics.

The hardness of MALACHITE figures at about 3.5 to 4 on the Mohs scale; its chemical constituent is carbonate of copper. Malachite was used in classical times and came back into fashion at the end of the eighteenth century, when huge deposits were discovered in the central Urals in Russia.

IV. FLUORITE, CALCIUM FLUORIDE

Fluorite was very popular in ancient times; Pliny records impressive vases made of *murra* (fluorite) with bright, glowing variations. The stone bears streaks of pink and violet and was frequently used in England (where it was known as 'blue John') by Matthew Boulton in the creation of his vases and candelabra with ormolu mounts. The variety streaked with green, from light green to emerald, is commonly known as EMERALDINE and was used in Imperial Rome and in Florence in the second half of the sixteenth century. LAPIS LAZULI falls between hardness grades 4 and 5, and is composed of lazurite, sodium alumosilicate, and calcium, with some sulphur. It was particularly admired and prized by the Grand Dukes of Florence. The stones were mined in Afghanistan and brought to Europe from ports in India and Persia. In the second half of the eighteenth century, deposits were found in Siberia. In general, the most highly prized variety is one of very brilliant blue flecked with yellow iron pyrites. Occasionally it bears large white or grey lime spots, which can be used to pleasant effect in mosaic work.

V. APATITE, CALCIUM FLUOROPHOSPHATE OR CHLOROPHOSPHATE

Porphyry falls between 5 and 6 on the Mohs scale. It is a magmatic effusive rock, which can be dark red or green with white markings.

VI. FELDSPAR, TRISILICATE OF ALUMINIUM, POTASSIUM OR SODIUM

VII. QUARTZ, ANHYDROUS BIOXIDE OF SILICIUM

Between points 6 and 7, all the siliceous materials – i.e. all the varieties of quartz of similar hardness and defined as PIETRE DURE or SEMI-PRECIOUS STONES – are found. CHALCEDONY was widely used from classical times, particularly the varieties known as ORIENTAL CHALCEDONY, honey-coloured and translucent, and CARNELIAN, which varies between dark red and pale yellow and was imported from Arabia, Persia, and India. Also from India was HELIOTROPE, dark green and subtly veined with small blood red spots. In the region of Volterra, near Florence, were vast deposits of a pale whitish to yellowish chalcedony, which was used in the Grand Ducal workshops in Florence to represent flesh colour. The variety of chalcedony in which the streaks are parallel or concentric, in a wide range of colours, is commonly called AGATE; this has different names according to its colour and provenance. The composition of JASPER is similar to that of chalcedony. The stone bears a variety of different names: BLOODSTONE, when the streaks are predominantly blood red; BOHEMIAN when it consists of various tones of speckled green (this is the stone that is characteristic of the items produced at the court of Rudolph II in Prague; SICILIAN JASPER bears alternate streaks of yellow, green, and pink; FLORAL is characterised by small spots that are alternately opaque and translucent. The variety of jasper known as BARGA is found near Lucca, in Tuscany, and was extracted during the Medici period; it is a dense dark red with white streaks. The so-called Corsican Jasper is in fact a calcareous stone, vivid green in colour and densely flecked with greyish white. JADE is typically green, sometimes streaked with brown. It was used in the East from ancient times; in Europe it was used in the late-sixteenth century in the production of carved urns; it was occasionally used in the Grand Ducal workshops in the second half of the eighteenth century.

ROCK CRYSTAL has a hardness of 7 and is as transparent as glass; it looks particularly handsome when cut (i.e. vases) and Milanese craftsmen became famous for this work. The colourless variety was mainly extracted in the Alps, near St. Gotthard; the mauve or AMETHYSTINE variety was frequently used in the Florentine workshops, particularly to represent flowers or grapes; the yellowish variety known as SMOKED or CITRINE was often confused with, or used as a substitute for, the more valuable topaz.

VIII. TOPAZ, ALUMINIUM SILICATE WITH FLUORINE

IX. CORUNDUM, ALUMINIUM SESQUIOXIDE

X. DIAMOND PURE CRYSTALLIZED CARBON

Information about the provenance of hard- and softstones can be garnered from a number of sources between the sixteenth and eighteenth centuries. Giorgio Vasari[1] discusses the processing of marble and porphyry. Agostino del Riccio (1597) has left what almost amounts to a treatise on different stones, quoting many interesting works with which he was familiar. Of particular interest is the manuscript dating back to 1718 and produced by the stoneworker Giuseppe Antonio Torricelli (1662–1719), who worked at the Florentine court; passages relating to the origins of the stones used in the Grand Ducal workshops are quoted in Appendix C. The works of the Tuscan naturalist Targioni Tozzetti (1768–79) are scientific in approach and provide detailed information on Tuscan stone deposits. More up-to-date research into the sources and types of stones most frequently used is contained in the seminal volume on antique marble by R. Gnoli (1971) and in the essays of A. Pampaloni Martelli and F. Rossi,[2] and more recently, in the work of A. M. Giusti,[3] who gives information on techniques as well as materials.

NOTES

1 Vasari 1568, vol. 1, pp. 45–55.

2 *Splendor di pietre dure* 1988, pp. 268–79.

3 Giusti 1992, pp. 267–98.

APPENDIX C

Techniques

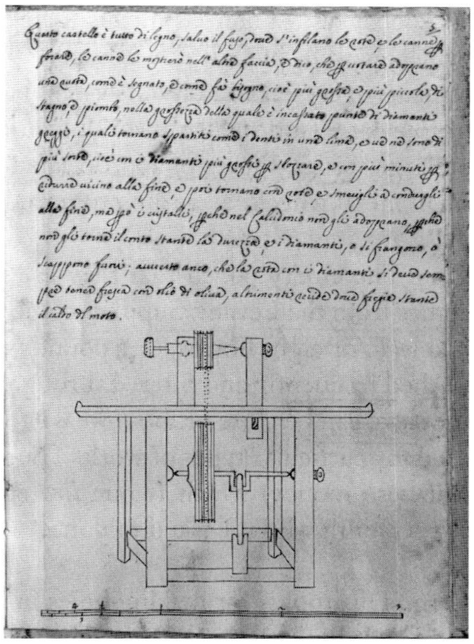

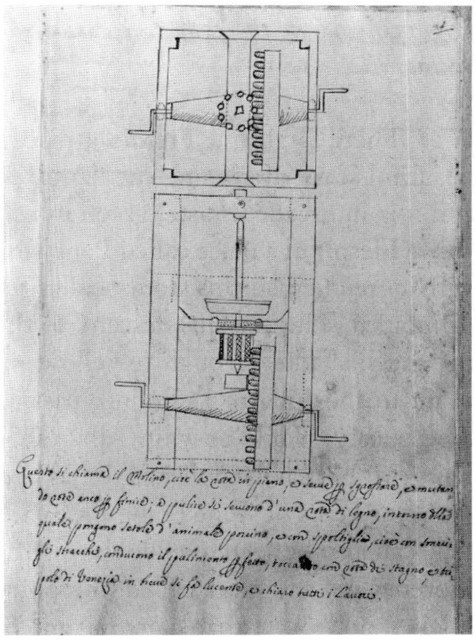

Manuscript in the Library of the Kunsthistorisches Institut, Florence, no. N2836, by Giuseppe Antonio Torricelli (1662–1719), 1714.

Designs for equipment for working pietre dure *(used in Milanese workshops) in the service of his Serene Highness the Grand Duke of Tuscany.*

C.1 This is called the mill, or flat wheel and it is used to remove grease, or, with a different wheel, for finishing; for cleaning, a wooden wheel is used with pigs' bristles fixed to it; with a scraper or emery strips the cleaning can be perfectly carried out; by touching up with a metal wheel and Venice tripoli (an abrasive powder) everything soon becomes bright and shining.

C.3 This framework is used for cutting all kinds of pieces quickly and well; when it cannot do the job a copper saw is used. It is useful for all kinds of work because it has a row of spindles with wheels of lead and tin which can carry out a number of different operations. At the points marked above the wheel there is a ring that protects the emery. The points marked B show the *tugatto* that causes the equipment to rotate.

C.5 This framework is made entirely of wood, apart from the spindle on to which the wheels and rods to be drilled are threaded (I shall show the rods on the other side). As I said, to turn it a wheel is used, as indicated, and it can be large or small as appropriate, made of tin and lead into the thickness of which are set fragments of uncut diamonds. These are spaced like the teeth of a file and they rotate; the diamonds are of various sizes, the larger ones to rough-hew and the smaller ones to reduce the stones almost to a finished state (they are finally finished with an emery wheel). This cannot be used on chalcedony nor will it work on crystal because of the hardness of the stone: the diamonds either break or jump out of their setting. Take note also that the wheel with diamonds should always be kept oiled with olive oil, otherwise the heat generated by the motion causes it to break where there is friction.

C.7 These are the quills used for drilling; there are large and small ones, of many varieties. The copper pipe fixed to the top of the iron spindle does not touch it, otherwise the emery might make a hole in it.

C.9 This frame is similar to the previous one, but it is turned by means of a large wheel attached by a rope; it is used for large items because it measures three hands.

C.11 These tools are used for rough cutting, then the latch is used to tear things apart. With the pliers and hammer all kinds of stones can be worked. The pliers are of soft iron and there is a larger version as well.

C.13 This frame is used as well. It is turned by a wheel under the bench like the others. It is used for small items because it is very steady. The cord that holds the wheel is a violin string. To make small holes a small iron drill is used with a slightly pointed diamond in the tip. The stone is fixed firmly into the drill and fixed into place with metal wire behind the diamond. Using olive oil it will make a hole for you very quickly for one *soldo*, for two (or one *scudo*) it will do whatever you require.

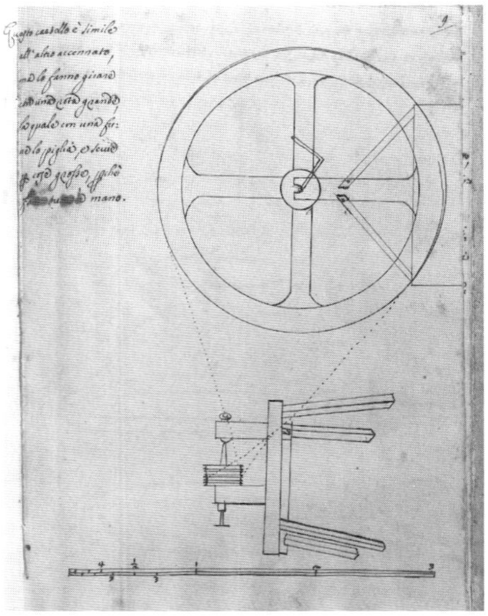

C.15 The stones worked here are chalcedonies from the mountains of Switzerland; the colour is a bit sad but I have seen some beautiful cups made of it. They work agates, and these are sardonyx; I have seen small boxes made of this, with lids of the chalcedony described above: they could not have supported lids of the same agate, but the colours are well-matched. They also work green jasper, and I have seen a large chalice just started in this material, fluted inside and out. I have seen other stones as well, but just small pieces to be used for making baubles – some lapis, remains of crystal and crystal paste. I have seen these pieces of equipment with three or four large and small all working at once; they go very fast and can easily be used on large stones. Pieces of appropriate size can be cut and then reduced on large and small metal wheels, according to need. This is at the Porta Ticinese.

C.17 The emery polish that they use is a leaden beige colour; it is very good and comes from the Levant. Supplies come from Venice and I have been told that it costs two *soldi*, or eight florins, or a pound (which is similar to the Florentine florin). It is washed frequently and filtered through bunting laid in a sieve made for the purpose: the sieve can be close or loose weave to separate the coarse, medium and fine emery used for particular types of work. The saws and wheels that they use cost 28 *soldi* (in Milanese money) which is one *lira* and five *soldi* in Florentine money, or so the coppersmith whom I asked told me.

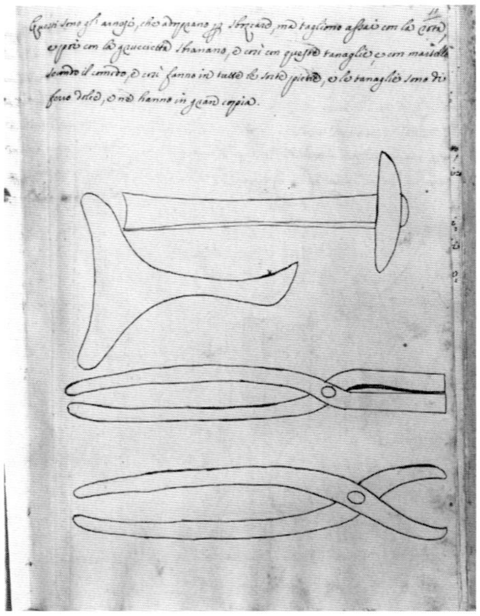

C.19. This tool is for making holes in large and small items as required. By changing the drill, the hole can be as deep as necessary. The sprocket is raised as the drill goes deeper.

C.21 *Treatise on* pietre dure *and* pietre tenere *as worked in the gallery of His Royal Highness and in the chapel of S. Lorenzo; on marble and other stones, even the most ordinary.*

C.22 There is also at Fiesole a place named Monte Magherini, where there is a beautiful seam of granite; the baptistery of the Duomo in Florence is made of this and it is in excellent taste, green in colour and polishing up to a nice shine. A mile above Fiesole at a place called Pera Monda there are several seams that are light blue with a green crust; this stone shades through to blue and is very suitable for mosaic or intarsia. These seams descend to the River Mugnone above La Querciola. Here the green shades through to yellow, which is perfect for leaves. The seam goes up again to the Villa di Pratolino, passing the road to Bologna below the bird cage. These seams would be white Albarese limestone if they were not curved; the stone is quite soft but can be polished. It has been used for bas reliefs, although so soft. There are some veins of stone going though His Royal Highness' garden in Florence, and they can also be seen outside the city from S. Miniato to the Porta Pisana, and from Florence out to a place called Campora. These veins are of different thicknesses (the thickest no stouter than a *braccio*) and occur one on top of the other ... This stone is called *forte* and is used by masons and sculptors; of this the facade of S. Michele degli Antinori is living proof, as are many other buildings of vast size like His Royal Highness' palace, the palace of the Duca Strozzi and many other churches and buildings in the same stone and equally large ...

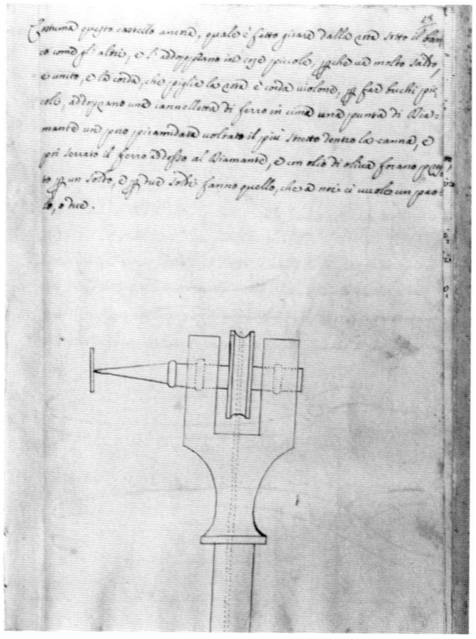

C.24 Let us move on to the State of Siena which is liberally supplied with stone. First of all, they have a yellow marble very similar to antique marble; this can be used in

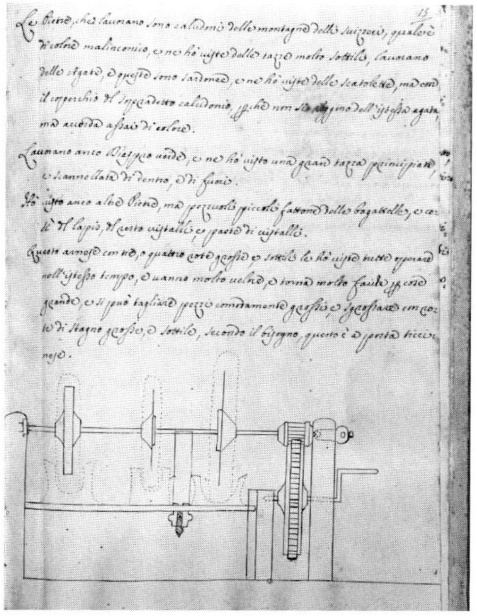

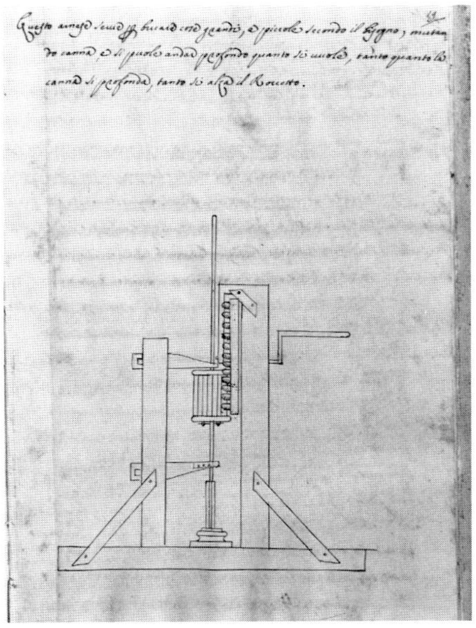

blocks or inlaid and can be polished to a good shine. They also have two red marbles, one at Caldana, the other at Moscona: the Moscona marble is dark and goes well with white; it makes good panels and floors and polishes well. Caldana marble is speckled like French marble; the colour is paler, it polishes well and can also be used for tables. They possess various kinds of alabaster, one at Montalto and the other at Montalcino, in quite large seams. The Montalcino alabaster is densely veined, buff and white in colour; the Montalto marble has large spots on it, is buff, white and yellowish in colour; they also have a seam of what is called 'quince', because of its colour, and all these polish well. In the town of Istria there are two large seams, one white with veins of a ferruginous red, very similar to Greek marble; the other is white spotted with red like the French mixture; these are not quarried, however, because the town is in ruins and the roads are no longer passable. Nevertheless the marble is very handsome, though a little on the hard side and difficult to work with metal tools. At Corneto in the same area there is an interesting alabaster

C.25 with buff coloured spots and what look like knotty onions in the white spots; these look like olive stones when the alabaster is made into tables, and the stone polishes beautifully. Here above Florence, six miles out just above the church of the Antella in a place called Picille belonging to Signor Palmieri there is a vein a little larger than a yard wide of a marble called Puzzenera; lengths of this are five to six yards, speckled and it polishes well. At Prato there are several seams of spotted green, softish, and similar to serpentine; it polishes well. There are some veins of red there too, marked with white but rather dark. There is a seam of granite there too which is a bit rough and scratchy; because of its roughness it is used for making equipment for mills. There are also some black seams but Albarese limestone in this colour is not very attractive. The river Brana at Pistoia is crossed by various black seams, the same seams passing through Fignline di Prato; in the Brana there is some handsome stone, the finer the seam the blacker it is. Some of the veins are one third of a *braccio* wide and resemble the black marble of Verona. There are seams three yards wide, but the larger they are the less good the quality of the stone, as I said before. These marbles are Albarese, i.e. limestone deposits which are naturally white but the finer the vein the more colourful they are. Believe me, this depends on the quality of the stone. Above and below the seam there are veins of a sort of beige stone, the kind that could be used for making allum. In the captaincy of Pietra Santa there is a village called Stazzena where the locals are called by the name of Seravezza; here there are big, broad seams from which big pyramids and fat columns have been excavated; this marble is a mixture of white, purplish pink, greenish and grey and the colours are frisky ...

C.26 Follow these seams westwards and they become more visible at Morsa di Carrara where marble is quarried for making statues, *bardiglio* and also black and yellow and black and white, all of good quality from very large seams, and all of good use to the gentlefolk of Carrara. At Librafiatta, between Pisa and Lucca there is a seam of flecked black and white marble similar to antique marble, but it is to be seen in a place that makes it difficult to quarry because it is so steep. In Monte S. Giuliano there is a seam of pale red marble, called *rosso di S. Giuliano*. There is also a greyish white marble but it is not suitable for making statues. At Corliano there is a further seam of red (though this is very hard and difficult to work with metal tools), and a pinkish marble veined in white. At Barga there are several seams of very beautiful white and red jasper.

C.28 There is also black jasper and a seam of soft black ... Above these seams lie other seams right up to the top of the mountain, and they are all Albarese limestone.

Higher up the mountain, where it is cooler, there are soft veins of black. It would be a good black but it has a beige crust beneath and above it, and at the ends; it is black inside and very handsome but the veins are only a fifth or a quarter of a *braccio*, so that there is only about a third left of good black. Now let us turn to Sicily where near Catania can be found a number of different jaspers; one yellow and green vein has streaks in bands, or rather a streak on the edge and one in the middle, and it is about a yard broad; another red and white seam resembles Barga marble except that neither the red nor the white is as beautiful and the speckles are smaller. There are also seams about a yard wide containing ravishing pieces speckled with white and red, and all of them polish well. There are also veins of yellow and white jasper, the white being mainly crystalline i.e. a translucent chalcedony, with small spots of different shapes. When one side is polished the yellow looks like the yellow inside chalcedony; the stone surrounding these pieces is soft and yellow. There is so much of the binding material that it gets condensed, consuming a good proportion of the stone, and is converted into chalcedony.

C.29 To return to our own Maremma, near Volterra, on an estate owned by Signor Maffei at a place called Monte Rugoli, chalcedony of all colours is to be found: white, white and yellow, white and red, purplish, black, red, scarlet, green, spotted white, dark and a hundred other shades ... I had in my possession a dark blue translucent stone from Sardinia, quite soft but with a good lustre and sometimes the colour is dark red, which is excellent for mosaic work; though small, it looks like the spongey kind of rock that grows in water with a high sulphur content. This comes from land owned by Commendatore Peruzzi. In Genoa there is a green stone with playful markings, and a versatile type of marble; I have seen columns eight yards long. They also have slate of all sizes, large seams of it which they uncover and hack off with a pick as they require it; they leave the piece to stand overnight.

C.36 Near Bologna, at Monte Corone on an estate belonging to the Principi Pompili, there are chalcedonies weighing fifteen and twenty pounds apiece; these are dark beige, almost black, with whitish middles. They are not all of the same colour, however, and differences of shade depend on their location... At Levane in the Valdarno there is a hill of white silica sand which is mixed with flints, bare, however, not like the English sand, and harder than the Parisian sand. Near the city there is a seam of red and white marble, the flecks smaller than in the French marble, and darker; I have seen large columns of this with a good shine. At Spello, near Assisi in Umbria, there are seams of travertine of the same type. At Marino, not far from Rome, there are big seams and large workshops can be seen. Near Cerola, by the Adriatic coast, there is a large seam of veined alabaster. Above the city of Verona, in the Veneto, there are beautiful black seams: small white granules of *Panico* attach themselves to this, and they are so abundant that in three or four years they have built up to the size of a tenth of a yard and have hardened, becoming part of the stone. The granules most recently attached can be scratched off with the fingernails. On an estate belonging to the Guarnacci family near Volterra, in a place called Gesseri there are some seams of alabaster as white as snow, as well as some white and yellow. The white is cloudy and is used to make figures, vases and a hundred little knick-knacks which are exported all over the world. Here there is also *scagliola*, to be found above the shafts of the salt mine; these alabasters are at the entrance to the salt mines. At Roccastrada, near Siena, there are agates up to two *braccia* in size. The markings are flat, becoming layered like an onion as in other agates, because this stone is made from hardened alabaster. The edges are never watertight and this means there are always knots and earth in it; if this were not so it would be the most beautiful stone on earth. In colour it is amethyst and white, beige, rich and fanciful rather like the alabaster of Montalcino and without faults; it is easy to work and polishes as well as

Flemish agate, though it is a little less hard...

Near Padua there are some veins one or two *soldi* wide which have formed chalcedony, producing pieces up to eight pounds. The most beautiful of these are like translucent agate, crystalline and very hard. Above Lake Maggiore, on the Boromei estates, there are large seams of white marble large enough for statuary; the Duomo in Milan is built of this. There are also seams of white, buff and reddish granite known as *sarciccio* which is used for the stonework of large buildings - staircases, doors and other fire-resistant items. There is also a beautiful veined alabaster with playful greenish veins. In Turin there is a handsome black with straight white veining which polishes up like crystal. In the Grisons, at the place called Bigini, there are lumps of good-quality chalcedony weighing up to twenty-five and thirty pounds each; it is harder than the oriental version because it has a livelier grain, and can be polished to perfection. Its crust is limestone, and it is tawny and soft red by turns, with translucent stripes between the colours (these stripes do not look translucent until the stones are polished). Inside they are salty and spongey. I have opened some that just had the tawny chalcedony crust, and inside were full of broken stone that looked like grimy grey salt ...

C.38 From the Pyrenees come certain agates with a greenish outer cover and layered like an onion. The red, white and blue are invaluable for making flowers. There are also veins of amethyst. This stone occurs between other stones; it is made of mountain crystal that is so prolific, the crystals cluster close enough to one another to form another stone.

C.39 The mountain of St Gotthard in Switzerland is near Basle; it is entirely formed of stone and is more than three leagues high, all one stone. The colour of the stone is like wood or chestnut, and it is wavy round the edge, the waves sometimes breaking off unexpectedly at the top. There are wavy parts round the base as well, with nodes in them. The village men go out and attach a ring five or six yards wide to the rock and go inside (using the ring like a funnel) and just as they are about to expire they make a hole about half a yard deep and a few inches wide and fill it with explosive, tap it hard with a wooden pole, leaving a little space for the wick. Then they make two holes in the funnel and fix a piece of wood across so that the stopper cannot blow out. They put in a long wick, light it and retire to a good distance because sometimes bits of mountain are blown off, which is terrifying. Once the blast has died away, they run back to look at the crystal which comes out of the spaces between the stones. As soon as they can they wrap the crystal in cloth so that the air does not get to it while it is damp because this would crack it. If it is tied up in a cloth it dries gradually and no harm comes to it. They find crystals that are tiny and some that are huge – up to 200 pounds.

C.40 The mountain called Plener shares the same seams of marble, granite and other minerals as St Gotthard. At Rostenbergh there is a silver mine that begins at Schioz and goes on beyond Rostenberg; many people are employed in the mine in which malachite and a dark blue stone are also found. Also to be found there is the 'star', which when it is large is known as the 'herbarium'; it has other properties too. The 'star' occurs on its own like a truffle, but it is made of stone (fairly soft, though). Initially it is small and shaped like a bladder; from its exit come vapours that look like individual stars. If the bladder is cut in half in a horizontal section all the little star-shaped puffs of vapour can be seen inside. If it is allowed to enlarge the stars merge together and the poor little 'star' becomes a 'herbarium' ... In the River Soli, that runs through Bavaria near Raicracovia, nephrite or jade can be found, not as hard as the oriental jade nor as translucent. This jade occurs in lumps like the oriental jade and has all the same properties which I will describe to you when I deal with oriental jade. In the Untersberg, which in Italian is called the Monte dell'Albagia, near Salzburg, there are seams of marble thirty yards thick, and I have seen vast statues seven and eight yards high made of it in the Cathedral at Salzburg. There are seams of marble (*palvi*?) and seams of beige and red granite throughout Germany. In Bohemia, below the city of Prague on the other side of the River Malte runs a seam of red jasper with beige and flecks.

C.42 Zughedol by P. P. Benedittiniand under this seam there are *Prombole* of pure jasper which, when opened, look as if there were flames and smoke inside. Another seam is very hard with markings similar to porphyry but paler in colour. In the Mountain of the Giants, above the city of Tunnan in the region of Valistain there is a spring called Radesna whose water is whiter than snow; this water issues forth at the base of Monte Casacco and brings with it *grisoliti*. The people of Tunnan keep such a close eye on it that it is difficult to find the stones although there are always some there. They are green and slightly smoky, not as translucent as the oriental stones, and of the same hardness as rock crystal. From here eastwards to mount Coristec there are pieces of green jasper similar in shape to heliotrope. The mountain is made entirely of purplish stone, like a salt violet with lots of little drops of green in it, softish, and some green bits the size of a walnut; where you see these drops, or this green, the green changes into a hard translucent lump of agate. To make crowns you only need to make a hole in them and polish them because they are round already. You don't need to bother with excavation because the stone of which the mountain is composed does not hang on to them tightly; it is quite soft and can easily be broken up with a pick. People have often tried to sink mines in different places, imagining there to be copper inside the mountain, but they have not found any. In fact, the stones that they have extracted have not been too soft; they have turned out to be jasper. The pieces that have been found on the ground are fine and have cut well; their colours are green and lively, agated with some red.

C.43 At the top of the mountain near Tariodnicche and Coristec, amethysts are to be found.

C.44 In Saxony there is a beautiful red, with wavy veins like alabaster but as hard as jasper from the seam. The stripes are longitudinal along the edge. They also possess seams of a green that they call soft serpentine. They turn this on a lathe as if it were wood and make all sorts of things from it – drinking glasses, kettles. From one piece they make six or seven items. It is heat resistant and they claim such unheard of properties for it that I had to tell them I thought it was nonsense.

At Laccheverte there is a wonderfully coloured agate; streaked, rather soft but translucent. It takes patience to polish it but it becomes unrecognisable, people working on it should not lose heart.

In Flanders, at Blumiz, there are a number of seams of black marble, which is frequently used in Italy.

C.45 There is also a pinkish jasper with white veins, very hard and of good quality and size. From Spain we get red *broccatello*, with yellow, buff and white marks. This is a marble that can be worked with irons, it can be carved and is useful for table panels and other items; it polishes well. There is also porphyry with particular markings and with lighter parts in it; it is not as evenly coloured as the Egyptian porphyry but it is just as hard. This is harder than other granites beccause it has been ground up more than they have.

From France we get lapis lazuli. It is different from the Persian lapis: the mine contains a lot of copper therefore the lapis is very green. It polishes well. There is a soft red stone, flecked with white and beige: this is a good mixed marble, very popular because it can be used for anything. There is also a jasper that we call French floral: finely speckled in red and white, very beautiful but no pieces larger than about a yard.

We use four different sorts of mixed stones and we term them 'antique' because no-one remembers where they were mined. There is a yellow one, called oriental, then red antique, green antique and white and black antique. These are all mixed marbles. The red sometimes (but rarely) has a few white veins amongst the flecks. The white and black is stunning, the white markings as well as the black; the white binds the marble together and is as white as snow. The green is flecked with white and a lot of the flecks are square in shape, the white being on the green side. The yellow has very yellow, sometimes dark yellow, markings – of its own basic material. There are three types of granite and Rome is full of great columns and pyramids made from them. One is white and black, finely mixed. Another is red and white with a tiny bit of black, and another white, black and reddish with larger flecks like the other red one. Only the white and black is so much finer. They are all antique and known as Egyptian granite. Porphyry and serpentine are also antique granites, also thought to be from Egypt. Porphyry is dark red lightly dusted with white and black. Serpentine is green flecked with white and a minute dusting of black. There is no difference between the hardness of porphyry and serpentine; both are harder than other granites. From Cyprus comes a beautiful red jasper, with cloudy red markings – all red with a few flecks of beige chalcedony. It polishes well.

Bibliography

A

ACCASCINA 1963
Accascina, Maria, 'A Messina, I mischi Trabischi, rabischi', *Antichità Viva* vol. 2, nos. 9–10, November–December 1963, pp. 45–52.

ALCOUFFE 1988a
Alcouffe, Daniel, 'Le "maitre aux dragons": les créations de l'orfèvre parisien Pierre Delabarre', *Revue de l'Art* (Paris), 1988, pp. 47–56.

ALCOUFFE 1988b
Alcouffe, Daniel, *1851–1900: Le arti decorative alle Grandi Esposizioni Universali*, Idealibri (Milan), 1988.

ALCOUFFE, DION-TENNENBAUM, and LEFEBURE 1993
Alcouffe, Daniel, A. Dion-Tennenbaum, and A. Lefébure, *Furniture Collections in the Louvre*, 2 vols., Editions Faton (Paris), 1993.

ALDROVANDI 1562
Aidrovandi, Ulisse, *Delle statue antiche che per tutta Roma, in diversi luoghi e case si veggono*, 1562. Reprint, Hildesheim, Georg Alms Verlag (New York), 1975.

ALFIERI, BRANCHETTI and CORNINI 1986
Alfieri, Massimo, Branchetti, Maria Grazia and Cornini, Guido, Mosaici Minuti Romani Del '700 e del '800, exh. cat., 15 October–30 November, 1986.

ALFTER 1986
Alfter, Dieter, *Die Geschichte des Augsburger Kabinettschranks*, Druckerei Joh Walch (Augsburg), 1986.

AMERICAN HOROLOGIST 1975
'Two Collections Donated to Los Angeles Museum', *American Horologist and Jeweler* 44, no. 4, 1975, (Denver, Colorado), pp. 44–45.

ARTE DEL MOSAICO 1928
La società 'Arte del mosaico', 14–15 October, 1928.

AVERY C. & EMPERATORI A. 1975
Mosaics from the Gilbert Collection, summary catalogue, V& A (London), 1975.

B

BACCI and FORLANI TEMPESTI 1961
Bacci, Mina, and Anna Forlani Tempesti, *Mostra di disegni di Jacopo Ligozzi*, exh. cat., Uffizi, Gabinetto Disegni e Stampe (Florence), 1961.

BAER 1980
Baer, Winfried, 'Ors et pierres des boîtes de Frédéric le Grand', *Connaissance des arts*, no. 346, (Paris), December 1980, pp. 100–105.

BAER 1993
Baer, Winfried, *Prunk-Tabatièren Friedrichs des Grossen*, exh. cat. Potsdam-Sanssouci, Higmer Verlag (Munich), 1993.

BALDINI, GIUSTI, and PAMPALONI MARTELLI 1979
Baldini, Umberto, Anna Maria Giusti, and Anna Paula Pampaloni Martelli, *La Cappella dei Principi e le Pietre Dure a Firenze*, Electa (Milan), 1979.

BALDINUCCI 1846
Baldinucci, Filippo, *Notizie dei professori del disegno da Cimabue in qua*, 7 vols., Ranalli (Florence), 1846.

BANDERA 1969
Bandera, Luisa, 'Due ebanisti per il Principe Demidoff', *Arte Illustrata* 2, nos. 17–18, May/June 1969, pp. 66–69.

BERMAN 1991
Berman, Avis, 'East Side Renaissance', *Architectural Digest*, vol. 48, no. 12, November 1991, pp. 176–183, ill. pp. 176–7.

BERNOULLI 1891
Bernoulli, J. J., *Die Budnisse der Römischen Kaiser*, vol. 2, *Von Galba bis Commoders*, Union Deutsche Verlags Gesellschaft (Stuttgart, Berlin, Leipzig), 1891.

BIERMANN 1914
Biermann, Georg, *Deutsches Barock und Rokoko* (Leipzig), 1914.

BOCCONI 1930
Bocconi, Schimo, *The Capitoline Collections*, Enzo Pinci (Rome), 1930.

BOESEL 1978
Boesel, Richard, 'Cosimo Fanzago a Roma', *Prospettiva* 15, (Florence), October 1978, pp. 29–40.

BORGHINI 1584
Borghini, Raffaello, *Il riposo di Raffaello Borghini in cui della pittura e della scultura si favella de' più illustri pittori e scultori e delle più famose opere loro ci fa menzione*, 1584. Reprint, 2 vols., M. Rosci (Milan), 1967.

BOURNE and BRETT 1991
Bourne, Jonathan, and Vanessa Brett, *Lighting in the Domestic Interior: Renaissance to Art Nouveau*, Sotheby's (London), 1991.

BUKOVINSKA 1972
Bukovinska, Beket, 'Dalsi Florentske mozaiky z Prahy', *Umeni* 5, no. 20, 1972, pp. 363–71.

C

CAMPORI 1879
Campori, Giuseppe, *Della lavorazione del Porfido e delle pietre dure d'intarsio e di commesso nella Corte degli Estensi. Atti e memorie delle Deputazioni di storia Patria dell'Emilia*, vol. 5 (Modena), 1879.

CANTONE 1969
Cantone, Gaetana, 'La controversia tra Cosimo Fanzago e i certosini (II) – Il Cappellone di S. Antonio e la Cappella Cacace in S. Lorenzo Maggiore', *Napoli Nobilissima* 8, part 6 (Naples), 1969, pp. 227–35.

CANTONE 1984
Cantone, Gaetana, *Napoli Barocca e Cosimo Fanzago*, Edizioni scientifiche italiani (Naples), 1984.

CARRE 1971
Carre, Louis, *A Guide to Old French Plate*, Eyre and Spottiswoode, London, 1931, reprint 1971.

CASEY 1978
Casey, Rick, 'The Miraculous Mosaics', *SA, The Magazine of San Antonio* 1, no. 12, (San Antonio) February 1978, pp. 30–32.

CATALOGO DELLA ESPOSIZIONE 1897
Catalogo della Esposizione Artistica a scopo di beneficenza (Florence), 1897.

CATELLO 1981
Catello, Elio, 'Modelli per argentieri di Orazio Scoppa', *Arte Cristiana* 69, fasc. 6, no. 678, 1981, pp. 145–50.

CAUSA 1967
Causa, Raffaello, *A proposito della Certosa di San Martino (II) Napoli nobilissima*, vol. 6, fasc. 3–4, 1967, pp. 89–97.

CEFARIELLO GROSSO 1993
Cefariello Grosso, Gilda, *I chini a Borgo S. Lorenzo*, Opus Libri (Florence), 1993.

CHAPMAN 1991
Chapman, Martin, *The Gilbert Collection of Gold and Silver: Recent Acquisitions 2*, Los Angeles County Museum of Art (Los Angeles), 1991.

CIVILTA DEL '700 A NAPOLI 1979
Civiltà del '700 a Napoli 1739–1799, exh. cat., Centro Di (Florence), 1979.

CIVILTA DEL '600 A NAPOLI 1984
Civiltà' del '600 a Napoli, exh. cat., Electa Napoli (Florence), 1984.

CLARKE 1986
Clarke, T. H. *The Rhinoceros from Dürer to Stubbs 1515–1799*, Sotheby's Publications (London), 1986.

COCCOLUTO 1861
Coccoluto, Ferrigni [pseud.], *Viaggio attraverso l'Esposizione Italiana del 1861 – Guida critico-descrittiva con Pianta del Palazzo delle Esposizioni, Florence* (Florence), 1861.

CONNAISSANCE 1987
'L'Or de l'Europe sur la 5e Avenue', *Connaissance des Arts* 11, no. 421 (Paris), March 1987.

COZZI 1986
Cozzi, Mauro, *Alabastro, Volterra dal Settecento all'Art Deco*, Cantini (Florence), 1986.

CRYSTAL PALACE 1851
The Crystal Palace Exhibition Illustrated Catalogue, 1851. Reprint, Dover Publications (New York), 1970.

D

DANIELS 1975
Daniels, George, *The Art of Breguet*, Sotheby Parke Bernet (London and New York), 1975.

DAVIS 1884
Davis, Charles, *A Description of the Works of Art Forming the Collection of Alfred de Rothschild*, 2 vols. (London), 1884.

DAYTON JOURNAL 1921
Dayton Journal, 9 October, 1921, p. 3.

DELLA PERGOLA 1971
Della Pergola, Paola, *Opere in mosaico, intarsi e pietra paesina*, De Luca (Rome), 1971.

DESIGNERS WEST 1987
'Conversation with an Avid Collector: An Interview about the Collection of Rosalinde and Arthur Gilbert', *Designers West* 34, no. 5 (Los Angeles), March 1987, pp. 114–20.

DETROIT INSTITUTE OF ARTS 1981
The Golden Age of Naples: Art and Civilization under the Bourbons 1734–1805, 2 vols, exh. cat., 1981.

DI CASTRO MOSCATI 1987
Di Castro Moscati, Daniela, 'The Revival of the Working of Porphyry in Sixteenth-Century Florence, *Apollo* 126, no. 308, October 1987, pp. 242–48.

DI CASTRO, PECCOLO, and GAZZANIGA 1994
Di Castro, Alberto, Paola Peccolo, and Valentina Gazzaniga, *Marmorari e Argenti a Roma e nel Lazio tra Cinqecento e Seicento*. Edizioni Quasar (Rome), 1994.

DISTELBERGER 1980
Distelberger, Rudolf, 'Pierres Précieuses du Liechtenstein', *Connaissance des Arts*, no. 343 (Paris), September 1980, pp. 61–66.

DRAGADZE 1988
Dragadze, Peter, 'Having It All', *Connoisseur* 218 (London), January 1988, pp. 82–91.

E

EFIMOVA 1968
Efimova, E. M., *Western European Mosaic of the Thirteenth–Nineteenth Centuries in the Collection of the Hermitage, Leningrad*, Sovietsky Khudozhnik (Leningrad), 1968.

F

FABIANSKI 1985
Fabianski, Marcin, 'Studies in Duquesnoy: His Literary Sources and Imitators', *Antichità Viva* 5–6 (Florence), 1985, pp. 40–49.

FICORONI 1744
Ficoroni, Francesco, *Le vestigia e rarità di Roma antica* (Rome), 1744.

FIGUEIREDO 1992
Figueiredo, Cristina, 'Caixinhas de Rape em Ouro', *Quilate*, 6 (Oporto), June/July 1992, pp. 11–23.

FINOCCHIETTI 1863
Finocchietti, Demetrio Carlo, 'Delle Arti e delle Industrie applicate ai mobili', *Politecnico* 19, 1863, pp. 3–41.

FITTIPALDI 1980
Fittipaldi, Teodoro, *Sculture Napoletano del Settecento*, Leguori editore (Naples), 1980.

FITTSCHEN and ZANCHER 1983
Fittschen, K., and P. Zancher., *Katalog der Römischen Porträts in dem Capitolinischen Museen un den anderen Kommunalen Sammlungen der stadt Rom*, 2 vols., Philipp von Zabern (Mainz am Rhein), 1983.

FLEMING 1955
Fleming, John, 'The Hugfords of Florence (Part 1)', *Connoisseur* 136, no. 548 (London), November 1955, pp. 106–10.

FLOWER 1951
Flower, Margaret, *Victorian Jewelry*, Duell, Sloan and Pearce (New York), 1951.

FOCK 1972
Fock, C. Willemign, 'Goldsmiths at the Court of Cosimo II de' Medici', *The Burlington Magazine* 114, vol CXIV, no. 826 (Vienna), January 1972, pp. 111–17.

FOCK 1974
Fock, C. Willemign, 'Der Goldschmied Jaques Bylivelt aus Delft und sein Wirken in der mediceischen Hofwerkstatt in Florenz', *Jahrbuch der Kunsthistorischen Sammlungen in Wien* 70 (Vienna), 1974, pp. 89–178.

FORLANI TEMPESTI 1993
Forlani Tempesti, Anna, 'Callot et Stefano della Bella: fetes et "caramogi"', in *Jacoues Callot (1592–1635)*, Louvre (Paris), 1993, pp. 481–510.

FRANCHINA 1990
Franchina, L., *Dizionario Biografico degli Italiani*, vol. 38, s.v. 'Flaminio del Turco', Istituto della enciclopedia Italiana fondata da Giovanni Teccani (Rome), 1990.

FREYBERGER 1991
Freyberger, Ronald, 'The Duke of Hamilton's Clock Cabinet', *Christie's International Magazine* 8, no. 6, June 1991, pp. 10–13.

FRIEDRICH DER GROSSE 1992
Friedrich der Grosse: Sammler und Mäzen, exh. cat., Hirmer Verlag (Munich), 1992.

FURIETTI 1752
Furietti, Giuseppe Alessandro, *De Musivis, ad SS. Patrem Benedictum XIV*, Salvioni (Rome), 1752.

FUSCO and HESS 1994
Fusco, Peter, and Catherine Hess, 'A Rediscovered "Commesso" Portrait', *The Burlington Magazine* 136, no. 1091, (London) February 1994, pp. 68–72.

G

GAMER 1971
Gamer, Jörg, 'Prunkschrein der Kurfürstin Anna Maria Luisa de' Medici', in *Europäische Barockplastik*, exh. cat., Kunstmuseum Düsseldorf (Dusseldorf), 1971, pp. 399–401.

GERE 1989
Gere, Charlotte, *Nineteenth–Century Decoration: The Art of the Interior*, Harry N. Abrams (New York), 1989.

GIUSTI 1989
Giusti, Anna Maria, *Masterpieces in Pietre Dure: Palazzo Pitti, the Uffizi and other Museums and Monuments in Florence*, Electa (Milan), 1989.

GIUSTI 1992
Giusti, Anna Maria, *Pietre Dure: L'arte europea del mosaico negli arredi e nelle decorazioni dal 1500 al 1800*, Allemandi (Turin), 1992.

GIUSTI 1995
Guisti, Anna Maria, Opificio delle Pietre Dure di Firenze Guida al Museo, Venice, Marsilio, 1995.

GIUSTI, MAZZONI and PAMPALONI MARTELLI 1978
Giusti, Anna Maria, Paolo Mazzoni, and Anna Paula Pampaloni Martelli, *Il Museo dell'Opificio delle Pietre Dure a Firenze*, Electa (Milan), 1978.

GNOLI 1971
Gnoli, Raniero, *Marmora Romana*, Edizioni dell'Elefante (Rome), 1971.

GONZALEZ-PALACIOS 1975
González-Palacios, Alvar, 'Il quadro di pietra', *Balaffi arte* (Turin), October 1975, pp. 42–43, 108.

GONZALEZ-PALACIOS 1976
González-Palacios, Alvar, 'I mani del Piranesi', *Paragone*, no. 315 (Florence), May 1976, pp. 40–47.

GONZALEZ-PALACIOS 1977a
González-Palacios, Alvar, *The Art of Mosaics*, Los Angeles County Museum of Art (Los Angeles), 1977.

GONZALEZ-PALACIOS 1977b
González-Palacios, Alvar, 'Taccuino delle Pietre Dure: Attorno al Foggini', *Antologia di Belle Arti* 1, no. 1, Federico Zeri and González-Palacios (eds.), Fabrizio Apolloni & Mario Tazzoli Editore (Rome), March 1977, pp. 57–64.

GONZALEZ-PALACIOS 1977c
González-Palacios, Alvar, 'Un'autobiografia del Ghinghi', *Antologia di Belle Arti no.* 3, Federico Zeri and González-Palacios (eds.), Fabrizio Apolloni & Mario Tazzoli Editore (Rome), 1977, pp. 271–85.

GONZALEZ-PALACIOS 1982a
González-Palacios, Alvar, *Mosaici e pietre dure, Firenze – Paesi germanici – Madrid. I guaderni dell'antiguariato*, Gruppo Editoriale Fabbri (Milan), 1982.

GONZALEZ-PALACIOS 1982b
González-Palacios, Alvar, *Mosaici e pietre dure, Mosaici a piccole tessere. Pietre dure a Parigi e a Napoli. I quaderni dell'antiouariato*, Gruppo Editoriale Fabbri (Milan), 1982.

GONZALEZ-PALACIOS 1984
González-Palacios, Alvar, *Il tempio del Gusto, Roma e Regno delle due Sicilie*, 2 vols., Longanesi (Milan), 1984.

GONZALEZ-PALACIOS 1986
González-Palacios, Alvar, *Il tempio del Gusto – Le arti decorative in Italia fra classicismo e barocco. La Toscana e l'Italia Settentrionale*, 2 vols., Longanesi (Milan), 1986.

GONZALEZ-PALACIOS 1988a
González-Palacios, Alvar, 'Itinerario da Roma a Firenze', in *Splendori di pietre dure. L'arte di corte nella Firenze del Granduchi*, exh. cat., Giunti (Florence), 1988, pp. 24–42.

GONZALEZ-PALACIOS 1988b
González-Palacios, Alvar, 'Il Laboratorio della pietre dure del Buen Retiro a Madrid, 1762–1808', in *Splendori di pietre dure. L'arte di corte nella Firenze dei Granduchi*, exh. cat. Giunti (Florence), 1988, pp. 260–67.

GONZALEZ-PALACIOS 1988c
González-Palacios, Alvar, 'La Manifattura di Luigi XIV ai Gobelins', in *Splendori di pietre dure. L'arte di corte nella Firenze dei Granduchi*, exh. cat., Giunti (Florence), 1988, pp. 240–49.

GONZALEZ-PALACIOS 1991a
González-Palacios, Alvar, *Fasto Romani Dipinti Sculture Arredi dai Palazzi Romani*, Leonardo de Luca (Rome), 1991.

GONZALEZ-PALACIOS 1991b
González-Palacios, Alvar, 'Lavori di Sibiho, Casa Vogue', *Antiques*, no. 12 (Milan), March 1991, pp. 84–89.

GONZALEZ-PALACIOS 1993
González-Palacios, Alvar, *Il gusto dei Principi*, 2 vols., Longanesi (Milan), 1993.

GONZALEZ-PALACIOS and ROTTGEN 1982
González-Palacios, Alvar, and Steffi Röttgen, *The Art of Mosaics: Selections from the Gilbert Collection*, Los Angeles County Museum of Art (Los Angeles), 1982 (rev. ed. of González-Palacios 1977a).

GOODISON 1974
Goodison, Nicholas. *Ormolu: The Work of Matthew Boulton*, Phaidon (London), 1974.

GRANDJEAN 1964
Grandjean, Serge, *Inventoire après le décès de l'Impératrice Joséphine à Malmaison*, Ministère d'Etat (Paris), 1964.

GRANDJEAN 1981
Catalogue des tabatières, boîtes et étuis des XVIIIE et XIXE siècles du Musée du Louvre, Paris, 1981.

H

HABSBURG-LOTHRINGEN 1983
Habsburg-Lothringen, Géza von, *Gold Boxes from the Collection of Rosalinde and Arthur Gilbert*, privately printed, 1983.

HAGANS 1977
Hagans, Orville R., 'In the Spotlight', *Horological Times* 1, no. 5 (Cincinnati, Ohio), May 1977, pp. 30–31.

HARRIS 1973
Harris, Eileen, *The Furniture of Robert Adam, Academy St. Martins Press* (New York), 1973.

HANISEE GABRIEL 2000
Hanisee Gabriel, Jeanette, *Micromosaics*, Philip Wilson Publishers (London), 2000.

HAYWARD 1976π
Hayward, J. F., *Virtuoso Goldsmiths and the Triumph of Mannerism 1540–1620*, Rizzoli/Sotheby Parke Bernet (London), 1976.

HEIKAMP 1963
Heikamp, Detlef, 'Zur Geschichte der Uffizien-Tribuna und der Kunstschranke in Florenz und Deutschland', *Zeitschrift für Kunstgeschichte* 26 (Berlin), 1963, pp. 193–268.

HERALD EXAMINER 1977
'The Art Mistaken for Paintings', *Los Angeles Herald Examiner, California Living* (Los Angeles), 24 April 1977, pp. 16–18.

HILLIER 1975
Hillier, Bevis 'The Gilbert Collection of Mosaics', *Connoisseur* 188, no. 758 (London), April 1975, pp. 268–73.

HOFMANN 1968
Hofmann, Von Walter Jurgen, *Schloss Pommersfelden: Geschichte seiner Entstehung*, (Nurnberg), 1968.

HOLZHAUSEN 1935
Holzhausen, Walter, *Johann Christian Neuber* (Dresden), 1935.

HORSWELL 1971
Horswell, Jane, *Bronze Sculpture of 'Les Animaliers' Reference and Price Guide*, Antique Collectors' Club (Woodbridge, Suffolk), 1971.

I

IRMAN 1986
Irman, Deborah, 'Pieces of a Lost Art: The Dazzling, Puzzling Gilbert Mosaics', *Almanac* 18, no. 4 (Franklin Center, Pennsylvania), September/October 1986, pp. 13–21.

J

JOHNSON 1977
Johnson, Sammye, 'Masterful Micromosaics and Monumental Silver', *SA, The Magazine of San Antonio* 2, no. 12 (San Antonio), December 1977, pp. 38–41.

JONES 1987
Jones, Dalu, (ed.), *A Mirror of Princes: The Mughals and The Medici*, Marg Publications (Bombay), 1987.

K

KLAR 1929
Klar, Martin, 'Die Tabatieren Friedrichs des Grossen', *Der Cicerone* 21, 1929, pp. 7–18.

KOEPPEL 1992
Koeppel, Fredric, 'Up to Snuff', *Memphis Commercial Appeal Playbook* (Memphis, Tennessee), 10 April 1992, pp. E12–13.

KREISEL 1968
Kreisel, Heinrich, *Die Kunst des Deutschen Möbels*, vol. 1, C. H. Beck (Munich), 1968.

KREISEL 1970
Kreisel, Heinrich, *Die Kunst des Deutschen Mobels*, vol. 2, C. H. Beck (Munich), 1970.

KUNSTGEWERBEMUSEUM 1989
Kunsthandwerk von Mittelalter bis zur Gegenwart, Kunstgewerbemuseum (Berlin), 1989.

KUNSTHISTORISCHES MUSEUM 1987
Kunsthistorisches Museum, Sammlungen Schloss Ambras: Möbel, Verlagsanstalt Tyrolia (Innsbruck), 1987.

L

LANKHEIT 1962
Lankheit, Klaus, *Florentinische Barockplastik: Die Kunst am Hofe der letzten Medici, (1670–1743)*, F. Bruckman, (Munich), 1962.

LAPIDARY JOURNAL 1977
'Los Angeles County Museum Receives Gift of Silver and Mosaic Collection', *Lapidary Journal* 31, no. 1, April 1977, pp. 198–201.

LE CORBEILLER 1970
Le Corbeiller, Clare, 'James Cox: A Biographical Review', *Burlington Magazine* 112 (London), June 1970, pp. 351–58.

LEDOUX-LEBARD 1965
Ledoux-Lebard, Denise, *Les ébénistes Parisien du XIXe siècle (1795–1889). Leurs Oeuvres et leurs margues*, F. De Nobele (Paris), 1965.

LEDOUX-LEBARD 1984
Ledoux-Lebard, Denise, *Le Mobilier Français du XIX siècle*, F. De Nobele (Paris), 1984.

LIECHTENSTEIN 1985
Liechtenstein, The Princely Collections, exh. cat., Metropolitan Museum of Art (New York), 1985.

LIZZANI 1970
Lizzani, G., *Il mobile romano*, Gorlich (Milan), 1970.

LOUVRE 1994
Luigi Valadier au Louvre, exh. cat., Louvre (Paris), 1994.

LUDMANN 1985
Ludmann, Jean Daniel, *Les Grands Apartements du Palais Rohan de Strasbourg*, Musées de Strasbourg (Strasbourg), 1985.

M

MACKOWSKY 1904
Mackowsky, Werner, *Giovanni Maria Nosseni und die Renaissance in Sachsen, Diss Dresden*, Beiträge zur Bauwissenschaft (Berlin), 1904.

MADRUGA 1975
Madruga, Real A., 'Cosimo Fanzago en las Agustinas de Salamanca', *Goya* 125 (Madrid), 1975, pp. 291–97.

MAKAY 1977
Makay, James, *Western Sculptures in Bronze*, Antique Collectors' Club (Woodbridge, Suffolk), 1977.

MALLET 1993
Mallet, Mallet & Son (Antiques) Ltd (London), 1993.

MANSUELLI 1960
Mansuelli, Guido, *Galleria degli Uffizi: Le sculture*, 2 vols., Poligrafico dello Stato (Rome), 1958, 1960.

MASSA 1983
Massa, Renata, *Dizionano Biografico degli Italiani*, vol. 28, s.v. 'Corbarelli', Istituto della enciclopedia Italiana fondata da Giovanni Teccani (Rome), 1983.

MASSINELLI 1990
Massinelli, Anna Maria 'Magnificenze medicee: gli stipi della Tribuna degli Uffizi', *Antologia di Belle Arti*, no. 37, (Rome) 1990, pp. 111–134.

MASSINELLI 1992
Massinelli, Anna Maria, 'Small Gemstone and Precious Metal Artifacts from the Medici Collections', in *Out of the Opulent Past: Italian Treasures from the Etruscan Age to Renaissance*, exh. cat., New York Grey Art Gallery (Florence) 1992, pp. 211–25.

MASSINELLI 1993
Massinelli, Anna Maria, *Il Mobile Toscano*, Electa (Milan), 1993.

MASSINELLI 1994
Massinelli, Anna Maria, 'Vasijas en piedras duras y metales preciosos provenientes de las colecciones Mediceas', in El oro de Italia, exh. cat., Museo Nacional de Belles Artes (Buenos Aires), 1994.

MAURICE 1976a
Maurice, Klaus, 'Augsburg Clocks', *Connoisseur* 193, no. 775, September 1976, pp. 34–38.

MAURICE 1976b
Maurice, Klaus, *Die deutsche Raderuhr. Zur Kunst und technik des mechanischen Zeitmesser im deutschen Sprachraum. Zweiter Band. Katalog und tafeln*, Verlag C. H. Beck (Munich), 1976.
MONACI 1977
Monaci, Lucia, *Disegni di Giovanni Battista Foggini, 1652–1725*, exh. cat., L. Olschki (Florence), 1977.

MONCRIEFF 1991
Moncrieff, Elspeth, 'Master of Mosaics', *The Antique Collector* 62, no. 2, February 1991, pp. 72–75.

MORIGIA 1595
Morigia, Paolo, *La nobiltà di Milano* (Milan), 1595.

MORROGH 1985
Morrogh, Andrew, *Disegni di architetti fiorentini 1540–1640*, exh. cat., Leo S. Olschki (Florence), 1985.

N

NEUMANN 1959
Neumann, Erwin, 'Materialen zur Geschichte der Scagliola', *Jahrbuch der Kunsthistorischen Sammlungen in Wien* (Vienna), 1959, pp. 75–156.

NICHT 1980
Nicht, Jutta, *Die Mobel im Neuen Palais, Postdam-Sanssouci*, Druckerei 'Freundschaft' (Berlin), 1980.

NICLAUSSE 1947
Niclausse, J., *Thomire, Fondeur, Ciseleur: Sa vie, son oeuvre* (Paris), 1947.

NOCQ and DREYFUS 1930
Nocq, Henry, and Carle Dreyfus, *Tabatières boîtes et étuis orfèvreries de Paris XVIIIE siècle des collections du Musée du Louvre*, La Semeuse (Paris), 1930.

NORTON and NORTON 1938
Norton, Richard, and Martin Norton, *A History of Gold Snuff Boxes*, S. J. Phillips (London), 1938.

O

OTTOMEYER and PROESCHEL 1986
Ottomeyer, H., and P. Proeschel, *Vergoldete Bronzen. Die Bronzearbeiten des Spätbarock und Klassizisimus*, 2 vols., Klinkhardt und Biermann (Munich), 1986.

P

PALAIS DE SAN DONATO 1880
Catalogue des objets d'art et d'ameublement, Tableaux dont la vente aux enchères publiques aura

lieu à Florence, au palais de San Donato le 15 mars 1880 et les jours suivant (Paris), 1880.

PAMPALONI MARTELLI 1978
Pampaloni Martelli, A., *Museo dell'Opificio delle Pietre Dure a Firenze*, Florence, 1978.

PANE 1984
Pane, Roberto, 'Marmi mischi e aggiunte a Cosimo Fanzago', in *Seicento napoletano. Arte Costume e Ambiente*, exh. cat., Electa (Naples), 1984, pp. 100–138.

PARRONCHI 1988
Parronchi, Antonio, *Raffaello Sorbi*, Lito Terrazzi (Florence), 1988.

PASSERI 1772
Passeri, Giovanni Battista, *Il Libro delle vite de'pittori scultori e architetti che hanno laborati in Roma*, Settari (Rome), 1772.

PAYNE 1981
Payne, Christopher, *The Price Guide to Nineteenth-Century European Furniture*, Antique Collectors' Club (Woodbridge, Suffolk), 1981.

PELLI BENCIVENNI 1779
Pelli Bencivenni, Giuseppe, *Saggio Istorico della Real Galleria di Firenze*, 2 vols., Stamperia Granducale (Florence), 1779.

PIAZZA 1992
Piazza, Stefano, *I marmi mischi nelle chiese di Palermo*, Selleno 1 (Palermo), 1992.

PINTO 1977
Pinto, Sandra, 'Gruppo di famiglia in un interno', in *Scritti in onore di U. Procacci*, vol. 2, Electa (Milan), 1977, pp. 614–20.

PLAISIR DE FRANCE 1969
'Le Cabinet, meuble rare entre tous', *Plaisir de France*, (Paris), November 1969, pp. 24–29.

PLINIO 1988
Plinio Secondo (Pliny the Elder), *Storia Naturale*, books 26, 33–37, Einaudi (Turin), 1988.

PRADERE 1989
Pradère, Alexandre, *French Furniture Makers: The Art of the Ebéniste from Louis XIV to the Revolution*, The J. Paul Getty Museum (Los Angeles), 1989.

PRAG 1988
Prag um 1600, Kunst und Kultur am Hofe Kaiser Rudolfs II exh. cat., Luca Verlag Freren (Vienna), 1988.

PRZYBOROWSKY 1982
Przyborowsky, Claudia, 'Die Ausstattung der fürstenkapeLle an der basilika von San Lorenzo in Florenz', Diss., Technischen Universität, Berlin, 1982.

Q

QUELLMALZ 1990
Quellmalz, Werner, *Die Edlen steine Sachsens*, Deutscher Verlag für grundstoffindustrie (Leipzig), 1990.

R

RADCLIFFE and THORNTON 1978
Radcliffe, Anthony, and Peter Thornton, 'John Evelyn's Cabinet', *Connoisseur* 1978, pp. 254–62.

RAGGIO 1960
Raggio, Olga, 'The Farnese Table: A Rediscovered Work of Vignola', *Bulletin of the Metropolitan Museum of Art* 7, no. 7, March 1960, pp. 213–31.

RICCIO 1959
Riccio, Bianca, 'La vita di Filippo Lauri di Francesco Saveno Baldinucci', *Commentari* 10 (Milan), 1959, pp. 65–75.

RICHARDSON 1983
Richardson, Nancy, 'A Pride of Boxes', *House and Garden*, 155, no. 5 (Los Angeles), May 1983.

RICHARDSON 1985
Richardson, Nancy, 'All about Style', *House and Garden*, 157, no. 6 (Los Angeles), June 1985, pp. 54–58.

RIZZO 1984
Rizzo, Vincenzo, 'Contributo alla conoscenza di Bartolomeo e Pietro Ghetti', *Antologia di Belle Arti*, new series nos. 21–22, 1984, pp. 98–110.

ROSSI 1967
Rossi, Ferdinando, *La pittura di pietra*, Giunti (Florence), 1967.

ROSSI 1970
Rossi, Ferdinando, Mosaics: A Survey of the History and Techniques, Praeger Publishers (New York, Washington, London), 1970.

RUBSAMEN 1980
Rubsamen, Gysela, *The Orsini Inventories*, J. Paul Getty Museum (Los Angeles), 1980.

RUOTOLO 1974
Ruotolo, Renato, 'La decorazione intarsia e commesso a Napoli nel periodo tardo-manierista', *Antichità Viva* 13, no. 1 (Florence), 1974, pp. 55–56.

S

SCHRODER 1988
Schroder, Timothy B., *The Gilbert Collection of Gold and Silver*, Los Angeles County Museum of Art (Los Angeles), 1988.

SEIDEL 1901
Seidel, Paul, 'Die Prunkdosen Friedrichs des Grossen', *Hohenzollern Jahrbuch* 5 (Berlin), 1901, pp. 74–86.

SELING 1980
Seling, Helmut, *Die Kunst der Augsburger Goldschmiede 1529–1868*, 3 vols., C. H. Bech (Munich), 1980.

SHERMAN 1971
Sherman, Anthony, *The Gilbert Mosaic Collection*, Pendulum Press (West Haven, Connecticut), 1971.

SMITH 1931
Smith Clifford, *The Complete History of Buckingham Palace* (London), 1931, p. 140.

SNOWMAN 1966
Snowman, A. Kenneth, *Eighteenth-Century Gold Boxes of Europe*, Faber and Faber (London), 1966.

SNOWMAN 1990
Snowman, A. Kenneth, *Eighteenth-Century Gold Boxes of Europe*, 2d ed., Antique Collector's Club Limited (Woodbridge, Suffolk), 1990.

SOLODKOFF and HABSBURG-LOTHRINGEN 1983
Solodkoff, Alexander von, and Géza von Habsburg-Lothringen, 'Tabatieren Friedrichs des Grossen', *Kunst und Antiquitäten* 3 (Hanover), May–June 1983, pp. 36–42.

SOMERS COCKS and TRUMAN
Somers Cocks, Anna and Truman, Charles, *The Thyssen-Bornemisza Collection: Renaissance jewels, gold boxes and objets de vertu*, Sotheby's Publications (London), 1984.

SPECTOR 1991
Spector, Danny, 'Cajas de Oro/Gold Boxes', *Aboard*, November/December 1991, pp. 93–100.

SPLENDORI DI PIETRE DURE 1988
Splendori di pietre dure. L'arte di corte nella Firenze dei Granduchi, exh. cat., Giunti (Florence), 1988.

SULLIVAN 1991
Sullivan, Meg, 'Gold boxes that are up to snuff', *Los Angeles Daily News* (Los Angeles), 17 November 1991, pp. 16–17.

SYKES 1985
Sykes, Christopher Simon, *Private Palaces: Life in Great London Houses*, Chatto & Windus Ltd (London), 1985.

THE ILLUSTRATED EXHIBITOR 1851
A tribute to the world's industrial jubilee, (London), 1851.

TREASURES FROM THE ROYAL COLLECTION 1988
Treasures from the Royal Collection, exh. cat. The Queen's Gallery, Buckingham Palace (London), 1988.

TRUMAN 1991
Truman, Charles, *The Gilbert Collection of Gold Boxes*, exh. cat., Los Angeles County Museum of Art (Los Angeles), 1991.

TRUMAN 1993
Truman, Charles ed., *Sotheby's Concise Encyclopedia of Silver*, Conran Octopus (London), 1993.

TUENA 1988
Tuena, Filippo, 'Appunti per il commesso romano: il Franciosino maestro di tavole e il Cardinal Giovanni Ricci', *Antologia di Belle Arti*, nos. 33–34 (Rome), 1988, pp. 54–69.

TUENA 1989
Tuena, Filippo, 'I marmi commessi nel tardo rinascimento romano', in *Marmi antichi*, De Luca (Rome), 1989, pp. 80–97.

TUENA 1990
Tuena, Filippo, 'Cosimo I e le pietre dure', *Antologia di Belle Arti*, no. 37 (Rome), 1990, pp. 135–47.

U

UGURGERI AZZOLINI 1640
Ugurgeri Azzolini, Iacopo, *Le pompe sanesi* (Pistoia), 1640.

V

VALADIER 1991
Valadier, Sacro e Profano, exh. cat., Trinity Fine Art (Florence), 1991.

VALERIANI 1991–92
Valeriani, Roberto, 'Un orologio di Giuseppe Valadier', *Antologia di Belle Arti*, nos. 39–42 (Rome), 1991–92, pp. 107–10.

VASARI 1568
Vasari, Giorgio, *Vite de' più eccellenti pittori, scultori e architettori*, 9 vols., (Florence), 1568. Reprint ed. G. Milanesi, Sansoni (Florence), 1878–85.

W

WILLS 1971
Wills, Geoffrey, *English Furniture 1550–1760*, Doubleday and Company (New York), 1971.

WILSON 1980
Wilson, Janet, 'Collecting Mosaics, Piece by Piece', *Realities*, no. 11 (Pennsylvania), May/June 1980, pp. 99–101.

WITTKOWER 1985
Wittkower, Rudolf, *Art and Architecture in Italy, 1600–1750*, Penguin Books (London), 1985.

Z

ZOBI 1853
Zobi, Antonio, *Notizie storiche sull'origine e progressi dei lavori di commesso in pietre dure nell'I. e R. Stabilimento di Firenze*, Stamperia Granducale (Florence), 1853.

ZUCKER 1977
Zucker, Martin, 'A Great Collection of Time Artistry: How It Was Made', *Smithsonian* 8, no. 2 (Washington D. C.), May 1977, pp. 84–90.

Exhibition History

Each catalogue entry indicates the work's exhibition history. The following is a key to the abbreviations used in the entries.

Bath, 1973
Octagon Room, *International Art Treasures Exhibition.*

Berlin, 1929
Schloss Monbijou.

Darmstadt, 1914
Jahrhundert Austellung Deutscher Kunst, 1650–1800.

Dayton, 1921
School of Industrial and Fine Arts at the Dayton Museum of Art, October (see bibliography for Dayton 1921).

Florence, 1971
Palazzo Strozzi, *Mostra internazionale dell'antiouariato.*

Jerusalem, 1995
The Israel Museum, *Princely Taste, Treasures from Great Private Collections*, 21 March–17 June.

London, 1851
Crystal Palace, *The Great Exhibition of the Works of Industry of All Nations*

London, 1968
Victoria and Albert Museum, *The British Antique Dealers' Association Golden Jublilee Exhibition.*

London, 1973
Christie's, *Fanfare for Europe.*

London, 1975
Victoria and Albert Museum, *Mosaics from the Gilbert Collection*, 16 July–31 August (see bibliography for Avery and Emperatori 1975).

London, 1984
Victoria and Albert Museum, *Rococo Art and Design in Hogarth's England*, 30 May–16 September.

London, 1990
Wartski, *Eighteenth-Century Gold Boxes*, 2–17 October (travelled to New York).

Los Angeles, 1975
Los Angeles County Museum of Art, *The Gilbert Mosaic Collection*, 14 January–2 March.

Los Angeles / Atlanta / San Antonio / Richmond / Seattle, 1977
Los Angeles County Museum of Art, *The Gilbert Collection: Monumental Silver and the Art of Mosaics*, 28 April–10 July (travelled to Atlanta, San Antonio, Richmond, Seattle, and Chicago).

Los Angeles, 1986
Los Angeles County Museum of Art, *Gold Boxes from the Gilbert Collection* (travelled to Richmond and New York).

Los Angeles, 1991
Los Angeles County Museum of Art, *Gold Boxes from the Collection of Arthur and Rosalinde Gilbert*, 14 November 1991–8, March 1992, (travelled to Memphis; see bibliography for Truman 1991).

Los Angeles, 1993
Los Angeles County Museum of Art, *Pleasure Gardens of the Mind: Indian Paintings from the Jane Greenough Green Collection*, 11 March–13 June.

Memphis, 1994
Dixon Gallery and Gardens, Selections from the Gilbert Treasury, Memphis, 1 April–July 1994.

Munich, 1992
Kunsthalle der Hypo-Kulturstiftung, *Friedrich der Grosse: Sammler und Mazen*, 28 November 1992–28 February 1993.

Potsdam, 1993
Stiftung Schlösser und Gärten, Potsdam-Sanssouci, *Prunk Tabatièren Friedrichs des Grossen*, 14 March–25 April (see bibliography for Baer 1993).

San Francisco, 1996
Fort Mason Center, Festival Pavilion, San Francisco Fall Antiques Show: *The Art Of Gold Boxes: Selections form the Arthur Gilbert Collection*, 24–28 October 1996.

Index